STUDIES IN GERMAN HISTORIES
Series Editors: Roger Chickering and Thomas A. Brady, Jr.

# German Encounters with Modernity

# German Encounters with Modernity

## Novels of Imperial Berlin

Katherine Roper

Humanities Press International, Inc.
New Jersey and London

First published 1991 by Humanities Press International, Inc.
Atlantic Highlands, N.J., and 3 Henrietta Street, London WC2E 8LU.

©Katherine Roper, 1991

**Library of Congress Cataloging-in-Publication Data**

Roper, Katherine.
    German encounters with modernity : novels of imperial Berlin / Katherine Roper.
        p. cm. — (Studies in German histories)
    Includes bibliographical references and index.
    ISBN 0-391-03695-5
    1. German fiction—19th century—History and criticism. 2. Berlin (Germany) in literature. 3. Berlin (Germany)—Civilization. 4. Germany—Civilization—19th century. 5. National characteristics, German. I. Title. II. Series.
PT771.R67 1991
833'.8093243155—dc20                                            90-38585
                                                                     CIP

**British Cataloging-in-Publication Data**
A CIP record for this book is available from the British Library.

Parts of the present work appeared in a slightly different version in *Fact and Fiction: German History and Literature, 1848–1924*, Gisela Brude-Firnau and Karin J. MacHardy, eds., Series: Edition Orpheus (Francke Verlag: Tübingen, 1990), and are reprinted with permission.

All rights reserved. No reproduction, copy, or transmission of this publication may be made without written permission.

Printed in the United States of America

For Stefan

# Contents

| | | |
|---|---|---|
| | *Acknowledgments* | ix |
| | Introduction: The Novel as an Arena of German Struggle | 1 |
| 1. | The Prologue: Karl Gutzkow's *Knights of the Spirit* | 21 |
| 2. | "Berlin Becomes a World-City!" | 40 |
| 3. | Storms of the *Gründerjahre*: The Imperiled *Bürger* | 55 |
| 4. | The Unfinished Revolution | 73 |
| 5. | The Struggle for Survival: The Cultural Combatant | 91 |
| 6. | The Working-Class Struggle | 109 |
| 7. | Dis-ease in the Metropolis | 127 |
| 8. | The Outsiders: Berlin's Jews | 146 |
| 9. | Coming of Age: Women in Berlin Society | 164 |
| 10. | The Aristocracy: A Crisis of Honor and Means | 185 |
| 11. | The Westward Procession: Into the Idler's Paradise | 200 |
| 12. | The Changing of the Guard | 219 |
| | Conclusion | 237 |
| | *Bibliography* | 246 |
| | *Index* | 261 |

# Acknowledgments

I am deeply grateful to St. Mary's College, whose granting of sabbatical and other released time allowed me sustained periods of concentration to research and write this book. A succession of faculty development grants from the college enabled me to present several papers at annual conferences of the German Studies Association, where I received invaluable feedback. The staff of the Historical Commission of Berlin provided welcome assistance during a research visit to Berlin.

Of the many people who have responded to my queries and ideas over the years of this project, a number deserve special mention for their assistance, though, of course, they bear no responsibility for faults that remain. Gordon Craig helped me conceive the topic, offered suggestions about approaches and strategies over its evolution, and read a large portion of the manuscript in its early stages. Whatever clarity the book has achieved is due in large measure to the persistent efforts of Karen Christensen, Judith Gruber, Judith Innes, Christine Rosen, and Eleanor Swift. As participants in an ongoing writing group, they made countless provocative inquiries about excerpts from all stages of the writing. Colleagues at St. Mary's College subjected drafts of the introduction and conclusion to lively discussion at faculty colloquia, and Chester Aaron, Benjamin Frankel, and Carl Guarneri augmented this with helpful written comments. The formal commentaries of the following colleagues in the German Studies Association provoked new perspectives and reexaminations of cherished assumptions: Ann Taylor Allen, Marion Deshmukh, Peter Jelavich, Vernon Lidtke, Ronald Ross, and Jacqueline Weisheit. The editors of this series, Roger Chickering and Thomas A. Brady, Jr., gave the manuscript careful scrutiny, offering worthwhile suggestions for its final revisions. Keith Ashfield, Judith Camlin, and William Zeisel at Humanities Press International all contributed to seeing the manuscript smoothly through the process of publication. Finally, I dedicate this book to my husband, Steve Roper, in loving gratitude for his unstinting editorial, gastronomical, and moral support.

# Introduction: The Novel as an Arena of German Struggle

The novels of Imperial Berlin comprise an extensive body of material that shows Germans wrestling with the new experiences of nationhood and modernity. Their contents offer abundant evidence about contemporary views of the German past, present, and future. Taken together they constitute a significant piece in the complicated puzzle of why the society of Imperial Germany, as it underwent the social and economic upheavals of modernization, sustained the rule of traditional elites in new authoritarian forms.[1] The novels' importance as a historical source lies in the intricate connections their authors, witnesses to a rapidly changing German society, made between the individual lives of their characters, the environment of Berlin, and the formation of a modernizing nation. These connections—and the values and perspectives behind them—are the focus of this study.

German unification had a startling effect on Berlin. In 1871, when the Prussian chancellor Otto von Bismarck created the new German empire through an intricate diplomatic and military chess game, Berlin became the capital. Within a few years the city that had long been the residence of the Hohenzollern kings burgeoned into Germany's only *Weltstadt*, or metropolis. This speedy transformation meant that Berlin underwent with particular intensity the maelstrom of experiences we call modernity.[2] Some of the most vivid reactions came from the countless artists and literati who gravitated to Berlin in the decades following unification. Seeing the city as "the Mecca" in which "to celebrate the spirit of the time to the fullest," they immersed themselves in urban life and brought forth abundant creations attesting to their experiences.[3] Through the imaginary realms they created in their works they hoped to contribute to building a national culture that both took cognizance of modernity and validated Germany's newly won preeminence. Such a culture, they believed, would become the hallmark of German nationhood.[4]

I have chosen to focus on the novel in the belief that this genre reveals particularly well the processes by which these reactions developed. With its ability to range widely through time and space, to focus in detail on characters and situations, and to communicate narrational comments, characters' thoughts, and conversations, the novel can offer a multi-faceted interpretation of social reality. Although the product of imagination, it is written within a historical time with the intent of conveying understanding of some aspect of human experience. While historians would be foolhardy to treat any novel as an exact mirror of the society it attempts to portray, they should not ignore the novel's role as a repository of social discourse. Behind the fictional creation lies a network of social perspectives, both conscious and unconscious, that the novelist communicates to readers through myriad means. In this sense a novel is a social document that yields insight into the consciousness of the society in which it was created.[5]

If all novels are thus potentially valuable historical sources, those of the late nineteenth century are especially so. Their authors' newly awakened commitment to "realism" meant they would try to depict the interaction between the individual and the surrounding society explicitly and accurately.[6] As social, economic, and political institutions become increasingly central to the lives of fictional characters, so do authors' perspectives on these institutions become increasingly visible to the historian. Literary realism in Germany was sparked by the revolutionary upheavals of 1848, whose vicissitudes brought profound awareness of new social uncertainties. The novels of Imperial Berlin, written in the broad context of this movement, exemplify many dimensions of the social consciousness that motivated it. Their explicit geographical and historical settings embody attempts by observers of German society to transform social reality into fiction and thereby to articulate a vision of modernity. Their characters, surroundings, and myriad social situations offer detailed testimony from Germans, that is, the authors, who were struggling with problems they thought exemplified the modern age.

Central to this struggle was a belief that literature should play a leading role in steering German society through the uncertainties of modernity.[7] This belief was frequently articulated in the novels themselves. Take, for example, the novelist who has a character remark, "The preachers are really doing too little. A good writer can affect more people than a whole consistory!"[8] Another contends that, "It is given to the poet and to the social writer to contribute in their ways to the solution of difficult problems, to intervene everywhere, to provoke now and then, to awaken enthusiasm for noble action, and to rouse the general populace."[9] Still another proclaims on his title page: "The novel is social therapy."[10] The most explicit statement about the implications of this belief comes from Berlin novelist Conrad Alberti. Writing in 1885 about Gustav Freytag's phenomenally popular *Soll und Haben* (*Debit and Credit*) (1855), Alberti asserts that any German with the slightest claim to being cultured has read the novel one, two, even three times. Long after the author or even the title might have been forgotten, he continues, the contents are working on the thinking and emotions of the reader: "And thus the work forms a rock-solid component of the mass of great material that ceaselessly and omnipotently provides the education and uplifting of a whole nation. That is the highest goal, the greatest triumph of the author."[11]

Alberti's hope that the novel would contribute to national regeneration was widely shared, and the fact that many novelists of Imperial Berlin conceived of their works in such terms is a significant element of their historical import. Simultaneously confronting the challenges of a modernizing society, and also the new experience of nationhood, they saw themselves as morally responsible for challenging outlooks and institutions that embodied the old ways. In spite of disparate ideological and stylistic inclinations, such writers dedicated themselves to an unspoken common task: engaging through their works in a struggle for Germany's soul. In diverse ways they explored, envisioned, and criticized the forms that German nationhood either was taking or might take. Unification, they urged, represented but the first stage of a still unfinished German revolution that would bring genuine national greatness.[12]

Creating even a fictional national greatness, however, proved to be difficult. A truly German revolution, it was frequently implied, would effect a spiritual or moral transformation in the nation. Such expectations grew from deep-rooted cultural ideals of spiritual freedom and inwardness (*Innerlichkeit*).[13] But for authors of Berlin novels, the context of a modernizing society provoked insistent questions about the relation of such private ideals to public ideals of civil liberty, economic justice, or political democracy that motivated other European revolutions. Their hopes for the German revolution were also affected by powerful historical memories of 1848 and 1871, whose social and political upheavals proved perplexing. It is not suprising that the meaning of the revolutionary year of 1848 was puzzling to German observers, but novels make it clear that the "glorious" year 1871 was hardly less so.[14] After the jubilation over the defeat of France had subsided, many wondered how the diverse states that had been brought together would ever form a genuine national unity. The novels of Imperial Berlin repeatedly attest to such puzzlement by using the capital as an arena in which to depict distinctively German struggles with nationhood and modernity. By linking the city with national symbols, they portray it as a catalyst for change throughout the rest of Germany, a unifying force amid a diverse conglomeration of particularist and religious traditions.

When analyzed chronologically, however, a succession of Berlin novels suggests that as the society of Imperial Germany matured, the authors' hopes for the unfinished revolution became increasingly elusive. What began as confident attempts to envision a modern nationhood yielded, by the early twentieth century, to signs of confusion and fatalism. Increasingly, doubts supplanted new visions, and resignation silenced calls to social engagement. The nature of these doubts and the origins of this resignation can be found in individual novels. By examining a sequence of fictional episodes, the historian can uncover distinct moments in which the social criticism of the Berlin novelists, as German proponents of modernity, collided with cultural legacies, historical mythologies, class prejudices, and political indifference.[15]

These moments provide insights into a developing national consciousness. Many take the form of jarring encounters between positive images of historical legacies and negative perceptions of the modern age. Images of individualism and self-cultivation from the Enlightenment collide with perceptions of cultural vulgarity and of a modern society forcing its members into uniform molds. Images of a stable Prussian polity, especially in the eighteenth-century reign of

Frederick II, collide with perceptions of political uncertainty and threats of disorder in Imperial Germany. Images of a people united in common cause with the state, as in the 1813 war of liberation against Napoleon, collide with perceptions of a contemporary German society divided into hostile social classes and particularist rivalries. Images of venerated generations from the past embodying virtues of duty, simplicity, and hard work collide with perceptions of modern generations who are self-indulgent, materialistic, or bereft of patriotic commitment. In addition to invocations of deep-seated cultural mythology, all Berlin novels use city landmarks to convey meaning. The appearance of such symbols as the triumphal Brandenburger Tor, the ostentatious mansions of the newly rich, or the multi-storied tenements housing the working masses become indicators of an author's intent. Similarly, the incorporation of dramatic episodes of contemporary history, such as the crash of 1873, the assassination attempts on Emperor William I in 1878, or the ascendancy of William II in 1888, identifies and interprets what authors saw as turning points in the progress of the new Germany.

Such tensions, symbols, and historical experiences, recurring in many novels, suggest a kaleidoscope, whose multi-colored and multi-shaped pieces fall into a new arrangement with each turn. Each arrangement is unique, just as each novel is unique, but a long sequence of rearrangements shows increasingly familiar pieces making up each view. Despite much diffuseness, these kaleidoscopic patterns can be interpreted in terms of categories and trends that correspond to novelists' notions of social structures, chronological periods, and multifarious dimensions of "modernity." The interplay between the distinctiveness of individual novels and recurrent patterns in a range of them, analyzed in their historical context, provides evidence for my contention that these authors used their works to explore challenges of modernity and thereby to engage a wide-ranging struggle over German identity.

To suggest the many dimensions of this struggle, I propose to analyze a spectrum of Berlin novels in terms of the historical implications of the social reality they create. Believing that a focus on the development of specific episodes will best reveal the processes by which assumptions and values emerge from fictional situations, I have chosen to leave the categorization of various phenomena, the examination of formal or structural patterns, the study of rhetorical strategies, and contextualist analysis to others.[16] Rather, I use the treatment of a crucial social issue in a single novel as something of a case study, to show how one observer used fiction to work through a question of Germany's contemporary development. The implications of such discernible "signs of authorial control," interpreted in the context of other scholarship, can suggest how this material becomes part of the identity formation of Imperial Germany. Affirming one's belief in authorial intent becomes a perilous enterprise in the light of some current theoretical systems, which proclaim "the death of the author" in a literary text that "eclipses and transcends its author's intentions."[17] Nevertheless, I am convinced that to ignore the clear evidence of such intent in the Berlin novels is to miss a central element of their import as documentary testimony to the cultural imagination of Imperial Germany. These novels represent significant instances of social discourse, created by novelists with the aim of communicating social meaning to their readers.

In searching for such instances, I culled a select number of germane episodes from a large and diverse body of material. I soon discovered that the "Berlin novel" resisted any all-embracing definition. To qualify as a "Berlin novel," a work had to be listed in that category in the various bibliographies or otherwise contain a demonstrable presence of Berlin. This presence most often meant that Berlin was the predominant setting, but I also included novels in which the influence of Berlin was a significant dimension of a plot whose main setting lay elsewhere (for example, Wilhelm Raabe's *Villa Schönow* or Theodor Fontane's *Der Stechlin*). I chose to limit my scope to works with at least a modicum of literary pretension, because I believe that popular genres such as colportage novels, even were they readily available in sufficient numbers, pose distinct analytical problems that demand extensive and separate treatment from the novels that predominate in the bibliographies and literary histories I depended upon. Of the more than three hundred titles I compiled, consisting primarily of middlebrow novels, I have chosen to concentrate on about fifty in the forthcoming chapters.[18] The choice required my reading as widely as possible, but the necessity of reducing the original list was underscored when, following the well-meant suggestion of a sympathetic colleague, I tried to dip into alternate chapters of a novel and quickly realized that I could make little sense of a work without reading it in its entirety.

I applied three criteria for selecting novels to read: the contemporary renown of an author or of a particular work, the suggestiveness of an individual title, and the publication date. A survey of secondary literature on Imperial Berlin and a sampling of its literary periodicals yielded names of novelists whose works were widely discussed, such as Theodor Fontane, Friedrich Spielhagen, and Max Kretzer, to name some of the best known. A wide reading of works by such figures would ensure contact with prominent elements of the cultural atmosphere. Bestsellers like Paul Lindau's *The Westward Procession*, when they could be identified from haphazard publication figures, also represented widely received social perspectives. Since my foremost interest remained the novels themselves rather than their reception, however, I also sought works whose titles indicated an explicit social or political focus, such as *From Brandenburg to Bismarck*, *Kurfürstendamm*, or *The Third Reich*—and an irresistible *Demonic Berlin*.[19] Finally, to achieve a selection that was fairly well balanced chronologically, I chose some novels, still with attention to the first two criteria, on the basis of their publication dates.

As I read, I looked for material depicting German encounters with modernity and was rewarded with limitless images, situations, and episodes that signified authors' consciousness of an emergent new age. A multitude of characters confronted a metropolis whose traffic, crowds, and new buildings were literally dizzying. Fathers of struggling families suddenly became victims of depression-caused unemployment. A young pregnant wife was widowed without any means of support. Another endured the bewildering experience of divorce. An aristocratic family contended with genteel poverty. An architect found himself blacklisted because he had taken the workers' part in a strike. A composer strove to create music that would express the dissonances of modernity. A member of the Reichstag struggled to achieve political effectiveness. A Jewish physician battled anti-Semitism. And a pastor worked to foster Christianity in a secularized, materialistic age. These and myriad other situations provide the raw material in which values and attitudes toward modernity were articulated in a specifically German context.

The conceptions of modernity that emerged, far from coalescing into a precise construct, were impressionistic depictions of urban hustle and bustle, brash new social groups, new technology, new kinds of economic misery, new moral values, new assaults on individuality, new intellectual perspectives, and new literary ideals. The multi-faceted scope of these impressions—limited only by the capacity of the reader to pick up threads and follow them—provides a rich and complex tapestry of German perceptions of the modern age.

Of the 130 novels I read, I found none irrelevant to my concerns. However unpromising some seemed because of tedious or trivial plots, every one articulated some sort of provocative social dimension related in a noteworthy way to Imperial Berlin and suggested implications for problems of German identity. Reading additional novels would provide additional material, which would surely result in new viewpoints on the ideas presented in the coming chapters. But on the basis of the many novels I have read but chosen not to analyze here, I am confident my choices represent a good cross section.

My principal criterion for selecting novels to discuss involved judging their relevance to issues of nationhood and modernity. Most novels of Imperial Berlin have fallen into well-deserved literary obscurity, and many have been disparaged by later critics for simplistic or prejudicial portrayals of social reality. I am convinced, however, that the contents of such literature, despite any tendencies toward sentimentality or "pamphleteering" they might manifest, offer valuable insights to the historian who analyzes them as social artifacts rather than as failed art or false ideology.[20] An author's provocative use of Berlin and its society to convey social meaning to readers, then, became my paramount standard for choosing a novel. Although the selection of material by such intuitive means may seem arbitrary, the imposition of a theoretical system on the selection, I believe, would result in material that is even more arbitrary by excluding that which does not conform to theory. I am drawn to invoke here Marc Bloch's comment about how a good historian resembles the ogre of legend: "Wherever he smells human flesh, he knows that there he will find his prey."[21]

As topical chapters evolved I reviewed works pertinent to the theme of each and defined from them a range of issues as sub-topics clustering around each theme. I then selected novels that best developed these issues, either in abundance of detail or in problematic suggestion, and from them identified episodes that would best reveal such development. To avoid confusing overlap, in most cases I confined my treatment of any one novel to a single chapter, concentrating usually on a work's handling of one issue at the expense of another. The fictional episodes that form the basis for this study were thus winnowed in two ways: they represent only a fraction of passages pertinent to a given theme and concern only a small segment of the social issues articulated within any single work.

What I offer is a topical and generally chronological interpretation of ways in which Berlin novels confronted German nationhood and modernity. The diverse episodes, characters, and situations to be considered attest to the immense complexity authors saw as they surveyed their society. The literary means by which they created their portrayals also underscore a wide variety of perspectives: from panoramic social vistas to a concentration on a single family; from idealist meditations to virulent parodies; from reportage to stream-of-consciousness ravings; from sentimentality to scathing satire. In their political commentary the novelists manifested ideologies that ranged from arch-conservatism to socialism. And they represented at least four literary generations. Although all produced works that attempted to come to terms with the emergent modern age, their articulation of what they saw offers a spectrum of images, symbols, values, hopes, and fears.

Like these novels, this study encompasses diverse realms of human experience even as it considers how each relates to central themes. To suggest the spectrum of issues a single novel can expound, I have chosen to treat as a prologue a pathbreaking novel published two decades before German unification. Karl Gutzkow's panoramic *Die Ritter vom Geiste* (*Knights of the Spirit*) enunciates virtually all the issues later works address. It provides a superb entry into the novels of Imperial Berlin.

The next five chapters focus on novels written during the reign of William I and the regime of Bismarck, analyzing them as attempts to come to terms with the German unification and its aftermath in the burgeoning metropolis. Many novels of these years, as we will see, posed questions about how the victories of the recent wars were to be translated into genuine national greatness. They also revealed the onset of serious concerns about cultural, economic, and political developments that cast their shadow over German achievements. Their multifarious portrayals of conflict—ranging from drawing-room encounters to what were seen as Darwinian struggles for survival—indicate the array of alternatives novelists confronted in their search for the unfinished German revolution. Their outcomes nevertheless suggested confidence on the part of authors that, however dire the situations they had portrayed, Germans truly dedicated to the national good would overcome the obstacles to national rebirth.

Chapters 7 through 11, drawing on novels from the 1890s and beyond, show fictional depictions of new obstacles. Spiritual crisis and cultural malaise, virulent anti-Semitism, clashes between the sexes, and crises of values within the ruling classes—all contributed to a growing pessimism that left little scope for visions of the unfinished revolution. Still, the notion of national regeneration had not died, and the last chapter analyzes how three novelists pondered the future of Germany by reconsidering the emergence of the post-Bismarckian generation around 1890. All three reveal pessimism about the capacities of this generation, but then they diverge—into cautious hope for a democratic Germany, wishful thinking about a resurrected Bismarckian spirit, or all-out cynicism toward the imperialistic Germany that had emerged. The last view, providing the most prophetic fictional version of the actual unfinished revolution, unfolds in Heinrich Mann's *Der Untertan* (*The Loyal Subject*), whose portrait of a German society inundated by the values of a belligerent and conformist new generation offered a not-so-timely warning in a work whose serialization was interrupted by the outbreak of war. Although Mann's novel represents an extreme, it can also be seen as but the despairing culmination of a long sequence of fictional efforts to discover the revolution that would bring a humane, peaceful Germany. Taken in succession, the novels of Imperial Berlin give a remarkable rendition of attempts to discern and determine the course of a fateful German odyssey.

In looking at the novel as a social product, we confront six basic components of its existence: its contents, its author, its literary context, the social context in which it was created, its publication, and its readership.[22] The contents, as repositories of social discourse, are my principal focus, but during the period in which they were created, each of the other components was undergoing its own version of a collision between traditional ways and modernizing forces. Such collisions meant drastic upheavals in the conditions under which an onslaught of contemporary novels was produced.

Many ambivalences toward modernity in Berlin novels corresponded to tensions that authors themselves were experiencing as members of a newly emerging writing profession. Even by the early nineteenth century the prospects for a literary boom were attracting a host of would-be writers to a seemingly prestigious realm.[23] They discovered, however, that the writer's liberation from dependence upon aristocratic patronage brought new perils. Goethe gloomily characterized this insecurity when he commented that German poets lacked rank and eminence, "making it mere chance which talent would end in honor or ignominy."[24] While it is impossible to conceive of Goethe as the beneficiary of chance alone, the situation he described certainly applied to less exceptional authors. Any desire for popular recognition, moreover, collided with a deeply held ideal that defined writers as a sequestered elite pursuing timeless truths. The word poet (*Dichter*), as the embodiment of this ideal, designated not the genre in which they wrote, but rather their lofty pursuits. In contrast, the word author (*Schriftsteller*) evoked connotations of esthetic indifference and of writing for financial gain. The transition from *Dichter* to *Schriftsteller* implied such a crass descent that even late in the century some literary figures were still urging peers to avoid *Schriftstellerei*.[25] Writing literature about contemporary society meant having to overcome such scruples.

A related source of uneasiness derived from the middle-class ties common to the professional endeavors of all writers, whatever their social origins. A majority of German authors after 1848 came from "the sphere of a provincial middle class" and brought middle-class values to their work, even as they sought a critical distance from their class.[26] Aristocratic authors, if they wished to be published, had to adopt enough of a middle-class outlook to overcome qualms about entering commercial ventures. The few authors from the working class and peasantry had to gain enough access into middle-class society to find a publisher, a process involving immense adjustments in social bearing and perspectives.

Especially acute among writers was a problematic relation to the middle-class work ethic. One dilemma had to do with conflicts between notions of financial success as the measure of work and abhorrence of what seemed vulgar striving for possessions (*Besitz*).[27] Another involved conflicts between self-conceptions of writers as artisans and beliefs that only a cultural elite could bring forth great literary creations.[28] A third dilemma entailed conflicts between ideals of self-cultivation (*Bildung*) and fears that systematic work was the province of the philistine. As an educational ideal, *Bildung* had profound cultural connotations, ranging far beyond any academic program to encompass an intensely purposeful esthetic and spiritual cultivation by the individual. Some who saw themselves as exemplars of the cultivated middle class (the *Bildungsbürgertum*), however, cringed at the thought of being defiled by the values of the propertied middle class (the *Besitzbürgertum*), and used this attitude to justify avoiding the mundane demands of work while they awaited creative inspiration.[29]

For most writers, however, tensions over professional identity were overshadowed by financial worries. The ideal of the writer worshipping at the shrine of esthetic purity did not, of course, leave room for vulgar questions of money, but even for those untroubled by such qualms, compensation was usually scant. Unknown authors were likely to be paid nothing until the success of their works had been established, and they might even be required to subsidize their publication. Few novelists could hope to live from proceeds of the book editions of their works, and turning to journalistic writing for support meant learning to work quickly and abandoning perfectionist instincts.[30] Such concerns were not unique to nineteenth-century German authors, for it is an axiom that "literature does not feed its creator."[31] In Germany, however, novelists' financial troubles were intensified by their ambivalence toward commercial aspects of writing, and this ambivalence expressed itself in many problematic fictional encounters with cultural commercialism.

In sum, nineteenth-century German writers were likely to find themselves beset by professional insecurities and mired in conflict with deeply held cultural values, even as many confronted their world with an exuberant sense of a new literary mission. The result, in the words of Fritz Martini, was "doubt, irony, and resignation on the one hand, and faith in progress, optimism for the future, and affirmation of life on the other."[32] Signs of such ambivalence permeate novels of Imperial Berlin. Moreover, the dilemmas of the writer as a member of a middle-class profession contributed to perceptions of wider crisis even as some members of the German middle class began to celebrate their apparent triumph as standard-bearers of the modern age.

Another source of modernizing pressures on Berlin novels came from the struggles that surrounded a rapidly expanding book trade. Novels depicted a crisis most frequently in terms of writers who had to deal with their new "patrons," the publishers. In one such novel, for instance, the narrator declares that "the grievances of authors toward the publishers are limitless and unanimous." He then cites examples from Cervantes to Heine to argue against the imbalanced relationship that allowed a publisher to mutilate—or kill—the creation of an author. Indeed, the publisher in this novel, a cold-hearted businessman, has a keen sense of the book market but lacks any literary insight. A stream of supplicating writers lies at his mercy, but an inclination toward mercy is totally absent in his dealings with them.[33]

Such a view, however plausible from the author's perspective, overlooked the enormous risks that confronted a publisher who tried to respond to technological innovations in paper production, lithography, and the growing necessity to discern the reading needs of "an anonymous and steadily expanding public."[34] As population growth, universal suffrage, and expanding education brought increasing demand for books, controversies multiplied. The copyright law of 1867, for instance, only partially settled the disputes that prompted it. Some hailed it as the liberation of a national literature because it released German classics to the public domain, but although the profusion of inexpensive editions fed patriotic appetites, the German reading public was not thereby elevated to higher realms of literary taste.[35] Moreover, the new law's protections for living authors inhibited the production of comparably low-priced contemporary works and put them beyond the reach of most Germans. Another controversy erupted over guildlike restrictions governing the book trade. While aggressive newcomers called for free enterprise (*Gewerbefreiheit*) to end stagnation in the industry, established publishers countered that price wars and gimmicks were already ruining it. Similar conflicts broke out at the retail level when small dealers, protesting large firms' practice of giving discounts, were answered with appeals to *Gewerbefreiheit*. Although the Organization of German Book Dealers finally produced regulations to protect the provincial bookseller, the running of a small bookstore remained risky, involving consequential decisions about how many and what books to stock in order to stay afloat.[36]

Censorship, both direct and indirect, was still another menace with which the book trade had to contend. Indirectly, critics could be manipulated by self-appointed moral guardians among editors and publishers to provide judgments by which desired cultural and social values could be propagated. Similarly, the awarding of literary prizes became a means by which the cultural establishment maintained control.³⁷ Although most official censorship in Germany supposedly was ended after 1848, succeeding decades brought new waves of control over the book industry. Censorship in the form of lese majesty (*Majestätsbeleidigung*) and "trash and filth" laws brought arrests, trials, and confiscations.³⁸ The distribution of books could become a militant activity for cautious publishers and book dealers.³⁹

Given the liabilities threatening the fate of any contemporary novel and the limited numbers in which most such books were published and sold, one might question whether novels had much influence in nineteenth-century Germany. Two other innovations, however, serialization and lending libraries, enabled new novels to reach a much wider audience than a description of book sales suggests.

The practice of serializing novels in newspapers and periodicals proved especially important to authors. The average first printing of a novel was about eight hundred copies, and even works of well-known writers might be published in no more than two thousand copies for the first edition. In contrast, periodicals like the popular *Gartenlaube*, which serialized innumerable novels, had an estimated one million readers. By the end of the century a few newspapers far exceeded even that figure.⁴⁰ Although some authors expressed distaste for allowing literary works to be serialized (a distaste embodying the tension between *Dichter* and *Schriftsteller*), most welcomed the increasingly substantial payment and the success that serialization often meant. Even popular authors like Wilhelm Raabe found they could maintain life and limb only by "unbroken involvement" with periodicals.⁴¹

Since the winning of new readers was the principal aim in the competition for novels among periodicals, this brought pressures similar to those in the book trade. Newspaper readers often besieged editors with letters of outrage or praise that affected subsequent publishing decisions. For example, the serialization of Paul Heyse's novel *Kinder der Welt* (*Children of the World*) in Berlin's venerable *Spenersche Zeitung* in 1872 provoked a storm of protest and subscription cancellations that contributed to the paper's subsequent demise.⁴² Reader disapproval of Fontane's *Irrungen, Wirrungen* (*Differences, Confusions*) as a "shocking story of harlotry" did not have such dire effects on the *Vossische Zeitung*, but it did make editors cautious about publishing further novels by even so popular an author.⁴³ Editors often exhorted novelists to avoid controversy even while encouraging them to appeal to readers' social concerns. The successful newspaper novelist, while depicting social misery and class conflicts, would learn to manipulate these into endings that would divert readers from the hardships of the daily struggle for survival: "[The reader] can at least triumph in this struggle in his imagination, at the hero's side. That is why he demands the happy outcome, which finally follows from trials of every sort."⁴⁴ Although such thinking encouraged the production of socially harmless novels, even the conventional happy ending reveals authorial attitudes about prevailing social values.

Another institution for distributing literature was the library—not free public libraries, which were slow to be established in Imperial Germany, but commercial enterprises known as lending libraries (*Leihbibliotheken*).[45] The exact number is impossible to discover since many were associated with stationery stores, book stores, and newspaper shops, but between 1865 and 1890, the number of officially designated *Leihbibliotheken* rose from 779 to 2,629. Holdings ranged from several hundred books in village libraries to six hundred thousand at Borstell's in Berlin, with the likely average being about three thousand volumes.[46] Although catalogues are scarce, all evidence suggests that the libraries' principal holdings consisted of novels, which borrowers read in abundance and likely passed on to other family members.[47] The typically low publication figures for novels published as books bear no relation to the number of readers, since most copies of first-edition novels went directly to the lending libraries. Up to ninety percent of the reading public made use of these libraries, including, in the words of a contemporary, "old maids, petty pensioners and bureaucrats, students of all levels, clerks, actors and singers, teachers, and dignitaries' families."[48] Evidence that all classes used them comes from the increasingly disdainful complaints that books were "smeared from so much use and yellowed from spilled coffee." It was shocking, exclaimed a critic, that "our most elegant ladies" actually took such books in their hands.[49] Underscoring the dangers of such folly, one novel portrayed a young woman who contracted a fatal disease from a lending library book because her wealthy father was too cheap to buy books for her.[50]

Not surprisingly, the proliferation of lending libraries also spurred protest among authors and produced further strife within the book trade. In the belief that libraries were reaping profits at their expense some authors tried unsuccessfully to garner royalties from the rental of their works. Others exhorted readers to support the development of a national literature through regular book purchases.[51] Contrary to appearances, however, most lending librarians, like most book sellers, reaped only a marginal income. To maintain the core of regular customers upon which they depended, they had to set relatively low rates and stock an unprofitable variety of books. Librarians instigated a controversy of their own by attacking newspaper novels as unfair competition with the high-priced book publications they were forced to buy.[52] Some contemporaries seemed to recognize that libraries and bookshops complemented each other, but disputes continued to rage. Despite such mutual suspicions, the various elements of the literary trade promoted a phenomenal rise in the production and distribution of imaginative literature.

All this literary output was aimed at a readership whose rapidly mutliplying numbers reflected myriad goals and interests. The problem of determining who reads a particular novel has been vividly expressed in the analogy of an author who throws a bottle into the sea: "The castaway imagines the rescuer to whom he sends his message, feels himself dependent on him, but does not really know to what distant shores the sea will carry his appeal."[53] Such bewilderment was intensified by the social transformations of the late nineteenth century. As novelist Friedrich Spielhagen explained it, the formerly easy equation between social class and *Bildung* was being eliminated; an author might find enthusiastic readers—and militant opponents—in any class, "from the palace to the cottage." The problem was compounded "by the diverse, often contradictory perspectives and needs of the city versus the country dweller; and again by the inhabitants of great cultural and commercial centers versus those of the provincial towns and villages."[54]

Nineteenth-century scholarship failed even to articulate the problem of determining readership, and when twentieth-century scholars raised questions about the reception of literary works, they were often shouted down by proponents of other schools of criticism.[55] Practitioners of research into literary reception continue to be cautious about method. Defining the expectations of the reading public, assessing the causes of opposition to a literary work, formulating research techniques appropriate to the period under study, identifying sources beyond reviews, letters, and diaries—such tasks point to the complexities of problems whose answers demand the effective use of a range of scholarly disciplines.[56] Beneath these complexities, however, lies ground for some broad inferences about a reading revolution transforming the reading public in Imperial Germany.

Two essential assumptions in postulating a social group of readers is that its members are literate and possess some sort of leisure time.[57] Despite a rapid growth in literacy by the middle of the nineteenth century, the level of reading for about fifty percent of the public was no more than elementary. The kind of leisure likely to be devoted to novel reading, moreover, must be relatively sustained, since odd moments during a work day, if used for reading at all, would most likely be restricted to newspapers. Leisure, then, includes "regular free time" in the evening as well as "periods of non-activity" such as Sundays, holidays, illness, and retirement.[58] Which literate groups in nineteenth-century Germany had such leisure, and to what extent was it devoted to reading novels?

Reinhard Wittmann approaches the question of the democratization of reading by inquiring how modernization affected the reading habits of every level of society. He challenges conjectures that the readership of middlebrow literature extended in any significant way into the working class or the peasantry. Evidence, Wittmann argues, suggests that the lower classes' involvement in the nineteenth-century reading revolution was inhibited by their social environment and economic situation. The overwhelming majority of marginally literate people was concentrated in the urban working classes and rural poor. Long, exhausting working hours left them little time or inclination for reading. In addition, living conditions made reading difficult, since a whole family would often crowd into one heated and usually ill-lit room. The prohibitive cost of books made the reading of contemporary literature still less accessible. Newspapers, because of price and because of their suitability for brief periods of free time, became increasingly popular, however, and made serialized novels the most likely contact of the lower classes with the works under study here. Even this likelihood was offset by the elementary reading level of many. Those who read for entertainment were more likely to turn to the sensationalist colportage novel hawked by door-to-door salesmen in cheap individual instalments.[59]

The novels that concern us made greater intellectual demands than the colportage novels. Their readers should be sought among the fifty percent of the population delineated by Wittmann as having adequate reading skills. Most fell into the broad category of the middle class, or *Mittelstand*, whose members, despite their diversity, tended to be better educated than the working class. They were also likely to have more spare time, were more inclined to use such time for reading, and were more likely to enjoy at least some privacy in their living quarters.[60] To be sure, few members of the middle class had the income to sustain regular purchases of contemporary literature, and even those who did, some evidence suggests, balked at the expense.[61] Whatever the book-buying practices, however, a qualitative and quantitative revolution was underway in middle-class reading habits as the traditional re-reading of a few time-honored works became transformed into a demand for "increasingly changeable, multifarious, entertaining stimulation through reading." Wittmann explains this demand as a product of modern society, commenting that the railway era had transmuted a sense of hurry to modern humanity that extended to reading.[62] A dramatic increase in the consumption of contemporary novels was a significant dimension of this revolution.

Although Wittmann links the consumption of novels to the emergence of an industrial society filled with competitive pressures, he also suggests that the majority of novel readers might have been housewives and ladies of leisure. Although research on this possibility is inconclusive, similar notions caused nineteenth-century observers to belittle the supposed woman reader as someone who, "enmeshed in her domesticity, lives a fantasy life with only the most childish ideas of the surrounding world." Some critics also disparaged authors who, by directing their works to such a woman, were producing "a world equally unrealistic as the one in her head."[63] Novels echo such beliefs as when a physician-character scoffs at a friend for wasting his time with fiction: "That's something for women, who don't know the world and who believe it really exists just as it's shown in books."[64]

Whether or not women were indeed the main consumers of fiction, the pronounced social criticism in most Berlin novels makes it clear that authors were addressing themselves to a more serious public than the stereotypical lady of leisure on her chaise longue. Some even made the point that supposed female weaknesses were more a state of mind than of gender. One such novel, whose epigraph dedicates the work to "All those gentlemen who are not ladies," opens with an attack on "women's literature," adding that one day a long column would march for "the true woman."[65] The opening manifesto of the naturalist periodical *Die Gesellschaft* is equally strident about encouraging a virile literature by bringing about "the emancipation of periodical literature and criticism from the tyranny of 'debutantes' and 'old maids of both sexes.'"[66]

The issue beneath such appeals has less to do with gender than with readers' motivations for reading novels at all. These are even more difficult to establish than the identity of the readers themselves. Nevertheless, literary sociologists have suggested three basic reasons for reading novels beyond a purely esthetic pursuit: escape, fashion, and social understanding. Although the apportioning of readers into such categories is not my concern here, the diversity of purposes for reading novels underscores the tentativeness with which their social role must be interpreted.

Escape from daily pressures was likely the most popular reason for reading novels. As the above comments about women's fantasy world show, the social significance of such escape was controversial in the last century. Today such controversy continues, with some critics assessing recourse to "wish-fulfillment literature" as a harmless pleasure and others arguing that even seemingly banal wish-fulfillment fosters dangerous social, nationalistic, and political prejudices.[67] Robert Escarpit counters such a sweeping condemnation by commenting that, "There are a thousand ways to escape and it is essential to know from what and towards what we are escaping."[68] Historians, according to this argument, should first determine how the need for escape might be related to such critical events as wars, revolutions, or political upheavals and only then evaluate the implications of a particular form of escape. Drawing such implications from individual novels will underlie much of the forthcoming analysis.

Critics in Imperial Germany frequently argued that people read novels simply because they were fashionable. In 1908 one critic described the phenomenon in terms of "an often dizzying reversal of public opinion, which drops today what yesterday it was still raising to the heavens."[69] Another observer, an early sociologist of literature named Levin Schücking, also emphasized the pressure of fashion on literary tastes by noting that anyone who wanted to keep up with the times was "forced to come to terms with new publications that were attracting attention."[70] Robert Escarpit has underlined the idea by showing that literature might be used to promote social ambitions or to affirm identity with a desired social group.[71] That Berlin novelists embraced some such hypothesis is shown by countless cynical portrayals of the molding of cultural taste by the pressures of the salon. Again, however, through such criticism they made it clear that they intended their own works to serve more socially responsible purposes. The idea that readers might choose a novel with the aim of understanding the world and their place in it, and of changing it for the better, appealed to many authors. Although well aware that such was not likely to be readers' principal motivation, they clearly hoped their works would awaken social consciousness in their readers if it was not already there.

Beyond all these rationales for reading, moreover, readers brought an intricate network of subjective values and social influences to the novels they read and thus took from them varying messages. The evidence suggests that most of the readers of the novels of Imperial Berlin were middle class, and that for many novels the majority were probably women. Although this readership was more likely to consist of urban rather than rural people and of Prussians rather than non-Prussians, it was by no means limited to those groups. Literary critiques in provincial newspapers, serializations, and the proliferation of lending libraries meant that Berlin novels were read and discussed all over Germany. To varying degrees, Berlin novels addressed the commonality of Germans confronting a bewildering array of new experiences. In that sense these works represent German encounters with nationhood and modernity.

The complexities of understanding the role of contemporary novels in the development of a national identity are immense. To explain their popularity in Imperial Germany involves a complicated chicken-and-egg problem: an abundance of novels poured forth, but whether they caused or resulted from the growth of the publication industry or from the rapid growth of the reading population is far from clear. Indisputably, however, novels became an extraordinarily popular form of entertainment in the last decades of the century, and this fact contributes to their importance as a historical source. In one novel a character says, "Sage mir, was du liest, und ich sage dir, was du bist."[72] This slogan, freely translated as, "You are what you read," assumes that by immersing readers in social issues that have been translated into human situations, novels become part of the process by which social and national values are formed. With this assumption in mind, I now turn to the question of what sorts of messages they transmitted.

# Notes

1. On recent scholarly controversy over German development, see "Kolloquien des Instituts für Zeitgeschichte," *Deutscher Sonderweg—Mythos oder Realität?* (Munich, 1982); David Blackbourn and Geoff Eley, *The Peculiarities of German History: Bourgeois Society and Politics in Nineteenth-Century Germany* (Oxford, 1984); and Harold James, *A German Identity: 1770–1990* (New York, 1989).
2. See Lothar Müller, "Die Großstadt als Ort der Moderne: Über Georg Simmel," in Klaus R. Scherpe, ed., *Die Unwirklichkeit der Städte: Großstadtdarstellungen zwischen Moderne und Postmoderne* (Reinbek bei Hamburg, 1988), 14–36. See also Marshall Berman, *All That Is Solid Melts into Air: The Experience of Modernity* (New York, 1982); Peter Berger, Brigitte Berger, and Hansfried Kellner, *The Homeless Mind: Modernization and Consciousness* (1973; New York, 1974); and Hans-Ulrich Wehler, *Modernisierungstheorie und Geschichte* (Göttingen, 1975).
3. Gerhart Hauptmann quoted in Adalbert von Hanstein, *Das jüngste Deutschland: Zwei Jahrzehnte miterlebter Literaturgeschichte* (Leipzig, 1905), 3. Here, as elsewhere, the translations are mine except when noted. See also Julius Hart, "Auf der Fahrt nach Berlin," in Jürgen Schutte and Peter Sprengel, eds., *Die Berliner Moderne, 1885–1914* (Stuttgart, 1987), 249–252. On the wider context of this pro-urban culture, see Andrew Lees, *Cities Perceived: Urban Society in European and American Thought, 1820–1940* (New York, 1985), 189–255, 312, and Andrew Lees, "The Civil Pride of the German Middle Classes, 1890–1918," in Jack R. Dukes and Joachim Remak, eds., *Another Germany: A Reconsideration of the Imperial Era* (Boulder, Colo., 1988), 41–59.
4. Or, to use another term, they were helping to *invent* German identity through their

discourse. James J. Sheehan, "The Problem of the Nation in German History," in Otto Büsch and James J. Sheehan, eds., *Die Rolle der Nation in der deutschen Geschichte und Gegenwart* (Berlin, 1985), 3–5. See also Lees, *Cities Perceived*, 89.
5. On the enormously complex relation between fiction and history see Dominick LaCapra, *History and Criticism* (Ithaca, N.Y., 1985), 115–134, Hayden White, *The Content of the Form: Narrative Discourse and Historical Representation* (Baltimore, 1987), 44–48; and Gisela Brude-Firnau and Karin J. MacHardy, eds. *Fact and Fiction: German History and Literature, 1848–1924* (Tübingen, 1990). For a lively exchange on approaches to literature and society see *American Historical Review*, 94 (1989), 581–626 and 1326–1332.
6. Fritz Martini, *Deutsche Literatur im bürgerlichen Realismus, 1848–1898*, 4th ed. (Stuttgart, 1981), 1–115. See also Friedrich Spielhagen, *Beiträge zur Theorie und Technik des Romans* (Leipzig, 1883); J. P. Stern, *On Realism* (London, 1973); and Roger Hillman, *Zeitroman: The Novel and Society in Germany, 1830–1900* (Bern, 1983), 13–24.
7. Martini, *Deutsche Literatur*, 1–4.
8. Karl Gutzkow, *Die neuen Serapionsbrüder* (Breslau, 1877), III, 184.
9. Hans R. Fischer, *Was Berlin verschlingt* (Berlin, 1890), 1–2.
10. Peter Hille, *Die Sozialisten* (Leipzig, 1886).
11. Conrad Alberti, *Gustav Freytag: Sein Leben und Schaffen* (Leipzig, 1885), 151.
12. On the legacy of revolutionary expectations within national movements, see Walter Bußmann, "Das deutsche Nationalbewußtsein im 19. Jahrhundert," in Werner Weidenfeld, ed., *Die Identität der Deutschen* (Munich, 1983), 64–82.
13. On notions of *Innerlichkeit* in German culture see Richard Münch, *Die Kultur der Moderne*, Vol. II: *Ihre Entwicklung in Frankreich und Deutschland* (Frankfurt am Main, 1986), 686–709.
14. See, for instance, Werner Conze, " 'Deutschland' und 'deutsche Nation' als historische Begriffe," in Büsch and Sheehan, *Die Rolle der Nation*, 32–35.
15. On the juxtaposition of optimism and pessimism in late nineteenth-century culture see Blackbourn and Eley, *Peculiarities of German History*, 217.
16. For examples of each of these approaches see, respectively, Hans-Werner Niemann, *Das Bild des industriellen Unternehmers in deutschen Romanen der Jahre 1890 bis 1945* (Berlin, 1982); Elizabeth Langland, *Society in the Novel* (Chapel Hill, N.C., 1984); Russell A. Berman, *The Rise of the Modern German Novel: Crisis and Charisma* (Cambridge, Mass., 1986); and Nancy A. Kaiser, *Social Integration and Narrative Structure: Patterns of Realism in Auerbach, Freytag, Fontane, and Raabe* (New York, 1986).
17. Frederick Crews, "The Parting of the Twains," *New York Review of Books*, 36, 12 (20 July 1989), 42. On the debate over authorial presence see *American Historical Review*, 94 (1989), 585, 614–615, and 1326–1332.
18. The two best sources for authors and titles are Hans Zopf and Heinrich Gerd, eds., *Berlin-Bibliographie (Bis 1960)* (Berlin, 1965), 457–483, and Wilhelm Kosch, *Deutsches Literatur-Lexikon*, 2nd ed. (Bern, 1949), I, 138–142.
19. Paul Lindau, *Der Zug nach dem Westen* (1886); Ludovika Hesekiel, *Von Brandenburg zu Bismarck* (1873); Rudolf Lothar, *Kurfürstendamm* (1910); Johannes Schlaf, *Das dritte Reich* (1900); Robert Saudek, *Dämon Berlin* (1906).
20. On the "important and instructive" nature of "subliterature" see David H. Miles, "Literary Sociology: Some Introductory Notes," *German Quarterly*, 48, 1 (1975), 28; on the perils of critics' attempting to establish works of literature as an "ideological instrument" see White, *Content of the Form*, 80–82.
21. Cited in Robert Darnton, *The Great Cat Massacre and Other Episodes in French Cultural History* (New York, 1984), 263.

22. A good introduction to the interaction of these components is J. A. Bull, *The Framework of Fiction: Socio-Cultural Approaches to the Novel* (London, 1988). See also Rudolf Schenda, *Die Lesestoffe der kleinen Leute: Studien zur populären Literatur im 19. und 20. Jahrhundert* (Munich, 1976).
23. Walter Horace Bruford, "Der Beruf des Schriftstellers," in Hans Norbert Fügen, ed., *Wege der Literatursoziologie* (Neuwied, 1968), 270. See also Friedrich Spielhagen, "Produktion, Kritik und Publikum" (1883), reprinted (with deletions) in Max Bucher, Werner Hahl, Georg Jäger, Reinhard Wittmann, eds., *Realismus und Gründerzeit: Manifeste und Dokumente zur deutschen Literatur, 1848–1880* (Stuttgart, 1976), II, 613–618.
24. *Dichtung und Wahrheit*, Part II, Book 10; quoted by Bruford, in Fügen, *Wege der Literatursoziologie*, 269. See also Fritz Hodeige, "Die Stellung von Dichter und Buch in der Gesellschaft: Eine literarsoziologische Untersuchung," *Archiv für Geschichte des Buchwesens*, 1 (1956), 153–163; and Ernest K. Bramsted, *Aristocracy and the Middle-Classes in Germany: Social Types in German Literature, 1830–1900*, rev. ed. (Chicago, 1964), 279–289.
25. Reinhard Wittmann, "Das literarische Leben 1848 bis 1880," in Bucher, *Realismus*, I, 197. See also Ulrich Engelhardt, *"Bildungsbürgertum": Begriffs- und Dogmengeschichte eines Etiketts* (Stuttgart, 1986), 147. On specific aspects of the distinction between *Dichter* and *Schriftsteller*, see Paul Levesque, "Jahrhundertwende, Fin de Siècle, Wilhelminian Era: Re-examining German Literary Culture 1871–1918," *German Studies Review*, 13, 1 (February 1990), 9–25.
26. Martini, *Deutsche Literatur*, 22. See also Bramsted, *Aristocracy and the Middle-Classes*, 333.
27. Wittmann in Bucher, *Realismus*, I, 200. See also Berman, *Modern German Novel*, 86, and Ronald Gray, "Writers and Politics: 1871–1918," in James Hardin, ed., *German Fiction Writers, 1885–1913* (Detroit, 1988), 542.
28. Bramsted, *Aristocracy and the Middle-Classes*, 333. See also Martin Halter, *Sklaven der Arbeit—Ritter vom Geiste: Arbeit und Arbeiter im deutschen Sozialroman zwischen 1840 und 1880* (Frankfurt am Main, 1983), 51–59.
29. See, for example, Walter Müller-Seidel, *Theodor Fontane: Soziale Romankunst in Deutschland* (Stuttgart, 1975), 289. On the difficulties of translating *Bildungsbürgertum* into English see Werner Conze and Jürgen Kocka, eds., *Bildungsbürgertum im 19. Jahrhundert* (Stuttgart, 1985), 12–13.
30. Reinhard Wittmann, *Buchmarkt und Lektüre im 18. und 19. Jahrhundert: Beiträge zum literarischen Leben, 1750–1880* (Tübingen, 1982), 165–177. See also Bramsted, *Aristocracy and the Middle-Classes*, 272–279; Eva Wolf, *Der Schriftsteller im Querschnitt: Außenseiter der Gesellschaft um 1900? Ein systematischer Vergleich von Prosatexten* (Munich, 1978), 29–31.
31. Robert Escarpit, *Sociology of Literature*, translated by Ernest Pick (Painesville, Ohio, 1965), 37.
32. Martini, *Deutsche Literatur*, 23.
33. Robert Springer, *Banquier und Schriftsteller* (Berlin, 1877), 25–35. See also Siegfried Unseld, *The Author and His Publisher*, translated by Hunter Hannum and Hildegarde Hannum (Chicago, 1980), 1–44.
34. Robert Escarpit, *The Book Revolution* (London, 1966), 115, and Bucher, *Realismus*, I, 163.
35. Bucher, *Realismus*, I, 166, 178, 240–251; Wittmann, *Buchmarkt*, 130–134; and Peter Uwe Hohendahl, *Building a National Literature: The Case of Germany, 1830–1870*, translated by Renate Baron Franciscono (Ithaca, N.Y., 1989), 329–331.
36. Wittmann in Bucher, *Realismus*, I, 170, and Escarpit, *Book Revolution*, 145. See also Johann Goldfriedrich, *Geschichte des Deutschen Buchhandels vom Beginn der Fremd-*

Introduction 19

   herrschaft bis zur Reform des Börsenvereins im neuen Deutschen Reiche (1805–1889) (Leipzig, 1913; reprinted 1970), Chapter 10.
37. Wittmann, Buchmarkt, 185–191.
38. See Gerhard Schulz, "Naturalismus und Zensur," in Helmut Scheuer, ed., Naturalismus: Bürgerliche Dichtung und soziales Engagement (Stuttgart, 1974), 93–121, and "Symposium: The Censorship of Literary Naturalism," in Central European History, 18, 3/4 (September/December 1985), 326–364.
39. Escarpit, Book Revolution, 148.
40. Bucher, Realismus, I, 190–191, 209. See also Eva D. Becker, "'Zeitungen sind doch das Beste': Bürgerliche Realisten und der Vorabdruck ihrer Werke in der periodischen Presse," in Helmut Kreuzer, ed., Gestaltungsgeschichte und Gesellschaftsgeschichte. Festschrift für Fritz Martini (Stuttgart, 1969), 395; Rudolf Hackmann, Die Anfänge des Romans in der Zeitung (Dissertation, Berlin, 1938), Parts I and II.
41. Becker, "Zeitungen," 382. Friedrich Spielhagen even adapted his widely discussed theory of the novel to the conditions of the periodical press. Bucher, Realismus, I, 209–210.
42. Bucher, Realismus, I, 209, and Becker, "Zeitungen," 396–408. Heyse's awareness of the dangers of popular censorship of social novels is suggested by dialogue within his controversial novel. Paul Heyse, Kinder der Welt, 11th ed. (Berlin, 1886), I, 142f.
43. Peter Demetz, "Theodor Fontane als Unterhaltungsautor," in Annamaria Rucktäschel and Hans Dieter Zimmermann, eds., Trivialliteratur (Munich, 1976), 190–204.
44. Hackmann, Anfänge des Roman in der Zeitung, 62, 35.
45. See Georg Jäger and Jörg Schönert, eds., Die Leihbibliothek als Institution des literarischen Lebens im 18. und 19. Jahrhundert: Organisationsformen, Bestände und Publikum (Hamburg, 1980), 7–195.
46. Bernd von Arnim and Friedrich Knilli, Gewerbliche Leihbüchereien: Berichte, Analysen und Interviews (Gütersloh, 1966), 18, 82, and Bucher, Realismus, I, 189.
47. Bucher, Realismus, II, 643. On Leihbibliothek holdings in an earlier period, see Georg Jäger, "Die Bestände deutscher Leihbibliotheken zwischen 1815 und 1860. Interpretation statistischer Befunde," in Reinhard Wittmann and Bertold Hack, eds., Buchhandel und Literatur (Wiesbaden, 1982), 247–313.
48. Quoted by Wittmann in Bucher, Realismus, I, 241 and 188. Statistics on users are difficult to garner, but a 1963 survey of lending library customers shows that modern-day readers come from all ranks and occupations, with stereotypical housewives, however, forming a disproportionate number. Arnim and Knilli, Leihbüchereien, 163–170.
49. Arnim and Knilli, Leihbüchereien, 16.
50. Conrad Alberti, Die Alten und die Jungen (Leipzig, 1889), II, 251. For other complaints about unhygienic aspects of using library books see Bucher, Realismus, II, 618–620, 626–630, and Peter Vodosek, ed., Auf dem Weg zur öffentlichen Literaturversorgung: Quellen und Texte zur Geschichte der Volksbibliotheken in der zweiten Hälfte des 19. Jahrhunderts (Wiesbaden, 1985), 153–155.
51. Arnim and Knilli, Leihbüchereien, 40–42. The sentiment expressed by Gustav Freytag in 1852 that "every well-to-do citizen has the duty of spending a fixed amount of his budget for a home library" continued to be uttered in later decades. Bucher, Realismus, II, 629; see also Berman, Modern German Novel, 68–75.
52. Bucher, Realismus, II, 635–647.
53. Escarpit, Sociology of Literature, 18. This analogy, of course, also provides grist for the mill of the "death of the author" theory. See above, n17.
54. Bucher, Realismus, II, 614.
55. Wittmann in Bucher, Realismus, I, 227. See also Peter Uwe Hohendahl, ed., Sozialgeschichte und Wirkungsästhetik (Frankfurt am Main, 1974), 9–48, and Terry

Eagleton, *Literary Theory: An Introduction* (Minneapolis, 1983), especially Chapters 1 and 2.
56. Karl Robert Mandelkow, "Probleme der Wirkungsgeschichte," in Hohendahl, *Wirkungsästhetik*, 82–96. See also Rudolf von Gottschall, "Die Lektüre des heutigen Lesepublikums," *Deutsche Revue*, 33, 1 (1908), 160.
57. Maria-Rita Girardi, *Buch und Leser in Deutschland* (Gütersloh, 1965), 28.
58. Escarpit, *Sociology of Literature*, 93–94.
59. Wittmann in Bucher, *Realismus*, I, 228–237, and Wittmann, *Buchmarkt*, 199–204, 138–142. See also Heinz Sarkowski, "Der Buchbetrieb von Tür zu Tür im 19. Jahrhundert," in Wittmann and Hack, *Buchhandel*, 221–246.
60. Wittmann, *Buchmarkt*, 204–210.
61. Wittmann in Bucher, *Realismus*, 237–239. See also Conrad Alberti, "Der Deutsche und das Buch," *Die Gesellschaft*, 4 (1888), 5–13, and Alberti, *Die Alten und die Jungen*, I, 203.
62. Wittmann in Bucher, *Realismus*, I, 239–241.
63. Ibid., 253. See also Walter Hofmann, *Die Lektüre der Frau: Ein Beitrag zur Leserkunde und zur Leserführung* (Leipzig, 1931), and Schenda, *Die Lesestoffe der kleinen Leute*, 147.
64. Conrad Alberti, "Wir Riesen," in *Riesen und Zwerge* (Berlin, 1888), 15. An echo of the negative connotations of a female readership is also heard in Rudolf von Gottschall, "Die Lektüre des heutigen Lesepublikums," *Deutsche Revue*, 33, 1 (1908), 158.
65. Hille, *Die Sozialisten*, 2.
66. *Die Gesellschaft*, 1, 1 (1 January 1885), 1.
67. For examples of these two views see, respectively, Fritz Hodeige, "Die Stellung von Dichter und Buch in der Gesellschaft: Eine literarsoziologische Untersuchung," *Archiv für Geschichte des Buchwesens*, 1 (1956–1958), 165, and Friedrich Heer, *Die Rolle des Buches in der Geistes- und Meinungsbildung* (Vienna, 1962), 6–7.
68. Escarpit, *Sociology of Literature*, 91.
69. Gottschall, "Lektüre des Lesepublikums," 166.
70. Levin Schücking, "Die Aufnahme beim Publikum," in Hohendahl, *Wirkungsästhetik*, 52, 63.
71. Escarpit, *Sociology of Literature*, 90. Another argument holds that the consumption of literature in bourgeois society is a display of culture that signifies an ordering of the world through capitalist possession. Berman, *Modern German Novel*, 67.
72. Karl Bleibtreu, *Die Auskunftei* (Munich, 1910), 100.

# 1

# The Prologue: Karl Gutzkow's *Knights of the Spirit*

In comparison to other European cities Berlin is young, having originated not as a prehistoric settlement or a Roman garrison but in the early thirteenth century as two fishing villages, Berlin and Cölln, straddling the Spree.[1] For almost two centuries the two hamlets remained independent by taking advantage of a hiatus in the power of neighboring feudal lords. This independence, however, came to an end in the fifteenth century, when a succession of Hohenzollern electors wrested control from the communal government and, building a palace on the Cölln side of the Spree, established Berlin/Cölln as their residence in the realm that became known as Brandenburg Prussia. Thus began a tense relationship that lasted into the twentieth century. As Berlin historian Walter Kiaulehn put it, "Berlin became the Prussian capital and later the imperial capital against her will."[2] In the late seventeenth century, with the military victories of the Great Elector against Sweden, the Hohenzollerns began to bring glory to the city. These and subsequent wars took a heavy toll, but interspersed were long periods when Berlin developed as the administrative, military, and economic center of Prussia. The fates of the dynasty, Prussia, and Berlin became inextricably intertwined.

At the end of the seventeenth century Frederick I, the first Hohenzollern to bear the title of king, commissioned a gridwork of streets to the west of the palace on the Spree, thereby initiating an expansion that would become a hallmark of Berlin—the "west" serving as the symbol of the city's splendor and modernity.[3] His wife, Sophia Charlotte, reinforced the process by planting the first of the linden trees that resulted in the elegant boulevard, Unter den Linden. It became lined with architectural landmarks as well as stately trees and culminated in the most famous landmark of all: the Doric columns of the Brandenburg Gate.[4] The two districts north and south of the Linden, Dorotheenstadt and Friedrichstadt, became the main sites of new building, while the easterly districts enclosed by the town's old tariff wall remained agrarian through the eighteenth century.[5] Other Hohenzollern palaces in Charlottenburg, to the west, and Potsdam, to the southwest, which led to a steady flow of traffic through Brandenburg and Potsdam gates, reinforced Berlin's westward focus.

The city's architectural transformations were accompanied by cultural ones as well. In 1700 philosopher Gottfried von Leibniz founded the society that evolved into the Prussian Academy, which for more than a century served as Berlin's major intellectual center. The reign of Frederick II (1740–1786) attracted still more writers and thinkers to the city, and they contributed to the emergence of a Berlin enlightenment under the influence of such figures as playwright Gotthold Ephraim Lessing, philosopher Moses Mendelssohn, publisher Friedrich Nicolai, and educator Friedrich Gedike. Berlin theaters also attained growing renown for their premieres of dramas by Goethe and Schiller. Not until 1810 would the city have its own university, but, as if to make up for lost time, it soon became the leading university in Germany. The early nineteenth century also saw spirited exchanges among scholars, artists, courtiers, and diplomats in the Jewish salons that dominated the city's cultural life.[6] Berlin thus laid claim to the sobriquet "Athens on the Spree," a title invoked with both pride and irony.[7]

A distinctive Berlin character was also emerging, and many decades later Berlin author Theodor Fontane tried to define its historical elements. Berliners, as Fontane described them, descended from both Slavic migrants from the east and Germanic conquerors from the west who first settled the swampy territory known as the Mark, which surrounded the future city. The Markish people were characterized by humble virtues: frugality, a sense of order, and a strong feeling of duty. Their vices involved the extremes of their virtues: miserliness, pettiness, and a tendency to exaggerate the smallest effort made for someone else.[8] These humorless, narrow-minded Berliners became transformed into "real" (*richtigen*) Berliners in the eighteenth century, with the injection of a singular wit and a tolerant rationalism into their character. Berliner humor, according to Fontane, derived from the court, where an appreciation of repartee flourished by the time of Frederick II. All who wanted to gain royal notice, Fontane explains, had to cultivate a "sharp Sanssouci-idiom," which then traveled from the officer corps down the ranks of the Frederician army and, as retiring soldiers settled in Berlin to practice their crafts, to other commoners.[9] Berliner rationalism, on the other hand, originated with the educated middle class, whose "gospel of enlightenment and religious equality" found literary expression in Lessing's *Nathan der Weise*.[10]

Another decisive element of Berlin's identity came with the wars of liberation against Napoleonic France in 1813. This uprising emerged from the difficult years following Prussia's humiliating defeat in 1806 and Berlin's occupation by French troops. The patriotic sentiments behind the 1813 effort were rooted in the political, cultural, and military reforms through which a shaken Prussian government sought to generate the popular support so lacking in 1806. Philosopher Johann Gottlieb Fichte helped kindle the popular fervor with a series of Sunday lectures, in 1807–1808, entitled "Addresses to the German Nation," which called upon Germans to sacrifice themselves "for the common weal" by reaffirming age-old virtues of modesty and duty.[11] A further incentive, a decree of 1808, restored the communal government the Hohenzollerns had destroyed in Berlin almost four centuries earlier.[12] Thus originated the mythology of 1813: a united citizenry defending Prussia.

The revolution of 1848 provoked a far more ambiguous mythology, but one equally important as that of 1813. One image derived from March 1848, when Berliners threw up barricades and forced Frederick William IV to agree to political reforms. As in 1813, Berlin citizens could be seen as banding together to defeat an oppressive enemy, but this time the enemy was Hohenzollern absolutism.[13] Seven months later the revolutionaries, beset by internal conflict, left the way open for the army to retake the city and reinstate dynastic rule. Irresponsible mobs, some said, had subverted a stable and benevolent Prussian state.[14] The complexities of 1848 are immense, but what is important here is the question of how Germans would assess the upheaval. As we will see, the image of revolution remained compelling. Equally compelling was the notion that the true German revolution must not unfold in the rowdy manner of 1848 but must find another, uniquely German, path.

Berlin's identity thus developed with a number of pronounced dichotomies. Distant memories of her early communal government provoked ongoing resentment toward Hohenzollern domination, even as it was indisputably this dynastic rule that was bringing the city to the forefront of European affairs. Sensitive notions of Berlin as a cultural backwater competed with the splendid image of Athens on the Spree. Caricatures of the Berliner as a churlish Marker or provincial philistine were being challenged with new, and perhaps equally negative, stereotypes of the Berliner as an unrefined parvenu. And legacies of Berlin as the center of Prussian tradition were clashing with ideals of the city as the progenitor of German nationhood.

What no one challenged, however, was the belief that Berlin stood in the vanguard of German modernity. By mid-century Berlin's modernization was in full swing. Her population in 1850 had reached 428,000, triple the level of fifty years earlier.[15] The old wall was rapidly being dismantled to make way for new construction. New districts were beginning to appear: industrial Moabit to the north, elegant Tiergarten to the west, and commercial Köpenick to the south. A network of railways emanating from the city marked Berlin's transformation into an industrial and financial center. In this atmosphere of rapid and bewildering change novelists tried to come to terms with what was happening.

Cities have appeared in literature since ancient times, but their use as a vehicle of social understanding is a modern phenomenon that coincides with the rise of the novel. As Volker Klotz argues, the novel, with its openendedness and its ability to roam widely and imaginatively, is uniquely suited to the portrayal of a city's "spatial breadth and diversity . . ., its social complexity, the intertwining and the conflict between private life and public commerce and professional life."[16] The crucial period of the city novel's history was the early nineteenth century, when novelists in England and France began to define the city they were experiencing. As they opened their eyes to their surroundings, these authors observed the misery of many urban dwellers and found themselves compelled to portray it.[17] Perceptions of material poverty were often overshadowed by a sense of spiritual poverty that resulted from the impersonal bureaucracies and bewildering social forces of the modern city. The antagonism authors saw between the individual and the city became a central theme in their works and created ambivalence toward modernity even among those who embraced it. In contrast to opponents of modernity, however, who expounded a nostalgic return to rural ways or the recreation of a mythical past, city novelists sought to understand how the individual might come to terms with the city.[18] The terms of their search provide keys to their values and perspectives and to those of their age.

German authors were relatively slow to confront the problem of coming to terms with the city. The city novel originated in countries that experienced the twin revolutions of modernity—political and economic—before Germany. But the early example of Dostoyevsky integrating St. Petersburg into his novels shows that modernity could not have been the sole prerequisite. In this light we might hypothesize that Germany's lack of national unity, and her corresponding lack of a capital or center, may also have impeded the development of the city novel in German culture.

Berlin's emergence as the center of Germany in the nineteenth century coincided with the rise of the German city novel, but even into the twentieth century some still questioned whether Berlin had yet developed a sufficiently clear identity for "the Berlin novel" to be written. As literary historian Paul Alfred Merbach commented in 1913: "The metropolis is still too young and lacks special characteristic qualities and features. It is only the summation and concentration of many things that are to be found throughout Germany."[19] Nevertheless, Merbach overcame such skepticism enough to identify historical stages by which Berlin came to be treated fictionally. In the process he created an operative definition of the Berlin novel as a genre. Reaching back to 1773, he identified a first novel "baptized with water from the Spree," and alluded to scores of others that followed in the next half century. But despite some critical social perspectives, these novels, in Merbach's view, had not yet attained the status of "Berlin novels," because they still portrayed Berlin as an isolated entity rather than as the center of a dynamic state. All this changed, Merbach asserted, with the historical novels of Willibald Alexis (1798–1871), whose depictions of such key moments as the aftermath of the defeat of 1806 showed Berlin as becoming "the real capital of a political entity, newly conscious of its existence and its coming development."[20] The statement refers to Alexis' 1852 novel *Ruhe ist die erste Bürgerpflicht* (*Calmness is the Citizen's First Duty*), but Merbach could better have applied those words to a novel by Karl Gutzkow (1811–1878) published two years earlier.

Gutzkow can rightfully be described as the father of the Berlin novel because he used the city in his fiction as a means of provoking his readers to come to terms with their own age.[21] The literary convention of using Berlin to show the impact of modernity on human existence was pioneered by Gutzkow in his panoramic work, *Die Ritter vom Geiste* (*Knights of the Spirit*). Published as a serialization beginning in 1850, and numbering three thousand pages in its first book edition, the novel develops intricate plots and subplots through which to survey a German society reeling from the shocks of 1848. Berlin is shown as a whirlpool of political activity and social intrigue, the restless center of a Germany undergoing profound change. Those with the fortitude to persevere in reading the long volumes will discover a monumental prologue to the novels of Imperial Berlin that introduces virtually every theme that subsequently appears.[22]

Central to Gutzkow's literary purpose was an intense social awareness whose beginnings he located in 1830, when news reached Berlin that Parisian revolutionaries had forced the abdication of Charles X. Prior to that day, he writes in his autobiography, he had pursued a conventional academic path at the university, following the wishes of his strict Pietist parents. News about the dramatic events in Paris caused him to abandon that path: "I picked up a newspaper *for the first time* . . . . Scholarship was now behind me; history lay before me."[23] Seeking to understand currents swirling through France, Gutzkow became aware of Germany's immobility after two decades of Metternich's dominance: "All of Europe was astir; only Germany continued to snore."[24] After concluding that both the academic and legal professions toward which his studies had been leading were also dormant, he immersed himself in self-assigned literary exercises.[25] He saw that writing alone offered a chance for freedom, and by the mid-1830s he had become a prolific and outspoken representative of the literary generation known as the "Young Germans."[26] Gutzkow's literary engagement would also become an attribute of countless successors.

Succeeding years took the writer to almost every literary center in the German Confederation and included frenetic activity: editorial involvement in a multitude of journals; publication of articles, critiques, poems, short stories, novels, and plays; and a stint as producer in the royal theater at Dresden. His experiences contributed to a growing conviction that German authoritarianism was doomed. Its destruction would result from the sum of pressures from "little events," he wrote later, instigated by people from all classes, whom he compared to the "rats who noiselessly gnaw the great net in which the bravest lion is held captive."[27] At first, Gutzkow's own gnawings were anything but noiseless, and the effects of a controversial novel published in 1835 included a prison term and prohibition of the work by the German diet.

During the 1840s Gutzkow's political frustrations grew, but significantly, these did not lead to action. When he journeyed from Dresden to Berlin in March 1848, he was seeking, by his account, only a chance to work on his latest drama. His expectations rested on memories of the city in the mid-1830s, when it had been impossible to conceive of any "upheaval in the gray monotony."[28] Hence, his astonishment to watch from his hotel window as crowds of Berliners let their discontents erupt into revolutionary action. Neither at this point, however, nor in the months after he returned to Dresden, did Gutzkow join, much less lead, any revolutionary party.[29] Literary engagement did not include political action.

The experience of 1848 nevertheless had a decisive effect on Gutzkow's expansive portrayal of post-revolutionary German society in *Ritter vom Geiste*. His intricate working out of a multitude of reactions to the revolution offers a complex rendition of the dilemmas and ambivalences with which German critics of the old order defined the present and faced the future. Even as the novel confronts a modernizing era, it reveals fears on the author's part that made it as difficult for him to articulate a vision of a future German revolution as it was to commit himself to action in the one just past.

Gutzkow's overriding impression of post-revolutionary society was of disparate components, which he sought to encompass by creating a new kind of novel. The traditional narrative of one event following another (*Nacheinander*), he explained in the preface, was inadequate to his purpose. The only way to grasp social reality was to discern the interworkings of its parts, a technique he called "side by side" (*Nebeneinander*).[30] Applying this technique to social classes, he would have "kings and beggars" encounter each other and would show what led to—and came out of—such encounters. In actuality, kings do not meet beggars, but scores of characters representing the spectrum of German society do meet one another. These encounters show multifarious social groups reacting to new forces. The Prussian king, Frederick William IV, appears in several episodes that suggest a dreamy aloofness from modern realities. The aristocracy, which comes under a good deal more scrutiny, is represented by princes, officers, and countesses, who respond with fear, bewilderment, or militance as they confront threats to their ascendancy. The middle class, whose representatives include businessmen, clergymen, artists, political agitators, police spies, innkeepers, and, of course, their wives, sisters, and daughters, is shown not only caught between subservience to the nobility and fear of the lower classes but also in a growing crisis of its own values. In contrast to the neglect of other authors, Gutzkow also provides many characters from the lower classes and distinguishes representatives of traditional groups—servants, peasants, petty artisans, and fallen women—from an emergent industrial proletariat to create portentous images of an inexorably growing force that makes new social demands.

In addition to encounters between classes Gutzkow clearly envisioned a physical *Nebeneinander*, an approach that he compared to a warship, "where the co-existing life in a hundred cabins and compartments, in which no one has a view of the other, still can be seen as a visible unity."[31] Applying the metaphor of the ship's compartments to his fictional geography, Gutzkow depicts three distinct settings: Hohenberg, a country estate some distance to the southwest of Berlin; Tempelheide, a bucolic village immediately south of Berlin (that is, Tempelhof); and Berlin itself, referred to not by name but as the residence, capital, or sometimes metropolis (*Weltstadt*). The human traffic between these settings suggests their unity, and this interaction becomes an important dimension of Gutzkow's social portrayals.

The novel, by drawing sharp contrasts with the outlying countryside, establishes Berlin as the center of political activity, as the social center (country nobility repeatedly become enmeshed in repercussions of developments there), and as the cultural and religious center, all of which strengthens "the magnetic pull of the capital."[32] One passage reveals that Gutzkow already thought of Berlin as a world capital. In a rare use of the city's name, he has a character contrast its setting with the freedom associated with mountains and the humility evoked by the expanse of the sea. "Unfortunately, Paris, Vienna, and Berlin lie neither in the mountains nor on the sea. The ambiguity of the flatland dominates us," he observes. "The reverie induced by the vista of naked earth and endless blue sky—*that* is supposed to spawn the ideas that will save the world."[33] The uninspiring connotation of Berlin's geography is the point of this remark, but notable also is the ease with which the speaker lists Berlin with Paris and Vienna as centers charged with saving the world.

Although the novel does not pursue the comparison, Berlin did share one striking similarity with Vienna and Paris: all three cities had recently undergone revolutionary upheavals. The experience of 1848 forms an omnipresent backdrop, and the sudden thought of Dankmar Wildungen, one of the major characters, might stand as epigraph for the whole novel: "The revolution is not yet over!"[34] Indeed, the thought of the unfinished revolution permeates the novel. Political criticism of the Prussian regime is unrelenting, both from various characters and from the narrator, whose many references to the reactionary politics of the court, the ministry, and the military are laced with scorn. Moreover, Prussia's new experience with elections, parliaments, and political parties provides another result of 1848, as does the portrayal of other forms of popular pressure, such as working-class action. The unanswered questions have to do with whether democratic or authoritarian pressures will prevail.

At the heart of these questions is Gutzkow's uncertainty about the effects of modernity on human civilization. Even as he portrays a new economic dynamism and discerns prospects for a broadening of freedom, he allows characters to argue about modern society's inherent corruption, hypocrisy, and deception.[35] More pessimistic still are images of a brutal modernity, but even the rendering of a notion of pervasive struggle for survival vacillates between optimism and pessimism, as these ruminations of Dankmar show:

"We were catapulted into this world, defenseless and without guidance. We have to struggle with our bare hands for any advantage—I don't want to say for happiness or joy of living, but only for the possibility of existing, of winning. We are like hungry wild beasts falling without mercy over whatever booty we can seize, and we restrain ourselves only by whatever quantity of religion, morality, conscience, and benign temperament we acquired at birth. . . . Being human is the one universal bond that envelops us, but does this really confer any advantage other than that of all living things: the noble power of the animal?"[36]

Dankmar's parenthetical comment that bare survival is all that can be realistically asked of life holds little promise for human endeavor. On the other hand, his reference to the calming force of civilized virtues suggests a conviction that through moral development humanity can overcome its brutal propensities. But his query about the distinction between humans and other animals manifests doubts about humanity's moral preeminence.

Such vacillation over human nature is compounded by warnings from various characters about economic and political conditions, but these warnings yield only ideological confusion. Louis Armand, a veteran of French working-class activity, for instance, puts forth a purely economic critique when he tells a group of reform-minded German friends, "Our civilization has bequeathed us a robber state." He explains this in terms of an unrestrained power of capital, whose ruthless exploitation will surely cause the oppressed to take to the barricades if it is not counteracted.[37] The person who agrees most fully with this prediction, however, is a renegade officer, who ignores the point about an ascendant capitalism when he replies that his feudal confreres would like nothing better than an excuse to instigate a bloodbath. The yielding of the specter of an oppressive economic system to one of violent confrontation between an ill-prepared populace and a brutal military system thus blurs the question of the real enemy to the German revolution.

The fact that no character comments on the ideological clutter in such exchanges suggests that Gutzkow himself is the victim of what the novel puts forth as another hallmark of the era: the struggle of competing ideas. The onslaught of scientific theories, political ideologies, esthetic experiments, and moral claims, the novel suggests, is producing intellectual chaos. References to such chaos abound, but it is personified in one character, referred to as "a true son of the nineteenth century," who is ridiculed for devouring every intellectual fad to come forth, from collecting etchings to new acquaintances to new ideologies.[38]

Religion is shown to be another victim of such anarchy, as evinced in countless conversations ranging from reincarnation to practices of oriental religions to quests for personal salvation. These preoccupations aside, Gutzkow is more concerned by what he depicts as the insidious force of institutionalized religion. The novel is especially virulent about "Jesuitism," a seemingly rampant phenomenon equated with hierarchical rule, manipulation of people, persecution of ideas, and subservience to Rome.[39] Protestants can also display these tendencies—particularly the Masons, who come in for similar attacks.[40] Even the more spiritual Pietists are reproached on the grounds that their preoccupation with otherworldly doctrines distracts them from the crises of the modern age.[41] Contemporary Christianity, according to repeated messages, has relinquished any claim to spiritual leadership.

Having thus depicted a society beset by class conflict, weighed down by despotic political and religious institutions, permeated by lying and corruption, and mired in a confusion of ideas and values, Gutzkow attempts to create a positive alternative in the spiritual knighthood of his title. But the "knighthood," a group of reform-minded men from a wide social spectrum, never surmounts the difficulty of envisioning such an alternative. "Public concerns had captivated all of them," the narrator reports of their first meeting. "At least for the moment every barrier had fallen."[42] A major outcome of this meeting, however, is the group's inability to agree on a program of action, which leads Dankmar to conclude, "We must give up the notion of calling forth positive creations and content ourselves with simply promoting the spirit in which they can grow."[43] Although this spirit involves a commitment to egalitarian ideals, the "knights of the spirit," as they decide to call themselves, have trouble reconciling this with their conception of themselves as spiritual aristocrats.[44] Their uneasiness about democratic practice becomes especially evident in their resistance to collaboration with the lower classes. As Dankmar puts it, "We have to preach some other equality than popular assemblies, for example. Equality with the masses is no longer the goal of thoughtful people."[45] The knights' commitment to working for the downfall of absolutism makes them a subversive organization but one without concrete political goals.

In a society whose institutions are shown to be fomenting new forms of brutal struggle, the spiritual knights exemplify Gutzkow's hope for a counter-struggle that would transform minds. *Ritter* in this way reinforces a myth reaching back to the age of the French Revolution—that Germany's unfinished revolution would not emerge from political programs but would instead take a spiritual form.[46] A major theme connects the knights with a medieval branch of the Knights of St. John, who are described as a crucial counterweight to the spiritual and secular powers of the Middle Ages.[47] The modern knights, by implication, will form a similar counterweight to monarchical absolutism and institutional religion. Another religious association is included in the messianic imagery the knights frequently use to characterize their mission.[48] Although the knights are beset by a succession of defeats, the novel's underlying message emerges intact: a revolution of the spirit will someday transform a compartmentalized, oppressed society into a unity based on freedom and justice. The abstractness of this vision, however, does not speak to the array of political and social crises Gutzkow depicts in the German society of 1850.

The most compelling issue was the continued existence of an aristocratic ruling class and the monarchy whose power sustained it. Through intricate details the novel depicts institutions by which the nobility bolstered its power in the aftermath of 1848.[49] But despite this institutional bulwark, the novel also stresses the anomaly of hereditary privilege in the modern era. An array of aristocratic characters shows not only the rural, land-owning nobility to be predictably isolated, but even most of the urban aristocracy are shown consorting mainly with each other, living in a dreamworld of hollow reassurances they have erected to shield themselves from modern realities.

The most concrete representation of their sentiments is their widespread membership in the *Reubund* (League of Remorse). The name clearly evokes the *Treubund* (League of Loyalty), an actual organization formed in post-1848 Prussia that sought to exorcize the revolutionary scourge by ceremonies and oaths of fealty to the monarchy. Although Gutzkow's *Reubund*, like its historical counterpart, is not restricted to aristocrats, it is dominated by them. Their efforts are depicted as the expression of a group seeking to absorb the glitter emanating from the monarchy while fearfully guarding its own property and privilege.[50] Some dissension crops up about whether the league should support the modest constitution the revolution extracted from Frederick William IV, but the overriding image of the league is that of a pillar of monarchical absolutism.

Not only does the novel attack ultra-royalists by depicting them as defensive and selfish, it criticizes the king himself. Myriad references convey an impression of a monarch who cultivates the adulation of the privileged while remaining aloof from modern realities.[51] The few appearances of the royal couple occur not in Berlin but in secluded surroundings such as the garden of Schloß Solitude (the Sans Souci Palace in Potsdam). Such settings correspond to allusions to Frederick William IV as a romantic king who, along with his queen, is striving to create "a chimerical, pastoral Arcadia, where love and charity could be the only occupation of their lives." One character, after an audience with the royal couple at Schloß Solitude, contrasts their serene manners with Berlin, where "despair is chewing up everything into millions of disconnected atoms."[52] Underscoring this contrast are a sudden shrill whistle and a lowered barricade across the road leading from the palace: the departing carriage has to halt to allow a roaring train its passage, only a short distance from the royal idyll.

The images of a rigid, isolated nobility are offset by some aristocratic characters who display openness to new ideas and sensitivity to other classes—a situation that, however open-minded, confuses Gutzkow's notion of a future revolution. Indeed, the central political character, Prince Egon von Hohenberg, becomes an exemplar of revolutionary leadership from above. Egon first appears disguised as a vagabond, having returned to Germany from France, where he has lived incognito as a carpenter and received a political education from a socialist mentor. His commitment to democratic change takes an ironic course, however, when growing political involvement causes him to lose faith in the goal of popular democracy and become convinced that an enlightened aristocracy is the best vehicle for realizing the unfinished revolution.[53] After a brief stint as a member of the Prussian assembly he resigns, having decided the body is only an arena for self-serving power struggles.[54] To the dismay of his friends in the spiritual knighthood he accepts a summons to head an aristocratic ministry. Like the leaders of Prussia's reform period of 1806, Egon envisions a ministry whose work will negate revolutionary pressures by earning popular support. But the year is 1850, not 1806, and the memory of 1848 seems such a threat that Egon uses his position to persecute and imprison, and does not even spare his old comrades.[55] He is eventually defeated by a reactionary tide springing from what the narrator enumerates as deeply rooted institutions: "from the historical state, from the common front of the old castes, from the military memories, from the Junkers with their arrogance and selfishness, from the power of the bureaucrats."[56]

Gutzkow, despite referring to Egon as a dictator and "a fanatic believer in his own infallibility,"[57] ends his novel by allowing him to justify his repressive actions. What many mistook for aristocratic pride, Egon tells his comrades, was really his belief that the time had not yet come to tear down the structure of the old society.[58] That Gutzkow intends no hint of self-serving rationalization is indicated when Egon's tearful mentor thereupon embraces his former pupil. This portrayal of Egon as a defeated hero seems to validate Egon's belief that the aristocratic state in Prussia was the best hope for the present. That the author arrived at this conclusion by default is suggested by his treatment of two plausible alternatives to aristocratic rule: the middle class and the workers.

*Ritter* articulates a crisis of middle-class confidence that resounds through subsequent Berlin novels. While the middle class was the logical heir to the revolution of 1848, the various failures and defeats of middle-class characters in the novel make it difficult to see them as the standard-bearers of the age. Some historians have hypothesized that when the German middle class failed to unify Germany by constitutional means in 1848, it lost a significant chance to assume political leadership. This novel might be seen as documentation of that theory, but it is more plausible that Gutzkow intended to warn rather than to sound a death knell. His warning took the form of dividing the middle class into two types that later authors would label the "*Bürger*" and the "bourgeois," and denouncing the latter as anathema to German values. This distinction would make visions of the unfinished revolution problematic because it denigrated the activities of that portion of the middle class most directly associated with modernity and because the traditional virtues identified with the *Bürger* left limited scope for social or political leadership.[59]

Numerous characters embody the virtues of a hard-working, unpretentious *Bürgertum*, but at the forefront stands Dankmar Wildungen, the jurist who organizes the spiritual knighthood. Energetic and intelligent, he ceaselessly invokes visions of an age of religious, judicial, intellectual, and moral freedom for all humanity and works to build a network of people to spread the message. But another noteworthy element of Dankmar's personality is his refusal to become involved in electoral, monarchical, or working-class politics. He is convinced that parliaments are only arenas for empty debating and selfish pursuits, that the monarchy is but a despotism based on a patriarchal lie, and that working-class movements simply use their egalitarian slogans to cover materialistic goals.[60] The sum of these attitudes argues for staying aloof from politics on the grounds that they inevitably compromise one's integrity. What to Gutzkow is a sign of *bürgerlich* virtue also forms a fateful justification for middle-class political withdrawal.

Franz Schlurck, a sought-after Berlin attorney, epitomizes an affluent new middle class whose feverish ambitions contrast sharply with the down-to-earth pursuits of the traditional *Bürger*. Schlurck's house, located "in the middle of the city, close to the venerable city hall, surrounded by a number of ancient neighboring churches," symbolizes the tensions in his personality. The exterior of the house epitomizes old Berlin; inside, however, modern comforts and luxuries bespeak all the latest fashions.[61] The contrast between the medieval exterior and the modern interior signifies a transformation of the *Bürger* into the bourgeois, which develops in Schlurck as an extreme confusion over values.[62] The capitalist mentality of this new class is depicted through Schlurck's involvement in intricate, doomed business deals over disputed property. His maneuvering leaves him cynical about politics and almost everything else; in his own words he is "a fanatic of irony."[63] One of the real ironies about Schlurck is that when Dankmar first meets him, he sees him as a possible role model.[64] No such thoughts remain after Schlurck's pathetic suicide.

The contrast between the solid old values and the cynical new ones is also drawn through dozens of other middle-class characters. These dichotomies involve the *bürgerlich* cultivation of genuine friendship versus the bourgeois frenzy for new social contacts; belief in the rationalistic ideals of the Enlightenment versus submission to the era's spiritual confusion; and, most visibly, a modest material existence versus accumulation of luxury. That middle-class society as a whole is following Schlurck's lead is a clear possibility. Through much of the novel his daughter Melanie seems even more restless and materialistic than he. Or, to take another example, in a chapter entitled "New People," Gutzkow, in describing a fashionable new district to the west (an allusion to the Tiergarten district beyond Potsdamer Tor), refers to the prominence there of "houses built on speculation."[65] Such images instruct the German middle class to worry less about oppressive political institutions than the need to protect its traditional values against modern onslaughts.

Gutzkow is clearly awed, however, by other signs of modern onslaught, as shown by his description of Berlin sites that attest to a new age of industrialization and of the masses. For example, his depiction of a vast amusement park named the Fortunaball (the Kroll establishment on the northern edge of old Berlin) conveys amazement at the scale in which modern enterprise could attend to human pleasure: a world of "gardens, halls, galleries, loges, tunnels, swings, carrousels, and slides."[66] An even more striking testament to the new age is the view from the grounds, where one looks across a meadow to a fortress-like building belching smoke, the Willingsche machine factory (the Borsig works in the Oranienburger district to the north). The narrator invokes the far-flung travels of its monstrous locomotives as worldwide testimony to "the activity of combined human labor and natural forces."[67]

Gutzkow's awareness of the human costs of such achievements is manifest in his depiction of a conglomeration of slum dwellings designated by their address, Brandgasse Nr. 9. From these surroundings emerges Gutzkow's depiction of an urban proletariat—a milestone in German literature. Gutzkow places this fictional address in the oldest section of Berlin, which means the Königsstadt, on the right bank of the Spree, but if the exteriors of "old sandstone and thick, blackened oak beams" resemble Schlurck's, the interiors comprise networks of tenements in which "each room offered a new picture of want and misery." With multi-storied apartments and courtyards lined up behind one another, Brandgasse Nr. 9 is a mid-century prototype of the infamous *Mietskasernen* (rental barracks) that became Berlin's solution to the housing crisis of its industrial masses.[68] As with Schlurck and his apartment, the inhabitants and buildings of this location are undergoing a social transformation, in this case from the age-old human misery of the "old dens of thieves" into a modern counterpart: the economic misery of the industrial working class. The latter is personified in the poverty-stricken but dignified Eisold family. Detailed descriptions portray the hardships endured by Karl Eisold, a young machine worker, along with four generations of his family, in a cramped fourth-floor tenement.[69] In the words of a critic writing in the 1890s, the lives portrayed in Brandgasse Nr. 9 "showed our nation for the first time how much poverty and misery, how much subordination and depravity, but also how much diligence and virtue dwell in the garrets and basements of the German city."[70]

Nevertheless, Gutzkow's portrayal of the Eisold family stops short of advocating working-class action. The one episode of such protest, a confrontation between the infant organization of machine workers and the military, receives less than three pages of treatment, and more significantly, is viewed only from an upper-floor hotel window (much like Gutzkow's own experience in March 1848). Modeled after the April 1849 riot on Dönhoffplatz, the incident is strangely abstract, with the salvo of shots on the square below fading into the background of conversation in the hotel room.[71] Only in the next chapter do readers learn that gentle Karl Eisold has died in the exchange, "a poor victim of the political agitation."[72]

Karl's funeral becomes the occasion for Gutzkow to disclose his apparent answer to working-class suffering. The mourners are being stirred up by an inflammatory eulogy when a middle-class character steps forward to calm the crowd. He urges them not to let their anger rule their actions but to believe rather in the just order that will someday emerge from the quiet labors of the "world spirit": "It will not rest on the division of worldly goods, which will only bring about murder and fire, but on a changed understanding of the state. Work toward that! Not toward destruction but toward new understanding . . . That is the goal; we can reach it only in the victory of the spirit, not in the victory of materialism."[73] The import of this scene is contained in the implication that the threat of "materialism," rather than the reality of human exploitation, is the real enemy. The speaker's injunction to the working class to eschew direct action in favor of moral endeavor provides scant answer to the grievances Gutzkow has depicted, but such an answer will echo through virtually every subsequent portrayal of working-class action in Berlin novels. It reflects a fundamental ambivalence of middle-class authors toward the victims of the conditions they so forcefully decry.

Such ambivalence toward the working class is evident in the sharply contrasting means by which Gutzkow portrays it. If the Eisold family shows his empathy, a strange character named Fritz Hackert exemplifies his uneasiness. An unlikely representative of the proletariat, Hackert is the illegitimate son of a prominent noblewoman and a copyist by profession. Depicted as crafty and diabolical, he lives on the fringes of Berlin society. His habit of sleepwalking becomes a symbol of a "terrible spirit of restlessness in the middle of sleep," whose wider connotations are revealed by Dankmar:

> "Hackert is a person of animalistic instincts. And is he not actually the expression of the masses themselves? . . . If I were a politician, I'd take note of the similarities between Hackert and the masses: vacillating, immature, half-grown, sometimes generous, then again petty, sometimes assertive, then again cowardly, sometimes touching, then again repulsive, sometimes poetic, then again prosaic, sleepwalking, expectant, but in the light of day intellectually asleep. I would ask myself: How do we restrain such a phenomenon? How do we improve it?"[74]

These notions of the masses as a lesser order of creation needing to be controlled provide scant basis for common cause between the middle and working classes against political oppression.

And yet such oppression intensifies in the novel to the point that staying in Berlin becomes impossible for members of the spiritual knighthood. Police spies, lurking all over, put hundreds, including members of the "knights," under surveillance. Searches, house arrests, and orders to leave the city abound. Dankmar goes into hiding but is found and imprisoned for suspicious activities.[75] Soon the "knights" are dispersing from Berlin to fight their battles in secrecy and to await the day when society will be redeemed by true reform. Although the exodus means the abandonment of an immediate challenge to the ruling institutions, the novel concludes by affirming a belief that absolutism will inevitably collapse from an infusion of what Gutzkow calls a "republicanism of the spirit." This transformation, the novel implies, would put Germans in the forefront of humanity, a hope that Gutzkow earlier made explicit when he wrote: "Our people, organized in the way they should be, could light the way toward universal benevolence and justice for all peoples and through their actions show why sages like Kant and Herder, preachers of eternal peace, were born in Germany."[76] Similar hopes would continue to be uttered by other novelists long after unification, but Gutzkow's essential qualifying phrase, implying a new form of political organization, would be more easily forgotten. Indeed, even Gutzkow's novel shows the ease with which authors could depict situations that called for political change and still remain captivated by the heritage of cultural scruples against acting directly to bring about such change.

*Ritter vom Geiste* solidifies a notion of national regeneration emanating from

Berlin, even as it remains ambiguous as a call to political engagement. Although persecuted people are fleeing the city at the end of the novel, Berlin, as the center of new social, economic, and political forces, has been shown to be the center of the German future.[77] Gutzkow clearly intended the unfinished revolution to have national implications, for although the novel does not address specific issues of unification, it refers repeatedly to the prospects for German nationhood. In one passage, for instance, dealing with different approaches by which Germans could proceed, a character warns that if they resort to a disruption of the inherited order, they "run the risk of losing [their] most precious possession, [their] venerable spiritual achievements."[78] As *Ritter* underwent successive editions, Gutzkow used the prefaces to ponder the national implications of his novel in the light of historical developments.

Most pertinent is his preface to the fifth edition. Published in 1869 on the eve of German unification, it links the idea of the unfinished revolution with the coming of Bismarckian Germany. Asking rhetorically whether his novel of almost twenty years ago has become passé, Gutzkow answers that it holds "unchanging validity for every future age."[79] Not only has his portrayal of the working class been borne out, he avers, but his protagonist Prince Egon has proven to have remarkable similarities to the foremost German politician. He urges readers to test the parallels between Egon and Bismarck by examining a designated chapter.[80] The depiction of Egon in that chapter does show fortuitous similarities with Bismarck's later retreats and illnesses,[81] but more interesting is what Gutzkow's reference reveals of his sense of Bismarck's motives. In this chapter Egon is a lonely, embittered, exhausted politician who is becoming convinced of the "deep internal rottenness of the state he is defending and of its agents as well."[82] By choosing in 1869 to link this passage with the most powerful political figure in Germany, Gutzkow seems to suggest that Bismarck too knew he served a state based on lies and deception.[83]

Despite this negative tone, Gutzkow concluded his novel with a positive image of Egon, as we have seen. His comparison thus included the possibility that he saw Bismarck, too, as a true reformer. The ambiguous implications of these few words point to deeper ambiguities in *Ritter vom Geiste*. Although the novel manifested a strong commitment to the unfinished revolution, its failure to condemn aristocratic rule unequivocally instilled considerable confusion in its characters' revolutionary hopes. Although the novel denounced social privilege and economic injustice, it allowed much of the force of those denunciations to be dissipated by the self-doubts and fears of those who would bring about a new age of justice. Although it expounded an ideal of a Germany based on humane values, it retreated from advocating particular action to bring them to fruition. Gutzkow's allusions to Bismarck in his 1869 preface suggested, moreover, a further blurring of political and social vision. The problems Gutzkow encountered in articulating a vision of the unfinished revolution in *Ritter vom Geiste* were to be compounded in subsequent novels by other authors who dealt with experiences surrounding the era of unification.

## Notes

1. On Berlin's early history see Richard Dietrich, ed., *Berlin: Zehn Kapitel seiner Geschichte* (Berlin, 1981), and Eberhard Bohm, "Die Frühgeschichte des Berliner Raumes," in Wolfgang Ribbe, ed., *Geschichte Berlins*, Vol. I (Munich, 1987), 3–135.
2. Walter Kiaulehn, *Berlin: Schicksal einer Weltstadt* (Munich, 1958), 42.
3. Werner Hegemann, *Das steinere Berlin* (1930; reprinted Braunschweig, 1976), 59. For later manifestations of this westward theme see Chapter 11.
4. Alexander Reissner, *Berlin, 1675–1945: The Rise and Fall of a Metropolis—A Panoramic View* (London, 1984), 11. See also Kiaulehn, *Berlin*, 58–81.
5. The locations of the gates of the old wall are preserved today as squares and subway station names. For maps and descriptions see Dietrich, *Berlin: Zehn Kapitel*, 201–211.
6. See Alfred Zastrau, "Im Jahrhundert Goethes," in ibid., 131–158; Anthony J. LaVopa, "The Politics of Enlightenment: Friedrich Gedike and German Professional Ideology," *Journal of Modern History*, 62 (March 1990), 34–56; Ludwig Geiger, *Berlin 1688–1840. Geschichte des geistigen Lebens der preußischen Hauptstadt*, 2 vols. (Berlin, 1892–1895); and Deborah Hertz, *Jewish High Society in Old Regime Berlin* (New Haven, Conn., 1988).
7. The origins of "Spreeathen" are attributed to Frederick II, who exclaimed as crown prince: "Berlin werde Athen! Ich nehme das Omen an." Eduard Spranger, *Berliner Geist* (Tübingen, 1966), 67. See also Gordon A. Craig, *The Germans* (New York, 1982), 261–280.
8. Theodor Fontane, "Die Märker und das Berlinertum," *Aus dem Nachlaß von Theodor Fontane* (Berlin, 1908), 295–297. See also Peter Wruck, "Fontanes Berlin: Durchlebte, erfahrene und dargestellte Wirklichkeit," in Peter Wruck, ed., *Literarisches Leben in Berlin, 1871–1933*, 2 vols. (Berlin, 1987), I, 22–87.
9. Fontane, "Die Märker und das Berlinertum," 301–305. Gordon Craig suggests sixteenth-century origins for Berlin humor in *The Germans*, 275.
10. Fontane, "Die Märker und das Berlinertum," 306.
11. Carl E. Schorske, "The Idea of the City in European Thought," in Oscar Handlin and John Burchard, eds., *The Historian and the City* (Cambridge, Mass., 1963), 101.
12. Hans Herzfeld, "Allgemeine Entwicklung und politische Geschichte," in Hans Herzfeld und Gerd Heinrich, eds., *Berlin und die Provinz Brandenburg im 19. und 20. Jahrhundert* (Berlin, 1968), 15–18.
13. Günter Richter, "Zwischen Revolution und Reichsgründung (1848–1870)," in Wolfgang Ribbe, ed., *Geschichte Berlins*, Vol. II: *Von der Märzrevolution bis zur Gegenwart* (Munich, 1987), 605–635.
14. Ibid., 636–654.
15. On comparative population growth of major European cities, see Hans Herzfeld, "Berlin als Kaiserstadt und Reichshauptstadt," in *Das Hauptstadtproblem in der Geschichte, Jahrbuch für Geschichte des Deutschen Ostens*, I (Tübingen, 1952), 166–167.
16. Volker Klotz, *Die erzählte Stadt: Ein Sujet als Herausforderung des Romans von Lesage bis Döblin* (Munich, 1969), 15. See also Friedbert Stühler, *Totale Welten: Der moderne deutsche Großstadtroman* (Regensburg, 1989), which appeared too late to be incorporated into the discussion; and Susan Merrill Squier, "Literature and the City: A Checklist of Relevant Secondary Works," in Susan Merrill Squier, ed., *Women Writers and the City: Essays in Feminist Literary Criticism* (Knoxville, Tenn., 1984), 288–294.
17. Klotz, *Die erzählte Stadt*, 131–166, and Andrew Lees, *Cities Perceived: Urban Society in European and American Thought, 1820–1940* (New York, 1985), 15–90.
18. On the wider cultural context of this pro-urban sentiment see Lees, *Cities Perceived*,

189–218. On further approaches to analyzing perceptions of the city see William Sharpe and Leonard Wallock, eds., *Visions of the Modern City: Essays in History, Art, and Literature* (New York, 1983), and Handlin, *The Historian and the City*.
19. Paul Alfred Merbach, "Der Berliner Roman: Eine Skizze seiner Entwicklung," *Groß-Berliner Kalender* (Berlin, 1913), 194. See also Klaus Günther Just, *Von der Gründerzeit bis zur Gegenwart: Geschichte der deutschen Literatur seit 1871* (Bern, 1973), 45–51.
20. Merbach, "Der Berliner Roman," 193.
21. On Gutzkow's influence on the Berlin novel see, for example, Kiaulehn, *Berlin*, 340, and Julius Rodenberg, *Unter den Linden* (Berlin, 1888), 235.
22. Heinrich Spiero designated the novel as indispensable for understanding nineteenth-century Berlin society in his article, "Vom Berliner Roman: Rückblicke und Ausblicke," *Germanisch-romanische Monatsschrift*, 6 (1914), 215.
23. Quoted in Peter Hasubek, *Karl Gutzkows Romane "Die Ritter vom Geiste" und "Der Zauberer von Rom": Studien zur Typologie des deutschen Zeitromans im 19. Jahrhundert* (Dissertation, Hamburg, 1964), 28.
24. Peter Müller, ed., *Gutzkows Werke*, IV: *Rückblicke auf mein Leben, 1829–1849* (first published 1875; Leipzig, n.d.), 140.
25. Ibid., 16.
26. See Rainer Funke, *Beharrung und Umbruch, 1830–1860: Karl Gutzkow auf dem Weg in die literarische Moderne* (Frankfurt am Main, 1984).
27. Quoted by R. J. Kavanagh, "Portrait of the Artist as a Young German: Karl Gutzkow's Political Attitudes and 1848," in Francis Barker et al., *1848: The Sociology of Literature* (Essex, 1978), 68. On Gutzkow's conflicts with censors and critics see ibid., 69–70, and Gutzkow, *Rückblicke*, 181–193.
28. Gutzkow, *Rückblicke*, 139.
29. Ibid., 395–423. One moment of action did occur on 19 March, when a conservative leader shoved Gutzkow forward to address calming words to the crowd before the palace. See Karl Gutzkow, "Ansprache an die Berliner im März 1848," in his *Vor- und Nach-Märzliches* (Leipzig, 1850), 105–119, and Ernest K. Bramsted, *Aristocracy and the Middle-Classes in Germany: Social Types in German Literature, 1830–1900* (1937; reprinted Chicago, 1964), 79, fnl.
30. Karl Gutzkow, *Die Ritter vom Geiste*, 6th ed., I (Berlin, 1878), v (preface to the first edition, 1850). On Gutzkow's technique see Gerhard K. Friesen, *The German Panoramic Novel of the 19th Century* (Bern, 1972), 82–87; Eda Sagarra, *Tradition and Revolution: German Literature and Society, 1830–1890* (New York, 1971), 207–212; and Roger Hillman, *Zeitroman: The Novel and Society in Germany, 1830–1900* (Bern, 1983), 20–21.
31. Gutzkow, *Ritter*, I, ix (preface to the third edition, 1854).
32. Ibid., I, 115. Although Gutzkow designated Berlin locations with disguised names, they were recognizable to readers familiar with the city.
33. Ibid., II, 95–96.
34. Ibid., II, 12. See also Gutzkow's statement of 1848: "Noch sind wir in der Zeit der Neubildung, noch in der Zeit der Gährungen." Karl Gutzkow, *Deutschland am Vorabend seines Falles oder seiner Größe* (Frankfurt am Main, 1848), 113.
35. Gutzkow, *Ritter*, III, 193.
36. Ibid., II, 376.
37. Ibid., III, 163. No explicit reference to Marx occurs in the novel.
38. Ibid., IV, 195, 77.
39. See especially the chapter entitled "The Jesuit," ibid., III, 81–90.
40. One such individual is a pastor who, in a chapter entitled "The Lutheran Pope," is described as a secret Jesuit because of his love of hierarchy. Ibid., II, 41.
41. Ibid., II, 84.

42. Ibid., III, 166.
43. Ibid., III, 175.
44. Ibid., I, 110. See also the exchange between Dankmar and Louis Armand over the question of spiritual aristocracy, ibid., 379.
45. Ibid., I, 100. See also his statement to the effect that a democracy based on the vote of the majority is a loss "für das Edlere"; Gutzkow, *Deutschland am Vorabend*, 51.
46. Grounded in the philosophies of Kant and Hegel, the notion of spiritual freedom became associated with an acceptance of a strong state authority. Gutzkow, of course, finds such acceptance problematic at the least. See Leonard Krieger, *The German Idea of Freedom* (Boston, 1957), 88–138.
47. Gutzkow, *Ritter*, I, 34. For other discussions of knightly orders, secret organizations, and their relevance to the modern age see I, 77, 83, 352; II, 115, 374, 378; III, 189; IV, 333. On Gutzkow's use of this theme see Victor Klemperer, *Die Zeitromane Friedrich Spielhagens und ihre Wurzeln* (Weimar, 1913), 45–47.
48. See, for instance, Gutzkow, *Ritter*, II, 374–377.
49. See Bramsted, *Aristocracy and the Middle-Classes in Germany*, 81–91. Gutzkow's emphasis on the connection between the political institutions and social predominance of the nobility proved to be unique among Berlin novelists.
50. Criticisms of the *Reubund* can be found in the following passages: Gutzkow, *Ritter*, I, 73, 84, 100; II, 150; IV, 35.
51. Elsewhere Gutzkow was still more critical, blaming the failure to unify Germany on the Prussian dynasty in general and Frederick William IV in particular. Gutzkow, *Deutschland am Vorabend*, 103, 131.
52. Gutzkow, *Ritter*, I, 333; III, 16.
53. Ibid., III, 10.
54. Ibid., III, 93.
55. Ibid., IV, 47. A temporary impediment to Egon's career arises when he uncovers evidence that he is actually the son of his mother's middle-class lover, but he quickly rationalizes to himself that the lie he is living matters little in a society based on lies. Ibid., IV, 306.
56. Ibid., IV, 309, 394. On the Prussian reform experience see Krieger, *German Idea of Freedom*, 148–165.
57. Gutzkow, *Ritter*, III, 314, and IV, 46.
58. Ibid., IV, 409–410.
59. The internal divisions of the middle class were far more complex than those suggested in this and later novels. See Dietrich Rüschmeyer, "Bourgeoisie, Staat und Bildungsbürgertum. Idealtypische Modelle für die vergleichende Erforschung von Bürgertum und Bürgerlichkeit," in Jürgen Kocka, ed., *Bürger und Bürgerlichkeit im 19. Jahrhundert* (Göttingen, 1987), 101–120.
60. Gutzkow, *Ritter*, II, 15, 310; III, 127.
61. Ibid., II, 2–3, 22.
62. See, for example, the following passages: ibid., I, 60, 344, 352, 355; II, 22, 45; IV, 401.
63. Ibid., I, 76.
64. Ibid., I, 61.
65. Ibid., I, 319.
66. Ibid., II, 200.
67. Ibid., II, 217. On Borsig as symbolic of German industrialization see Robert Springer, *Berlin: Die deutsche Kaiserstadt* (Darmstadt, 1878), 90; Friesen, *German Panoramic Novel*, 88; and Herzfeld, ed., *Berlin und die Provinz Brandenburg*, 70 and 361. On the railway as symbol of national culture see Harold James, *A German Identity: 1770–1990* (New York, 1989), 80.
68. Gutzkow, *Ritter*, II, 159, 164. Julius Rodenberg's retrospective description of

Königsstadt confirms the atmosphere portrayed by Gutzkow. See his article, "Im Herzen von Berlin," reprinted in *Der Berliner zweifelt immer: Feuilletons von damals* (Leipzig, 1979), 153–161. On policies that encouraged the building of Mietskasernen see Hegemann, *Das steinere Berlin*, Chapters 14, 22, and 23.

69. Gutzkow, *Ritter*, II, 179–184. See also Sagarra, *Tradition and Revolution*, 210.
70. This statement by literary historian Johann Proells is quoted in Rudolf Hackmann, *Die Anfänge des Roman in der Zeitung* (Dissertation, Berlin, 1938), 46. Gutzkow's scenes of urban misery seem to draw heavily on Eugène Sue's *Mystères de Paris* (1842). Martin Halter, *Sklaven der Arbeit—Ritter vom Geiste. Arbeit und Arbeiter im deutschen Sozialroman zwischen 1840 und 1880* (Frankfurt am Main, 1983), 31.
71. Gutzkow, *Ritter*, IV, 157–159. See also Hasubek, *Karl Gutzkows Romane*, 80, and Friesen, *German Panoramic Novel*, 104–108.
72. Gutzkow, *Ritter*, IV, 165.
73. Ibid., IV, 182.
74. Ibid., IV, 192; II, 199. Victor Klemperer explains Gutzkow's strange choice of Hackert as symbol as evidence of a lack of an overall vision of the proletariat. Klemperer, *Zeitromane*, 57.
75. See passages beginning on the following pages: Gutzkow, *Ritter*, IV, 49, 190, 205, 344.
76. Gutzkow, *Deutschland am Vorabend*, 43.
77. In the novel Gutzkow does not mention the Frankfurt Assembly's effort at unification in 1848.
78. Gutzkow, *Ritter*, IV, 14. Elsewhere Gutzkow was unremitting in his belief that the German people must be at the center of any plan for unification. Gutzkow, *Deutschland am Vorabend*, 43, 77, 235.
79. Gutzkow, *Ritter*, I, xiii.
80. Ibid., I, xiv. See also Book 9, Chapter 6 (IV, 286–312), which he cites to his readers.
81. The third edition, published before Bismarck's political ascendancy, includes the same parallels. Karl Gutzkow, *Die Ritter vom Geiste* (Berlin, 1855), V, 129–185.
82. Gutzkow, *Ritter*, 6th ed., IV, 308 (compare *Ritter*, 3rd ed., V, 174).
83. On Gutzkow's hostility to Bismarck see Ludwig Maenner, *Karl Gutzkow und der demokratische Gedanke* (Munich, 1921), 138–140.

# 2

# "Berlin Becomes a World-City!"

In 1868 Berlin journalist Robert Springer published a book whose title exuberantly proclaimed, *Berlin wird Weltstadt* (*Berlin Becomes a World-City!*).[1] Although the book's affectionate portraits of woefully provincial Berliners might suggest Springer's proclamation was premature, the descriptions of the city depicted remarkable changes. Most visible, perhaps, was the dense traffic, which consisted of a dozen types of conveyances from the milk wagon to the omnibus to the new firefighting wagons (a system that merited a whole descriptive chapter). A succession of trains transported growing numbers of humans and quantities of goods in and out of the city. Specialty shops, also proliferating, distributed imported merchandise to all corners of the city. The New Museum on Museum Island attested to Berlin's growing cultural renown, and the expansive marble stockmarket building across the Spree made a startling contrast with its humble predecessor. As the center of the newly formed North German Confederation, Berlin had also taken its first official step toward becoming the capital of Germany.

The human activity behind all these developments translated into dramatic increases in population and a rapid expansion of the city.[2] "The city wall of Berlin," Springer announces, "is falling victim to the metropolitan spirit."[3] Although many of the old gates have already disappeared, he continues, their names remain to evoke the particular character of the new districts beyond. Because the character of each such district named in Berlin novels has significant connotations, a brief summary of Springer's geographical survey is in order.

At the city's southwest side lies the site of Potsdamer Tor, Berlin's busiest intersection as well as a symbolic social confluence, with the aristocratic Wilhelmstraße to the north; Leipzigerstraße, the elegant shopping street, to the east; the Potsdamer railroad station to the south; the Potsdamerstraße with its cafés and restaurants to the southwest; and the bourgeois mansions by the Tiergarten to the northwest. North of Potsdamer Platz is the Brandenburger Tor, topped by its victorious quadriga facing eastward toward the magnificent buildings along the Linden, and opening to the west on the Tiergarten, Berlin's Bois de Boulogne. Across the Spree the city's character changes sharply at

Oranienburger Tor. Located at the northern end of the main north-south thoroughfare, Friedrichstraße, this is the gateway to Berlin's "Fire Country." "Everywhere you smell soot and iron," Springer reports, "everywhere you hear the throbbing of machines and the pounding of sledgehammers; everywhere you see workers with their blackened, bearded faces and their powerful arms. This is the empire founded by Borsig and extended by its competitors."[4] Rosenthaler Tor, to the northeast, still leads to the sandy Gesundbrunnen, renowned for its mineral baths before more elegant spas eclipsed it.[5] Frankfurter Tor, to the east, denotes the realm of Berlin's traditional poor, where unemployed silkweaving apprentices wander the streets in their dressing gowns. Hallesches Tor, at the southern end of Friedrichstraße, forms another social conjunction of modest residential neighborhoods, the breweries of the Kreuzberg area (a favorite destination for outings), and the concentration of barracks and exercise grounds at Tempelhof (attesting to Berlin's role of garrison).

The transformation of Berlin became an overriding theme of fictional portrayals of the city, but images of a city devoid of identity—or at least still in the process of establishing one—competed with exuberant proclamations like Springer's. Historian Heinrich von Treitschke, for instance, likened Berlin to a gangly adolescent with limbs jutting out of ill-fitting clothes. The city's sorry reputation, Treitschke explained, resulted from the throwing together of a mass of people into densely populated confines, which caused "every crime, every popular vulgarity, every fraud, every social conflict" to be magnified and exposed to derision throughout Germany.[6] Wilhelm Raabe produced another revealing image with his 1886 novel, *Im alten Eisen* (*Of Old Iron*), whose title referred both to the old iron one character collected for her junkshop and to the scrap iron a local company bought and melted down for re-use. While Raabe did not explicitly apply the theme to Berlin, the story did suggest that the city seemed to melt down its people and recast them for new use.[7]

This chapter deals with dilemmas of Berlin's transformation into a *Weltstadt* as depicted in novels set in the crucial period surrounding German unification. Not only do they contain expansive portrayals of the physical upheaval reported by Springer and the identity crisis described by Treitschke, but they also show the authors, Berliners themselves, engaging in the struggle to recast the old Berlin rather than discard it to rust in the scrap heap. Underlying all this is their attempt to understand how these changes relate to the experiences of German nationhood.

A useful model for this process has been suggested by sociologist Peter Marris, who proposes that the ambivalences with which societies confront change can be compared to the experience of bereavement. Just as the death of a husband means a period of disorientation as the widow reformulates her life to accommodate the loss, so the passing of a traditional society involves disorientation and readjustment. Like the bereaved, Marris suggests, people who experience the turmoil of modernization react with conflicting desires: "to return to the past, which seems in retrospect a haven of security and meaningful satisfactions; or to realize at once a new self, a modern man confidently handling the possibilities of a progressive nation." Neither wish, of course, is immediately feasible, but the two must be integrated "through a long process of reinterpretation" comparable to the widow working out her grief.[8]

Berlin novelists engaged in such a process of reinterpretation as they confronted German unification. Beneath the sense of triumph, their works reveal feelings of loss and ambivalence, which can be interpreted as attempts to redefine an unfamiliar world in ways that would provide a sense of continuity with the world that had been lost. Four such novels, published over fifteen years, are the subject of this chapter.[9] The clearest expression of bereavement is Ludovika Hesekiel's *Von Brandenburg zu Bismarck* (1873), which articulates the loss felt by an arch-conservative Prussian at the time of unification. Julius Rodenberg's *Die Grandidiers* (1878), though far more celebratory of unification, shows the ambivalence with which people of diverse particularist origins confronted the reality of living and working together in the new German capital. Wolfgang Kirchbach's novella about Berlin in his collection *Die Kinder des Reiches* (*Children of the Empire*) (1883) pursues this ambivalence by asking whether Berlin deserved to be the capital and how the old Berlin could be reformulated into the new. Conrad Alberti, finally, in his novella "Majestätsbeleidigung" ("Lese Majesty") (1887), links the physical and psychological disruptions of a modernizing capital with new forms of patriotism demanded by unification. All four works vacillate between feelings of loss over old Berlin and Prussia and feelings of hope for the new city and the new Germany.

Ludovika Hesekiel's unabashedly anti-democratic *Von Brandenburg zu Bismarck* is the most conservative work used in this study. Focusing nostalgically on the aristocracy and its supporters from early 1849 to the Prussian victories in Schleswig-Holstein in 1864, it provides a melancholy picture of the prospects for Prussian loyalists in the aftermath of Germany's triumph. The protagonist, Gerda Thurn, is the daughter of a novelist/journalist who closely resembles Hesekiel's own father, Georg Hesekiel. Like his real-life counterpart, Dr. Thurn is a pillar of a conservative Berlin literary circle whimsically named "Tunnel over the Spree" and has devoted his professional life to serving the monarchy and the institutions that support it.[10] Within the self-conceived, as well as socially imposed, limitations of her womanhood Gerda helps her father with his writing projects, reads compulsively, and, most important, lends her ardent support to the Prussian king. After her father's death Gerda devotes herself to carrying on his work. *Von Brandenburg zu Bismarck* represents Hesekiel's commitment to the same task.

The novel is based on the belief that 1848 meant not just a disruption but a tragedy for Prussia. Through the activities of the father-daughter pair it traces the regeneration of Prussia to her ultimate ascendancy in the newly united Germany. "If Prussia has been defeated," Dr. Thurn comments early in the novel, "then it's happened only in order to rise again still more magnificently, like the phoenix from the ashes."[11] The unequivocal message is that this phoenix will be the Hohenzollern dynasty surrounded by its supporters.

Given this focus, Hesekiel is less concerned about the role of democrats in fomenting the March revolution than the question of royalists' responsibility. In one uneasy passage the narrator denies that guilt can be placed on "the aristocracy, the absolutists, the members of the right," and yet with the next sentence confirms their role by alluding to "how the reaction atoned after 1848 for what it had caused before then."[12] The terrible experience was a blessing in disguise, for it mobilized royalists to form a wall of "honor and loyalty" around the throne, which strengthened it for the task of unification that lay ahead. A passage that begins defensively thus ends militantly.

In light of this militance it is hardly surprising that Hesekiel gives a far more approving picture of the *Treubund*, the association of loyalists who rallied around the monarchy, than Gutzkow did with his *Reubund*.[13] Nor is it surprising that Hesekiel's alarm about a democratizing era extended even to this group. What is striking, however, is the degree of similarity between Hesekiel's fears and those of the liberal Gutzkow, as is suggested by a comment in one of Hesekiel's episodes. Members of the *Treubund* are converging in June 1849 on a beer garden at Kreuzberg to celebrate Prussia's military victory over a revolutionary uprising in Baden. The scene is replete with popular imagery of Berlin, with goblets of *Weißbier* and plates of the humble Berlin sandwich, *belegte Stullen*, lining every table. Prussian imagery also prevails, with celebrants dressed in Hohenzollern black and white, with repeated rounds of the Prussian anthem, and with a succession of toasts to the monarchy. Thurn, however, complains about the rowdiness and adds, "I see a lot of people here who jeered at the king just as loudly in the March days as they're now toasting him."[14] He endures the discomfort, however, in deference to his belief that Prussia can survive only if the nobility succeeds "in uniting with the *Volk* to become a strong support for the throne against the growing power of speculation and of the proletariat."[15] With this remark Thurn not only shows uneasiness about the *Volk* but specifically excludes from it the bourgeoisie and the proletariat, the same two groups Gutzkow distrusted because of their materialistic concerns. Elsewhere Thurn refers to himself as a "knight of the spirit," and beneath the phrase lies the same fear articulated in *Ritter* that aristocrats of the spirit will be overrun by egalitarian forces.[16] This is indicated by Thurn's comment to the effect that "people of rank" (*die Vornehmen*) will always be despised, especially "the intellectually superior" (*die geistig Vornehmen*).[17] To be sure, Hesekiel draws far different conclusions than Gutzkow, but both authors reveal similar anxieties about a leveling era.

Hesekiel's ideal of a traditional hierarchical society is aptly expressed in a passage that links this ideal with her discomfort over the newly emerging city. She uses a description of the transformation of Wilhelmstraße to suggest a lost social harmony. In quieter times, the narrator comments, the elegant palaces and marble statues of the upper part of the street (north of Leipzigerstraße) gave way to modest houses and shops in the lower part. Implied in the description of "the most original of all Berlin streets" was a bygone continuum between the aristocracy and commoners.[18] Thurn's "beloved, comfortable old house," with its "broad, colorful, tree-filled garden" had been located on the modest end of the street. Like so many Berlin houses, however, it was torn down to make way for "a modern building." And implied by the nostalgic reference to the street's former quietness was the jarring intrusion of traffic noise. The disappearance of the old character of Wilhelmstraße, reflecting a wider loss of the old Berlin, resulted from the demands placed upon it by its transformation to German capital.

Hesekiel's sadness over this loss is clear. She makes no pretense over her uneasiness about German unification, even as she struggles with the realization that this is the logical outcome of the ascendancy of her beloved Prussia. The novel's title honors Count Friedrich Wilhelm von Brandenburg, who until his death in 1850 headed a Prussian ministry that, as Gerda puts it, blazed the trail that would eventually be followed by William I and Otto von Bismarck.[19] Even Prussia's abject capitulation to Austrian power in the Moravian town of Olmütz finds justification. Hesekiel refers to the 1850 agreement, in which Prussia renounced any efforts at unification, as a costly but necessary step by which Frederick William IV eradicated the last vestige of the revolution and thus laid the foundations for Prussia's—and Germany's—future.[20] Hesekiel also dutifully applauds the Prussian victories in Bismarck's war in Schleswig-Holstein. But while Gerda's "soul cheered," she is also painfully aware of the truth of a friend's assessment that "Germany is gaining ground only at the cost of Prussia."[21] The internal conflict is too much for Gerda, who declines and at the end of the novel lies on her deathbed. Although able to see the glory of the new Germany, she is convinced she can never embrace the dawning age: "[My heart] is sick," she says. "Let me go home now; the new German sun that is rising into the sky would only blind this old Prussian lady."[22]

In contrast to Hesekiel, who portrays grief over Prussia, Julius Rodenberg in *Die Grandidiers* depicts unification as a time of tumultuous but salutary change. Yet elements of loss appear in his novel as well. Somewhat like Hesekiel's mourning the loss of Prussianism to Germany, the sense of loss in Rodenberg has to do with the struggle of non-Prussian immigrants in Berlin to adapt to their surroundings while still retaining a sense of their origins. The dilemma is shown to be particularly critical right before the Franco-Prussian war.

One of the earliest Berlin novels to focus on the theme of immigrants, Rodenberg's work tells the story of the descendants of a French Huguenot family, the Grandidiers, with the growing crisis between Prussia and France as a backdrop for the conflict between George Grandidier and his son. Having lived in Berlin since the reign of the Great Elector, the family seems far removed from immigrants of the unification period, but the Grandidiers' cultural ties to the family's original homeland have remained alive, and their sense of belonging in Berlin remains tenuous even after two centuries. Other themes invoke historical experiences between Prussia and France, as when members of another branch of the family—modern counterparts to the Huguenots—arrive penniless, having fled persecutions of Napoleon III. Another image, evoking the Great Elector as would-be "liberator" of Alsace two centuries earlier, allows Rodenberg to portray a victorious Prussia bringing that promise to fulfillment by reuniting a sundered Alsace with its German homeland in 1870.[23] Finally, the healing of the seemingly irreparable breach among the Grandidiers coincides, by Rodenberg's design, with the return of the triumphant Prussian army to Berlin on 16 June 1871. German unification thus becomes a cleansing experience for a family as well as for a society.

Lest his message be construed to apply only to Berlin's "French colony," Rodenberg supplements it with episodes about immigrants from other German states. Like the Grandidiers, they experience loss but are enjoined to accustom themselves to Prussian ascendancy and to acknowledge the positive effects of that ascendancy for Germany.

The setting for one such episode is a beer hall in the heart of old Berlin; the narrator introduces it by wryly enumerating its various incarnations as the "Democratic Beer Hall" in 1848, the "New Prussian Beer Hall" ten years later, and now, in the late '60s, the "North German Beer Hall," all reflective of the owner's attempt to remain current. The picturesque interior, whose "roughnesses" (*Unebenheiten*) are likened to those of the recently formed North German Confederation, is dominated by a large painting that depicts the Confederation's border on the Main, where Napoleon III symbolically stands as the only obstacle to German unity.[24] This episode indicates, however, other obstacles in the form of Germans themselves. Among the regular customers on this particular day are a Prussian, a Saxon, a Bavarian, a Hanoverian, and a Hessian, and it is not long before insults begin to fly. The embittered Hanoverian accuses his Prussian drinking comrade: "You Prussians are beggars, a poor, starving people living off our money."[25] The others chime in with their agreement.

The tense situation is resolved by a rag-tag revolutionary from 1848, "the Colonel." Rodenberg allows this charismatic figure to relate an experience that actually happened to the author: seeing the elector from his native Hesse brought into Berlin as a Prussian prisoner after the war of 1866.[26] Despite vivid memories of wrongs perpetrated by this ruler, the Colonel admits that he could not avoid a wrenching feeling upon seeing his former ruler humiliated. He uses the story to suggest to his listeners that as Germans they must learn to overcome such feelings and support Prussia in the context of what is best for Germany. Through this story, the Colonel proposes that loyalties to one's native land must now be supplanted by loyalties to Germany, and this, in turn, means accepting Prussia's centrality in the nation.

The Colonel makes another leap in interpreting present events when he tells the now attentive group that Bismarck has become "a revolutionary center to this Prussia." The man who in Hesekiel's novel was only one of a succession of figures leading Germany to unity becomes in this work Germany's savior, described as a combination of a St. George with sword and a St. Peter with keys. Moreover, Bismarck is made into the legitimate heir of 1848 when the Colonel explains, "What we tried with insufficient means, another person has taken up, and if he succeeds with the task, the revolution will be completed; we Germans will become the greatest people on earth and Germany the world's leading nation."[27] The Colonel then proposes a conciliatory toast to Prussian honor. With this character Rodenberg urges that Germans translate their revolutionary defeat and the loss of their particularist origins into redeeming change by embracing Bismarckian politics. The pub, a meeting ground for Germans from all over, suggests Berlin as a city in which Germans would be reconciled and educated in their common interests. With didactic scenes like this *Grandidiers* assumes a clear role in the formation of a German identity.

Rodenberg uses the war of 1870 to complete the process of education. Upon reading about the imminence of war, George Grandidier remembers how when he once led his small son through Berlin, he explained the meaning of all the heroic statues, and "how he instructed him in his duty toward the fatherland, double in fact for those whom the fatherland had taken up when they were fugitives from persecution, poor and homeless."[28] A few moments later the mailman, who brings that day's paper containing the news of the outbreak of war, snaps to attention when he meets Grandidier and declares that if his majesty should call, he will respond: "Here I am, Friedrich Anton Thielemann, discharged as a sergeant from the fusiliers' regiment, letter carrier in the postal district of Treptow; if need be, I'm ready to go!"[29] Ensuing scenes show young men being sent off to service by proud fathers.

But ambivalence about the war is widespread as well, and it is not restricted to Berlin's French community. One scene shows the meeting hall of the North German diet, filled with restless people assembled to hear from Bismarck himself the words of France's declaration of war and the Confederation's response to it. Bismarck becomes the master of the situation in the hall by showing himself to be the master of the international situation beyond. His careful address "had a liberating effect on the assembled people; the pressure of uncertainty was taken away, and everyone felt himself confronting the irreversible reality." At the end of the speech the hall erupts in cheers. In the visitors' gallery the exuberant Colonel reiterates the notion of Bismarck as the legitimate heir of the revolution when he tells another spectator of the wonder of him, an old 48er, raising his hat to the Junker: "What we wanted then is now being realized by him—the German will have a fatherland again."[30]

If the uncertainties have ended, the reality of loss is only beginning, as Rodenberg takes his readers through Germany to war-torn settings in Alsace. Long lines of exhausted soldiers, processions of the wounded being carried to makeshift hospitals, a camp for French prisoners of war, civilians fleeing the destruction—all these sights meet a group making its way westward with the

Colonel. They receive news of the German conquest of Strasbourg with quiet relief: "For all them it was as if the suffering of a dear relative had come to an end."[31] An important thread from earlier in the novel is tied when the Colonel steps onto a train platform covered with bivouacking soldiers and recognizes one of the men who had hurled insults against Prussians back in the Berlin beer hall. The Colonel queries him about others present that day to learn where they have fought—and who has fallen: "Prussians, Hanoverians, Hessians, and Westphalians," all buried peacefully next to one another, it is reported.[32]

The exchange presages Rodenberg's message of redemption: "The seriousness of the times, the great and solemn concern for the fatherland, had purified all hearts, so that no vanity had a place anymore. Everyone had done his duty according to his abilities, and everyone had found his peace."[33] The last scene, some months later, shows the triumphant return of troops to Berlin. The breach between Grandidier and his son has been healed, and the elder man, walking among the jubilant throngs, returns to the place where he had instructed his son so long ago, at the statue of the Great Elector overlooking the palace and the Spree. Now he lays a laurel wreath at its base and murmurs that this monument should not be forgotten among all the others that have been decorated for the occasion. With this scene Rodenberg responds to the disruption of German unification by placing Prussian tradition in its center.

Julius Rodenberg's own activity after unification focused on efforts to end the schisms in the society around him. In 1874 he became founding editor of *Deutsche Rundschau*, the cultural journal that would flourish for sixty years until disbanded by Josef Goebbels. Its intent of bringing cultural unity to the new empire was grounded in the fact of its publication in the new capital. Berlin as the center of Germany was an underlying theme of every issue. In an 1884 article Rodenberg declared his belief when he wrote that, "for all important expressions of our nation, Berlin will some day be the center." While urging his readers to be patient in awaiting the day, he lauded "this new magnificence transforming Berlin into the most beautiful of cities" and affirmed that Berlin's new glories derived from a combination of the victory of 1870 with the two centuries of tradition that had spawned the idea of a German empire.[34]

Such reassurances, however, only suggest the continuation of the doubts about a unified Germany that *Grandidiers* had portrayed among Berlin's immigrants. The feeling of being torn (*Zerrissenheit*) that descendants of French immigrants had experienced would reappear in other Berlin novels portraying the aftermath of unification. This feeling seemed part of the experience of living in Berlin, and one manifestation was the persistent question of whether Berlin was truly the center of Germany.

The beer hall episode in *Grandidiers* depicted resentment against the ascendancy of Prussia over other German states. When Berlin was catapulted into the role of German capital similar resentments caused critics to disparage the city. Vienna, as the seat of Habsburg rule, had dominated central Europe for centuries, and, even after the defeat of 1866 excluded Vienna as Germany's capital, none but the most fervent Berliner could believe that the city on the Spree would supplant the historical majesty of its Danube rival.[35] Critics could also point to other cities within the new empire whose German character might better have prevailed except for the overpowering Prussian militarism. Weimar's literary brilliance, Munich's artistic energy, Frankfurt's political tradition, Hamburg's economic power—all fueled anti-Berlin fires that broke out regularly after German unification. Such criticism, to be sure, ignored Berlin's own long-standing claims to being the political, as well as the intellectual, artistic, and economic center of Germany.[36]

That doubts about Berlin as capital could reflect worries over national identity is exemplified in a novella written by a 25-year-old Munich author named Wolfgang Kirchbach. Part of a larger work celebrating unification, "Reichshauptstadt" ("Imperial Capital") is one of the few fictional works to address the question of *whether* Berlin should be capital. *Die Kinder des Reiches*, the collection in which it appeared, argues that Germany's strength lies in the very diversity that made unification so difficult. "Reichshauptstadt," the first and longest story, intertwines this argument with themes of loss and change in Berlin. Kirchbach's eagerness to embrace the new Berlin is countered by a simultaneous lament for the passing of its provincial traditions. His ambivalence about the changing Berlin suggests a wider uneasiness about whether the German future may also mean the abandonment of down-to-earth values at the heart of these traditions.

At the same time, however, Kirchbach sounds another note for the future: strident nationalism. The impetus to write *Kinder des Reiches*, a paean to the new empire, came, according to his account in the introduction, from the experience of being born in London of German parents who went into exile after 1848. Kirchbach's key memory is related as a conversation overheard between two German friends, who explained that their elders had fled "because they had exalted a free and unified fatherland, because they did not want Germany to be a country of humiliation."[37] According to this explanation Germans were motivated to go into exile because of the failure of unification and shame over episodes like the agreement of Olmütz (Kirchbach makes no mention here of the political persecution that writers like Gutzkow emphasized). This interpretation makes the next leap easy: the "glorious years 1870–1871" brought the freedom, unity, and pride to Germany that the generation of 1848 had failed to achieve. At one level, Kirchbach's stories imply this through hints of the wounded national pride for which Germany would become famous. At another level, however, the stories criticize the selfishness and intolerance Kirchbach sees in the new Germany and seriously question the prospects for freedom.

Kirchbach uses the contrast between the old and the new Berlin to plead for humane values he sees as endangered. One dimension of this contrast is the two generations of a Berlin family, with the old personified by a postal clerk named Bredow and the new by his two socially elevated sons, one an ennobled hero of the Franco-Prussian war and the other a prominent jurist. The elder Bredow is intensely dedicated to his post, leads a modest life whose major excitement is a Sunday outing to Kreuzberg, proudly uses Berlin dialect, and possesses a wry, self-ironic sense of humor. The younger Bredows, however, consort with more refined circles and are embarrassed by their father's reversion to dialect and other quaint ways. They try to persuade him to retire from his humble job, but he scoffs, saying that as long as "his" 85-year-old Kaiser is not ashamed to work for the fatherland neither is he.[38] Another sort of contrast emerges when the younger son announces his engagement to a Jewish woman. Bredow, a strong advocate of Berlin's tradition of tolerance, is pitted against his wife, elder son, and daughter-in-law. As Bredow puts it, "Old Fritz himself brought the Jews to Berlin. That's good enough for me!"[39] Lest readers sympathize with the rest of the family, the narrator comments that in "those days" Germany, and not least the capital itself, was the scene of "unbelievable hatred" (*unerhörte Feindschaft*) against Jews. The elder Bredow is the antidote to these hatreds as well as to the pretensions of modern Berlin.

Like Rodenberg, Kirchbach uses family tensions to reflect wider tensions in Berlin and German society. In Bredow's thoughts, "The discord at home reminded him of the discord in the city . . . . His fears about an arduous new war [the war scare of 1875], about violent struggles of nations and races stood before him as before many others and swept over his soul along with the thousand ills of his age and the inner confusion of his own experiences."[40] A few pages later Bredow snaps to himself in Berlin dialect, "I'm sick of these times with all the Jew-baiting and fears and threats of war; even my family's fallen into miserable bickering. I've had it with the times and with my century; I'm getting out!"[41] He thereupon leaves home on an odyssey through the city he has never had time really to see. But this is hardly a tour of nostalgia.

Instead, the narrative of Bredow's wanderings makes a dramatic shift of focus from a society in conflict to a society bursting with modern dynamism. The marvels of the new streetcar system, the maneuvers of the military establishment, the passions of political meetings, the array of museums, the cosmopolitan hotels on Unter den Linden, the cafés, the zoo—all evince Berlin's transformation to *Reichshauptstadt*. And all contribute to Bredow's transformation from a loyal Prussian civil servant into a patriotic son of Germany. As a proud Berliner he stops a passerby to affirm that "Berlin is the rightful capital of the German Reich because you notice immediately from the people on the street that all the German peoples are represented here."[42] The narrator also stresses that the transformation of the city has only just begun: "We decline to describe any further what Herr Bredow saw and admired because just as he found everything in an unfinished state, so would we give the German people a very unfinished impression of their capital."[43]

The specific connection between Bredow, Berlin, and the times in this story can be tenuous, but Kirchbach clearly felt such a connection and wanted his readers to do so also. While many other authors conveyed dilemmas of the modernizing city, few stated them explicitly in terms of the experiences of

German unification and Berlin's becoming the capital. The convergence of these themes in the character of Bredow culminates, through him, in the symbolic disappearance of the old Berlin. Chastened by a false arrest on suspicion of embezzlement and by his subsequent forced retirement from the postal service, Bredow vows that henceforth "no impure German word would cross his lips."[44] Not only does his dialect vanish but, with it, his Berlin humor. The old ways, he decides, are no longer proper in the new Berlin with its diverse population.

The last scene depicts the old man, somewhat in the likeness of Moses, overlooking a promised land he will not enter.[45] He senses his approaching death and takes his grandson on a last walk through the capital. Showing him its monuments, he stops in front of the chancellor's residence on Wilhelmstraße, where they catch a glimpse of Bismarck, and continues to the palace, where they glimpse the Kaiser himself. "You have seen a valiant generation of northern men," he instructs the boy, "who through their strong will and combined efforts have become the honor and glory of their great nation."[46] Bredow dies that evening. The loss of the old Berlin is conveyed as something that, although inevitable, should be painful to all Germans.

Kirchbach's hope for the future rested on his belief that the diverse groups in Berlin represented a true basis for German unity, but the novella gives scant sustenance to this hope. In addition to the dynamism of Imperial Berlin it depicts a city of social barriers, a society permeated by anti-Semitism, a bureaucracy that could falsely accuse a loyal servant, and a judicial system providing dubious safeguards against such accusations. The story neither acknowledges nor attempts to resolve the contradictions. Moreover, one passage picks up the ominous implications of the reference to German humiliation in the introduction. In a plea for understanding between Germans and Jews, Bredow's younger son simultaneously invokes a myth of international persecution by alluding to Germans and Jews as "two peoples who are hated in the world and who will be eternally hated because they long for their own realm (*Reich*) and want to keep it."[47] This linkage of the idea of Germany as a pariah nation with a plea for toleration strikingly demonstrates how strands of differing values could be interwoven.

Kirchbach was a young man at the time, but he resembled the elderly Bredow in that he overlooked a land he could not enter. Condemned by conservative critics as a representative of dangerous new literary trends, he was also ostracized by the emergent literary generation of naturalists. In a Reichstag debate of 1883 an angry government official alluded to the newly published *Kinder des Reiches* as evidence of the infection of German culture by the influence of French naturalist Emile Zola.[48] This attack, although unjustified by any critical comparison of the two authors, marked the beginning of interminable hostilities between conservative advocates of *Dichtung* and the naturalist notion of *Literatur*. Naturalist writers also suspected Kirchbach because of his association with the author Paul Heyse, whose works they scorned as elitist. Although Kirchbach contributed to naturalist publications, including an article satirizing Heyse's works, he was dismissed by leading naturalists as an author of mere romantic fantasies.[49] Linked to the new school by conservative attacks and yet ejected from it by virtue of his idealist leanings, Kirchbach became caught in a literary no-man's land comparable to the ones in which he had placed Berlin as capital and Germany as Reich: he had experienced too much to remain wholly committed to traditions that had nurtured him, and yet his refusal to deny those traditions brought collisions with the new forces.

A young author with no such ambiguities in his literary allegiances also wrestled with tensions between tradition and modernity, and also did so with an old Berlin character who fell victim to new forces. Conrad Alberti (1862–1918), who arrived in Berlin from Breslau in the early 1880s, soon became an outspoken proponent of the new naturalist movement. His first published fiction, which appeared under the title *Plebs* in 1887, consisted of three novellas that used images of the physical demolition of old Berlin as a backdrop for themes of lives being ruined by the new.

"Majestätsbeleidigung" deals most explicitly of the three with the conjunction of destruction and new magnificence. Set at the end of the '70s, it shows Berlin still far from settled in her new identity. The protagonist, Herr Dräsecke, is a prosperous descendant of a line of butchers who for generations have lived proudly in a charming house an ancestor was granted by Frederick II for distinguished service. Located near Alexanderplatz, the transition point between old Berlin (the central district of Berlin) and the city's eastern realms, the house embodies the family's proud tradition and its monarchical loyalties. Dräsecke might complain about certain ministers, the Junkers, or some new laws—but never about the dynasty. "Such is the Berliner of the old mold," the narrator explains, "progressive, even radical in his political outlook . . . but always patriotic and loyal to the throne."[50]

This loyalty is put to the test when modernity encroaches on the Dräsecke realm. The new elevated railway (*Stadtbahn*), the family learns, will pass right by their property. Dräsecke's immediate reaction is opposition: "What did the easing of traffic mean to him, or the grandeur of the system, or the glory of such an enormous undertaking for Berlin? He feared only the effects of vibration on the foundation of the house and the possibility of having to make repairs."[51] But he gruffly admits the necessity of such progress: "Berlin truly is becoming a world city."[52] The crisis worsens when plans are announced for the construction of a station that will condemn the Dräsecke property. The city proposes compensation sufficient to allow the family to exchange its uncomfortable, poorly lit quarters for a modern, well-furnished house in a new section of town, but the Dräseckes do not want to modernize.

Dräsecke's futile struggles against condemnation drive him to a desperate act. It is now summer 1878, and Berlin has been shocked by two assassination attempts on the Kaiser. One reaction is a burst of arrests for lese majesty, and

Dräsecke takes advantage of the fearful atmosphere by falsely accusing a civil engineer involved in the construction of the railway. On the basis of Dräsecke's testimony the engineer is convicted and imprisoned, but after a series of family crises over the act Dräsecke finally confesses to perjury. Convicted, Dräsecke enters a Berlin jail with a "Three Cheers! Long live the Kaiser!" The jubilation has to do with the fact that the Kaiser has reduced the sentence of his dutiful subject, but the cheer affirms the continuity of Dräsecke's loyalty. This happy ending does not alter the fact that the symbol of the family's long loyalty has been destroyed by the demands of progress.

The works discussed in this chapter articulated fears about loss: loss of the old Prussia, of the old Berlin, and of old values. Yet all of them, to varying degrees, embraced unification and heralded prospects for the German future. The themes and images in these novels suggest that German unification intensified the process of modernization by calling into question the foundations of the old Prussia, by throwing people of diverse loyalties together into one city and one nation, and by transforming Berlin into a dynamic but alienating metropolis. Beneath fictional visions of national harmony we have seen authors who confront dilemmas about class conflict, particularist rivalries, divided loyalties, and an aggressive new nationalism. Noteworthy is that such dilemmas arose from the presumably positive experience of unification, attesting to Peter Marris's premise that any fundamental social change gives rise to ambivalence.

When the change is clearly negative, such ambivalence can grow into horror. Many Berlin novelists discerned such a moment when the national celebration vanished into the economic crash of 1873. They saw this experience as a national trauma that scarred the soul of Imperial Germany. Their fictional treatment of this experience, moreover, became intricately bound with inherited perceptions of a deep crisis of middle-class values.

# Notes

1. Robert Springer, *Berlin wird Weltstadt: Ernste und heitere Culturbilder* (Berlin, 1868). The slogan derives from the 1840s, when it was used sarcastically. Maximilian Müller-Jabusch, *So waren die Gründerjahre* (Düsseldorf, 1957), 45.
2. In the half century following 1860, the population increased from 580,000 to 3,400,000. Martin Pfannschmidt, "Probleme der Weltstadt Berlin," *Zum Problem der Weltstadt* (Berlin, 1959), 4. See also Ingrid Thienel, *Städtewachstum im Industrialisierungsprozeß des 19. Jahrhunderts. Das Berliner Beispiel* (Berlin, 1973).
3. Springer, *Berlin wird Weltstadt*, 148.
4. Ibid., 156.
5. Soon this area would be packed with *Mietskasernern* to house the workers of the ever-expanding "Fire Country."
6. Quoted by Heinrich Spiero, *Das poetische Berlin: Alt-Berlin* (Munich, 1911), 39. Spiero also uses the image of clothes to point to Berlin's crisis of identity, ibid., 26. On Berlin's reputation for *Traditionslosigkeit* see Klaus Ziegler, "Die Berliner Gesell-

schaft und die Literatur," in Hans Rothfels, ed., *Berlin in Vergangenheit und Gegenwart* (Tübingen, 1961), 39.
7. For example, two middle-aged characters become recast into the guardians of two children left orphaned in a *Mietskaserne*; see below, 110.
8. Peter Marris, *Loss and Change* (New York, 1974), 64, 68.
9. On linking literature with a political date like 1870 see Klaus Günther Just, *Von der Gründerzeit bis zur Gegenwart. Geschichte der deutsche Literatur seit 1871* (Bern, 1973), 12–14. On the premise that "with the foundation of the Reich in 1871 the real work of national unification only began" see Geoff Eley, "State Formation, Nationalism, and Political Culture: Some Thoughts on the Unification of Germany," in his *From Unification to Nazism: Reinterpreting the German Past* (Boston, 1986), 61–84.
10. On this important literary association see Friedrich Behrend, *Die Geschichte des Tunnels über der Spree* (Berlin, 1919).
11. Ludovika Hesekiel, *Von Brandenburg zu Bismarck. Roman aus der Gegenwart* (Berlin, 1873), I, 18.
12. Ibid., I, 100.
13. See above, 30.
14. Hesekiel, *Von Brandenburg zu Bismarck*, I, 119.
15. Ibid., I, 23. On such a conception of *Volk* see Bedrich Loewenstein, *Der Entwurf der Moderne: Vom Geist der bürgerlichen Gesellschaft* (Essen, 1987), 10.
16. Hesekiel, *Von Brandenburg zu Bismarck*, II, 71.
17. Ibid., I, 62. For more on the notion of *Vornehmheit*, see below, 58–60.
18. Ibid., I, 34–35. On Wilhelmstraße see also Annemarie Lange, *Berlin zur Zeit Bebels und Bismarcks* (Berlin, 1972), 239–281.
19. Hesekiel, *Von Brandenburg zu Bismarck*, II, 258.
20. Ibid., I, 154. See also Lothar Gall, *Bismarck: Der weiße Revolutionär* (Frankfurt am Main, 1980), 110–111.
21. Hesekiel, *Von Brandenburg zu Bismarck*, II, 173, 250.
22. Ibid., II, 260. The arithmetic of the "old" Prussian's age indicates a woman in her early thirties—old, perhaps, to the 24-year-old author!
23. Julius Rodenberg, *Die Grandidiers: Ein Berliner Roman aus der französischen Kolonie*, 4th ed. (Stuttgart, 1912), 410. The novel was first published in 1878 as a well-received serial and then with further fanfare as a book. Heinrich Spiero, *Julius Rodenberg: Sein Leben und seine Werke* (Berlin, 1921), 80.
24. Rodenberg, *Die Grandidiers*, 213–215.
25. Ibid., 220.
26. Spiero, *Rodenberg*, 75; Rodenberg, *Die Grandidiers*, 225–226.
27. *Die Grandidiers*, 227.
28. Ibid., 330.
29. Ibid., 333. On Rodenberg's portrayal of the stages by which the French community responded to the war, see ibid., 345–356.
30. Ibid., 360.
31. Ibid., 397.
32. Ibid., 401. On the notion of the army as an "instrument of social integration" see Dennis E. Showalter, "Army, State and Society in Germany, 1871–1914," in Jack R. Dukes and Joachim Remak, eds., *Another Germany: A Reconsideration of the Imperial Era* (Boulder, Colo., 1988), 6.
33. Rodenberg, *Die Grandidiers*, 429.
34. Reprinted in Robert Springer, *Bilder aus dem Berliner Leben* (Halle, 1892), 41.
35. Some opponents of the reactionary Habsburg regime, however, looked favorably upon Berlin as opposed to Vienna. See Eberhard Faden, "Berlin Hauptstadt—seit wann und wodurch?" in *Jahrbuch für brandenburgische Landesgeschichte*, I (1950), 31.

36. Richard Dietrich, "Von der Residenzstadt zur Weltstadt: Berlin vom Anfang des 19. Jahrhunderts bis zur Reichsgründung," and Hans Herzfeld, "Berlin als Kaiserstadt und Reichshauptstadt, 1871–1945," in *Das Hauptstadtproblem in der Geschichte* (Tübingen, 1952), 111–165.
37. Wolfgang Kirchbach, *Die Kinder des Reiches* (Leipzig, 1883), I, 14.
38. Ibid., 27. Kirchbach later inserts into his text two poems his own grandfather wrote about being a letter carrier. Ibid., 144.
39. Ibid., 57. The reference is to Frederick II and his invitation for Jews to settle in the city.
40. Ibid., 62.
41. Ibid., 65.
42. Ibid., 106 and 108.
43. Ibid., 141.
44. Ibid., 163.
45. Ludovika Hesekiel's portrayal of a female Moses who cannot enter the promised land of the German reich is a noteworthy parallel to Kirchbach's Bredow.
46. Kirchbach, *Die Kinder des Reich*, 170.
47. Ibid., 49; similar references to Germany's being hated by other nations occur on 39 and 166.
48. Adalbert von Hanstein, *Das jüngste Deutschland: Zwei Jahrzehnte miterlebter Literaturgeschichte*, 3rd ed. (Leipzig, 1905), 27–28.
49. Werner F. Striedieck, "Wolfgang Kirchbach and the 'Jüngstdeutschen,'" *The Germanic Review*, 22 (February 1947), 46, and Karl Bleibtreu, *Revolution der Literatur* (Leipzig, 1885; reprinted, Tübingen, 1973), 32.
50. Conrad Alberti, *Plebs* (Leipzig, 1887), 96.
51. Ibid., 99. On the stages of *Stadtbahn* construction see Richard Dietrich, ed., *Berlin: Zehn Kapitel Seiner Geschichte* (Berlin, 1981), 255.
52. Alberti, *Plebs*, 102.

# 3

# Storms of the *Gründerjahre*: The Imperiled *Bürger*

The 1870s were a critical time for the German middle class. Given its growing economic power in an industrializing nation, it might have been expected to take advantage of the disruptions of unification to assert political and social leadership as well. Although the Bismarckian system retained many hallmarks of aristocratic rule, the role of the middle class in that system was ill-defined and thus might have allowed scope for new forms of power. As the decade passed, however, not only did the new institutions become less malleable, but fragmentation within the middle class lessened prospects for its political ascendancy. Despite achieving noteworthy improvements in its legal status, the middle class failed to launch a concerted challenge to aristocratic or monarchical authority.[1] Berlin novels of these years suggest two significant elements of a process that allowed the German middle class to forego attempts at political self-affirmation.

First, novels sustained the tendency to define middle-class goals in spiritual or moral rather than social or political terms. A crisis of the German *Bürgertum* was already depicted in Gutzkow's *Ritter*, which, as we have seen, portrayed a deepening tension between *Bildung* and *Besitz*—or between a middle class distinguished by its cultural commitments and one devoted to the amassing of material wealth. In novels of the 1870s this dichotomy deepened with repeated homage to intellectual rather than economic individualism and with advocacy of self-cultivation over social engagement. While such novels delineated an array of new urban pressures that threatened to turn individuals into cogs of a machine and political persecution that intruded into their day-to-day lives, they usually allowed criticism of institutions to dissipate before an ideal of freedom achieved by individual self-cultivation (*Bildung*).[2] Their overriding concern with inner autonomy led to the creation of many fictional Berliners who maintained their integrity and independence by cultivating the values of a bygone city whose citizens eschewed pretension, lived in humble surroundings, and developed their individuality through a disciplined life of intellectual and spiritual endeavor rather than through economic pursuits.[3]

Second, in novels treating the period following unification, these tendencies were intensified by bewildering economic upheaval. The early 1870s, which came to be known as the "founders' era" (*Gründerjahre*), saw the founding not only of the German empire but also of innumerable industrial and commercial enterprises. The boom began with Germany's receipt of a five-billion-franc indemnity from defeated France, which helped to fuel a frenzy of economic activity concentrated in Berlin. The euphoria came to a sudden end in 1873, however, with a stockmarket crash that led to the collapse of dozens of companies and resulted in a storm of social and political recriminations that swirled through Berlin and the rest of German society.[4] Berlin authors depicted the *Gründerjahre* in terms of a mania for reckless speculation that broke the bounds of the economic world and invaded heretofore sacred social and cultural realms. They interpreted the crash of 1873 as moral retribution against a German nation that had allowed itself to be tempted by the lure of easy riches. Through the lives of their characters they linked an accelerating crisis of middle-class values with a crisis of nationhood. Such a link articulated an expectation that Germany's salvation would coincide with the national renunciation of entrepreneurial values and a return to the spiritual virtues of self-cultivation. In focusing on the new capitalist middle class as the worst threat to Germany, authors dissipated their fictional challenges to aristocratic rule.

The first Berlin novel of the 1870s to probe the crisis in middle-class values was Paul Heyse's *Kinder der Welt* (*Children of the World*) (1872). Published a year before the denouement of the speculative boom, the novel did not specifically concern the *Gründerjahre*, nor did it even depict unification. But it did focus on the German *Bürger* reacting to the pressures of modern society and drew lessons about the need for a moral steadfastness that later novels about the *Gründerjahre* would underscore. In this novel Heyse depicted social evils that implied a clear call to action, but he refrained from developing middle-class characters who committed themselves to respond. His characters instead withdrew into the haven of traditional values, safe from the storms of the age but also removed from the possibility of steering their society through them.

Paul Heyse (1830–1914) claimed to have inherited his unshakable commitment to self-cultivation from his philologist father,[5] but his whole childhood seems an idyll of Athens-on-the-Spree. He thrived in the atmosphere of *Vormärz* Berlin, nourished by the classical curriculum of the venerable Friedrich-Wilhelm Gymnasium and stimulated by discourse, music, and poetry readings in Berlin's most rarefied cultural salons.[6] Heyse's idyll was transferred to a new setting in 1855, when he was called to Munich to join the intellectual circle at the court of King Maximilian II. Although this royal patronage died with the king in 1865, Heyse made an apparently effortless transition from court poet to author and achieved renown as a prolific writer of short stories, poetry, and literary commentaries.[7] A lifetime of honors as "*the* writer of the second half of the century"[8] culminated in 1910 when Heyse received the Nobel Prize for literature. Despite these successes, however, Heyse continued to affirm the proud values of his Berlin childhood.

*Kinder der Welt*, Heyse's most significant Berlin work, was published when his fame was already established. It was the first novel serialized in a Berlin newspaper. For both of these reasons it reached an especially large audience and provoked a storm of controversy over its defense of free-thinking and apparent condoning of extra-marital passion. Since Heyse is remembered in literary histories as the target of unrelenting naturalist criticism for his purportedly innocuous, harmonious themes, it is essential to recall how radical this novel seemed to readers of the 1870s. Indeed, popular displeasure over the novel was said to have contributed to the subsequent failure of the venerable *Spenersche Zeitung*, the newspaper that published it.[9] But even as Heyse challenged religious values, sexual taboos, and political oppression, he allowed his characters to find resolution by withdrawing from the public arena. This novel demonstrates how modernist social criticism could yield to the cultural tradition of inwardness (*Innerlichkeit*); it exemplifies a crucial element of middle-class crisis in Imperial Germany.

The ideal of spiritual withdrawal from the strains of day-to-day life is explicitly drawn by Heyse in the context of Berlin when he uses as his vehicle a cherished Berlin institution: the *Landpartie*, or country outing. Such an excursion was usually a social occasion that involved a group of family and friends who mounted an omnibus and escaped to one of the lakes or forests surrounding the city. An array of outdoor restaurants catered to *Landpartien* by providing everything from multi-course feasts to outdoor tables at which families could spread out their sandwiches and indulge in *Kuchen* or *Weißbier*, while enjoying the strains of the inevitable *Kapelle*. So well established became the convention that one cultural historian wryly remarked, "A novel without a *Landpartie* was simply not a Berlin novel."[10] It was a particularly useful literary convention, for in addition to lending authenticity to Berlin novels it allowed authors to remove characters from everyday settings so that they could open their hearts to spiritual concerns. Heyse used the *Landpartie* for precisely these purposes. A day-long outing to the popular Charlottenburg palace becomes an occasion for intense soul-searching. With its components of Berlin, the Hohenzollern rulers, and middle-class values this particular *Landpartie* becomes a striking example of the connections authors made between the crisis of the *Bürger* and the quest for German nationhood.

The episode is initiated by the protagonist, Edwin, an impecunious university lecturer (*Privatdozent*) who personifies the ideal of Athens-on-the-Spree. Enamored of a lovely newcomer to Berlin named Toinette Marchard, Edwin encourages her attempts at self-cultivation and delivers a succession of books to her elegant apartment. One day, when Toinette begins to weep over her desperately lonely situation, Edwin seizes the moment: "We should follow the example of nine-tenths of our fellow citizens and use the beautiful weather for a little outing."[11] With unaccustomed assertiveness he instructs her to dress plainly and leave her servant boy at home. At Charlottenburg all traces of the traditionally jocular *Landpartie* disappear as Edwin and Toinette stroll through the palace grounds to the mausoleum where King Frederick William III and his wife are buried. Once inside the pair is overcome by awe as they gaze at the marble statues.

As they emerge into the sunlight Edwin explains their reverie in terms of the spirit emanating from the royal couple:

"Neither of them was an intellectual nor deeply educated. But their inborn nobility gave them in crucial moments the incisive word and the right deed in their hearts, and a thoroughly middle-class sense of duty caused them always to appear truly princely and dignified [*vornehm*]."

Toinette takes up the word *vornehm* and continues:

"There is but one genuine dignity [*Vornehmheit*] and that is to remain true to oneself. . . . Whoever has nobility inside, lives and dies from his own grace and is thus sovereign. Everything else is wretched torment that angry, ordinary people who are uncomfortable in their own skins have devised to make life as bitter as possible even for their good-natured neighbors."[12]

With these broad strokes Heyse establishes as his ideal the spirit emanating from those who are true to themselves in a world of oppressive social forms. Such spirit is recognized in a refined bearing that comes from a middle-class notion of duty possessed by the morally noble.[13] Heyse's use of a Prussian king to evoke such a middle-class ideal appears to derive both from the esthetic qualities of the statues and the king's reputation for humble simplicity. He ignores the implications of idealizing a monarch notorious for his reactionary politics.[14]

Heyse further develops this humble notion of *Vornehmheit* by mythologizing the old Berlin. The novel counters jarring images of the "throng of rough and uncouth people" by focusing on islands of true humanity in the urban sea of "cheerless existences."[15] A major theme concerns the perils of social ambition, and two houses symbolize the alternative by being portrayed as realms in which unpretentious people devote themselves to modest undertakings and warm human relationships. One is an unadorned building just north of Unter den Linden, occupied by Meister Gottfried Feyertag, a prosperous shoemaker. He stays there, the narrator explains, because "it would have seemed to him to be base ingratitude to turn his back on the old witnesses and protectors of his good fortune without a compelling reason."[16] This shop, with its rear annex of cramped apartments, is a major setting for the novel, a place in which the artisan and educated classes mix. The second house provides even meaner surroundings for its occupant, the sculptor Philipp König. Once a sailors' dive, the dilapidated building sits on a narrow canal, inspiring König to praise "our dear Spree" with its "honest old barges."[17] He even induces a polite visitor to admit that the sluggish canal offers a piece of Holland and that the rusty bridge across it resembles Venice's Bridge of Sighs. König's "lagoon" is also notable because its location corresponds with that of the house of Heyse's earliest memories.[18]

The exemplary people who live in these settings show that Heyse's notion of

*Vornehmheit* has little to do with social rank. Superiority rests, rather, with those who avoid social ambition to remain true to themselves. Heyse further emphasizes this connotation of *Vornehmheit* by using Toinette's apartment as a contrast. When Edwin first stares in wonder at the heavily decorated drawing room, he quickly reminds himself not to be intimidated by the contrast with the austere furnishings of his quarters in Feyertag's annex.[19] In his espousal of simplicity Edwin reflects the attitude of the adult Heyse, who reminisces about his childhood: "In those days no one in the otherwise so cultivated houses of the *Bürger* had the least notion of an artistic furnishing of the rooms." Berliners, he continues, made "a virtue of necessity, and there was still no trace of social discontent."[20] The image of Berlin in simpler times serves here as a lament over the arrival of a new age.

Nevertheless, Heyse was not as alienated from modernity as these images suggest, for the novel is also a paean to a secularized modern humanity. With the title he defines this new humanity as those who see "the realm of their duties and rights, their troubles and their joys encompassed *here on earth*." He contrasts them with people who remain committed to godly realms, those for whom the thought of life without religion means "a feeling of loss, of hopeless desolation and abandonment."[21] Heyse rejects the notion that an age of freedom has dawned and shows that society still refuses its worldly children the freedom not to believe. The most explicit attack comes at the funeral of Edwin's brother, when a clergyman's intonations about "the error and depredation of this poor sinner" anger the mourners. One of them, a firebrand named Reinhold Franzelius, angrily denounces the minister for assaulting the young man's memory and urges those present not to allow themselves to be enslaved by visions of the hereafter.[22] When Reinhold is arrested and charged with "disruption of a public religious ceremony," Edwin becomes angry at his own passivity toward the "murmured formulas" by which society intervenes in life's important moments.[23] This realization might have become a call to action for Edwin, providing, in turn, a model of the German *Bürger* challenging repressive institutions. Instead, the novel makes no further reference to Edwin's passivity.

Reinhold's socialist agitation represents an even more compelling chance for middle-class social engagement. When beseeched by well-meaning friends to give up his dangerous activity, Reinhold offers a prescient view of the police harassment that would become a hallmark of Imperial Berlin: "There will be a lot of hullaballoo when they burst forth with their usual clumsy methods—arrests, house searches, confiscation of papers, warrants for conspirators."[24] But even the specter of such persecution leads to no further discussion of what the burgher's reaction should be. Reinhold eventually abandons his political action.

Thus, although Heyse clearly questions the extent to which individual autonomy can be maintained against the political pressures of the day, he does not pursue the implications of his words. He allows characters to turn away from social dilemmas and find internal resolution. Both Edwin and Reinhold leave Berlin for a provincial town, where they settle into quiet, harmonious lives with their respective families (Edwin having finally turned away from the tempestuous Toinette to marry the serene daughter of Philipp König). In the last chapters Edwin and his wife visit Berlin, six years after leaving it. New residential districts now spread westward along the Tiergarten, and König's old barrack on the "lagoon" has been replaced by a new building. The concluding scene, however, takes place in the timelessness of the Charlottenburg mausoleum, where the visitors are newly inspired: "Come! Let's go back into our lives, to our child, and to our friends."[25]

For Heyse the serenity inspired by the mausoleum meant resolution to crises of human experience. His esthetic inclinations caused him to concentrate on the intellectual and moral crises of the middle class.[26] Implicitly he acknowledged the new German state in his choice of a Hohenzollern monarch as the embodiment of the ideal of *Vornehmheit*, but in bringing resolution outside the emerging metropolis Heyse abandoned the social criticism that some of his Berlin episodes implied. That he raised such ideas at all, however, testified to the difficulty of ignoring them.

Other novelists were explicit about their belief that the crises of the middle class dovetailed with economic and political upheavals wrought by unification. By far the best known was Friedrich Spielhagen (1829–1911), whose immensely popular *Sturmflut* (1877) interwove themes of middle-class crisis with images of the *Gründerjahre* as a time of rampant speculation, corruption, and bankruptcy.[27] Although Spielhagen clearly intended the work to address concrete social and political problems in the new Germany, his diagnosis of the evils behind the crash of 1873 culminated in a moral lecture to fellow Germans that strayed from the challenges he had raised to the status quo.

The protagonist of *Sturmflut*, a sea captain named Reinhold Schmidt, is a middle-class exemplar who clings fiercely to his social identity. His militant independence ultimately earns him immense respect and a high post in the German government and makes him, to use one of Spielhagen's favorite metaphors, the smith of his own happiness.[28] Spielhagen's admiration for such middle-class initiative was deeply ingrained. Although his protagonist was modeled after a sea captain he met while working on the novel,[29] Schmidt also embodied characteristics Spielhagen attributed to two mentors from his youth: his father, a building commissioner in the Baltic port of Stralsund, and Friedrich August Mons, an older foster brother who became chief civil engineer of the Thuringian railway. The two epitomized, in Spielhagen's words, "the real type of Prussian official of the old mold: pure as gold in their intentions, dutiful to the last breath, unaffected by the enticements of personal gain, and, most important of all, loyal to the throne from head to foot." Reinhold, too, is a paragon of competence, trustworthiness, modesty, and loyalty. And, like the real-life models, the fictional protagonist is a "self-made man in the best sense of the word," in that he achieves a succession of worthy posts through diligence and competence.[30]

Other crucial elements of Reinhold's identity are his patriotism and his middle-class pride. Readers learn that Reinhold's commitment to Germany caused him to abandon the newly won command of a merchant ship to participate in the war against France. This commitment continually surfaces in conversations in which he takes the part of the new Reich in the face of particularist opposition and apathy.[31] Overriding even his patriotism, however, is a pride of class (*Bürgerstolz*) that attests to Spielhagen's own middle-class upbringing in a social environment dominated by a still-thriving Pomeranian nobility.[32] In Reinhold it means shunning anything that hints at aristocratic pretension, whether it involves using his uncle's preferred carriage or allowing an aristocrat to address him as "Lieutenant," even though he earned that rank in the war.[33] To be sure, he falls in love with the daughter of a tradition-bound nobleman, but this unremarked paradox seems not to compromise Reinhold's middle-class loyalties.[34]

In Reinhold Schmidt, Spielhagen created a middle-class character who was unusual in that he combined traditional virtues with active participation in the German regime. Even this outcome had problematic elements, but if Reinhold were the only prominent middle-class character in *Sturmflut* the novel would hardly exemplify *bürgerlich* crisis. His example is offset by two other Schmidts whose attitudes Spielhagen identifies as the real source of crisis in the rising German middle class. The first is Ernst Schmidt, Reinhold's uncle, depicted as an "old intractable revolutionary" from 1848.[35] The second is Ernst's son, Philipp, who, as an unstoppable speculator in the economic bonanza of the *Gründerjahre*, represents a still greater danger to the *Bürgertum*. These two Schmidts personify the perils Spielhagen sees for the German *Bürger*, who either petrifies his goals or deserts them for the lures of materialism.

The cantankerous Ernst Schmidt, owner of a prospering marble-cutting plant in Berlin, has vivid memories of the barricades in 1848. The anger that motivated him then still prevails. As he explains, "I instinctively hated monarchical and princely rule as an institution suited to an immature people or a people grown senile, but one that must be rejected with disgust by a people who have become conscious of their own power."[36] On 18 March 1848, when he was taken prisoner and threatened by an officer with raised sword, Ernst's life was saved by the timely arrival of a dispatch. He shouted after the departing officer that the next time they met, it would be his turn to exact revenge. Twenty-four years later Ernst finds himself facing the same officer, now a retired general forced by circumstances to discuss a possible marriage between his profligate son and Ernst's daughter. The dignified General von Werben seems far removed from the brutal young aristocrat who had threatened a freedom fighter with death as he tells Ernst that the struggle begun in 1848 now is continuing "in the field of law and justice." Victory, he says, will go that group "who first understands this ground and is able to grow the strongest roots in it."[37] Ernst, however, believing that even civility means a betrayal of his integrity, soon drives the general away with insults.

Beneath Ernst's stubbornness is a conviction that the legacy of 1848 has been betrayed. For him the uprising was the real German revolution and republicanism its necessary outcome. "The old true German middle class was republican," Ernst growls.[38] This comment indicates the deep hostility to the Bismarckian regime of one who sees himself not only as a 48er but also as the embodiment of true Germanism. Unification, he says, was prepared by men like himself, "at the barricades in the March days, on the benches of the Frankfurter Assembly, and everywhere, every time it was possible for people to put their shoulders to the wheel."[39] It was the work of "thousands upon thousands of patriotic hearts and minds who were not granted aristocratic titles and estates." In Ernst's view Bismarck has received credit for the work of many, and for accepting the adulation he merits contempt. "I don't think there's anyone in the whole world who hates that man as much I do," Ernst adds.[40]

Another cause for contempt is Bismarck's readiness to compromise, a quality Ernst sees as faithlessness to one's ideals. In one scene, when Reinhold pleads with his uncle to give in to the strike demands of workers at his factory, Ernst explodes, "Is my name Bismarck? . . . Will they sink into breathless silence as soon as I stand up?"[41] When Reinhold comments that he could do worse than learn from Bismarck's ability to know when to trim his sails, Ernst counters with the refrain of the unwavering *Bürger*: "I can't give in without giving up myself, without ceasing to be the person I am."[42] For him the legacy of 1848 means unyielding dedication to principle. Reinhold is not the only one to question this trait. In the marriage exchange the general tells Ernst he is guilty of the sin he attributes to the nobility: he has forgotten nothing and learned nothing. Ernst later confesses that this judgment wounded him because he considered himself a man of reason, but he has come to realize how much truth the judgment contains.[43] He finally learns that fealty to oneself has its limits.

Ernst sees the ruin of his son Philipp as the result of transgressing those limits: "The principle of limitless freedom and commitment to absolute selfhood [*Selbstbestimmung*] taken to its logical extreme can or perhaps must lead weaker minds astray, as it has done with my [son]."[44] The case of Philipp is especially significant because he is designated early in the novel as a "man of the times," whose shrewd dealings have allowed him to parlay a plot of Berlin land into a fortune.[45] The price of his success is a break with his father, who becomes enraged by his son's speculation with property once intended for working-class housing. Ernst further denounces Philipp's involvement in joint stock companies, and accuses him of deluding small investors with his "sensationalist, deceptive prospectuses."[46] Philipp, in turn, rationalizes his father's anger as envy. He is also skeptical when his cousin Reinhold declines an investment tip with the maxim, "Caution is the mother of wisdom." "And the grandmother of poverty," Philipp shoots back. "Then I am her real grandson," replies Reinhold.[47] Such *bürgerlich* caution against investing seems at first absurd.

Philipp's gains are astonishing, and he celebrates them by commissioning a magnificent mansion on Wilhelmstraße and opening it to Berlin society with a sumptuous ball. As guests consume the inevitable lobster salad and glasses of the finest champagne, Philipp receives a toast to his achievements. "The proverb says that everyone is the smith of his own happiness. At every forge there is a smith," begins the speaker, proceeding to extoll Philipp's "anvil of honesty" and the "hammer of his success."[48] This paean to the self-made man, however, becomes the ironic prelude to catastrophe.

To depict the intricate financial, political, and social background to this catastrophe—the crash of 1873—Spielhagen focuses on a massive financial project. It involves a proposal to extend the railroad from "Sundin" (Stralsund, the Baltic port where Spielhagen grew up) across the island of Rügen, and a related proposal to build a strategic harbor at its terminus to justify the extension. The harbor's location becomes a matter of critical importance, since estate owners' land values will soar or languish according to the route of the railroad. A formidable opposition develops among those who believe the project to be both wasteful and strategically unsound.[49] Meanwhile, an equally formidable consortium of promoters gradually prevails through intricate maneuverings.[50] The basic issues involve conflicts between individual profits and national security. The novel characterizes them as primarily moral rather than economic conflicts, whose outcome is critical to Germany's integrity.

Spielhagen uses storm images to connect the Baltic setting of the railroad project and the speculative frenzy in Berlin. As Reinhold Schmidt explains, a change in the prevailing winds means a shift in the flow of Baltic waters, which in a severe storm can cause a flood tide from the east to sweep over the coast and wreak havoc. Another character then extends the scenario to the currents of money flowing into Germany (in the form of France's enormous indemnity):

> "Those who are knowledgeable prophesy that such unnatural situations cannot last indefinitely, that a reversal of current, a reaction, a stormflood has to set in, which just like the natural phenomenon will crash over us, destructive and deadly, and its turbid, barren waters will sweep over places upon which people thought they had built their empire and their domination for all times."[51]

Such predictions do not affect the multitude of speculators who pursue their interests through intricate networks of promissory notes, credit agreements, and property transfers.

The climax of the novel comes with the simultaneous outbreak of two storms, both modeled after actual historical events. The shift of winds predicted by Reinhold brings a raging storm that recalls the Baltic storm of November 1872. The figurative storm breaks over Berlin with a three-hour speech before the Prussian chamber of deputies by liberal politician Eduard Lasker. The speech to which the novel refers actually took place on 7 February 1873, and contained far-reaching accusations against prominent individuals associated with a vast Pomeranian railway project.[52] As the novel describes it, "The storm that rushed out of today's debate will tear the roof from many a factory and many a mansion that this morning still seemed to be solid, and it will shake the foundations of the stock market and bring others to utter disgrace!"[53] Spielhagen causes the storm to swirl first through the top levels of Berlin society and to hit Philipp Schmidt's mansion at the moment of his triumph. Realizing his financial house of cards is collapsing, Philipp has taken four million marks from his banker's vault to cover his obligations, and now, even as the toasts continue, the police arrive to arrest him. As word begins to spread, the ball disintegrates into an apocalyptic scene: "In chaotic waves tumbling over one another, the horrified crowd pushes and whirls out of the brilliantly lit house into the dark street through which the storm was howling."[54]

The last quarter of the novel becomes a tale of heroism and ruin in which each of the three Schmidts meets the fate his actions have forged for him. Reinhold, vindicated in his warnings about the harbor location, becomes the hero. He carries out courageous rescues in the storm, wins the approval of General von Werben for his daughter's hand, and, in recognition of his merits, is called to a high post in Berlin. Through him the *bürgerlich* ideal of devotion to king and country comes to fruition.[55] Philipp, on the other hand, meets ruin. News of his suicide causes his father's heart to beat "strongly and proudly again." The fact that Philipp left the stolen funds untouched seems not to affect Ernst's judgment; his son's act proves, he concludes, "that even for him there was a level of shame he would not exceed."[56] In this moral code the disgrace of prison exceeds the value of life itself.

Ernst Schmidt uses his personal tragedy to draw universal meaning for Germany's future. Not only has he lost his son, but his daughter has died heroically along with her fiancé, the general's son. In the last scene Ernst presides over a ceremony of contrition and reconciliation when people from across the social spectrum flock to the double funeral. Through a metaphor of the storm Ernst tells the assembled mourners that the gale has roared through the German countryside and through German hearts. They all have contributed to the catastrophe by "restlessly engaging in the sordid struggle over yours and mine, the wild, ugly struggle without shame or pity; wanting no peace and giving no pardon; recognizing no right other than that of the conqueror scornfully trampling the defeated." In the wake of the storm they—all Germans—must rededicate themselves to the honor of humanity and to the glory of Germany.[57] Through this eulogy Spielhagen propounds an idea that became deeply ingrained in German mythology: the crash of 1873 represented a moral judgment against the Germans, and their redemption would come only through their repentance of the greed that had led to it.

The scene of atonement at the end of *Sturmflut*, however, provides little basis for an age of national regeneration. Reinhold's entry into the Bismarckian government suggests a kind of political consolidation of the middle and aristocratic classes, but it glosses over the serious political tensions portrayed between the liberals of 1848 and the imperial regime. The economic storm, contrary to the novel's portrayal, was not simply a product of German failings but part of a wider crisis that extended to Vienna and New York. By focusing on "the desolation that the curse of the billions [the French indemnity] brought in its economic and moral effects on Germany," Spielhagen gave credence to the notion that a divine judgment was being levied on German society.[58] The apparent social harmony of the last scene derived from wishful thinking rather than from a reconciliation of classes. Although Spielhagen depicted a seemingly democratic gathering in the long funeral procession, he grouped the mourners in traditional hierarchy, with the military at the head followed by other members of the aristocracy, and, finally, the commoners bringing up the rear. The presence of countryfolk and seamen might most plausibly be explained in terms of paying respects to their social betters. The building of bases for true social harmony involved far more difficult tasks, which the novel suggested but did not pursue.

Still another implicit argument of *Sturmflut* was the notion that the crisis centered in the willingness of Germans to adopt capitalist practices alien to their deepest values. Reinhold's refusal to put his modest savings into investments involving any risk seems justified when all who seek to participate in the economic boom are brought to ruin. Those who have not died have fled, and the novel implies that the fatherland will be redeemed only without them. The very economic activity that, until 1873, seemed a testimony of German success was the source of its ruination. Middle-class traditions had been desecrated by a *Selbstbestimmung* that meant unbridled pursuit of profit. In calling on Germans to repudiate the intrusion, *Sturmflut* gave strength to the notion that the real threat to German society came from a selfish and corrupt middle class whose identity had become intertwined with images of economic crash and national failure.

Numerous other novelists took up the evils of speculation and the dangers of *Egoismus*, but few treated the crash itself.[59] Karl Gutzkow, however, used his last novel, the three-volume *Die neuen Serapionsbrüder* (*The New Serapion Brethren*) (1877), to probe—even more deeply than Spielhagen—the mentality of the *Gründerjahre*. Like Spielhagen, Gutzkow set his novel during the years when Germans were exulting over their new-found status as a great power. Both authors, in fact, symbolized this exultation by depicting the seemingly insatiable demand for victory monuments. But the ways in which the sculptor-characters of each novel react to this sudden demand reveal the differing ironies drawn by Spielhagen and Gutzkow toward unification.

In *Sturmflut* the irony centers in what Spielhagen saw as the mistaken assumption that a German nation could be created by proclamation. A sculptor conveys this when he tells Ernst Schmidt he has dealt with the onslaught of orders for statues by dusting off a long-since-finished statue of Homer, replacing its head, and transforming it into a victorious Germania. The symbolism of such a transformation does not escape the cynical Ernst: "A venerable old torso, which an artist unconcerned about means has topped with a new head that doesn't belong to it—that seems to me a splendid picture of the new German unity."⁶⁰ For the sculptor, however, the use of the Homer statue is but a temporary expedient while he works on a massive, newly commissioned monument whose pedestal will depict Germany in the figures of actual people he knows. The real German victory, he explains, lies in the strength of individual Germans from all walks of life, and they, rather than a victorious war, will build true national unity. For Spielhagen the irony of the Germania statue would be overcome by social harmony.

Gutzkow, on the other hand, saw the traffic in victory statues as an overriding tendency of the new age: the commercialization of all human experience. In *Die neuen Serapionsbrüder* he uses Meister Althing, the head of a respected sculpture studio, to show the commercial pressures on the artist. Althing's hair has turned gray over the problems of maintaining his artistic integrity amid middlemen and current fashions.⁶¹ Gutzkow contrasts the plainness and modesty of Althing's studio with "other studios, in which creators of the civil and military monuments commissioned by the royal court use their spare time to make 'Victorias,' which will always sell."⁶² Victory statues are but one symptom of the national epidemic of profit-seeking.

Another sign of Gutzkow's perception of changed times is that no spiritual knights struggle against such commerce. The book's title, rather, denotes a loose organization of professional men, modeled after a group of poets and raconteurs founded in 1818 by Berlin *Literat* E. T. A. Hoffmann. Known as the *Serapionsbrüder*, Hoffmann's group met for weekly discussions intended to provide haven from the perils of philistinism in the post-Napoleonic age.⁶³ Gutzkow's version of their successors, the "New Serapion Brethren," schedule their luncheon conversations on Monday, the day the newspapers are not published. The members of this group are not out to reform the world, nor do they regard themselves as leaders of the German destiny.⁶⁴

In fact, Gutzkow's luncheon group reveals significant confusion over such destiny in its repeated discussions of problematical issues arising from recent events. One member, referring to the lack of recognition given Germany by other nations, comments, "Our victories seem to them to be undeserved and only accidental!"⁶⁵ It is apparent, however, that some members of the group are also unsure as to whether Germany has earned her triumphs. When one asserts that unification has meant an "intoxication of joy and pride in deeds that are unparalleled throughout history," another counters that it has resulted in nothing more than "the phenomenon of the go-getter" and adds, "Everything is full of this careerism! The national resurgence is becoming paralyzed by it."⁶⁶ Gutzkow underscores this remark by allowing the discussion to languish suddenly as participants become aware of their own precarious positions in the national clamor for success. As the narrator notes, "The crash was already underway." The only really great idea of the day, one member concludes, is all too simple: to have money. From German greatness to money: the speed with which the discussion travels this distance is a telling instance of Gutzkow's judgment about the sorry moral condition of the new Reich.

Gutzkow elevates the stockmarket frenzy into a symbol of the age and portrays the mentality of the *Gründer* as an insidious disease. Representatives of the mentality include, of course, a range of unscrupulous speculators and lawyers involved in financial swindle, but also among them is the novel's most conscientious businessman, the owner of a railroad equipment factory. Stricken by the death of his wife, he wants to sell the factory and decides the quickest means of doing so is to turn it into a joint stock company. Thus, "unconsciously, completely innocently, with the noblest intentions, he joined the *Gründer*, who in those days still came across as being so harmless."[67] Joint stock companies, Gutzkow implies, as hallmarks of the *Gründerjahre*, are an inherent evil.

The *Gründermentalität* is not, however, restricted to the economic realm. A whole range of other self-serving individuals parade through the novel, including a painter who never tires of prating about his twenty-one medals of distinction, a calculating clergyman from the provinces trying to make his mark on Berlin society, a socialist agitator turned social climber, a dilettantish composer nicknamed "The Narcissist," and a beautiful but rootless young woman in a degrading pursuit of fortune. All these figures proclaim with their actions what one character calls "the gospel of the new age: promote only yourself and see how far you can get ahead!"[68] Consumed by the fear that they might be left behind in the rush, they drive themselves to ruin, alcoholism, prison, or death.

Gutzkow adds an explicitly urban dimension to his depiction of the times when he shows modern Berlin as a source of nervous tension for all its inhabitants. The book opens as the *Serapionsbrüder* listen to a physician lecture on "sidewalk disease" (*Trottoirkrankheit*), which he describes as a previously unknown condition brought on by the crowding, the random contact of its inhabitants with one another, and the nervousness created by constant pressures and demands of the hurried pace of life in Berlin.[69] The narrowness of the sidewalk, the doctor explains, in forcing all classes together, creates this nervousness. The novel personifies the condition in a solicitor who seems to thrive in the atmosphere of the *Gründerzeit*, "always busy, always racking his brains for ways to make money with decorum."[70] When the strain of these involvements culminates in suicide, however, the attending physician wonders aloud, "Is it perhaps possible that we have here a victim of the sidewalk disease?"[71]

Here the crisis of the *Bürger* is depicted in terms of the pressures of the emergent metropolis. The survivors, like those in Spielhagen's novel, are those who embody down-to-earth, *bürgerlich* virtues, like the sculptor Meister Althing and his son Ottomar. The tone of the ending, however, is far closer to that of *Kinder der Welt* than *Sturmflut*. Ottomar Althing, the closest parallel to Heyse's Edwin, draws the moral that in this age the best goal is to become "a hero of the insignificant."[72] His father, the sculptor, stays in the capital but vows, "This time I'm not going to get the sidewalk sickness!"[73] The storm has left devastation in its wake, but Gutzkow's survivors retreat to the havens of their personal lives. Gutzkow draws no vision for Germany's future beyond that of a serene *Bürgertum* tending its humble affairs.

∙ ∙ ∙

The three novels considered in this chapter probed limits of middle-class selfhood in the 1870s. All three confronted dilemmas of a *Bürgertum* cut loose from its traditional moorings, and each sought to find a haven for the buffeted individual. Although all three levied sharp criticisms against a social and political regime that harassed and even persecuted the individual, they aimed still sharper attacks at a new middle class, portrayed as frantic with social ambition and unrestrained in its material pursuits. Whatever the authors' intent, this focus had the effect of deflecting attention from institutions they had challenged and of strengthening ideals of middle-class withdrawal and political acquiescence.

Heyse, whose novel predated the storms of the *Gründerjahre*, defined his crisis in terms of social and legal persecutions against children of the modern age. He allowed Edwin finally to find a haven in a happy marriage in a small town far from the pressures of Berlin, where, miraculously, local religious pressures to remove him from his teaching post subsided in the face of student support. Society's intervention in individual lives, although depicted in seriously threatening terms, simply dissolved in the end. Edwin epitomized Heyse's conviction that an individual need not become victim of the forces around him, but it was the author's prerogative as creator rather than a portrayal of an actual social change that led to this outcome.

Both Spielhagen and Gutzkow connected their characters' crises with the economic upheavals of the early '70s. Spielhagen came closer to defining such an identity along with a positive role for the German *Bürger*. Like Heyse he depicted individuals who were being buffeted by a rapidly changing society, but he defined the crisis as a direct result of German unification. The crash, in Spielhagen's view, had forced Germans to face the moral dimension of German unity. *Sturmflut* raised the hope of a cleansing effect to follow: a far-reaching social reconciliation based on each German's dedication to the fatherland. The *Bürger* here was not only the smith of his own happiness but, by implication, the smith of well-being for Germany. In contrast, Gutzkow's characters, much like Heyse's, vowed commitments to family and private endeavors. No knights of the spirit were dispersing in this novel to further the German revolution.

All three novels nevertheless raised the question of Germany's future direction. What George Mosse has characterized as a general "longing for a specifically German identity" during these years is evident.[74] In episodes and themes dealing with the fatherland the three authors sought to define a positive national myth to substitute for the ominous trends they discerned. That their efforts remained unfulfilled had partly to do with their inability to provide their characters, as representatives of the German *Bürgertum*, with values that would challenge rather than tolerate the ills of the present. All three novels depicted intolerable effects of German society on their characters, yet none put forth a real challenge to its institutions.

In addition to abandoning a call to social engagement, these novels depicted tensions within the middle class by portraying capitalist enterprises as anathema to *bürgerlich* and to national integrity.[75] Such beliefs contributed to the alienation of the *Bildungs-* from the *Besitzbürgertum* and intensified confusion about the direction Germany should take to show she had indeed earned her victories. The crisis of middle-class identity in novels of the *Gründerjahre* thus compounded a crisis of national identity. The internal tensions that authors depicted prevented them from conceiving of a unified middle class capable of asserting itself against aristocratic rule and of agitating for reform. Even Spielhagen's conclusion, which had the middle-class Reinhold preparing to serve Germany under a reactionary monarch in an aristocratic ministry, raised more questions than it answered, for the political constitution of the German Reich contained a strange mixture of traditional authoritarian forms and seemingly democratic institutions.[76] Yet, in the early years of the new Reich it still seemed an open question as to which part of the mixture would prevail, as novels that took up political themes confirm.

## Notes

1. That this political failure did not in itself betoken the wider failure of a bourgeois revolution in Germany has been plausibly argued by David Blackbourn and Geoff Eley in *The Peculiarities of German History: Bourgeois Society and Politics in Nineteenth-Century Germany* (Oxford, 1984).
2. The most precise contemporary statement of these views was made by German sociologist Georg Simmel in his 1903 lecture, "The Metropolis and Mental Life," translated in Richard Sennett, ed., *Classic Essays on the Culture of Cities* (New York, 1969), 47–60. See also Richard Münch, *Die Kultur der Moderne*, Vol. II: *Ihre Entwicklung in Frankreich und Deutschland* (Frankfurt am Main, 1986), 683–709; and Jürgen Kocka, "Bürgertum und Bürgerlichkeit als Probleme der deutschen Geschichte vom späten 18. zum frühen 20. Jahrhundert," in Jürgen Kocka, ed., *Bürger und Bürgerlichkeit im 19. Jahrhundert* (Göttingen, 1987), 21–64.
3. See, for example, Karl Bleibtreu, *Geist* (Munich, 1906), 57. Hajo Holborn declares that the creation of these ideals was the "work of German burghers"; the "effort to realize virtue was taken very seriously by [them]." Hajo Holborn, *A Short History of Modern Germany, 1648–1840* (New York, 1968), 352 and 314.
4. On these developments see Gordon A. Craig, *Germany, 1866–1945* (New York, 1978), 61–85. See also Hans Otto, *Gründerzeit: Aufbruch einer Nation* (Bonn, 1984).
5. Paul Heyse, *Jugenderinnerungen und Bekenntnisse*, 5th ed. (Stuttgart, 1912), I, 16. On the "cult of spiritual sovereignty of the individual" see Leonard Krieger, *The German Idea of Freedom* (Boston, 1957), 167, 177, 492, and also W. H. Bruford, *The German Tradition of Self-Cultivation; "Bildung" from Humboldt to Thomas Mann* (Cambridge, 1975).
6. Michail Krausnick, *Paul Heyse und der Münchener Dichterkreis, Abhandlungen zur Kunst- Musik- und Literaturwissenschaft*, Vol. 165 (Bonn, 1974), 41.
7. On this as a typical literary transition see Eva D. Becker, "'Zeitungen sind doch das Beste': Bürgerliche Realisten und der Vorabdruck ihrer Werke in der periodischen Presse," in Helmut Kreuzer, ed., *Gestaltungsgeschichte und Gesellschaftsgeschichte: Literatur-, Kunst- und Musikwissenschaftliche Studien. Festschrift für Fritz Martini* (Stuttgart, 1969), 384.
8. Max Bucher et al., *Realismus und Gründerzeit* (Stuttgart, 1976), I, 321.

9. Becker, "Zeitungen," 396; Rudolf Hackmann, *Die Anfänge des Romans in der Zeitung* (Dissertation, Berlin, 1938), 16.
10. Walter Kiaulehn, *Berlin: Schicksal einer Weltstadt* (Munich, 1958), 343; see also 349.
11. Paul Heyse, *Kinder der Welt*, 11th ed. (Berlin, 1886), I, 243–244.
12. Ibid., I, 256–257. On the German ideal of beauty as repose see George L. Mosse, *The Nationalization of the Masses. Political Symbolism and Mass Movements in Germany from the Napoleonic Wars through the Third Reich* (New York, 1975), 25–26, 35.
13. The contention of Richard Hamann and Jost Hermand that this ideal became associated with power and position in the late nineteenth century is not borne out in this novel. Richard Hamann and Jost Hermand, *Die Gründerzeit* (Berlin, 1965), 198–213.
14. Frederick William III still evokes sharply differing images, characterized in one history as "the oppressive symbol of the old era," and in another as "the 'simple' king [whose] aversion to luxury [and] great personal modesty . . . made him impervious to all flattery." See Golo Mann, *Deutsche Geschichte des 19. und 20. Jahrhunderts* (Frankfurt am Main, 1958), 145, and Hajo Holborn, *A History of Modern Germany: 1840–1945* (New York, 1969), 375.
15. Heyse, *Kinder der Welt*, I, 85.
16. Ibid., I, 1.
17. Ibid., I, 59.
18. Heyse, *Jugenderinnerungen*, I, 12; Krausnick, *Paul Heyse*, 33. The novel's description implies a location at Weidendamm at Kupfergraben.
19. Heyse, *Kinder der Welt*, I, 72.
20. Heyse, *Jugenderinnerungen*, I, 35, 37.
21. Heyse, *Kinder der Welt*, I, 221 and 217.
22. Ibid., II, 33–34.
23. Ibid., II, 39. On this unrealized call to action see George Brandes, *Creative Spirits of the Nineteenth Century* (New York, 1923), 94.
24. Heyse, *Kinder der Welt*, I, 167.
25. Ibid., II, 335.
26. Heyse's focus on the "children of the world" has also been interpreted as reflecting the pragmatism of the Gründerzeit. Klaus Günther Just, *Von der Gründerzeit bis zur Gegenwart: Geschichte der deutschen Literatur seit 1871* (Bern, 1973), 43.
27. Kiaulehn refers to Spielhagen as "the Gutzkow of the Gründerjahre" in his *Berlin*, 354. See also Bernd Neumann, "Friedrich Spielhagen: *Sturmflut* (1877): Die 'Gründerjahre' als die 'Signatur des Jahrhunderts'," in Horst Denkler, ed., *Romane und Erzählungen des Bürgerlichen Realismus: Neue Interpretationen* (Stuttgart, 1980), 260–273.
28. Imagery of smithing occurs throughout Spielhagen's writing; he opens his memoirs with the injunction that all people should try to be "Hammer und Amboß zugleich." Friedrich Spielhagen, *Finder und Erfinder: Erinnerungen aus meinem Leben*, I (Leipzig, 1890), 8.
29. Friedrich Spielhagen, "Wie ich zu dem Helden von 'Sturmflut' kam," *Neue Beiträge zur Theorie und Technik der Epik und Dramatik* (Leipzig, 1898), 214.
30. Spielhagen, *Finder und Erfinder*, 119, 62, 406.
31. Friedrich Spielhagen, *Sturmflut*, in *Sämtliche Werke* (Leipzig, 1883), XIII, 72, 111. Subsequent references to this two-volume novel will be to I or II, corresponding to XIII or XIV, respectively.
32. On the origins of Spielhagen's *Adelshaß* see Spielhagen, *Finder und Erfinder*, 90–94.
33. Spielhagen, *Sturmflut*, I, 172, 80.
34. It has also been argued that Reinhold embodies the class compromise between the nobility and middle class that developed in Imperial Germany. Neumann, "Friedrich Spielhagen," 269.

35. Spielhagen, *Sturmflut*, I, 84.
36. Ibid., I, 363.
37. Ibid., I, 368.
38. Ibid., I, 126. On the ideal of the republic in literature see Leo Lowenthal, *Erzählkunst und Gesellschaft: Die Gesellschaftsproblematik in der deutschen Literatur des 19. Jahrhunderts* (Neuwied in Berlin, 1971), 165.
39. Spielhagen, *Sturmflut*, I, 112.
40. Ibid., I, 114.
41. Ibid., I, 251.
42. Ibid., I, 252. On Spielhagen's attack on "liberalistischer Egoismus" see Neumann, "Friedrich Spielhagen," 269.
43. Spielhagen, *Sturmflut*, II, 337. Spielhagen later wrote that he also had the reputation of a man who had forgotten nothing but had learned nothing. *Finder und Erfinder*, 407.
44. Spielhagen, *Sturmflut*, II, 340. This statement refers to Ernst's son and daughter, but for the sake of simplification I am analyzing only the ruination of Philipp.
45. Ibid., I, 174.
46. Ibid., I, 260.
47. Ibid., I, 196.
48. Ibid., II, 257–258. Philipp Schmidt has been compared to Bethel Henry Strousberg, whose railway projects were central to the crisis of 1873. Maximilian Müller-Jabusch, *So waren die Gründerjahre* (Düsseldorf, 1957), 5–8.
49. Spielhagen, *Sturmflut*, I, 303, 310, 333.
50. See, for example, ibid., I, 211, 228.
51. Ibid., I, 70–71.
52. For Lasker's speech see *Stenographische Berichte über die Verhandlungen des preußischen Hauses der Abgeordneten*, 1872–1873, Vol. II, 934–951.
53. Spielhagen, *Sturmflut*, II, 227.
54. Ibid., II, 280.
55. Ibid., II, 446. Reinhold's Prussian loyalties seem to exceed his German loyalties when he proclaims his greatest wish is to serve "the king."
56. Ibid., II, 458.
57. Ibid., II, 459. Walter Kiaulehn also interprets 1873 as a "cleansing process." Kiaulehn, *Berlin*, 156.
58. Spielhagen, "Wie ich zu dem Helden," 219–220.
59. Max Kretzer's two well-known Berlin novels, *Meister Timpe* (1888) and *Der Millionenbauer* (1890), both set in the Gründerjahre, will be treated in Chapter 11, below, in the context of the time in which they were written.
60. Spielhagen, *Sturmflut*, I, 123. The statue may also reflect Spielhagen's vow to put the classics in the service of understanding the modern world. Spielhagen, *Finder und Erfinder*, 206–207. On his comparison of Reinhold to a Homeric hero see Spielhagen, "Wie ich zu dem Helden", 212–213.
61. Gutzkow, *Serapionsbrüder*, I, 33.
62. Ibid., I, 71.
63. On the origins of Hoffmann's group see E. T. A. Hoffmann, "Über das Serapionische Prinzip," *Gesammelte Werke*, Vol. V (Hamburg, 1965), 703, and Klaus Günzel, *E. T. A. Hoffmann. Leben und Werk in Briefen, Selbstzeugnissen und Zeitdokumenten* (Berlin, 1976), 348–349, 360–362.
64. It has also been argued that this sort of voluntary association attested to bourgeois ascendancy in German society. David Blackbourn and Geoff Eley, *The Peculiarities of German History: Bourgeois Society and Politics in Nineteenth-Century Germany* (Oxford, 1984), 224–226.
65. Gutzkow, *Serapionsbrüder*, II, 48.

66. Ibid., II, 201, 203.
67. Ibid., II, 51.
68. Ibid., II, 126, 237.
69. Gutzkow, *Serapionsbrüder* I, 4–10, and III, 185, 204. Toinette anticipated the syndrome when she characterized those who were not *vornehm* as "angry, ordinary people who are uncomfortable with themselves and invent all kinds of ways to make life miserable for their good-hearted neighbors." Heyse, *Kinder der Welt*, I, 257.
70. Gutzkow, *Serapionsbrüder* I, 53; the character in question is Justizrath Luzius.
71. Ibid., III, 204.
72. Ibid., III, 309.
73. Ibid., III, 304.
74. George Mosse, "Was die Deutschen wirklich lasen: Marklitt, May, Ganghofer," in Reinhold Grimm and Jost Hermand, eds., *Popularität und Trivialität* (Frankfurt am Main, 1972), 101.
75. See Otto Glagau, *Der Börsen- und Gründungs-Schwindel in Berlin* (Leipzig, 1876), v–vi; Gordon R. Mork, "The Prussian Railway Scandal of 1873: Economics and Politics in the German Empire," *European Studies Review*, I (1971) 35–48; Harold James, *A German Identity: 1770–1990* (New York, 1989), 72–77.
76. On the question of middle-class political power in Imperial Germany see Hans-Ulrich Wehler, "Wie bürgerlich war das Deutsche Kaiserreich?" and the commentary by David Blackbourn in Kocka, *Bürger und Bürgerlichkeit*, 243–287.

# 4

# The Unfinished Revolution

A painting by Anton von Werner depicts the dramatic scene enacted by Bismarck on 18 January 1871, in the Hall of Mirrors at Versailles, consummating the intricate diplomacy by which he transformed the military alliance of German states into the foundation for a unified Germany. "The Proclamation of the German Empire" shows a brilliant pageant of officers and princes cheering King William of Prussia, the new German emperor.[1] The painting does not portray, however, the reluctance with which William assumed the imperial title. It does not depict the grudging acquiescence of Prussia's political rivals to her ascendancy. Nor does it show any popularly elected delegates at the ceremony, for there were none. Once the cheering ended and the dignitaries returned to Germany, a prolonged struggle over the meaning of that moment ensued as competing individuals and groups sought to claim the victory for their cause. The dominance of the monarch, his chancellor, and the cheering officers in the scene at Versailles suggests that the outcome of the struggle was foreordained. Nonetheless, a new state was being created, and even Prussian authoritarianism, if it were to prevail, would have to undergo vast changes. A political revolution was underway.[2]

Berlin novelists who sought to come to terms with this revolution contributed to the process of creating a German political tradition that would influence its outcome. By setting their works in the new capital, they inevitably linked this emergent tradition with Prussia, the state that had led the way to national unity. Prussian political heritage was by no means monolithic, however, and novelists drew their ideals from four historical episodes that evoked differing mythologies. Two such episodes involved images of revolution from above: the reign of Frederick II as a model of enlightened absolutism and the reform period following 1806 as the prototype of a revolution by an enlightened aristocracy. In contrast, two equally vivid experiences, the wars of liberation in 1813 and the revolution of 1848, evoked images of revolution from below. These instances of popular uprising, moreover, came to have strikingly different connotations, with 1813 signifying a people taking arms to defend the Prussian government and 1848 signifying a people taking arms against that government. The conflicting mythologies of these four experiences point to differing paths by which the young German state might mature. A succession of fictional critiques exemplifies the resultant confusion over political goals and the difficulties of defining a coherent course for a state so precipitously created.

This chapter examines novels with a significant political dimension that depict the period from the ascension of William I to the succession of his grandson William II in 1888. They reveal a gamut of responses, from cynicism to uncritical patriotism to a search for liberal alternatives to a resounding endorsement of imperial rule. Taken together, they suggest that while some Germans accepted the Bismarckian regime only reluctantly, through a process of elimination, many came to embrace it as the fulfillment of the German revolution.

In contrast to Gutzkow's *Die Ritter vom Geiste*, political issues barely surface in his *Die neuen Serapionsbrüder*, but when they do emerge, they suggest a failed revolution. One comment is unequivocal about the new system: "You have destroyed too much! You've governed too quickly!"[3] The statement suggests a belief that Germany had broken with tradition and, paradoxically, that the new constitution actually destroyed the basis for German unity. Moreover, the characters in this later novel reveal none of the expectations about an unfinished revolution that sustained the spiritual knights in the earlier one. The likelihood that Gutzkow himself had abandoned such expectations is supported by his last preface to *Ritter*, written shortly before his death in 1878, in which he claimed he had wanted the novel only to provoke "a quiet examination" of progressive ideas among educated people.[4] Gutzkow did not even mention the spiritual revolution to which his novel had been dedicated, an omission that suggested it, too, now merited only "a quiet examination."

*Serapionsbrüder* contains no echoes of Dankmar Wildungen's statement in *Ritter* that "the basic rights of the people are basic duties to the knights of the spirit."[5] Instead, it portrays a society in which thoughtful people take refuge from political discourse. To that end, the statutes of the lunchtime club of the title forbid the discussion of politics. As one member explains, "It's a real achievement that one can sit down among men for a while without always talking about the Reichstag, elections, parties, the royal court, and the imperial parades."[6] When politics do intrude, human rights are not at the forefront of members' concerns. Bismarck's astonishing success, in their eyes, has resulted only in a surfeit of political liberalization: "Even the conservatives are liberal!"[7] Underscoring this supposed transformation, the narrator also remarks that the club statutes are not taken too seriously because of cynicism over constitutions, elections, and procedures. Adherence to English parliamentary forms, it seems, has become fanatical. An occasional reference to "faults in the mechanism" of the "imperial machine" is less a call to reform than testimony to the belief that in an age of "careerism" (*Strebertum*) politics have been reduced to procedural tinkering.[8] In the face of such degradation, questions of institutional change are irrelevant.

Another pervasive theme of *Serapionsbrüder* holds that German political unity had betrayed moral unity of the sort that motivated the national uprising of

1813. Whether this is the belief of Gutzkow, the lifelong democrat grown old and embittered,[9] or simply his perception of Germany in the late 1870s, the novel provides no vision of an unfinished revolution. Gutzkow's political resignation coincided with a wider loss of confidence among German liberals in the late 1870s, when the seemingly inexorable successes of *Realpolitik* caused many to abandon the hope for genuinely responsible political rule.[10] For them the legacies of 1806, 1813, and 1848 had not withstood the Bismarckian juggernaut.

Author Julius Stinde took another path to political acquiescence with his enormously popular Buchholz stories, published between 1883 and 1888.[11] In contrast to Gutzkow, Stinde, restricting his focus to ordinary people coping with everyday problems, refrained completely from political cynicism. The stories open with the narrator telling readers that every house in Berlin "is a home for those who live within it, and the street on which the house stands is a realm in which there are neighbors just as there are in a small town."[12] One such house is ruled by Frau Wilhelmine Buchholz. Although sometimes meddling, sometimes petty, and too often socially ambitious, she is a housewife who, in responding to the inevitable crises of life, unfailingly comes through with traditional Berlin virtues of humility, self-irony, and generosity. Thus personifying a German tradition of simpler times, Frau Buchholz could hardly seem further removed from the tumult of Imperial Berlin.

This tradition, her example implies, contains the means of moral regeneration for a whole nation.[13] In this context, the political conformism of the Buchholz family conveys a distinct message to German readers. A conspicuous instance occurs in an episode in which the family returns home from the public celebration of Bismarck's seventieth birthday.[14] Filled with inspiration, the husband pulls a book from the shelf and reads aloud the Kaiser's 1871 proclamation at Versailles: "God grant us, and our successors on the imperial throne, the ability forever to expand the German Reich, not with military conquests, but with the goods and gifts of peace, in the realms of national well-being, freedom, and culture."[15] The scene makes it clear that the Buchholzes believe this oath has been richly fulfilled. Frau Buchholz underscores this belief when, envisioning an expansive future for Berlin, she observes that growth will depend on the maintenance of peace. Business will applaud such a course with the exception "of powder mills and surgical-dressing factories, which are probably very annoyed that Bismarck hasn't begun a war for them."[16] Such faith in Bismarck rests on a renunciation of political criticism. When a friend blames his financial troubles on the lack of political freedom, the Buchholzes scoff: someone who cannot manage his own affairs cannot presume to know how Germany should be governed. When this friend becomes serious about staving off bankruptcy, the Buchholzes are pleased he has given up building "castles in the air."[17] Patriotic observances are clearly the only appropriate form of political activity.

Such docility in novels did not result from censorship by the political establishment, but it was welcomed by the regime. Bismarck let it be known that he greatly admired the Buchholz stories, and they came at a time when the regime itself was building monuments and enacting ceremonies that would legitimate the German Empire.[18] Stinde's unquestioning support for the regime testifies to the success of such efforts and to an ominous wish-fulfillment. By seeing the Bismarckian state of the mid-1880s as the realization of a new, peaceful Germany, authors like Stinde bolstered a popular assent to the political status quo. In exalting the fact that Bismarck's diplomacy had kept Germany out of war, they ignored the dangers of his alliance system and of the political repression at home (this was, after all, the decade of the Anti-Socialist Law). By cultivating an ideal of Berliners whose focus was upon family and neighbor, Stinde offered an antidote to urban alienation, but, in suggesting that real Berliners need not involve themselves beyond their own neighborhoods, such works gave readers misleading reassurance about the future of Germany.

Friedrich Spielhagen, a notable exception among writers who were becoming cynical or uncritically acquiescent, continued to ponder prosects for democratization in Bismarckian Germany. In two novels of the 1880s, *Was will das werden?* (*What Will Come of This?*) (1886) and *Ein neuer Pharao* (*A New Pharaoh*) (1889), he pursued the notion that the legacy of 1848 contained political answers for Imperial Germany, even while he wrestled with an awareness that authoritarian forms were hardening. The biblical passages upon which the novels' titles are based describe two different times of crisis and suggest a fundamental change in Spielhagen's outlook during the three years separating their publication. A world of fermentation and open possibilities in the first has been replaced in the second by oppression and rigidity. The two novels form a progression from hope for the unfinished revolution to near despair.

The title *Was will das werden?* manifests the religious cast Spielhagen gave to unification. Drawn from the book of Acts, it comes from an episode shortly after the crucifixion, in which followers of Jesus are beset by a whirling wind betokening the Holy Spirit. They are astonished to discover that, despite their diverse origins, they have been imbued with the ability to speak a single language. In Spielhagen's novel, a young revolutionary declares that the sudden appearance of "the holy spirit of truth" brings chaos in any age, and quotes the passage that raises the question for his own time: "And they were all amazed, and were in doubt, saying one to another, what will come of this?"[19] The rest of this passage clearly inspired Spielhagen, for in the succeeding verses Peter calms the people with words from the prophet Joel: "Your sons and your daughters shall prophesy, and your young men shall see visions, and your old men shall dream dreams" (Acts 2:17). This novel explores prophecies, visions, and dreams of young and old, men and women in Germany—all in search of a political answer to "what will come of this."

A *Bildungsroman* narrated by its protagonist, Lothar Lorenz, *Was will das werden?* has two chronological and geographical settings. The first volume, extending to the outbreak of the Franco-Prussian war, depicts Lothar's youth in a Baltic port that corresponds to Stralsund, the town of Spielhagen's youth. The second focuses on Lothar's living in Berlin from late 1876 to the onset of the political persecutions of 1878. Against these backdrops Spielhagen links Lothar's search for his own direction with Germany's search for nationhood. The parallel becomes clear through the spectrum of characters impinging upon Lothar's life in the first volume. They become personifications of Prussian political tradition, struggling to win the boy's soul.

The struggle begins when Lothar's unconscious secularism surfaces during confirmation instruction. The outraged pastor accuses Lothar of having inherited his "godlessness" from his free-thinking stepfather. The boy, wondering how to deal with the painful episode, seeks out two respected adults, a gymnasium professor and his stepfather. Both respond sympathetically, but their differing answers put him in a quandary between expedience and unswerving allegiance to ideals.

Professor von Hunnius, his aristocratic name to the contrary, has led a life committed to democratic change.[20] His answer to Lothar is couched in terms of pragmatic acquiescence. Invoking the tradition of 1848, Hunnius reveals he was a republican delegate to the Frankfurt Assembly. Now, as a member of the North German parliament, he is still fighting for German freedom. But in the interests of political effectiveness, he continues, he has abandoned republicanism to support the present path because it is the best road to unification. "Our beliefs can change, must change—political, scientific, why not also religious?" he asks.[21] Lothar should profess the established faith, Hunnius counsels, in order to take part in the work of changing society. Later, when urging Lothar to commit himself as a poet to the national struggle, he describes the poet as a warrior who must have "the courage to break his lyre and take up the sword."[22] Hunnius thus propounds a vision of *Realpolitik* grounded in liberal ideals that compelled many other German liberals as well.

When Lothar seeks his stepfather out in his carpentry shop, he is similarly urged to dedicate himself to working for German freedom, but the vision of Peter Lorenz contains no hint of political pragmatism. Like Hunnius, Lorenz reveals himself as a republican who might have supported monarchical rule in 1848 had the Prussian king accepted the crown offered by the Frankfurt Assembly. Instead, the revolution was defeated and Lorenz was sent to prison. Now, many years later, he bequeaths his defeated hopes to his stepson: personal hope of becoming an artist and political hope for a liberated Germany. The scene, filled with Christian symbolism, culminates as Lorenz describes a messianic vision he had in 1848: "[It was] the figure of a youth destined to portray the genius of the nation that is awakening and contemplating its right to freedom." Implying that Lothar is that youth, the stepfather predicts that through his artistic work he will help build "a united Germany in which only free people live."[23] In this vision the artist thus assumes the role of German messiah.

That night Lothar compares the day's events to the storm raging outside. In contrast to *Sturmflut*, however, Spielhagen here distinguishes the spiritual storm of Lothar—and of Germany—from the natural one. In nature, Lothar reasons, a stormy spring will be followed by a milder summer; in human affairs, no such certainty is possible. Indeed, other mentors with other visions complicate Lothar's quest for understanding. The two most influential, another teacher and the aristocratic uncle of a school friend, represent the claims of two other traditions on his allegiance: the idealism of the German enlightenment and the code of loyalty of the Prussian officer.

Professor Willy, the second gymnasium teacher, a fervent champion of German classicism, tries to influence Lothar to reject political concerns completely. Introduced to the reader while lecturing on Schiller, Willy attempts to inspire restless pupils to strive for transcendent esthetic realms. His implicit contempt for his pupils reflects a wider disdain for contemporary society. He makes this clear in his praise of an essay by Lothar on Lessing: "If, in the soul of only one youth among so many, a spark glimmers from the holy fire that glowed through Lessing's great soul; if, in spite of the banal, materialistic sentiment that touches the minds of present-day youth with its chilling breath, that spark is still not extinguished, then one need not despair."[24] Lothar, though trying to live up to Willy's expectations, commits an unpardonable sin. Signs of an impending "holy war" between Prussia and France inspire him to submit a poem entitled "Goethe und Bismarck" that proclaims both the man of ideals and the man of action as expressions of the "German spirit."[25] The juxtaposition appalls Willy, who accuses Lothar of descending to the level of the rest of his generation, whose admiration for Bismarck has taken away any understanding of their cultural heritage.[26] The break between Lothar and his professor is irreparable, but Willy has given him an unforgettable vision of a spiritually transcendant Germany.

A fourth mentor-figure, Major von Vogtriz, uses the outbreak of the Franco-Prussian war to implant a monarchical ideal into Lothar's hitherto republican heart. The war, the major explains, is divinely ordained, "in order that we will become a single, powerful nation [*Volk*] that from now on can dictate peace to the world, the peace for which our royal master longs so much."[27] History, by repeatedly opening Germany to plunder by weaker nations, has shown the Germans' need for monarchical leadership:

> "One has to take a people as it is; to demand things from them that they cannot do or to give them institutions alien to their being is like wanting to pick apples from a pear tree. A republic is nice—but for others, not for us Germans. Therefore, whoever touches our monarchy, which God's grace has given us and which with God's grace will lead us to the highest pinnacles of culture and freedom, is sinning against the body and spirit of the German nation."[28]

Overcome by emotion, Lothar grasps the major's hand and swears fealty to him and his king.

Successively, then, Lothar has sworn fealty to parliamentarism, republicanism, apolitical idealism, and monarchism. Each, at the moment of its presentation, seems a compelling answer to the uncertainty in the boy's heart. It is impossible, however, to remain true to all of them, much less to reconcile them. This is the dilemma Spielhagen wrestled with—through Lothar—as he sought the answer to Germany's future.

Lothar's counterpart is his classmate Adalbert von Werin, the character who invokes the passage from Acts and who in the second volume becomes a passionate advocate of a German revolution that will do away with the oppressive forces of Prussian tradition. Lothar envies Adalbert's certitude, and his friend acknowledges, "I'm completely firm-footed."[29] His steadiness, he explains, is a reaction against his parents, who represent Prussian tradition gone mad. Adalbert's father, a dutiful Prussian officer, committed suicide when falsely accused of a lapse. His mother, living in a world populated by demons, seeks revenge by writing lengthy "instructions" to Bismarck, which Adalbert ceremoniously seals with the family emblem—and then secretly burns. The process of surviving such turmoil, Adalbert tells Lothar, has not allowed him the luxury of internal confusion. He despises both the old Prussia that caused his father's ruin and the new Prussia, the focus of his mother's derangement.

Adalbert believes the real answer for Germany lies in the revolutionary message of early Christianity. In a crowded wine cellar he expounds his belief to Lothar, who, in patriotic fervor, is preparing to set off to the front on a mission for a local war supplier. Adalbert announces their ways must part because of Lothar's misguided enthusiasm. Lothar is incredulous: "What a great nation is striving for single-mindedly—putting its life and property on the line—you don't call that a goal? Love of the fatherland, the struggle of a nation for its endangered freedom, the humiliated honor—that's not a holy war?"[30] Adalbert answers that his goal concerns an earthbound humanity being sacrificed at the altar of war. True liberation will come not from the high priests of German politics but from the German people, just as it was not the Pharisees and Sadducees but the common people who spread the Christian gospel. Describing the scene of confusion in Acts, Adalbert repeats the question, "What will come of this?" He then raises his glass to the hope that the prevailing idols will one day lie broken at the feet of a liberated humanity;[31] thus the vision of a young prophet who scorns the triumphant path of Bismarckian Germany.

When this exchange is interrupted by news of the Prussian victory at Sedan, the cellar erupts into confusion, not unlike the biblical scene Adalbert has described. No holy spirit descends on this crowd, however. Rather, when Adalbert refuses to join in toasting Bismarck, the atmosphere turns vicious. In the ensuing scuffle Lothar, an innocent bystander, is seriously injured. Thus ends his chance of participating in the war.

This accident, moreover, begins a long period of aimlessness. In tying Lothar's life to the events of unification, Spielhagen implies that Germany, despite her new power, is aimless as well. Lothar's wanderings are of scant political significance, and in contrast to *Sturmflut*, Spielhagen makes little mention here of the *Gründerjahre*.[32] After six years, Lothar's odyssey takes him to Berlin, where he has come in order to break free from the narrow life of a provincial acting troupe he had joined.[33] Other characters from the first volume also make their way to the capital, motivated in each case by a political cause. It becomes clear from their actions that genuine national unity has not been achieved and that a new stage of Germany's struggle is underway.

Once in Berlin, Lothar, too, discovers a political mission. At first he buries himself in his stepbrother's carpentry shop in working-class Moabit, intending to prepare to become a poet by first engaging in the tangible work of the artisan. Later, when he happens to attend a workers' meeting and hears Adalbert giving a passionate and eloquent speech, Lothar realizes he is in the arena where the major battles of humanity will be engaged. He castigates himself for having lost sight of Hunnius' vision of him storming onto the political battlefield.[34] From this day onward he is drawn from the confines of the workshop into the struggle for Germany's political soul. In Berlin the question of "what will come of this" attains new urgency.

Opposition to the Bismarckian state reigns among a host of characters. The principal target is what they discern as the dichotomy between an outmoded, militaristic government and a modernizing society. Ironically, the now-promoted Colonel von Vogtriz enunciates the strongest attack when, disillusioned, he condemns the government's use of the army to repress popular demonstrations. "Where is the reform," he asks, "in which the people placed their hopes after the enormous sacrifices of war brought them to their hard-fought, long-sought goal?"[35] The mass of German people still live as pawns of the aristocracy, Vogtriz contends, in a system molded by notions of "blood and iron." Another character points to the impossibility of serving two masters: a monarchy whose rule by divine right is upheld by a medieval caste system and a modern economic system supposedly governed by scientific laws.[36] In still another passage Adalbert proclaims that the real malaise in Germany comes not from the frenzy of speculation but from the militaristic spirit behind Germany's triumphs.[37] The controversial nature of an attack on the military establishment is clear in the uneasiness of the normally sympathetic working-class audience Adalbert is addressing. Nevertheless, political critics in this novel agree that the social and military realms in Germany are working at cross purposes. The German revolution, their statements suggest, can be completed only with the end of the Bismarckian system.

This conviction is evident in the intensifying search for alternatives as reform-minded characters crisscross each other's paths. Even more fully than in the Baltic setting, the Berlin episodes recall the passage in Acts that foretells an age of many prophets with many visions. As Lothar remarks, the city is beset by a "revolutionary mood." By the end of the novel, however, this mood has dissipated. Vogtriz, having become a vehement opponent of conservatism, is forced to retire from the officer corps and retreats into an apolitical realm of scholarship. Adalbert's mother propounds another form of revolutionary hope—and then is defeated by it. Having recovered from her fixation on Bismarck, she becomes convinced that the revolution will begin with the young, and founds a home in Berlin for children of social outcasts. When two children in her care die, however, she interprets the tragedy as a condemnation of her ideology and kills herself. Finally, Adalbert, the apostle of German redemption, lapses into despair in a speech before a group of political friends. Reiterating the question, "What's to come of this?" he now replies, "I don't ask it anymore. I know nothing will come of it. That it will continue to be as it was and as it is."[38] When the police arrive to arrest him for his revolutionary activities, he declares he cannot face life in a cell and shoots himself.

If Adalbert personifies failed revolutionary expectations, Professor von Hunnius' outcome signifies the failure of a German liberalism that has corrupted its basic ideals. He came to Berlin, Hunnius explains, as a Reichstag member and editor of a political paper to work for the gradual transformation of the economic and moral condition of the German masses,[39] but the transformation Spielhagen depicts is Hunnius'. His lifelong willingness to compromise his goals culminates in a shocking surrender to anti-Semitic pressures. Liberalism is in trouble, he declares to Lothar, because people associate the movement with moneygrubbing Jews who have entered its ranks. Despite Lothar's objections, Hunnius insists the image is valid and avers that responsible Jews have the duty of shaking off ties with their unsavory kin.[40] Such condoning of anti-Semitism reveals a foreboding shadow in the liberal vision. Hunnius argues that liberals' inability to compromise their principle of toleration plays into the hands of anti-Semitic opponents. For Lothar the danger lies in the ease with which Hunnius does compromise the principle. Lothar's shock suggests the bankruptcy of Hunnius' commitment and, with it, of German liberalism.

Spielhagen gives the last word not to the German liberal (*Fortschrittsmann*) but to a Russian exile who sharply criticizes the aloofness of German intellectuals from the cause of genuine revolution. Count von Pahlen, alias Captain Edgar Smith (another instance of the image of smithing used for characters who hammer at Germany's destiny), is a self-proclaimed nihilist who aims to transform ruling groups.[41] "Let us revolutionize, if possible, the upper classes," he says once, "the nobility, the officers, the ministers, the upper ten thousand in scholarship, in art, and not least, in wealth."[42] At the end of the novel Pahlen has been ordered to leave Germany and is preparing once again to take up the wandering life of the political exile. In a conversation with Lothar and Hunnius he is angered by Hunnius' suggestion that, given his Russian origins, he cannot hope to understand the realities of German society. Pahlen counters that Germans do not understand the realities: the German intelligentsia are enveloped in their pride in their cultural heritage, oblivious of the chasm between them and the vast majority of their countrymen. In contrast, he continues, England and France, along with backward Russia, have a multitude of "educated, eminent, intelligent men, who live and work in the knowledge that their salvation can be found only in the fundamental alteration of social relationships in modern society."[43] German intellectuals, far from assuming leadership, have allowed their fear of liberty to overcome their commitment to it. The only salvation for German liberalism, Pahlen asserts, is for it to rebuild its faith in democracy.

Pahlen clearly does not expect such salvation to come from the likes of Hunnius and so turns to Lothar. He expresses a hope that echoes the long-ago wish of Lothar's stepfather: that someone with understanding of the oppressive realities will provide German society with insights through literature. Such an author, Pahlen urges, should face the Kaiser and the Reichstag with the words of the monk from Wittenberg: "Here I stand. I cannot do otherwise." Only when present-day Germans utter such words will the question, "What will come of this?" receive its proper answer and herald "a glorious new phase of an eternally striving humanity."[44] When Pahlen places his hand on Lothar's shoulder, the latter realizes the Russian means for him to take up the charge. This scene leaves little doubt as to Spielhagen's conviction that with this novel he has taken up the same charge.

Spielhagen's next novel, *Ein neuer Pharao*, portrays political disillusionment over a system grown considerably more authoritarian. The novel is set in 1878, the year in which two assassination attempts on the Kaiser became Bismarck's justification for the overhaul of domestic politics. The elements of this crisis—international instability, economic depression, realignment of political parties, debate over protectionism, and growing pressure on the social democratic movement—form a background to Spielhagen's continued quest to foster the ideals of 1848 in Imperial Germany.[45]

Although Spielhagen again uses a biblical image for his title, the Exodus passage to which it refers suggests not a nation being liberated by the "holy spirit of truth" but rather one sinking into bondage. The title derives from the story of Joseph, who was sold into slavery by his jealous brothers and then won the confidence of the pharaoh with his service. A subsequent passage denotes bitter times for Joseph's descendants: "Now there rose up a new pharoah over Egypt, who knew not Joseph."[46] The novel suggests that Germans who believe 1870 to be a tabula rasa have failed to recognize the legacy of 1848, symbolized in the image of Joseph. This failure, the novel further suggests, indicates a bankruptcy of values. *Ein neuer Pharao* represents Spielhagen's most searing condemnation of Bismarckian Germany.

The character who levies this attack is yet another of Spielhagen's smiths. "Charles Smith" is an alias adopted by a west German baron who took to the barricades in 1848 and then fled to the New World to escape a death sentence. Three decades later he arrives in Berlin with an American family that befriended him. Talking to the grown son of the family shortly after his arrival, Smith cites the Exodus passage, explaining that he has encountered a new pharaoh to whom he is a stranger. Smith's young friend suggests that the new pharaoh simply represents a new age. Is it not to be expected, he asks, that after thirty years he would find a changed Germany? Smith replies by comparing himself to a man who returns after years to find his village transformed into "a powerful city, or—a yawning wilderness."[47] Having left a society that seemed to be working toward a unity based on the solid values of the *Bürger*, he has returned to an ascendant empire ruled by an imperious nobility. Germany seems committed to a struggle to make "the nation powerful and dominant over others."[48] The pharaoh's not knowing Joseph signifies the thinking of a society that no longer recognizes its inherited values. The awesome new city of his homeland has become a moral wilderness.

Another element of Smith's desolate vision—a protest against capitalism—appears so fleetingly that it seems only to confuse the novel's depiction of Germany's malaise. "Manchesterism," as Smith explains it, is a brutal economic system whose unbridled competition threatens all nations living under it: "Unhappy, quarrelsome peoples wanting to shake off the fear gripping them, will turn outward and tear each other to pieces in the most horrible wars. The fruit of this will be the demise of culture and the ruin of all the achievements of civilization."[49] Smith does not pursue this prophetic vision, however, and he does not react to any diplomatic developments that might confirm or soften it, such as Bismarck's triumph as "honest broker" at the Congress of Berlin in 1878. Nor does Smith elaborate on the link he makes between capitalist competition and belligerent nationalism. But he continues his unremitting attacks on the atmosphere in Germany: "this swaggering, saber-rattling chauvinism; this loyalty, which in its Byzantine exaggeration actually imagines itself to be admirable; this careerism among young and old, for whom success is everything."[50] Like Ernst Schmidt in *Sturmflut*, he is convinced that a republic is the only acceptable system for a German people who have come of age politically.[51] Smith steadfastly clings to this answer even as friends insist on its futility.

Charles Smith's obstinate republicanism is one legacy of 1848, but in a physician-character named Dr. Brunn, Spielhagen creates a complementary figure, who, like Hunnius in *Was will das werden?*, is committed to working for change within existing realities. Brunn personifies a one-time insurgent who, becoming disillusioned with the Frankfurt Assembly's failure, placed his hope in Bismarck as the man who would enable the German people "to uphold in an equally glorious manner the powerful, decisive position they so gloriously won."[52] He does not seem to notice the lack of glory implied when he tries to persuade his friend that "in the land of true idealism, we can only make haste through the present wilderness of realism."[53] Crossing such a wilderness means acknowledging the present oppression and working to pass beyond it. Through Brunn, Spielhagen allows liberals to rationalize their support for the Bismarckian regime.

A third political type from 1848 emerges in a character named Ilicius, now a militantly conservative member of the Bismarckian regime and a founder of the conservative *Kreuzzeitung*. Once a "red republican," Ilicius is described by one observer as unabashedly opportunistic: "When the democratic business went awry, he changed saddles in all haste and threw himself with the fanaticism of a renegade into the service of the reaction, where his energy and lack of scruples led to notable accomplishments that earned the gratitude of the powerful."[54] In his zeal to defend the regime, Ilicius fails to notice that a political re-alignment is underway.[55] Signs of it are noticed by Ilicius' son, who laments that his father "either will not or cannot understand that another age has arrived: the age of Bismarck, who has decided to clean up the rotten old free trade system because that's the only way of getting the support we need for our army so we can get the damned social democrats to shut up."[56] The reference to Bismarck's turn to protectionism and the repressive Anti-Socialist Law denotes the shift in policy that came to be known as the second founding of the empire (*die zweite Reichsgründung*).[57] Ilicius' downfall comes about "with his official defense of views of the government that are actually no longer government views."[58] It takes the form of a letter conveying Bismarck's displeasure over Ilicius' Reichstag speech on the regime's proposed legislation "for defense against social democratic excesses." Clearly referring to May 1878, when Bismarck's first antisocialist legislation was defeated after brief debate, this episode makes Ilicius the scapegoat.[59] So stricken is he that his heart gives out.

Far from being portrayed as an anomaly, Ilicius is used to exemplify the rigidity of the typical 48er. Spielhagen echoes the self-description of Ernst Schmidt in *Sturmflut*, the unyielding ideals of Peter Lorenz in *Was will das werden?*, and the unwavering position of Charles Smith in the comments of one observer to Ilicius' son: "These old forty-eighters were all born doctrinaire and they stay doctrinaire even if they change colors ten times. Your father only changed them once, but then it was for good."[60]

Spielhagen's critique of doctrinaire ideology is offset, however, by signs that Germany's course is being determined by an oppressive, manipulative system and a middle class willing to compromise its values. A tumultuous time is portended, moreover, when the Kaiser is wounded in a second shooting only weeks after the first. Although nation does not set upon nation as Smith prophesied, a crazed crowd attacks the coach carrying away the assailant.[61] In Smith's view the authoritarian atmosphere will spawn more violence: "Everywhere under the deceptive conservative surface, I see radicalism at work and gaining ground, and not only in the lower classes, where its largely misunderstood phrases work with elementary force."[62] The Germany of 1878 is not his homeland, he decides, and he leaves for new exile. In a farewell at the train station, Smith praises Brunn's steadfastness, but avers that his Homeric heroism will not prevail in a world in which Homeric weapons are no longer used and in which the reigning Agamemnon is suspicious even of Brunn's kind. Returning to the pharaoh image, Smith prophesies that a Moses in the form of the "genius of humanity" will one day lead the nation from slavery. This leader will once again recognize "the Joseph of humaneness and idealism."[63]

Brunn is planning to stay, but, despite earlier expressions of cautious optimism, he knows that more than protective tariffs are needed to bring harmony to Germany. In the thronging Friedrichstraße he acknowledges to himself, "It is no longer the old Egypt—that's certain. And we still have to try to carry on the struggle—in spite of the new pharaoh."[64] The biblical passage from which Spielhagen drew his inspiration offers little hope, however: Joseph's descendants fall into slavery and their lives become "bitter with bondage." Although Brunn has the last word, his uncertainty and the departure of Charles Smith indicate the depth of Spielhagen's political despair. It is the despair of a German democrat who realizes his cause is lost.

The conclusion of *Pharao* reveals another element of Spielhagen's pessimism. In his farewell, Smith lashes out at a young literary generation rebelling against the ideals of the older: "And the *jeunesse dorée* with their *après nous le déluge*, these university-trained youths with their mockery of all ideology and their worship of practical success—aren't they providing an example that young artisans, workers, and proletarians are all too eager to follow?"[65] This outburst suggests that, like Brunn, Spielhagen sees himself as standing alone, fighting with weapons his successors deride. It also testifies to a widening chasm between two literary generations involved in the struggle for Germany's future. Spielhagen's attack on the "mockery of all ideology" was surely motivated by such criticism as was levied in 1884, when Heinrich and Julius Hart devoted a whole issue of their *Kritische Waffengänge* to showing how Spielhagen's works reflected "a whole epoch of German narrative literature" and embodied "pervasive defects in the German novel."[66] They concurred that novels should depict contemporary life, but denounced Spielhagen for allowing political themes to predominate and for making his characters into mere ideological mouthpieces.

The Harts' criticism has literary merit, but their hostility to Spielhagen's political themes marks a turning point in the fictional search for Germany's unfinished revolution. Indeed, Charles Smith's reference to the young generation's tendency to scoff at ideology is confirmed in an offhand comment by Conrad Alberti in an article on the French revolution: "A republic or a monarchy: in the future no one will even stir from his chair over the distinction."[67] But Spielhagen's character was not justified in equating their scoffing with an abandonment of ideals. Like their elders, young writers of the 1880s were sharply critical of German society, and they too sought a positive direction for German nationhood. They professed themselves to have given up on political solutions, however, especially any having to do with the legacy of 1848. Whether this anti-ideological stance justifies the label "neoconservative," applied by recent critics, is debatable, but it did have the effect of reinforcing the status quo.[68]

Conrad Alberti was one of the few members of his generation to deal with politics in novels of the 1880s. In his writing the conscious indifference to ideology suggested above was countered by childhood memories of the triumphant Germany of 1870, whose strength was symbolized neither in Bismarck nor in a people in arms, but in the Kaiser. This vision reflected not only the legacy of Frederician Prussia but also a modern world in which Germany struggled to secure her place. We have already seen an example of the transition from Frederician to imperial ideals in Alberti's novella, "Majestätsbeleidigung."[69] At the end, as Dräsecke makes his way to prison to serve his term for perjury, he glimpses the Kaiser and lets loose with a cheer. Modernity has won out, but the dynastic loyalty of the humble Berliner is sustained. Perhaps Alberti, a militantly proud representative of the modern age, was being ironic, but his later treatments of dynastic fervor suggest otherwise. In his first full-length novel, for instance, a character seeks respite from modern pressures by contemplating the statue of the Great Elector by the palace: "the bronze image of the forceful creator of Prussia [Staatenschöpfers], looking defiantly and boldly, like the genius of action he was, at the enslaved souls below, crumpled in chains at his horse's feet."[70]

Alberti's translation of dynastic loyalty into contemporary terms culminates in his best-known novel, Die Alten und die Jungen (The Old and the Young), published in 1889. His working title for this novel was Achtundvierzig und Siebzig (Forty-eight and Seventy),[71] and the conflict of these two generations will be treated in the next chapter. Pertinent here is Alberti's use of Hohenzollern imagery to develop his theme. The novel is set in 1888, the year in which three German emperors reigned in succession. Alberti links them to three generations and to three momentous years in German history: William I representing 1813; Frederick III, 1848; and William II, 1870. His portrayal of generational strife thus becomes fused with history, politics, and culture. The deaths of the first two rulers signify the demise of the generations of 1813 and 1848, with William II representing the arrival of a generation that will heal the conflicts rending German society.

Alberti idealizes the generation of 1813 as one whose steadfastness and sacrifice laid the groundwork for German unification. One character comments, "That's the famous generation of 1813, the one that kicked out Napoleon and founded the German empire."[72] Its legacy is personified in William I, who is memorialized for his role in creating "the German empire with his sinewy fist from the dozens of fragments, just as young Siegfried welded his victorious sword from small splinters; [he was] the shining representative of that wonderful third generation that only with its last breath, laid its spade aside and left the stage."[73]

The generation of 1848 presents a sorry contrast of muddled idealism and vulgar materialism, but although Alberti refrains from attributing these sins to Frederick III, he gives a confused rendition of his role as leader. Frederick is introduced as "the most handsome, best-loved man in Germany, the hope of the future," but he is also portrayed as the hope of the generation Alberti despised, who believed his reign would bring "the full triumph of their principles."[74] Moreover, although the course of Frederick's illness from throat cancer forms a major backdrop, Alberti does not use it to symbolize the disease of a whole generation. Instead, the narrator refers to him as the healthy element whose death means the end of the last hope "of improving these contorted, sick limbs from the great, healthy head, to make them straight, to change them; the only possibility of elevating this generation by one who was better than they was taken away."[75] Frederick's death puts the generation of 1848 "beyond salvation," under a cosmic judgment: "it was not to rule."[76]

Although Alberti also attacks representatives of the generation of 1870, he uses the ascent of William II to signify his belief that the new generation can succeed where its parents failed. The final scene shows the novel's protagonist, Franz Treumann, glimpsing the Kaiser as he passes beneath the Brandenburger Tor in his carriage. Franz's eyes are drawn upward to the quadriga atop the columns, its horses driven by a powerful victory goddess imbued with classical symbols of triumph. In the distance he can see a second monument—the victory column commemorating 1870—also topped by a forceful victory goddess. Surrounded by symbols of German destiny, Franz returns his glance to the face of the new Kaiser and discerns the "bold features of a leader and a judge, with nothing of a weakling, nothing of a dreamer, nothing of a tyrant, and nothing of a moneygrubber about them; the lines in his brow told rather of internal battles and storms, of honest combat and honestly won victory." He thinks to himself, "'You are of our generation and you seem born to be its leader. I believe in your strength and in your will.'"[77] The generation of 1870 now stands at the fore.

The Kaiser's appearances in "Majestätsbeleidigung" and *Die Alten und die Jungen* reveal a significant contrast in political perception. In both situations, a reigning monarch inspires a devoted subject, but with Dräsecke the loyalty extends only to the submissive fulfillment of duty. For Franz Treumann it becomes a commitment to active participation in the building of a new Germany. More than a leader in the Frederician mold who commands unquestioning obedience from his subjects, William II is depicted as the man who will mobilize the energies of a vigorous generation for achievements that will bring a third goddess of victory to Berlin. This victory statue would commemorate "the peaceful, inner victory that would liberate the fatherland and all humanity."[78] Would this monument ever be realized? Onward to battle, Franz answers.

Alberti's idea of the need for a moral transformation of the German nation is remarkably similar to Spielhagen's, whatever their generational and literary differences. Both saw a Germany weighed down by a self-serving aristocracy, by a dangerous militarism, by an oppressive political system, by a growing class conflict, and by an overweening materialism. Both asserted that artists and writers should work vigorously to bring about change. Both were conscious of internal struggles for nationhood; both were conscious of the failure of German liberals to prevail. The two authors' visions of how the unfinished revolution could be brought to fruition differed sharply, however. For Spielhagen the legacy of 1848 continued to provide the main hope, however unlikely. For Alberti that legacy was worse than useless: it was the cause of Germany's crisis. Only strong monarchical leadership, he concluded, could complete the revolution.[79]

Alberti's rejection of the tradition of 1848 was a fateful turn if it represented a rejection by his whole generation—as both he and Spielhagen claimed it did. The growing distrust for liberalism in particular and for political ideology in general not only stemmed from a rejection of the ideas of 1848 but also reflected a growing belief that politics involved nothing more than a struggle of the strong against the weak. Ideology matters little, remarks a character in a novel by Helene Böhlau: "The pessimist is one who stands at the side of those being devoured, the optimist at the side of those who are feeding; those who know they are feeding call themselves conservative, and those who feel themselves being devoured call themselves liberal. That's the whole game!"[80] The struggle over German nationhood was becoming defined in new terms—as a struggle for survival.

# Notes

1. Two versions of Werner's painting are reproduced and discussed in Peter Paret, *Art as History: Episodes in the Culture and Politics of Nineteenth-Century Germany* (Princeton, 1988), 167–180.
2. See Lothar Gall, *Bismarck: Der weiße Revolutionär* (Frankfurt am Main, 1980), and Ernst Engelberg, *Bismarck: Urpreuße und Reichsgründer* (Berlin, 1985), 557–602.
3. Karl Gutzkow, *Die neuen Serapionsbrüder* (Breslau, 1877), III, 294–295.
4. Karl Gutzkow, *Die Ritter vom Geiste*, 6th ed. (Berlin, 1878), I, xv.
5. Ibid., III, 196.
6. Gutzkow, *Serapionsbrüder*, I, 14.
7. Ibid., II, 200.
8. Ibid., II, 202–203. On the problematic relation of German liberalism to parliamentarianism see David Blackbourn and Geoff Eley, *The Peculiarities of German History: Bourgeois Society and Politics in Nineteenth-Century Germany* (Oxford, 1984), 253–260.
9. On the illnesses and mental disarray of Gutzkow's last years see R. J. Kavanagh, "Portrait of the Artist as a Young German: Karl Gutzkow's Political Attitudes and 1848," in Francis Barker et al., eds., *1848: The Sociology of Literature* (Essex, 1978), 65.
10. See James J. Sheehan, *German Liberalism in the Nineteenth Century* (Chicago, 1978), 79–177, and Dieter Langewiesche, ed., *Liberalismus im 19. Jahrhundert: Deutschland im europäischen Vergleich* (Göttingen, 1988).
11. *Die Familie Buchholz* achieved 86 printings by 1905. Annemarie Lange, *Berlin zur Zeit Bebels und Bismarcks* (Berlin, 1972), 680.
12. Julius Stinde, *Die Familie Buchholz: Aus dem Leben der Hauptstadt* (Berlin, 1885), I, 4.
13. Raabe explicitly expressed such hopes when a salt-of-the-earth *Berlinerin* is extolled with the wish that she could be multiplied and sent to every corner of Germany. Wilhelm Raabe, *Villa Schönow* in *Sämtliche Werke*, Third Series (Berlin, n.d.), II, 170.
14. Stinde, *Buchholz*, II, 117.
15. Ibid., II, 119. The book from which Buchholz is reading is *Fürst Bismarck* by Ernst Scherenberg.
16. Ibid., II, 41.
17. Ibid., II, 70–71; 177.
18. See George L. Mosse, *The Nationalization of the Masses: Political Symbolism and Mass Movements in Germany from the Napoleonic War through the Third Reich* (New York,

1975), and Eric Hobsbawm, "Mass Producing Traditions: Europe, 1870–1914," in Eric Hobsbawm and Terence Ranger, eds., *The Invention of Tradition* (Cambridge, 1983), 273–279.
19. Acts 2:12. To preserve the sense of the German translation, I have altered the King James text. Friedrich Spielhagen, *Was will das werden?*, in *Sämtliche Romane* (Leipzig, 1895), XXI, 385. Subsequent references to this novel will be to I or II, corresponding to XXI or XXII, respectively.
20. Ibid., II, 446.
21. Ibid., I, 86.
22. Ibid., I, 415.
23. Ibid., I, 115.
24. Ibid., I, 148. On the eighteenth-century origins of unpolitical individualism see Hajo Holborn, *A History of Modern Germany: 1648–1840* (New York, 1968), 308, 352–354.
25. Spielhagen, *Was will das werden?*, I, 356.
26. Ibid., I, 337, 361–363, 366–368. See also Russell A. Berman, *The Rise of the Modern German Novel: Crisis and Charisma* (Cambridge, Mass., 1986), 16.
27. Spielhagen, *Was will das werden?*, I, 286.
28. Ibid., I, 288–289.
29. Ibid., I, 171.
30. Ibid., I, 381.
31. Ibid., I, 385–386.
32. One minor character casually refers to *Gründungsschwindel* as the principal cause of the depression of the late seventies. Ibid., II, 89.
33. References in the last pages of the novel to effects of the new Anti-Socialist Law (passed in October 1878) indicate that the second volume is set in the late 1870s, not the mid-1880s as suggested in Fritz Martini, *Deutsche Literatur im bürgerlichen Realismus, 1848–1898*, 4th ed. (Stuttgart, 1981), 431.
34. Spielhagen, *Was will das werden?*, II, 95.
35. Ibid., II, 206; see also 324.
36. Ibid., II, 441.
37. Ibid., II, 92.
38. Ibid., II, 397.
39. Ibid., II, 348.
40. Ibid., II, 349–351. This distinction between the "good" Jew and the "bad" is common. For further treatment of it see below, Chapter 8.
41. Ibid., II, 448 and 445.
42. Ibid., II, 133.
43. Ibid., II, 449.
44. Spielhagen, *Was will das werden?*, II, 453. For enunciation of similar sentiments see Heinrich Spiero, *Das poetische Berlin*, Vol. II: *Neu-Berlin* (Munich, 1912), 93.
45. On the interaction of these developments see Gordon A. Craig, *Germany, 1866–1945* (New York, 1978), 85–98; Gall, *Bismarck*, 526–591; and Michael Stürmer, *Das ruhelose Reich: Deutschland, 1866–1918* (Berlin, 1983), 210–229.
46. Exodus 1:8. Friedrich Spielhagen, *Ein neuer Pharao*, *Sämtliche Romane* (Leipzig, 1897), Vol. XX, 133. The image of Joseph also appears briefly in Spielhagen, *Was will das werden?*, I, 48.
47. Spielhagen, *Pharao*, 134.
48. Ibid., 137.
49. Ibid. For a more explicitly apocalyptic vision in a Berlin novel see Botho von Pressentin, *Apokalypse* (Berlin, 1889), I, 212–213, and II, 218–219.
50. Spielhagen, *Pharao*, 367.
51. Ibid., 526.

52. Ibid., 127.
53. Ibid., 277.
54. Ibid., 42–43.
55. Another novel dealing with conservative politics of this period is Pressentin's *Apokalypse*.
56. Spielhagen, *Pharao*, 231–232.
57. Gall, *Bismarck*, 526–591.
58. Spielhagen, *Pharao*, 280. On the conflict between Bismarck and conservatives over the new policies see Gall, *Bismarck*, 545–547.
59. Spielhagen, *Pharao*, 426–437. A model for Ilicius might have been Karl von Hoffmann, president of the chancellory, who presented the bill to the Reichstag, or Friedrich von Eulenburg, dismissed as Prussian Interior Minister in March 1878 because of his continued commitment to free trade. See, respectively, *Reichstag Verhandlungen*, 1878, 2, especially 1496 and 1534, and Michael Stürmer, *Regierung und Reichstag im Bismarckstaat, 1871–1880: Cäsarismus oder Parlamentarismus* (Düsseldorf, 1975), 212.
60. Spielhagen, *Pharao*, 446–447.
61. Ibid., 500–502. Spielhagen's description is supported in Lange, *Berlin*, 390.
62. Spielhagen, *Pharao*, 526.
63. Ibid., 529 and also 410–413.
64. Ibid., 531 and also 367.
65. Ibid., 527. More conciliatory lines by Spielhagen about naturalists are quoted in Spiero, *Das poetische Berlin*, 93.
66. *Kritische Waffengänge*, Heft 6 (1884), 3, 41–44.
67. Conrad Alberti, "Entwicklung und Ergebnisse der 'großen Revolution,'" *Die Gesellschaft*, 5, 3 (October 1889), 1399.
68. See Russell A. Berman, *Between Fontane and Tucholsky: Literary Criticism and the Public Sphere in Imperial Germany* (New York, 1983), 80–83.
69. See above, 51–52.
70. Conrad Alberti, *Wer ist der Stärkere?* (Leipzig, 1888), II, 2.
71. Robert Plöhn, "Kritik," *Die Gesellschaft*, 5, 1 (April 1889), 561.
72. Conrad Alberti, *Die Alten und die Jungen* (Leipzig, 1889), II, 141 and also 137. On the mythology of 1813 see James J. Sheehan, "The Problem of the Nation in German History," in Otto Büsch and James J. Sheehan, eds., *Die Rolle der Nation in der deutschen Geschichte und Gegenwart* (Berlin, 1985), 10–11.
73. Alberti, *Die Alten und die Jungen*, II, 189. Hobsbawm questions the degree to which Germans revered William I as the founder of German unity, despite efforts to promote him as such. Hobsbawm, *Invention of Tradition*, 264.
74. Alberti, *Die Alten und die Jungen*, I, 309–311, and II, 190. Alberti wrote elsewhere that liberal hopes that Frederick would transform the political system were probably ephemeral. Conrad Alberti, "Der tote Kaiser," *Die Gesellschaft*, 5 (1889), 764. See also J. Alden Nichols, *The Year of the Three Kaisers: Bismarck and the German Succession, 1887–1888* (Urbana, Ill., 1987).
75. Alberti, *Die Alten und die Jungen*, II, 275.
76. Ibid., II, 42; 275.
77. Ibid., II, 284.
78. Ibid., II, 286. Actually, William I in his address in the Hall of Mirrors first put forth the idea of an inner peaceful victory; here the goal is bequeathed, apparently still unrealized, to his grandson. See above, n15.
79. See also Katherine Larson Roper, "Conrad Alberti's *Kampf ums Dasein*: The Writer in Imperial Berlin," *German Studies Review*, 7, 1 (February 1984), 75–82.
80. Helene Böhlau, *Das Recht der Mutter* (Berlin, 1906), 39.

# 5

# The Struggle for Survival: The Cultural Combatant

The 1880s brought critical new perspectives to the literary struggle for German nationhood. The young naturalist writers of these years, as suggested by Spielhagen's allusion in *Pharao*, conceived of themselves as standard-bearers of a revolutionary challenge to a culture fraught with illusion and corruption. Central to their movement was the premise that a truly modern literature would sweep away prevailing fantasies with a realism grounded in scientific principles. To realize this goal meant embracing the new theory that, they believed, had transformed the foundations of civilization: Darwinian evolution. The naturalists seized upon Darwin's notion of the biological struggle for survival (*Kampf ums Dasein*), transmuting it into a pervasive force in every realm of human society. As if the challenges of fusing science with art were not daunting enough, these would-be revolutionaries infused their task with a moral dimension as well. Humanity was evolving to new heights, and they, as artists, would lead the way. They must convert themselves, the young poet Hermann Conradi proclaimed in 1884, into "protectors and guardians, leaders and comforters, pathfinders and guides, physicians and priests of humanity."[1] Such notions proved susceptible to the still loftier idea of a cultural messiah who, drawing on a superior cultural heritage, would bring a gospel of regeneration to Germany—and, eventually, to all humanity.[2]

This chapter deals with novels that depict the unfinished revolution in terms of generational struggle over German culture, and, ultimately, nationhood. It focuses on characters representing the young generation who live in conscious tension with society and seek to resolve that tension through their chosen work. Such characters suggest a great deal about authors' conceptions of their own social role. Whether they interpreted the struggle for survival as a triumph or devastation for humanity would influence their will to become socially involved. How they conceived of their cultural mission would be of equal importance in determining the nature of their engagement. And finally, how they related their ideas of struggle and engagement to notions of nationhood would affect their contributions to a developing national consciousness. All of these questions became increasingly perplexing to young artists and intellectuals in Berlin novels of the 1880s.

As we have seen, similar figures had appeared in novels of the 1870s, but their existence as challengers to the existing culture was not, in the long run, particularly problematic. As young people, they took their economic insecurity for granted, and even though they stood outside the social mainstream, theirs was not a self-conscious alienation. Edwin, for instance, in Heyse's *Kinder der Welt*, struggles to complete a philosophical tract defining an age whose ethics are centered in scientific laws and everyday life.[3] Despite strong public opposition to the work's irreligious tendency, Edwin not only succeeds in having his book published but wins critical acclaim, after which he seems to forget his cultural struggles and immerses himself in family life. In *Die neuen Serapionsbrüder* Gutzkow devised a similar resolution for his young jurist, Ottomar Althing, who vows to dedicate himself "to the fulfillment of his duty to those dear to him and to the cultivation of his own mind and spirit."[4] Each character struggles with the pressures of a modernizing society and then retreats into a realm circumscribed by his individuality and artistic/intellectual integrity. Such an outcome loses sight of the social criticism in earlier situations in each novel.

Friedrich Spielhagen provided a more active charge in *Was will das werden?* by having his protagonist vow to serve his nation by becoming a poet. Although Lothar's idea of creating but a few building blocks for the new era sounds as humble as the commitments of Edwin and Ottomar, he differs in believing his work will lay the foundations "for the master who will come after me."[5] Still less constrained is the Christian imagery surrounding him, from his lifelong association with carpentry, to his being subjected to three temptations in the form of offers and enticements, to his giving freely of himself to whomever is in need, and to a young woman's deathbed confession that she has always thought of him as her messiah. The allusion becomes plain in Adalbert's appeal to Lothar, "Was it the scholarly Pharisees or the philosophical Sadducees who proclaimed the kingdom of God on earth? Wasn't it instead a carpenter's son?"[6]

Spielhagen, a generation older than his protagonist, did not place him in the company of the naturalist authors who would have been his contemporaries. Lothar's experiences in Berlin included encounters with poverty, but it was the poverty of the working class, not the artist. Nor did Lothar's artistic growth come from associating with artists' circles. It came, rather, with the exception of Adalbert, from his association with a range of activists from the older generation. Spielhagen's subsequent attack on naturalists in *Ein neuer Pharao* was the first sign in his writings that new generational battle lines were being drawn in the struggle for Germany's salvation.

Generational struggle and the artist's life in Imperial Berlin were first interwoven in *Die Betrogenen* (*The Betrayed*) (1882), by Max Kretzer (1854–1941). Soon to become Berlin's best-known naturalist novelist, Kretzer came closer than most other Berlin writers to being a native; he moved there with his family while still a boy. At one point the family's situation became so desperate that the thirteen-year-old had to work in a lamp factory, the first of a succession of jobs that competed with his formal education over the next decade. Then a fortuitous fall from a ladder laid the young man up long enough for him to write a series of stories for a socialist newspaper, followed in 1879 by the serialization of a first novel.[7] National recognition came later, however, with the publication of *Die Betrogenen*. The novel's theme of betrayal focuses on the vulnerability of proletarian women to economic lures and moral pressures from unscrupulous men, but an extensive subplot on artists introduces a German version of bohemian culture.

Kretzer's portrait, no doubt, was influenced by the appearance in 1881 of the German translation of Henri Murger's *Scènes de la Bohème*, a collection of sketches first published in Paris in 1851.[8] True bohemian existence, Murger wrote, was the "time of testing for the young person with talent, his way station before the crossroads leading either to the Academy or, to those who failed, to the charity hospital and to the morgue."[9] *Die Betrogenen* similarly distinguishes between an intensely purposeful artistic life and the aimlessness of those on the fringes of Berlin society.

Inevitable in the period of testing is artistic poverty. To introduce it, Kretzer's narrator relates the legend of a shoemaker who envies the artist's carefree existence. Magically, the devil whisks the shoemaker through garrets all over Berlin, showing him a thousand artists sleeping on sofas, rarely selling their paintings, and leading a completely dreary existence.[10] Should any readers doubt the legend's veracity, the narrator instructs, they should scan the Berlin address book to see how few of the listed artists have achieved renown.

*Die Betrogenen* presents three characters who respond differently to the problematic economic relation between the artist and modern society. Alexander Plagemann, a designer at a carpet factory, represents a failed artist forced into the normal workaday world. Describing himself as one "who sailed out with billowing sails of hope into the sea of his ideals," he watched his ship of dreams founder "on the cruel reef known as the struggle for survival."[11] A second artist-figure, Hannes Schlichting, sustains his commitment through a life of privation. A Westphalian painter of religious subjects, he also saw his dreams founder when he realized he could not hope to live off such painting in the secular environment of Berlin. He momentarily thinks of imitating the popular painter Hans Makart with a series of nude paintings. He cannot afford to hire models, however, and consoles himself with the reminder that Dürer and Cranach did not yield to such commercial temptations.[12] Refusing to sacrifice his art, he devises a routine that involves painting vases for a porcelain manufacturer three days a week and then settling in for a few blissful days of siege on his real work, his paintings. A third figure, Oswald Freigang, not only is able to subsist from his painting but eventually attains both critical acclaim and commercial success. Unlike Hannes, Oswald paints "scenes from the pubs, streets, and workplace," creating portraits of a new world driven by "steam and smoke." The insights his paintings give into the world of industrial Berlin bring growing acclaim, increased sales, and the success he "had so often longed for in his noble ambition."[13] Oswald embodies Kretzer's message that success need not be a sign of an artist's having sold out, and desire for recognition need not be a sin.

Both Hannes and Oswald have paintings exhibited and praised at the annual Berlin salon,[14] but their respective outcomes reflect Kretzer's judgment of each painter's style. Having characterized Hannes' style as "a half-forgotten, dead language," Kretzer has him depart in sadness from a Berlin whose environment has proven too alien. In contrast, having praised Oswald's modern style as "a freshly pulsating, living [language],"[15] Kretzer gives him the elements of a happy ending: successful in love and in art, he remains in Berlin. Both artists pass their period of testing, but only Oswald has won the *Kampf ums Dasein*. His realistic art makes him a spokesman of his age.

If *Die Betrogenen* introduces an artistic version of literary naturalism, it also depicts a major theme of that movement: the conflict of generations. Oswald's industrialist father reflects the older generation's incomprehension of artistic commitment. Oswald explains his father's obstinacy as a result of his being "a self-made man," who sees art as having nothing to offer those with something respectable to do, such as run a factory. Oswald, too, is a self-made man in his art, having gotten where he is without help from his wealthy father.[16] Not only is he making money from his chosen path; more important, he is winning social respect. When his father accuses artists of being a pack of beggars, Oswald answers that he is bringing honor to the family name and produces an enthusiastic critique of his work, which his father reads with puzzlement.[17] More surprising still is his realization that the son who shunned his machine factory has become a painter of machines. The old man, vowing to see the paintings for himself, goes to the crowded exhibition hall at the tip of Berlin's Museum Island. Facing a painting of gigantic machine works, the elder Freigang understands that his son is communicating realities of his age. He makes his way through the crowd and tells him, "You just keep painting your machines, and I will keep building them."[18] Such a change is difficult to imagine in the garret of an unknown artist. A combination of commercial success, public acclaim, and artistic merit spark the resolution to this generational conflict. Kretzer cannot seem to resist an outcome couched in the values of the parent generation.

The main focus in the novel, the ruined lives of working-class girls and women, exemplifies even more directly than the words about Oswald's style Kretzer's concern with coming to terms with the struggles of a rapidly industrializing society. The remark by the former artist about foundering on the reef of the struggle for survival applies in large measure to the novel's central developments. This character's use of the phrase made famous by Darwin attests to the pervasiveness of the Darwinian revolution in culture of the 1880s.

The publication of *On the Origin of Species* in 1859 astounded the European intellectual community by offering a sweeping scientific explanation for the development of biological species. Central to this explanation was Darwin's premise of "severe competition" among organic beings to attain the physical necessities for survival.[19] "The universal struggle for life," as Darwin termed it, became the means by which the process he called natural selection produced the gradual evolution of a species. When an accidental variation in a biological characteristic enabled one individual of a species to adapt more successfully to the environment than those without the trait, it not only became easier for it to survive but heightened its chances for successful propagation and, hence, for transmitting the favorable characteristic. The fittest members of a species would gain in numerical strength until those without the characteristic were eliminated. In turn, other variations would allow adaptation to new environmental conditions and allow the species to evolve further. Natural selection, then, in Darwin's view, worked positively, *"whenever and wherever opportunity offers*, at the improvement of each organic being in relation to its organic and inorganic conditions of life."[20]

Enthusiastic supporters soon translated Darwin's geographic and climatic conditions into social and economic conditions of human society and grafted his theory of struggle onto notions of human progress. In Germany, Ernst Haeckel, a professor of zoology at the University of Jena, not only popularized the theory but transformed it into a clarion call for national liberation. Having read *Origin of Species* in 1860, when it appeared in German, Haeckel was converted "in a virtual flash of immediate revelation and inspiration" and soon introduced its ideas to the public in heavily attended lectures.[21] Effortlessly, he leaped from biological science to German society, proclaiming, for example, that Darwin's insights could become the impetus "for the overthrow of 'tyrants' and 'priests,'— those, in other words, who stood in the way of German emancipation and freedom."[22] Over the next decade Haeckel continued his lectures and publications on the scientific, social, and philosophical implications of Darwin's theories. Such efforts transformed Darwinism in Germany from "a working hypothesis . . . into a philosophy of life."[23]

Evidence of its popular acceptance began to appear in novels, as in a comment in *Sturmflut* that Darwinism had become the true religion of the time.[24] More often, however, the catch-phrase *Kampf ums Dasein* cropped up in characters' conversations and in narrative description. Gutzkow's introduction of the Serapion Brethren, for example, alluded to the club's purpose of providing its members a respite from the *Kampf ums Dasein*, "which seemed to all the inhabitants of this city, even the propertied and the capitalists, to have become a hard, almost exclusive focus of life."[25] Few authors paused to define the phrase, but those who did showed an inclination to inject the struggle for survival with a conspicuous measure of German idealism.

An early attempt to wrestle—at least implicitly—with the idea was made in 1878 by Julius Hart in a Berlin novella entitled "Kein Ideal" ("Without Ideals"). Although the notion of *Kampf ums Dasein* is not the focus, the phrase occurs at both the beginning and the end, thus becoming a framework within which the story unfolds. The dilemma behind it—whether the realities of the modern age have eclipsed the possibility of living one's life according to ethical ideals—is articulated in a dialogue between two young men, Edwin and Benedikt. Edwin, the skeptic, argues that only practical results matter: "Shall I explain our times to you? It is a period of great deeds; we don't have the leisure anymore for musing and thinking, for indulging in childlike and childish ideals—oh, no, our minds are too powerful for that; we no longer simply *want*—we act."[26] Benedikt, citing cultural monuments to the human spirit, counters that to abandon ideals is to sink into egoism and hypocrisy. Each person must look out for himself first, Edwin replies: "The struggle for survival—" Benedikt interrupts: "The struggle for survival—how all of you have misunderstood that phrase and made it into a slogan to justify your selfishness."[27] Benedikt never specifies what the *Kampf ums Dasein* is, if it exists at all, but his interruption shows what it is not.

The rest of "Kein Ideal" develops the disaster awaiting those who so misconstrue the *Kampf ums Dasein*. Under the guise of adapting to the demands of an unphilosophical age, Edwin ignores mounting debts, casts aside love in favor of momentary passion, commits forgery, reveals state secrets, and plunges into hedonism, for which Berlin offers ample opportunity. The last scene has him fleeing by train with his equally depraved mistress and her jewels after having shot her husband. Edwin reassures himself that "the struggle for survival rages and burns in all corners; it's either you or me."[28] His attempt to make off with the jewels ends, however, when he rushes into the arms of waiting police. He thus falls victim to his own notion of the struggle for survival.

Through Edwin, then, Hart portrays the *Kampf ums Dasein* as a contemptible rationalization for modern excesses and posits idealism as the alternative. Other writers, however, were captivated by what they saw as the irreversible ascendancy of scientific doctrine that such notions as *Kampf ums Dasein* evinced. As literary scholar Wilhelm Scherer proclaimed in 1870, "Science is entering as the victor on the triumphal carriage to which we are all chained."[29] Few considered the negative image in Scherer's exuberant metaphor—a humanity chained to science—in the ensuing clamor for literary works that bespoke modernity.

The impetus for incorporating science into literature came from outside Germany. Works by authors such as Hippolyte Taine, Henrik Ibsen, and Ivan Turgenev had fomented discussion all over Europe on the interaction of the individual and his social environment.[30] New approaches to art, such as Taine's milieu-theory, strengthened the belief that scientific method offered the only means of understanding the human species.[31] Most influential, however, was Émile Zola's idea of a *roman expérimental*. Such a novel would depict characters in terms of hereditary and environmental factors that molded them, and would then subject them to "experiments" consisting of changing social conditions. The outcomes would be explained by their hereditary makeup, the pressures of their particular environment, and the accidental conjunctions of life.[32] Zola pursued this intent in the cycle of novels through which he traced the evolution of a single family, *Les Rougon-Macquart*. Although he did not limit himself to Darwinian theory, his characters were undeniably combatants in a universal struggle for survival.

In the early 1880s Zola's *roman expérimental* struck a chord in Germany that proved to be the clarion call of a literary revolution. The writer who sounded this call was Michael Georg Conrad (1846–1927), who in 1879 described literary conversations with Zola in a series of articles for the *Frankfurter Zeitung*. Conrad awakened the attention of a young generation of German writers to the man he called the "grand master of naturalism."[33] Having returned to Germany in 1882, Conrad settled in Munich, but through his naturalist periodical, *Die Gesellschaft*, his influence soon extended to Berlin.[34] Conrad's work was prominent among a host of publications proclaiming a literary revolution that would incorporate scientific theory.[35] Darwinism, as the epitome of modern science, became the banner.

The dilemma of how the legacy of idealism could be reconciled with scientific theory now surfaced with renewed intensity. A young Rhinelander named Wilhelm Bölsche (1861–1939) set himself the task of resolving it and in 1887 produced an essay that purported to do so.[36] Its lengthy title, *The Scientific Foundations of Literature: Prolegomena to a Realistic Esthetic*, embodies its premise that natural science is essential to the writing of realistic literature. But having postulated a world in which age-old questions of free will and love could be answered in terms of neurological impulses, Bölsche confronted an unintended moral vacuum.[37] He sought to fill it in two ways: by setting forth moral dimensions to the *Kampf ums Dasein* and by invoking German idealism as the necessary accompaniment to the scientific approach to literature.

Bölsche, though acknowledging the complexities of applying Darwinian theory to human experience, proceeded to do so anyway and in the process imposed moral purpose on the theory of evolution. The premise of the struggle for survival *did* apply to the human species, he argued, but the process worked differently than with other species, since humans were distinguishable more by intellectual capacity than biological characteristics. But intellectual adaptations—or achievements of individual genius—unlike the biological adaptations described by Darwin, could at once become the common property of humanity. This left the individual who created them with no apparent advantage in the struggle for survival.[38] To answer this dilemma Bölsche stepped further away from biological struggle. The achievement of individual genius brought an intangible gain: the knowledge of having contributed to humanity. This should be compensation enough, Bölsche argued, to the individual who loses his monopoly over the effects of his genius.

In a still greater leap from biological into cultural realms, Bölsche insisted that the struggle for survival aimed at the well-being of the entire species.[39] Such well-being could be furthered, he continued, if German writers would dedicate themselves to creating a healthy national literature. While such a literature should be grounded in the new scientific precepts of realism, in order to be "healthy," it should not focus exclusively on sordidness and brutality. Zola's *Nana* might be justified in portraying "sick people, in diseased situations and diseased developments," but the use of sickness should serve to illuminate "the true and the healthy."[40] True realism in the scientific age meant that literature should become the "educator of the human species."[41] Only by combining the highest idealism with scientific understanding could literature point the way toward a healthy, contented humanity—the final goal of evolution.[42] German writers, as the bearers of "a richer and deeper literature than that of neighboring countries," should resist embracing Zola as the messiah, Bölsche warned. "Do not forget that you belong to German literature, that Goethe and Schiller stand behind you." Germans should embrace their literary heritage and thereby show the world "that realism, in truth, is the highest, most complete idealism, in that it brings even the smallest part into the light of the whole, into the light of the Idea."[43] With this credo Bölsche believed he had spanned the chasm between German classicism and the literature of the scientific age. But his bridge, consisting of little more than faith, glossed over the contradiction between a supposedly value-free science and a value-laden tradition.

Nevertheless, this essay and other such manifestoes spurred a generation of writers to literary action. Their abundant responses reveal both confidence in their ability to create a new literature and concomitant naiveté about the enormous problems. "The law of natural selection rules inexorably even in art," wrote Berlin poet Arno Holz. "Art is not a sanatorium for asthmatics. It is the great world of the healthy."[44] With such sentiments young writers assumed the charge of leading humanity to a higher evolutionary stage. In the affectionate words of a recent critic, those who took up the call "were dreamers—progressive, optimistic dreamers, and all in all, with all their optimism, they were very lovable dreamers."[45] Their optimism, however, would be severely challenged by visions of the cruel *Kampf ums Dasein* that writers like Hart and Bölsche had sought to avoid.

The tension between the optimistic view and pessimism over the brutal conditions of modern society is vividly demonstrated in Conrad Alberti's six-volume *Kampf ums Dasein* cycle, published between 1888 and 1895. All but one of the novels are set in Berlin, where rapidly changing social conditions become the equivalent of climatic changes in Darwinian theory. Each novel takes up specific themes of struggle with the aim of revealing the scientific basis of the social phenomena that determine the struggle. These phenomena "are not a matter of mood or of happenstance, as often seems at first glance," Alberti wrote. "They are grounded in the universal, eternal law of the struggle for survival and its natural outcomes. They are not without rules, not irrational as fools contend: they have their logic, their strict development, their laws."[46] In his journalism Alberti echoed Bölsche's optimistic assertion that Darwinian struggle held the promise for the steady improvement of humankind. He urged, for instance, the inclusion of Darwinian theory in school curricula, arguing that showing a progressive, organic evolution of increasingly higher forms would inspire pupils to dedicate themselves to humanity.[47] When he tried to apply such precepts to the writing of fiction, however, he encountered more than a few difficulties in sustaining his optimism in the face of so much evidence of urban ruthlessness.[48]

All the *Kampf ums Dasein* novels show the destructive side of such struggle, but the first, *Wer ist der Stärkere?* (1888), relates it most directly to Imperial Berlin. Its dozens of references to trials of strength are all defined in terms of social and intellectual combat of the modern age. A major focus is the struggle against what Alberti depicts as the overwhelming weight of a rigid establishment, and it is waged by two characters in their respective professional realms. One, a successful architect named Otto Hilgers, suffers complete defeat, and the other, a provincial physician named Franz Breitinger, ultimately triumphs. Despite differing outcomes, both men's struggles reveal "natural laws" that contravene any positive notion of the *Kampf ums Dasein*: that human nature possesses a powerful resistance to change and that individuals who challenge this resistance will be seriously battered, even if victorious.

Otto Hilgers seems an exemplar in the urban struggle, having broken loose from the chains of poverty by deliberate action and hard work. He continues to live in working-class Moabit because he loves its dynamic human activity.[49] His dedication to the idea of progress inspires a deep concern for the situation of workers who, as he sees it, are building Berlin's new existence. When builders try to head off construction workers' demands by lowering wages, Hilgers takes up their cause and supports the subsequent strike. In the ensuing conflict he is blacklisted and struggles for his own survival. More painful still, strike leaders persuade the workers to accept the wage cut, reversing the position for which Hilgers has sacrificed his career. A final defeat occurs when the police order him to leave Berlin because of his activity. He realizes the blacklisting will extend throughout Germany and decides to emigrate to the New World. Germany thus loses a hero in the *Kampf ums Dasein*, and Hilgers is denied the satisfaction of continuing the work he has begun.

Franz Breitinger, on the other hand, triumphs, but his victory is clouded by moral cost. Arriving in Berlin with research showing the source of typhus to be in drinking water, Breitinger discovers that medical theory is the jealously guarded province of a closed academic establishment. His struggle to have his work published or even discussed by an obsequious Berlin press is repeatedly thwarted. "The martyrdom of being killed by silence," he complains, "is a hundred times worse than the inquisition."[50] Like Hilgers, Breitinger is ostracized for challenging existing powers, but he is saved from professional ruin when the French press prints an article describing the confirmation of his theory by French researchers. National rivalry causes the German establishment to take notice, and, overnight, Breitinger becomes a hero. Even the most pompous academician claims that he recognized the young man's genius all along. The bittersweet victory causes Breitinger to decide to adopt the brutal weapons of the surrounding society.[51] With him, then, Germany retains a victory in the *Kampf ums Dasein*, but a ruthless society has ruined his desperately needed ideals.

Although the optimistic view of struggle surfaces in Alberti's next novel, he succeeds in depicting only its promise, not its triumph. *Die Alten und die Jungen* (1889), as we have seen, becomes a paean to the dawning Wilhelmine era, but in focusing on a circle of young composers (with clear parallels to Berlin naturalists), it also seeks a vision that will bring the cultural regeneration of German society.[52] Alberti was undoubtedly influenced by Zola's depiction of Parisian bohemian circles in his novel *L'oeuvre* (1886),[53] but if Zola was an impetus, Alberti's clear interest lay in his own society. Under Alberti's pen the traditional conflict between old and young becomes transformed into an all-out struggle between two historical generations over the future of Germany and her culture. Multifarious characters and subplots form a search for means by which the generation of 1870, now coming of age, might rescue Germany from the desperate crisis fomented by its parent generation, 1848. German culture serves as an expression of the condition of the society and also as the means of its salvation.

Alberti defines the generation of 1848 as a prosperous middle class whose members are either hopelessly immersed in vulgar materialism or lost in a dreamworld. Their ascendancy means disaster for German culture, as is shown with three types. Most offensive are the parvenus, whom Alberti personifies in a wealthy Jewish investor and his social-climbing wife. The Jarociners' role in Berlin culture reflects their values, with their mansion the scene of ostentatious salons and cultural evenings. The money they pour into the arts becomes the means of their social ascent; they glory in their new-found power and use it to corrupt all they touch.[54] A second representative of 1848 is Professor Julian Stinkert, a pompous composer whose renditions of sentimental melodies at the Jarociners' affairs bring tears to the ladies' eyes. A newspaper proclaims Stinkert the successor to Beethoven, and the Kaiser bestows an order of merit on the "poet of the German soul"—both of which, in the eyes of the young generation, are apt commentaries on the woeful state of Germany's soul.[55]

The third type representing 1848 is more complicated, personified in a respected Berlin architect and his cultivated wife. The Hoffmeisters, however, show themselves to be far removed from modern realities, lost in a confused idealism whose consequences are professionally disastrous and personally tragic. Their dreamworld becomes exposed when Hoffmeister, who has attacked modern art as "crippled and deformed," designs a cathedral-like opera house that lacks all the practical necessities of a modern concert hall.[56] Another dimension of delusion is revealed in the Hoffmeisters' glorification of their composer-son, Paul. Although their ethereal ideas of art seem far removed from Paul's quest for tonalities of the modern age, they allow their veneration of his genius to blind them to signs of his impending downfall. Too late does Frau Hoffmeister acknowledge "the foolishness of their upbringing and of their self-idolization through their son."[57]

Alberti most sharply attacks the generation of 1848 for visiting its sins upon its children. Not only are the Hoffmeisters and Jarociners portrayed as central contributors to the ruin of their respective sons, but myriad other details contribute to the refrain about how the weaknesses of the parent generation have contaminated the generation of 1870. What, then, of the prospects for the younger generation? Having grown up with the intoxication of military victories and having become accustomed to repeated scientific and technological triumphs, its members are shown to be children of an age not only of grandiose delusions but of awesome achievement. Unified by their youth, their pugnacity, and their hope, they exude confidence in their ability to rise above their parents' petty, confined visions to effect an artistic revolution that truly expresses modern realities.[58] This confidence ignores, however, not only the inherited weaknesses of the parent generation but an array of distractions and obstacles to genuine artistic creativity.

The quest for such creativity is central to *Die Alten und die Jungen*, and Alberti rejects the notion that artistic genius alone will suffice. He advocates, instead, the necessity of disciplined, sustained commitment, but his argument becomes blurred by imagery that suggests still another version of artistic genius. For, despite dire warnings about the dangers of exaggerated notions of the artist's powers, Alberti is beguiled by the vision of a German cultural messiah. This tension emerges most clearly in his two central artist-characters—the genius, Paul Hoffmeister, and the would-be prophet, Franz Treumann.

Paul Hoffmeister is introduced as a composer who seeks to create a new music that will make its listeners whole persons—unified, he says, in their thinking, their feeling, and their doing. His works are described as powerful music of "the shrillest, most shrieking dissonances." "I don't want an art that rises above the contradictions, the horrors, and the battles of life," Paul explains, "because it doesn't take notice of them; I want one that portrays them and leads through them because it knows them."[59] His music is intended to awaken people "from this dull thoughtlessness that clings so strongly to what is meaningless, trivial, and spiritless," and force them to deal with their chaotic times.[60] The ethereal ideals of the parent generation are anathema to those brought up amid the political and technological revolutions of the 1870s. Children of the modern age, Paul insists, "wouldn't want to be people with two hearts anymore, two souls—creeping around by day, fearfully ducking to avoid bringing down the wrath of the police and only breathing easily in the evening when Schiller led them into those faraway, feudal middle ages and Mozart immersed them into a world resounding with harmony and melody that existed nowhere on earth."[61] Genuine harmony would be found instead only through a culture that encompassed rather than transcended modern dissonances.

This vision begins to crumble, however, as Paul falls under the sway of a hidden demon.[62] This takes the form of an excessive confidence in his own genius, a weakness for dissipation in café society and drink, and a disastrous mixture of passion and contempt for women. All this is worsened by a sudden conviction that Wagner's music cannot be surpassed. Paul's long decline ends in suicide.[63] Notably, Paul Hoffmeister and Frederick III die on the same day. Both deaths symbolize a lost hope for leadership in their respective generations.

For the generation of 1870, however, Franz Treumann, the protagonist, embodies an alternative hope: disciplined commitment rather than unbridled genius will fulfill the national promise. As Franz's story unfolds, however, the notion of genius proves to be difficult for Alberti to abandon. As a restless adolescent in Silesia, Franz questioned whether his artistic longings were the voice of genius or only a boyish fancy, but "he did know he had to give this voice freedom."[64] The road to freedom takes him to Berlin. Beneath wondrous expectations lies foreboding also, for, approaching Berlin in a fourth-class train compartment, he falls asleep and dreams of lying paralyzed in a grassy field, held by "an incomprehensible, irresistible force," as huge cliffs break loose upon him.[65] The nightmare is quickly forgotten, however, as Franz absorbs the intoxicating atmosphere of the capital. Most wondrous of all is what he perceives as the air of freedom, in which each person is answerable only to himself and has only to take advantage of this freedom to realize his dreams.[66]

After this first, exhilarating encounter, Berlin becomes for Franz, as for the artists in *Die Betrogenen*, a place and time of testing. He comes to realize that his is not the voice of genius but neither is it simply a schoolboy's fancy. Deciding that genius is not the first requirement for the cultural revolution Germany so urgently needs, he resolves to become a kind of John the Baptist, preparing the way for an artistic messiah of the future.[67] In a private ceremony Franz tramples a particularly offensive review from a popular newspaper and swears fealty to his art, "because he believed in it, as only a Christian—if there still were any—could have believed in his Savior."[68] The reward for his dedication is the awakening sound of new music: "strong, swelling melodies, which rose and fell in powerful harmony in his breast, hidden, silent, and still moving, today only audible to him but tomorrow for all humanity."[69] The exemplar of slow, disciplined work becomes infused by what sounds oddly like the voice of genius.

The intimation of Franz Treumann as cultural messiah becomes heightened by the contrast between him and other representatives of 1870, who are shown to possess neither genius nor a willingness to work. Scenes in artistic hangouts depict endless talk about the new musical revolution—and also diverse, even peculiar means by which to bring it about: by founding a conservatory, by forming national associations, by expelling the Jews, by making vegetarianism mandatory, by translating Nietzsche's philosophy into music, by experiencing another national humiliation like Jena, by drinking more, by getting rid of Bismarck.[70] Any unity of purpose crumbles into rivalry and backbiting of whomever happens to be absent. As to sustained work, one young man rationalizes that "neither Christ nor Mohammed kept working after they assumed their messianic roles."[71] Far from being messiahs, these characters are depicted as self-indulgent weaklings.

Franz's disillusionment with his peers, moreover, extends to the entire nation.

Lamenting "their secret ridiculing and whispering, their consuming megalomania, their petty jealousy," he asks rhetorically: "Weren't they just Germans; wasn't that same flame of disunity and quarrelsomeness flaring up in them that once made their ancestors into slaves of shrewd enemies, that characteristic that reached back long before forty-eight?"[72] An inherited inability to unify in common purpose thus becomes a crucial flaw in the cultural mission of the generation of 1870.

Behind the disunity and individual weaknesses Franz sees other debilitating forces that undermine his generation and its potential for leadership. Contaminated by the "megalomania" of the age of pretension, luxury, and upheaval, many members of the generation of 1870 have lost the capacity for serious thought and have sunk to the level of servants of Mammon—the very thing they vowed to combat.[73] The Bismarckian regime, moreover, has intoxicated many young people with dangerous notions of themselves as *Realpolitiker*.[74] The real Bismarck-hater of the novel, an ascetic apostle of Nietzsche, goes still further, maintaining that his artistic vision can be realized only with the departure of Bismarck, "who has interdicted the idealist instincts of our people and who is brutalizing and militarizing them."[75] A more subtle, yet insistent, theme portrays the dilution of German culture by foreign influences, as shown by Franz's perception of a mindless Francophilia that allows French works to dominate German theaters or infuses French phrases into daily use throughout Berlin.[76] Another assault on the Germanness of Berlin culture is the intrusion of East European Jews. In the train compartment at the beginning of the novel Franz shudders at the presence of a caftan-clad Galician and his family, whom he perceives as dirty, strong-smelling, and noisy. Upon arrival he acknowledges that as a newcomer, he shares their hopes and uncertainty, but he continues to notice the presence of East Europeans in Berlin and continues to be troubled by it.[77]

Berlin holds all the strands of Alberti's criticism together, and, as Franz's disillusionment grows, negative images of the city increase. The splendor he once saw becomes transformed into mindless uniformity; formerly magnificent buildings now blend together with factory-made regularity; formerly fascinating people on the street now hurry past each other, "hollow-cheeked, pale, gaunt, with shrill voices and unhappy, nervous expressions." The new Berlin, Franz thinks, is "a quickly built, brilliant, blinding facade behind which everything was desolate, bare, empty, unfinished, rough, and boorish." His mind lights upon the Jarociners, and he suddenly asks himself, "This man, why did he go under a Polish name? Why wasn't he named 'Berlin'?"[78] The city and the parvenu have become one. Berlin also embodies Franz's growing sense of isolation, as he asks himself how he could be living at the focal point of Germany and still be as lonely as "a flea in Saharan sands."[79] His despair seems absolute as he walks on the northern outskirts of Berlin "over the long, bleak stretches of sand at whose edge [he could see] the haze and columns of smoke that engulfed that hateful cavern of unhappiness, of disease, of depravity called

Berlin."[80] The city that was once his hope now embodies his defeat. The final image of Berlin, however, is contained in the scene of Franz finding new commitment at the Brandenburger Tor. Inspired by the symbols of German triumph, Franz answers the question of the next, peaceful victory by quickening his stride. Berlin is no longer the source of lavish dreams nor the cause of hopeless despair, but rather the place where the battle for Germany's future will be waged.

Franz Treumann embodies Alberti's hope for artistic leadership in this battle, but, given his isolation from the rest of his generation, those hopes seem weak indeed. At one stage midway in the novel, when Franz seeks to rally the most likely leaders of 1870, he is stunned by their refusal to his call to battle and asks himself, "Where, then, were our troops?"[81] Alberti did not, with this call, relinquish the vision of artists bringing salvation to German society. But through the array of representatives of 1870 he demonstrated how easily mere mortals could identify themselves as saviors and then show their humanness by falling prey to the innumerable social forces that militated against them.

The novels considered in this chapter portray pure-minded young characters who strive to maintain their integrity and to use that integrity to bring about the regeneration of German society. All these figures are imbued with a vision of the individual combatant struggling on behalf of his nation's culture. Novels by members of the older literary generation depict with confidence the ability of dedicated intellectuals and artists to further German culture through their work, whether quietly, as Gutzkow and Heyse envisioned, or as cultural leaders, as Spielhagen proposed. Kretzer and Alberti, members of the younger generation, wrote novels embodying similarly high expectations for the transformation of German culture, but their works reveal a growing concern with the notion of a struggle for survival and its effect on their struggle for Germany's soul. Kretzer's answer in *Die Betrogenen*, at least as it applied to generations, was that the economically successful older generation and the culturally committed younger one must strive together. This notion of reconciliation between generations, however, was completely rejected in Alberti's version of all-out conflict.

Still, Alberti's *Die Alten und die Jungen* conveyed the most explicit hope that the new age would bring the progressive evolution of the human species, as suggested by the positive version of natural selection. This hope rested on assumptions similar to those in Bölsche's essay on scientific literature: that the tenets of Darwinian evolutionary theory held true for the development of human culture and that a contemporary art grounded in the realities of the modern age could provide moral truths to an amoral or immoral society. Franz Treumann's confidence at the end rested on his belief that his commitment to moral ideals of national greatness, along with a clear-headed perception of modern realities, would bring German civilization to new heights. He might well be seen as an embodiment of Bölsche's idea that individual cultural genius could transmit evolutionary progress to all humankind. But once this leap was made, the focus shifted from transforming institutions to the individual combatant. Once the hope became posited in an isolated individual, the prospects for a whole society undergoing some sort of moral or spiritual regeneration diminished.[82]

Further weakening the hope for German regeneration is Alberti's implication that the failure of the generation of 1870 exemplifies a peculiarly German failure. Although the anxiety Alberti discerns in his generation might seem to inhere in the modern tension between the individual and society, he links rivalries and betrayals within the artistic community to ideas about the failure to achieve true German unity. Such emphasis on disunity opened the door to appeals for uncritical nationalism as the antidote to this perceived national failure.

None of these novels make such a call, however. Indeed, underlying the theme of individual struggle in all of them is an awareness of the wider struggles of a rapidly industrializing society. In particular, novelists truly committed to dealing with the modern age, as the young naturalists believed themselves to be, could not ignore the looming Kampf ums Dasein of a growing industrial proletariat. Whether these combatants were to be victims or conquerors, however, was not easily discerned, as Berlin novels dealing with the working class reveal.

# Notes

1. Quoted in Lotte Rausch, Die Gestalt des Künstlers in der Dichtung des Naturalismus (Dissertation, Gießen, 1931), 16. See also Manfred Brauneck and Christine Müller, Naturalismus: Manifeste und Dokumente zur deutschen Literatur, 1880–1900 (Stuttgart, 1987), 19–77.
2. On messianic imagery in literature of this period see Adalbert von Hanstein, Das jüngste Deutschland: Zwei Jahrzehnte miterlebter Literaturgeschichte, 3rd ed. (Leipzig, 1905), 165, 203, 240; Richard Hamann and Jost Hermand, Naturalismus (Berlin, 1972), 215–219; Hans Wilhelm Rosenhaupt, Der deutsche Dichter um die Jahrhundertwende und seine Abgelöstheit von der Gesellschaft (Dissertation, Bern, 1939), 12–14.
3. Paul Heyse, Kinder der Welt (Berlin, 1872/1886), I, 215; II, 306, 328.
4. Karl Gutzkow, Die neuen Serapionsbrüder (Breslau, 1877), III, 309.
5. Friedrich Spielhagen, Sämtliche Romane (Leipzig, 1895), XXII, 453; see also 18.
6. Ibid., XXI, 384.
7. The novel, Bürger ihrer Zeit, was published in book form in 1881 under the title Sonderbare Schwärmer. On Kretzer's early life see Günther Keil, Max Kretzer: A Study in German Naturalism (New York, 1928; reprinted, 1966), 14–15.
8. Helmut Kreuzer, Die Bohème: Beiträge zu ihrer Beschreibung (Stuttgart, 1968), 6.
9. Ibid. Kreuzer paraphrases Murger's statement from his expanded Scènes de la Vie de Bohème (Paris, 1883), 1ff.
10. Max Kretzer, Die Betrogenen (Berlin, 1882) I, 133.
11. Ibid., I, 11.
12. Ibid., I, 191. On Makart as symbol of artistic success see Richard Hamann and Jost Hermand, Die Gründerzeit (Berlin, 1965), 25, 186.
13. Kretzer, Die Betrogenen, I, 142–143.
14. Ibid., II, 309. On the workings of this important exhibition see Peter Paret, The

Berlin Secession: Modernism and Its Enemies in Imperial Germany (Cambridge, Mass., 1980), 19–21 and passim.
15. Kretzer, Die Betrogenen, I, 141.
16. Ibid., I, 14, 143.
17. Ibid., II, 299.
18. Ibid., II, 310.
19. Charles Darwin, The Origin of Species, 6th ed. (1872); reproduced in Philip Appleman, ed., Darwin: A Norton Critical Edition (New York, 1970), 116.
20. Ibid., 123. For pessimistic versions of natural selection, see Hans-Ulrich Wehler, "Sozialdarwinismus im expandierenden Industriestaat," in Imanuel Geiss and Bernd Jürgen Wendt, eds., Deutschland in der Weltpolitik des 19. und 20. Jahrhunderts (Düsseldorf, 1973), 134–139, and Peter J. Bowler, The Non-Darwinian Revolution: Reinterpreting a Historical Myth (Baltimore, 1988), 34–38.
21. Daniel Gasman, The Scientific Origins of National Socialism: Social Darwinism in Ernst Haeckel and the German Monist League (London, 1971), 6. On the extent to which Haeckel ran roughshod over Darwin's theory see Bowler, The Non-Darwinian Revolution, 82–90.
22. Gasman, Scientific Origins, 8, and Alfred Kelly, Descent of Darwin: The Popularization of Darwinism in Germany, 1890–1914 (Chapel Hill, N.C., 1981), 22–28. See also Wilhelm Bölsche, Haeckel: His Life and Work, translated by Joseph McCabe (Philadelphia, 1906), 144–171.
23. Eda Sagarra, Tradition and Revolution: German Literature and Society, 1830–1890 (New York, 1971), 254.
24. Bernd Neumann, "Friedrich Spielhagen: Sturmflut (1877): Die 'Gründerjahre' als die 'Signatur des Jahrhunderts'," in Horst Denkler, ed., Romane und Erzählungen des Bürgerlichen Realismus: Neue Interpretationen (Stuttgart, 1980), 265.
25. Karl Gutzkow, Die neuen Serapionsbrüder (Breslau, 1877), I, 2.
26. Julius Hart, "Kein Ideal," Deutsche Monatsblätter, I, 2 (May 1878), 115.
27. Ibid., 116. On the problems of translating "struggle for existence" into German see also Kelly, Descent of Darwin, 30–31.
28. Hart, "Kein Ideal," 141.
29. Quoted in Hanstein, Das jüngste Deutschland, 6, and subsequently in Richard Urban, Die literarische Gegenwart: 20 Jahre deutschen Schrifttums, 1888–1908 (Leipzig, 1908), 2.
30. See Maurice Larkin, Man and Society in Nineteenth-Century Realism: Determinism and Literature (London, 1977).
31. On the German reception of Taine's milieu-theory see Hamann and Hermand, Naturalismus, 117–120.
32. On Zola's roman expérimental and its influence on German naturalism see Günther Schmidt, Die literarische Rezeption des Darwinismus: Das Problem der Vererbung bei Émile Zola und im Drama des deutschen Naturalismus (Berlin, 1974), 120–126.
33. Hanstein, Das jüngste Deutschland, 34. See also Michael Georg Conrad, Von Émile Zola bis Gerhart Hauptmann: Erinnerungen zur Geschichte der Moderne (Leipzig, 1902), 39–40, and Vera Ingunn Moe, Deutscher Naturalismus und ausländische Literatur: Zur Rezeption der Werke von Zola, Ibsen und Dostojewski durch die deutsche naturalistische Bewegung (1880–1895) (Frankfurt am Main, 1983), 71–87.
34. See Agnes Strieder, "Die Gesellschaft": Eine kritische Auseinandersetzung mit der Zeitschrift der frühen Naturalisten (Frankfurt am Main, 1985).
35. For other influential works see Conrad, Von Émile Zola bis Gerhart Hauptmann, 66–67, and Hanstein, Das jüngste Deutschland, 50–81.
36. On Bölsche's association with Berlin naturalists see Katharina Günther, Literarische Gruppenbildung in Berliner Naturalismus (Bonn, 1972), 52, 60, 68, and 74, n132. On the development of his Darwinian ideas see Kelly, Descent of Darwin, 36–56.

37. Wilhelm Bölsche, *Die naturwissenschaftlichen Grundlagen der Poesie: Prologemena einer realistischen Aesthetik* (Leipzig, 1887), 18–24, 44, 52.
38. Ibid., 78–80.
39. Ibid., 70.
40. Ibid., 63. See also Wilhelm Bölsche, "Dem neunzehnten Jahrhundert," *Hinter der Weltstadt: Friedrichshagener Gedanken zur ästhetischen Kultur* (Leipzig, 1901), 11.
41. Bölsche, *Die naturwissenschaftlichen Grundlagen*, 71.
42. Ibid., 93. On the spectrum of other assumptions involved in literary applications of Darwinian ideas see George Levine, *Darwin and the Novelists: Patterns of Science in Victorian Fiction* (Cambridge, Mass., 1988), 13–21.
43. Bölsche, *Die naturwissenschaftlichen Grundlagen*, 91–92. On Bölsche's linking of idealism and realism see Fritz Bolle, "Darwinismus und Zeitgeist," in Hans Joachim Schoeps, ed., *Zeitgeist im Wandel: Das Wilhelminische Zeitalter* (Stuttgart, 1967), 265–267. On nineteenth-century notions of Germany's cultural *Sonderweg* see Peter Uwe Hohendahl, "Bürgerliche Literaturgeschichte und nationale Identität: Bilder vom deutschen Sonderweg," in Jürgen Kocka, ed., *Bürgertum im 19. Jahrhundert: Deutschland im europäischen Vergleich* (Munich, 1988), III, 200–231.
44. Quoted in Helmut Scheuer, "Zwischen Sozialismus und Individualismus—Zwischen Marx und Nietzsche," in Helmet Scheuer, ed., *Naturalismus: Bürgerliche Dichtung und soziales Engagement* (Stuttgart, 1974), 169, n9. See also Schmidt, *Die literarische Rezeption des Darwinismus*, 67–70.
45. Bolle, "Darwinismus und Zeitgeist," 268.
46. Conrad Alberti, *Mode* (Berlin, 1892), i–iii. See also Conrad Alberti, "Die zwölf Artikel des Realismus" (1889), in Brauneck and Müller, *Naturalismus*, 49–58. On the wide-ranging applications of Darwinian struggle to social conditions see Bowler, *Non-Darwinian Revolution*, 152–162.
47. Conrad Alberti, "Cicero oder Darwin?" *Die Gesellschaft*, Supp. 4 (July 1888), 223. This article is part of a long-standing debate over whether Darwinian theories should be part of the school curriculum. See Kelly, *Descent of Darwin*, 57–74.
48. Two novellas that form a prelude to the *Kampf ums Dasein* cycle, published under the title *Riesen und Zwerge* (Berlin, 1889), represent Alberti's most deliberate attempt to apply the hereditary and environmental notions to his fiction.
49. Conrad Alberti, *Wer ist der Stärkere? Ein sozialer Roman aus dem modernen Berlin* (Leipzig, 1888), I, 78. Otto Hilgers represents the classic "virtuous victim" described by George Goodin, *The Poetics of Protest: Literary Form and Political Implication in the Victim-of-Society Novel* (Carbondale, Ill., 1985), 51–55.
50. Alberti, *Wer ist der Stärkere?*, II, 27. The theme of being sentenced to death by silence was a favorite Alberti-image for the fate of naturalist authors.
51. Ibid., II, 333.
52. The parallels to naturalist circles are mentioned in Günther, *Literarische Gruppenbildung*, 16, and Rausch, *Gestalt des Künstlers*, 44.
53. On the importance of Zola's *L'oeuvre* see ibid., 23–25, 45, and Hanstein, *Das jüngste Deutschland*, 101.
54. Conrad Alberti, *Die Alten und die Jungen* (Leipzig, 1889), I, 123–124. See also Hamann and Hermand, *Naturalismus*, 37–47.
55. Alberti, *Die Alten und die Jungen*, I, 200; II, 216, 220, 222. A likely literary model for Stinkert was author and critic Paul Lindau, who was despised by naturalists. See the Hart brothers' "Lindau als Kritiker," *Kritische Waffengänge*, 2 (1882), 9–43, and Heinrich Spiero, *Das poetische Berlin: Neu-Berlin* (Munich, 1912), 35.
56. Alberti, *Die Alten und die Jungen*, I, 65, 87; II, 127, 130.
57. Ibid., II, 232. On the *Geniekult* of the *Gründerjahre* see Hamann and Hermand, *Gründerzeit*, 51–61.
58. Alberti, *Die Alten und die Jungen*, I, 87–88, 135–136. On the problem of defining

distinct German generations see Martin Doerry, *Übergansmenschen: Die Mentalität der Wilhelminer und die Krise des Kaiserreichs* (Weinheim, 1986), 30–43.

59. Alberti, *Die Alten und die Jungen*, I, 13, 62, 90–91, 98–100. Not surprisingly, Paul's goals are a musical counterpart of Alberti's. See Alberti, "Zwölf Artikel des Realismus," in Brauneck and Müller, *Naturalismus*, 49–58; and Conrad Alberti, *Der moderne Realismus in der deutschen Litteratur und die Grenzen seiner Berechtigung* (Hamburg, 1889).
60. Alberti, *Die Alten und die Jungen*, I, 201–202.
61. Ibid., I, 87–88.
62. Ibid., II, 152. Alberti's depiction of Hoffmeister can be seen to embody a long-held German fascination with and concomitant fear of "the mysterious and sometimes demonic creativity of the poet." See Fritz Stern, *Dreams and Delusions: The Drama of German History* (New York, 1987), 9.
63. Passages that describe Paul's downfall include Alberti, *Die Alten und die Jungen*, I, 258, 278; II, 68, 81, 152, 159, 164, 231, 268. On parallels with Claude Lantier in Zola's *L'oeuvre* and with other autobiographical characters see Rausch, *Gestalt des Künstlers*, 45–46, 48.
64. Alberti, *Die Alten und die Jungen*, I, 35.
65. Ibid., I, 3–4.
66. Ibid., I, 13.
67. Ibid., I, 210. See also Conrad Alberti, "Zur Psychologie des Genies," *Natur und Kunst: Beiträge zur Untersuchung ihres gegenseitigen Verhältnisses*, 33–50, and Jochen Schmidt, *Die Geschichte des Genie-Gedankens in der deutschen Literatur, Philosophie und Politik: 1750–1945*, Vol. II: *Von der Romantik bis zum Ende des Dritten Reichs* (Darmstadt, 1985).
68. Alberti, *Die Alten und die Jungen*, II, 176.
69. Ibid., II, 283.
70. Ibid., I, 74–85.
71. Ibid., I, 95.
72. Ibid., II, 17–18.
73. Ibid., I, 188. Carl Bleibtreu's novel of artistic circles in Berlin, *Größenwahn* (1887), attributes virtually all the ills of the age to ubiquitous megalomania.
74. Alberti, *Die Alten und die Jungen*, II, 13–14. It is not clear from the context whether this observation is Franz Treumann's or the narrator's.
75. Ibid., II, 24. See also Franz Treumann's reference to "diesem rohen, unfertigen, Militärstaate." Ibid., II, 142.
76. Ibid., II, 18, 23, 54, 119, 157. See also Conrad Alberti, "Sünden wider den vaterländischen Geist," *Die Gesellschaft*, 5, 1 (February 1889), 268–274, and Hanstein, *Das jüngste Deutschland*, 143–148.
77. Alberti, *Die Alten und die Jungen*, I, 3–10, 80.
78. Ibid., II, 6–8.
79. Ibid., II, 27, 55.
80. Ibid., II, 257–258.
81. Ibid., II, 26.
82. See Scheuer, *Naturalismus*, 155.

# 6

# The Working-Class Struggle

It might seem that alienated writers should have made common cause with the oppressed proletariat. Few, however, did so, and those who joined the most prominent working-class movement, the Social Democratic Party (SPD), usually found their membership short-lived. As we have seen, the principal notion of the German revolution to emerge in Berlin novels was the belief that Germany's salvation lay in a moral and cultural regeneration. This notion was accompanied by a strong preoccupation with the cultivation of individual integrity, an ideal that could hardly be expected to inspire middle-class authors to join working-class activists in espousing socialist revolution. Nevertheless, the awareness by novelists of miserable living and working conditions impelled many to articulate the social evils they saw.

The resulting vacillation between outrage over the suffering and anxiety over an unruly mob is evident in the works of virtually all novelists who treat the working class, beginning with Karl Gutzkow. *Die Ritter vom Geiste* sets a precedent in which working-class grievances are validated, but fear of the proletariat wins out. Gutzkow's comparison of the mysterious, sleepwalking Fritz Hackert to the masses conveys an image of a restless, potentially demonic force, and his portrayal of military power turned loose against a demonstration suggests a belief, moreover, in the futility of working-class action. In a preface written in 1878, Gutzkow emphatically distances himself still further from any advocacy of revolution. Instead, he asserts, he intended his novel to transpose the forbidden discussion of revolutionary ideas into "higher spheres," to forestall the need for reorganizing society "after the models of Marx and Lassalle, which will remain utopias—or at least so we hope!"[1]

Gutzkow's *Die neuen Serapionsbrüder*, even more critical of working-class activism, depicts ill-planned strikes, demagogic agitators, and rowdy meetings.[2] Other potent criticisms arise when middle-class characters argue that workers should focus on national ideals and suggest that their discontent has more to do with a malaise of the *Gründerzeit* than with genuine economic grievances.[3] Far from offsetting such attitudes with comparably strong statements by workers, Gutzkow has the character once declared to be "the new Lassalle"[4] meet a depraved, alcoholic end after he denounces the International, the "academic socialists," and the workers themselves as expressions of an absurd *Zeitgeist*.[5]

When novelists of the 1880s focused new attention on the role of industrial workers in the society of Imperial Berlin, their works expressed fears and prejudices similar to those of Gutzkow, but they also manifested a heightened awareness of the working class that resulted from a conjunction of literary trends. Directives about realism had long since induced novelists to become increasingly explicit about the social attributes of their characters. Increased consciousness of class boundaries caused many to feel compelled to incorporate the lower classes into art. The prominence of industrialization as a hallmark of modernity further increased writers' awareness of an emerging industrial working class, and ideas from the new discipline of sociology inspired them with notions of their times as an age of the masses.[6] Finally, Darwinian ideas induced writers to scan the urban environment for evidence of the *Kampf ums Dasein*, and many thought they had found it in Berlin's working-class districts.

The "social question" (*Sozialfrage*), the codeword by which all manners of people referred to the array of issues concerning the lower classes, thus made frequent appearances in novels of the 1880s. Its usual connotation of the self-evident, however, provides little clarity—and less consensus—over its meaning. To whom did it refer? Different novelists gave different answers, identifying the group in some instances as factory workers and their families; in others as the jobless from both the artisan and working classes; and in still others as a disreputable *Lumpenproletariat*. And what question was involved? Again, a spectrum of possibilities are implied, ranging from how to improve the workers' economic situation, to how to bring social justice (whatever that meant) to an oppressed group, to how to inculcate moral reform in a dissolute people, to how to control rowdy masses. Despite such ambiguities, two basic approaches emerged in novels. One, which focused on material and moral conditions, tended to define the poor as victims needing help. The second, which focused on organized action against these conditions, warned that *Kampf ums Dasein* would henceforth be fought with new weapons wielded by a no longer passive populace. Although the two approaches gave differing messages, both challenged ethereal notions about the social harmony that was supposed to result from the German revolution.

Wilhelm Raabe (1831–1911) provides a good example of how even novelists far removed from the naturalist movement expressed a growing consciousness of urban misery. *Im alten Eisen* (*Of Old Iron*) (serialized 1884–1886) shows two children lost in Berlin after their mother dies in squalor in a *Mietskaserne*. Although Raabe does not link the children's misery with the working class per se, he does criticize the failures of purveyors of social services to the poor, such as "the doctors, social workers, carpenters, undertakers, etc."[7] He also remarks on the unwillingness of neighbors in the tenement to help the orphaned children, noting that their indifference is "remarkably similar to that of their well-to-do fellow citizens in the most refined districts of the city."[8] The "humane healing power" of two middle-class individuals becomes Raabe's answer; they simply remove the children from the miserable environment he has depicted.

Other novelists made the issue still more problematic by suggesting that the working class might not deserve any better. An instance of this occurs in Spielhagen's *Was will das werden?* Upon arriving in Berlin, Lothar Lorenz finds his stepbrother Otto running a carpentry shop in Moabit from a squalid house whose swampy location by the Spree means perpetual dampness. One crisis after another hits his family as two children succumb to diphtheria; the apprentice leaves to follow the call of Pastor Renner (a thinly disguised version of the Christian Socialist leader Adolf Stoecker); and a supplier refuses to give more credit. These pressures aside, Otto turns out to be an inept carpenter whose shoddy window- and door-frames are difficult to sell. His wife copes as ineptly with the meager household budget as with the ubiquitous dust and mildew. Lothar is deeply ambivalent: "Anger flamed up over so much lack of understanding, foolishness and weakness, but then it melted into pity over so much misfortune, pain, and suffering."[9] He continues to vacillate between the so-called "social democratic" view—that the misery he sees derives from economic exploitation—and the feeling that the condition of Berlin's poor testifies only to their own inabilities. The novel's conclusion suggests that the unfinished revolution will come from above and will take place in spite of the stupor of those to be saved. Nevertheless, Spielhagen clearly intended his portrayals of severe economic pressures and disastrous living conditions to awaken readers' social consciousness.

The novelist who did most to promote such consciousness was Max Kretzer, whose *Betrogenen* was followed by *Die Verkommenen* (*The Ruined*) (1883), a novel with still more graphic treatment of the lower-class *Kampf ums Dasein*. Kretzer was heralded as Germany's answer to Zola, and two decades later a contemporary recalled, "We felt that a real writer of the Berlin people had come forth, one who had looked into the depths of the metropolis through his own experience, who had observed the terrible wheels of the machinery of the gigantic city with his energetic mind."[10] Kretzer's fascination with Berlin's poor soon reverberated through other works by other authors, provoking him to comment irritably that "a whole literary school has preyed upon *Die Verkommenen* in dramas, in novels, in short stories, in sketches, and characteristic descriptions."[11]

Kretzer denied that ideology motivated him to write *Die Verkommenen*: "I had to write, and to do that I didn't have to seek out a new 'ism' first. For everything was already there inside me."[12] What he saw as a strength—his intense feeling for the desperation of poverty—has also been seen, especially by Marxist critics, as his major weakness. As a Berlin historian noted, "He drew only the downtrodden and declassé; the ascendant, forceful, organized class of the proletariat—the future, in other words—he did not have the capacity to see."[13] The idea that Kretzer was motivated by emotion is plausible, coming as it does both from him and his critics, but it is also one-sided. More than an outpouring of feeling, *Die Verkommenen* offers well-researched details of conditions, explanations as to the sources of misery, and numerous suggestions for reform.

*Die Verkommenen* portrays the *Kampf ums Dasein* for Berlin workers in terms of laws of economic catastrophe and social exploitation. In contrast to Darwin's notion of natural selection of individuals best able to adapt to their surroundings, this novel proposes that human adaptation to the desperate environment of poverty means ruin, and that the struggle for survival can be won only by those able to break free. It attempts to explain why so many are defeated and how the few attain salvation.

The opening third of the novel focuses on the ruination of a single working-class family, the Merks. Through them Kretzer enunciates the view that disaster in the *Kampf ums Dasein* unfolds as a chain of crises (*Kette von Grausamkeiten*).[14] The first link in the Merks' chain is the depression of the late 1870s, "an after-effect of the golden age of speculation [*Gründen*] and swindle, which cast its shadow for years into the future."[15] Merk, an ironworker at Borsig, has been let go, along with hundreds of others, just as winter is approaching. For Merk the loss of his job constitutes a broken social contract. He entered adulthood with expectations of security, accepting in exchange the necessity of working long, arduous hours at subsistence wages. Now, without warning, he is told he is no longer needed and left to fend alone for his family's sustenance.[16] At this time the Merks are living in a cramped flat north of Rosentaler Tor. The grim quarters are typical, the narrator notes, of the "thousands of damp, mean, and suffocating workers' flats that take up the whole territory of this spread-out district."[17]

These conditions soon come to seem luxurious, however, as new links in the Merks' fate are forged. The second consists of the gradual pawning of clothing and furniture at a nearby shop whose chaotic stacks of household goods attest to the ruin of countless other families. A third comes with the formerly unthinkable decision to move into a cheaper flat on Gerichtstraße, located in "one of those dreadful *Mietskasernen* on the outskirts," in Wedding.[18] The narrator describes the building as a "cavern of misery" with seventy families piled one on top of the other, enduring screaming children, shrill quarrels, and constant turnover as tenants leave to take up the *Kampf ums Dasein* in some other forsaken place.[19] The Merks bring moral values that stand out in their new surroundings; curious neighbors note that their humble possessions are polished and in good repair and that, still more important, the children are clean, neat, and mannerly. After some months, however, the remaining furniture is broken down and the children are no longer as carefully dressed as when they arrived.

Two other links are forged when Ida Merk takes a factory job and her husband turns to drink. The mother's absence means terrible changes, especially for thirteen-year-old Magda, who now cares for the younger children while Merk searches in vain for work. She thus becomes one of the "small, innocent housewives, whom the perversity of existence usually prevents from actually becoming the role they now play."[20] Humiliated over his lack of work, Merk allows himself one day to be enticed by an unsavory neighbor named Ludwig Jakob into the mean basement tavern of their building. His two youngest children, left unsupervised in the family quarters while Magda is on an errand, play with live coals from the stove, and the infant burns to death. Merk's presence in the tavern is deemed negligence, and the bereaved father is sentenced to four weeks in jail. Alcohol becomes still another link when Merk, returning from jail, enters the tavern again and, inflamed by Jakob's needling, hurls a beer mug that kills the neighbor. Jakob's provocation mitigates the judgment against Merk, but he still receives a two-year sentence, leaving his family fatherless and burdened by taunts and gossip. "Modern circumstances," a character explains, are to blame for this disaster. "It's a chain of relations that can twist around even the best person; . . . unemployment is the devil that in the end can numb us against everything and drive us to evil, for that's the first link in the chain."[21]

Kretzer no doubt intended the Merks' story to symbolize the threat to the whole working class, but his ultimate concern lay with the children of Gerichtstraße. The rest of the novel follows five of them into adulthood: Rosa Jakob, eldest daughter of the man Merk killed; Magda and Franz Merk, the two oldest Merk children; Oskar Schwarz, the son of a widowed seamstress; and Leonhard Sirach, son of the widowed proprietess of a small produce shop. Depicted as alert, sensitive, and hard working, all succeed in leaving Gerichtstraße, but while two build the foundations for productive lives, the other three are utterly ruined. The only factor separating the two successes from the three tales of ruin is education. Both in the sense of upbringing and in its institutional sense, *Bildung* becomes the critical weapon in the struggle for survival.

Most predictable is the fate of Rosa Jakob, whose upbringing left nothing but scars. Her father, also an unemployed ironworker, was a rowdy drunkard who brutalized his unkempt children, especially Rosa, who had the task of coaxing him from the tavern. Her inevitable bitterness produces a twisted morality that is said to verify the aphorism that "the sins of the fathers shall be visited upon their children."[22] The novel also depicts Rosa's seduction by colportage novels sold by the ever-present hawker. Although the financial cost is great, Kretzer urges that the cost of the Cinderella-mythology inculcated by the novels is still greater. Seduced by a man who provides lavish entertainment and a luxurious apartment, Rosa triumphantly walks down Leipzigerstraße in her finery, seeing herself "as the factory girl transformed into the lady baroness in the cheap yellow pamphlets."[23] Like a flower planted in arid soil, the narrator remarks, she will bloom and wilt quickly without ever knowing why.[24] Indeed, she dies miserably in the "Charité" and is buried in a pauper's grave. With an upbringing consisting of the disastrous combination of a brutal father and a mythology of delusionary hopes, the novel argues, Rosa never had a chance.

Each of the other four children has a substantially better chance because of strict, careful upbringing in their respective families, but Magda Merk and Oskar Schwarz become two additional casualties in the *Kampf ums Dasein*. Their intellectual resources are shown to be inadequate to withstand the temptations of easy escapes.

Magda's downfall begins when, wanting to provide income for her family, she is lured into the dangerous activity of selling matches and flowers in the cafés around Friedrichstraße. One night, through the wiles of Rosa Jakob, she becomes intoxicated and is impregnated by an unscrupulous seducer. Frightened by this experience but unaware of her pregnancy, Magda turns back from the road to ruin by beginning a factory apprenticeship. The honest daytime work holds further perils, however, in the form of the other factory girls, whose frivolous longings are as much of an insidious influence as colportage novels. When the shame of her pregnancy forces Magda to flee Gerichtstraße, she loses herself irredeemably in the society of fallen women and the men who sustain them. Magda's "intellectual limitations became apparent on the day she allowed her notions about life to cloud her eyes like a thick fog," the narrator explains. "Thus she fell into the bubbling witches' kettle we call Berlin, and its evil society became her guardian."[25]

Oskar Schwarz, by confronting his "intellectual limitations," seems to come closer to salvation. As a boy, he spends long hours writing stories about life in the *Mietskaserne*, an activity his mother tolerates in the belief that it will prepare him to be a copyist. Oskar, however, has higher ambitions, and when his best friend, Leonhard Sirach, offers him the use of his humble library of classics, Oskar embarks on a period of intense study. All this ends once he takes a job in a publishing house of colportage novels and falls under the influence of a cynical, alcoholic writer. Soon Oskar, too, is producing the poisonous literary fare, and despite the shock of discovering his sister innocently reading one of the pseudonymous issues, he depends too much on the income to stop writing. A chain of disasters culminates in Oskar's succumbing to alcohol. Nature gave Oskar talent, the narrator explains, "without giving him the means to realize his gifts in a purified form." Even devoted study did not inculcate the discipline of work, for "as with all autodidacts, the compulsion of grandiose visions overwhelmed his artistic instincts."[26] Genuine purpose, this statement implies, grows only with sustained guidance.

This belief is confirmed by the examples of the two successful children. Although it is not clear what kind of schooling either Leonhard Sirach or Franz Merk had, there are hints that both received more education than the other three children. More explicit are references to the formal training each boy received in his respective art. With incredible sacrifice Frau Sirach enables Leonhard to attend a conservatory, where he receives the violin lessons that discipline his love of music and result in a successful debut. Franz, whose love of drawing is a luxury the Merks cannot possibly support, acquires a protector in the person of a down-and-out gentleman upstairs. The man first gets him involved in a Sunday art school and then guides him into an examination that results in a stipend from the art academy. A background character through most of the novel, Franz comes forth in the last scene in a convergence of the survivor and the ruined. Having come to the morgue to draw anatomy studies, he is led to two unidentified corpses whom he is horrified to recognize as his sister,

Magda, and her lover, Oskar. Overcome at first, "he then opened his portfolio and began to draw with care and love."[27]

Die Verkommenen implies three approaches to breaking the chain of disasters in the struggle of Berlin's poor: individual effort, reform of social conditions, and transformation of the economic system. For the individual, the examples of Oskar and Franz show the only hope to be the development of solid perspectives on one's abilities and the discipline needed to overcome the immense social obstacles to fulfilling them. Kretzer shows such preparation to be virtually impossible in the environment he describes, and thus also advocates that this environment be changed. Countless episodes in his novels cry out for improvements in conditions: for some type of unemployment insurance, for better housing, for education on the dangers of alcohol, and for action against exploiters such as the *Kolporteurs*, the procurers, the baby-farmers (or so-called "angel makers"), the pawnshop owners, and, not least, the sweatshop owners and purveyors of piece work. But although Kretzer gives readers a much-needed education by enumerating these problems, he does not question whether the institutions in Imperial Germany will allow for such reform.[28] He is equally vague about advocating action against an economic system that produces widespread unemployment and depressions.

The few remarks about socialism in *Die Verkommenen* suggest Kretzer's desire to delimit it as a purely moral force. For instance, he idealizes Frau Sirach's deceased husband for his dedication to the craft of glazing, his commitment to his family, and his unwavering solidarity with "the great army of the poor and the oppressed." Such virtues, the description implies, manifest Sirach's commitment to Lassalleanism, a "purely social creed that tolerated no political fragmentation."[29] Far from promoting political programs or class struggle, socialism in this context means "being humane, thinking humanely, feeling humanely, and acting humanely."[30] When Kretzer depicts socialist activism, however, he betrays uneasiness that stems in part from an ignorance that was widespread. For example, his novel *Die beiden Genossen* (*The Two Comrades*) (1882) allows its focus on ideological issues and on police persecution of social democracy to devolve into a melodrama of free love, thereby strengthening one of the most popular prejudices about socialism. But more basic to Kretzer's aversion is his conviction that by fanning the flames of class hatred, socialism is inimical to Germany's best interests.

This message is most explicit in his novel *Im Sturmwind des Sozialismus* (*In the Windstorm of Socialism*) (1883), in which two working-class characters dispute whether a strike will promote workers' goals or defeat their best interests. The debate culminates at a noisy meeting of workers. First, the labor organizer raises the crowd to euphoria with a speech extolling the strike as a first step toward a workers' state and a utopia of brotherhood. His opponent then reverses the mood with a barrage of counter-arguments: socialist promises are slogans without substance; its leaders are corrupt; the only true socialist was Jesus Christ; and, most telling, they, the workers, have too great a stake in the success of private capital to risk a strike. This speech wins over the audience—and the narrator as well, who declares, "Step by step he attacked social democracy; blow after blow fell on the hollow fantasy until it broke into pieces."[31] In a convoluted sequence of events the crowd's mood reverses once again, giving a sorry picture of the prospects for workers' choosing a reasoned course of action, and the confusing build-up climaxes with an apocalyptic vision: "The windstorm of socialism swept over the fevered heads and scourged the naked body of class hatred."[32] An actual apocalypse does not occur, however, and in the resolution the specter of class hatred has vanished.

Kretzer, however, was still plagued by the thought that socialism offered plausible answers to the economic misery he had so graphically portrayed, and in *Meister Timpe* (1887) he undertook his most systematic examination of industrial capitalism. Instead of focusing on factory workers, however, this novel turned to the artisan class, personified in the title character, Johannes Timpe. Owner of a prosperous wood-turning shop built over three generations, Meister Timpe is driven to ruin by competition from a mechanized factory. Inexorable economic forces drive the desperate Timpe to the unthinkable step of embracing social democracy, but, as with earlier novels, Kretzer reveals through the outcome an unshakable refusal to pursue the implications of his own vision into advocating fundamental change.

At one level the ruination of Johannes Timpe is the ruination of the *Kleinbürger* by the loss of his own values. It begins with the particularly modern ambition of parents to spare their children the hardships they have undergone. For Timpe this meant untold sacrifices so his son Franz would want for nothing in a household otherwise governed by austerity and dedication to work. His dreams are realized when Franz is hired as a clerk in a nearby firm, but the sacrifices produce an unintended result. Infused with ambition, Franz Timpe spurns the virtues that have guided his family for so long. He reflects his times, the narrator explains, in that he represents "the new generation of the early *Gründerjahre*, which was only trying to find easy ways to make money and to sacrifice the humble ways of the *Bürgertum* to the specter of pleasure."[33]

These disturbing signs form a prelude to the real trouble, which comes when Franz's boss, Herr Ferdinand Friedrich Urban, marries the widow whose property abuts Timpe's and begins to transform its parklike garden into a factory site. Morbidly fascinated by the felling of the venerable old trees, Johannes Timpe concludes, "What was falling there was old Berlin."[34] His own life begins to fall as well when Urban, angered by Timpe's refusal to sell him his property, launches a campaign to ruin him. He lays plans to produce machine-made umbrella handles in direct competition with Timpe's workshop and draws Franz Timpe into the brutal contest by inducing him to steal patterns from his father. Steadily losing orders, Timpe is soon forced to dismiss his apprentice and then his loyal assistant. At his neighborhood pub he rails against the economic pressures bearing down on his heretofore secure existence.[35] These conversations tie the demise of traditional ideals to the economic conditions of industrialization and to the materialism Kretzer believes the process spawned.

The episode with social democracy has three stages. Timpe strongly resists at first, asking, "How should he, the loyal artisan, who had never wavered in his love of monarchy and the hereditary dynasty, now in the autumn of his life abandon his deeply rooted views and go over to social democracy and swear allegiance to that blood-red flag that was supposed to be carried by storming masses over the corpses of half of humanity?"[36] Soon, however, he becomes incensed that the monarchy has not reciprocated his loyalty, and allows "hatred for the existing order in the state" to lead him to "the new savior."[37] His new-found obsession causes him to take the floor at an SPD meeting, where his call to bring down the factories allows the ever-present police agent to shut down the meeting. The crowd leaves the hall arm in arm, singing the workers' anthem, and as they march down the street the earth seems to tremble under the footsteps of the ever-growing mass. In the excitement, however, Timpe collapses in the hall, and when he awakens after weeks of delirium he denies that the social democratic apostasy ever took place. A short time later he is found suffocated by smoke from the fire he set to forestall eviction from his house and workshop. Scrawled on the basement walls are the words, "Long live the Kaiser!" Thus the old Berliner's answer to the threatening vision of marching masses: the Kaiser would prevail. Outside, the new Berlin is celebrating the new rail system with its inaugural train of dignitaries. The crowd's cheers echo in the distance, the novel concludes, "like the soft rumble of thunder from a retreating storm."[38]

The diminishing thunder suggests an unspoken middle-class wish that the threat of socialism would retreat before the progress of modernity. Despite such wishes, however, Berlin novelists, especially naturalists like Kretzer, were also vocal critics of the existing order, including the intense persecution of social democracy. The Anti-Socialist Law, a key element of Bismarck's program of political consolidation of 1878, was passed by a newly elected conservative Reichstag. It proposed to eliminate socialist subversion by prohibiting publications, meetings, and other activities of the recently formed Social Democratic Party or any other group manifesting so-called socialist tendencies.[39] Driven underground or into exile, social democrats endured a period of ideological and tactical confusion that lasted the life of the law, from 1878 to 1890. During this period novelists, despite their ideological qualms, were scathing in their portrayals of police persecution and other repressive measures undertaken in the name of the Anti-Socialist Law.[40]

Why, then, did they fail to embrace the movement victimized by this repression? Recent studies have posited numerous answers: the intolerance of Social Democratic leadership for the ideological vagaries of naturalist writers; the conflict in writers' minds between Nietzschean individualism and collective ideals of socialism; the attractiveness of a "social imperial regime" (*sozialen Kaisertum*) that seemed to obviate the need for a new political system; or the failure on the part of writers to undertake systematic study of economics and politics.⁴¹ Each of these explanations can be supported by portrayals in novels, but they should be augmented with the reminder that the SPD was in its infancy when it was banned. During the years it was outlawed, widespread popular confusion reigned over the actual nature of the party, and novels reflected this confusion, as we have already seen with Kretzer's fiction of the early 1880s.

Some novelists, however, gave sympathetic treatment to the development of the Berlin social democratic movement under the Anti-Socialist Law. Hans R. Fischer (1863–?) may be said to have initiated this trend with three semi-documentary works published between 1887 and 1890 that interspersed descriptions of shelters for the homeless, work houses, pawnshops, and prisons with human interest stories.⁴² Despite the abundance of statistics and factual description, these books had the hallmarks of fiction, and Fischer clearly thought of them as such when he wrote in one introduction, "It is a sign of the times that the social novel has achieved a significant place in contemporary literature. To the poet . . . is given the opportunity of contributing to the solution of difficult questions, to intervene everywhere, to provoke here and there, to awaken enthusiasm for noble actions, and to appeal to the general public."⁴³

Despite his stated intent, Fischer did not define what form such actions might take, but he did remind readers of those who were dedicating their lives to the socialist cause in his most explicitly political chapter, entitled "Zigeuner des Parteigetriebes" ("Gypsies of the Party Movement"). It depicts the first attempt of socialist leader August Bebel to speak publicly in Berlin since the onset of the Anti-Socialist Law eight years earlier. Fischer's account of the mass meeting of 19 March 1886 shows the party responding to the years of persecution with new dynamism. It conveys the uproar of a huge audience (10,000, by later estimate) growing impatient as they wait for the popular Bebel to appear. Once he begins to speak, Bebel, despite his careful choice of words, cannot forestall police agents from dissolving the meeting almost immediately, but the crowd cheers his brief attempt.⁴⁴ Fischer also uses the episode to give portraits of social democratic types, finally focusing on an aging agitator, Johann Baptist von Hofstetten. An actual leader of the early Berlin movement, he is depicted as poverty stricken after lifelong involvement in working-class causes.⁴⁵ In a postscript noting Hofstetten's recent death, Fischer describes the belated tribute paid by a long procession of mourners. The conjunction here of the obscure Hofstetten and a vigorous figure like Bebel gives two striking examples of the perils of being a social democrat in Berlin of the 1880s: anonymous destitution and incessant persecution.

Both were more fully spelled out in a novel by Hans Land entitled *Der neue Gott* (*The New God*) (1890). It centers on a young nobleman who, rejecting his family, becomes deeply involved in the outlawed social democratic movement. Of immediate interest here is the extent to which Land depicts the harsh realities of Berlin under the Anti-Socialist Law. Although Land does not give explicit dates, his portrayal of intensified police action suggests the early part of

1886, when the Prussian Minister of the Interior, Robert von Puttkamer, issued a spate of repressive decrees. Discussions over tactics for a Reichstag campaign correspond to events surrounding the election of 1887. Franz Mehring later characterized this period as the "death throes of the Anti-Socialist Law"; Land's novel exhibits clear signs of governmental desperation.[46] For the novel's characters, however, the end of persecution is not apparent amid police spying, censorship, arrests, expulsions from Berlin, and dissolved meetings. Despite these pressures, the novel also depicts the emergence of a newly invigorated party.[47]

*Der neue Gott* consists of thirteen episodic chapters, intended, Land explains in the preface, to convey dramatic developments of the era. The opening chapter introduces the major characters and themes in an unusual setting. A despondent Count Friedrich von der Haiden, wandering from his family's house, sees a procession of people carrying an unwieldy assortment of luggage and tools; he follows it across the Spree and into the Hamburger (Lehrter) station. Land thus depicts the send-off of a group of workers expelled under the Anti-Socialist Law. As the train pulls out, those remaining hide their tears with a militant cheer for the departing heroes. Two figures on the platform attract von der Haiden's attention with their angry exchange about a government that forces loyal citizens to leave their homes. One of the critics, a worker named Franz Herning, proves to be deeply involved in the SPD; the other is a sympathetic physician named Jakoby. The Anti-Socialist Law, Jakoby explains, is a misguided attempt to stifle an idea rooted in the misery of the German masses. Instead, the law has created martyrs and thus strengthened the movement's appeal, as forthcoming elections will show. Herning produces a proclamation for a workers' meeting, and von der Haiden impulsively signs it, thereby breaking ties with his past. By delivering the proclamation to the printer, Herning also draws new battle lines; despite the repressive law, workers will take action to seize their future. The rest of the novel pursues the ramifications of this moment.

A major theme of the book is how the atmosphere of Berlin under the Anti-Socialist Law has been poisoned by conflict and suspicion, both between and within classes. Von der Haiden's signature on the proclamation, for instance, leads to a stormy break with his father and his resignation from the officer corps. For disseminating the proclamation, Franz Herning, despite long years of service, is fired from his factory job. "You are one of our best workers," the factory owner tells him, "but I intend to keep my shop free of agitators because I don't want my business to be disturbed by police surveillance."[48] Such surveillance is no empty threat, and the meeting announced by the proclamation becomes an instance of its omnipresence. Since the meeting is tied to scheduled elections, it is legally permissible, but as soon as the inexperienced count ascends the podium and alludes to the possibility of revolutionary violence, police disband the meeting. The network of police spying is shown to make organizing extremely difficult—not least because of the distrust it sows within the workers' groups.

Most of the activists in *Der neue Gott* come from the educated classes. Incensed by the injustices around them, such characters as Jakoby work to improve the situation of the oppressed and thus tend to become central in the struggle. Their centrality might suggest that Land, like so many of his fellow novelists, lacks confidence in the ability of the working class to fight its own battle. Jakoby, however, also demonstrates Land's sense of the limitations of middle-class leadership. His dedication to the poor exemplifies a humane commitment, and it is he who refers to "the new God" of the title, defining it not as socialism but as a "grand compassion."[49] But although some have taken Jakoby's dictum to be the complete message of the novel,[50] it is noteworthy that he plays a scant political role and disappears completely from the last quarter of the book. The end focuses instead on von der Haiden, the alienated aristocrat, and Herning, the activist worker.

Even the count, after tumultuous experiences, is removed from the stage, but not before he overcomes his aristocratic weaknesses. His first attempt to be accepted in a crowded workers' pub is clumsy as he forces himself to sip gingerly from the schnaps bottle being passed. Having accepted an assignment to teach history in a clandestine school for workers, he strives to expand his material beyond the traditional "battles, commanders, and kings" and seems to succeed.[51] When internal conflicts cause him to be dismissed from his post, however, he is devastated. Near starvation and desperately isolated, he reveals the school's location to a police spy. His betrayal quickly results in arrests and ends with his being beaten senseless by angry working-class youths. Von der Haiden thus awakens to the fact that he, the aristocratic man of honor, has been too weak to withstand the misery that is routine for his comrades.

He redeems himself with his last act. As he trudges along an ice-bound canal, a breathless worker being pursued by police stumbles and falls. Unable to go on, the man shoves a packet of documents at von der Haiden, who then runs to the canal, across which stand comrades who will take the papers to safety. His last self-image is ironic: "He had to think of the messiah, who walked on water."[52] Unlike the messiah, the count cannot walk even on ice but falls through and drowns. This plunge through the ice had an actual precedent: on a January night in 1887 three workers making their way home from a secret meeting broke through the frozen Spandauer Canal and drowned. Their heroes' funeral in Moabit elevated them to the status of fallen warriors in the struggle for social justice.[53] Land's use of the frozen canal memorialized the victims, at least in the minds of contemporaries, and also implied the transformation of von der Haiden to a worker in service to the workers' cause.

The real hero, however, is Franz Herning. The only prominent working-class character, he is depicted from his first appearance on the station platform as a dedicated missionary who studies Marx at night in order to gain understanding he can communicate to his comrades.[54] At the workers' meeting he organizes, he addresses the critical question of the party's participation in city elections. Despite the unfairness of the three-class Prussian voting system, he argues, workers must make themselves heard at the polls.⁵⁵ A gray-haired comrade in the audience, invoking the memory of Lassalle in heavy Berlin dialect, begs the workers to retain their pride by not taking part in processes rigged against them. The hoots that meet the old man's plea imply Herning's position is winning, but the police dissolve the meeting before Herning can bring the issue to a vote. This meeting bears parallels to an actual meeting held on 17 November 1887; just as several working-class leaders emerged there, so Herning emerges in *Der neue Gott* as a strong working-class voice in favor of parliamentary action.⁵⁶ Soon he becomes a Reichstag candidate, whose campaign fliers evince the new politics: "Vote for Herning! Let the people help themselves. Let their native-born sons speak for them, not false prophets descended from the upper regions to redeem their chewed-up honor down below."⁵⁷ On the last page a victorious Herning stands before cheering voters; the workers will indeed help themselves.

The fictional moment of Herning's victory proclaimed a new era of German politics: the constitution created by Bismarck would be turned against the political and social system it had been intended to foster. Although other novels would also dwell on the ascendancy of electoral politics, none portrayed as explicitly as *Der neue Gott* the triumph of a worker—and with him, the working class—in the *Kampf ums Dasein*.⁵⁸

Far more frequently novelists kept their focus on the travails of upper-class protagonists. A striking example of this tendency is Felix Hollaender's *Jesus und Judas* (1891), which critics have often paired with *Der neue Gott*.⁵⁹ In contrast to Land, however, Hollaender uses Berlin under the Anti-Socialist Law as a setting in which to depict the growing madness and ultimate suicide of his tormented middle-class hero. Carl Truck is a student of jurisprudence whose emotional sensibilities, poverty-stricken existence, and intense commitment to working to usher in a new age of humanity link him to artist-figures in other Berlin novels. Hollaender draws an explicit connection when one character asserts that "all these young literary revolutionaries . . ., these advocates of the future, are really nothing but political revolutionaries—people who find the doors to action barred and take up pen instead."⁶⁰ The story of Carl Truck shows how the society of Imperial Germany has barred the road of political activism and also how the obstructions drive a sensitive soul to madness.

Carl's political vision interweaves Christianity, socialism, and Hegelianism, but Christianity predominates in the form of messianic delusions. Although Carl's socialism comes from his association with social democrats in Leipzig, it is grounded in his belief that the first true social democrat was Jesus and that the real social democratic program is to be found in the New Testament. The Hegelianism, a result of university studies, injects into Carl's philosophy a world soul as the force that will unite and liberate humanity.⁶¹ His real education, however, comes from two experiences of betrayal. The first is precipitated when his father, a staid Saxon bureaucrat, learning that his son's studies have been but a cover for outlawed socialist activity, breaks all ties. Carl worries that he has been a Judas to his family but then makes his father the betrayer by envisioning him as Peter, "three times denying [Jesus]."[62] The second betrayal, however, is worse: Carl is expelled from the party when he is accused of being an informant and the accuser is mysteriously murdered.[63] Unjustly or not, Carl's mentor in the party writes, the party cannot afford the internal controversy of trying to deal with wrongs against individual members.[64]

Each stage of Carl's isolation is accompanied by signs of progressive madness; some episodes attribute this to the pressures of persecution, while others suggest it derives from the awfulness of Carl's prophetic vision. Whatever its cause, an episode between Carl and a doctor friend in a sedate restaurant reveals the deterioration. Carl, expounding loudly on the World Soul, suddenly feels the doctor is observing him as a clinician and reacts by physically attacking him. As he is taken from the restaurant, he realizes "that the mental illness that had long been developing had burst forth."[65] He is saved from being committed when he manages to convince the examining physician that philosophizing about the World Soul has impeccable cultural precedents. Subsequent outbursts and new stream-of-consciousness ravings, however, denote the breakdown of a man exerting himself to comprehend the complexities of the modern age.[66]

Carl briefly thinks about giving up politics, for he knows the emotional toll of underground activity. Just before the outburst in the restaurant, his friend had joked about the comforts of an apolitical existence, saying in Berlin idiom, "I've copped out."[67] Carl rejected the idea of political withdrawal then, but now he ponders the luxury of being able to walk the streets of Berlin in "thoughtless well-being, secure from the police."[68] Even after his expulsion from the party, however, he cannot bring himself to abandon his opposition to the existing order. Still hoping to disseminate his ideas—and wanting also to support his now-pregnant mistress—he decides to write a series of essays entitled *Ideas for the Future*. Working with new intensity, Carl completes the first, which receives wide discussion in Berlin papers. A book dealer gives him an advance for the next, predicting its title alone will ensure its success: *Socialism and Anarchism: Second Essay of Ideas for the Future. Written by a Man in Despair.*[69] Carl's exuberance over the sale of his manuscript is short-lived, however, for on his return, an angry book dealer tells him the work has been confiscated under the provisions of the Anti-Socialist Law. The dealer has lost his investment and wants nothing more to do with the new gospel: "We aren't ready for your ideas yet."[70]

Carl is besieged by a crescendo of revelations. Imprisoned for a speech and tortured for refusing to cooperate with a police search, he vows to become the preacher of a new gospel, recalling that "the times now were the same as those centuries earlier, when great preachers moved from place to place, calling people to adhere to the new faith."[71] Once released he roams Berlin in new delirium and spots a crowd of frantic people swarming around two figures. Thinking they are handing out bread, Carl draws closer, only to see they are distributing some sort of paper. A crazed ecstasy grows: "Here at last are tidings from the messiah—and whoever read and understood them would triumph over his suffering."[72] With his last groschen he buys a copy only to find it is a newspaper—and the salvation sought by the pathetic crowd is in the want ads. Carl spends the rest of the day trudging from one place to the next: "And those are the tidings from the messiah: to beg, whine, and plead for work—but to find none."[73] New revelations assail him: "Anarchism and socialism were mere words. The final wisdom was nihilism in the most literal, boldest sense."[74] Carl's nihilism takes the form of a Judas deed: he sells his knowledge of the SPD organization to the police. Remorseful, he tries in vain to return the pieces of silver as his head swirls with biblical images: "And he, he was Jesus, Jesus with the soul of Judas."[75] Unlike his biblical prototype, Carl does not hang himself but takes the conventional Berlin mode of suicide by throwing himself into the Spree.

Hollaender gave ample evidence that Carl's madness exemplified the effects of police persecution on the mentality of the populace, but he also raised the possibility that Carl was a genuine prophet. For instance, a friend gauges Carl's mental state with an allusion to Mohammed and Jesus, asking whether they too were not "so consumed by their ideas that they heard inner voices, whose commands they believed were directing their works."[76] Hollaender gave further credence to the profundity of Carl's ideas by allowing his essays to be perceived as revolutionary and dangerous to the status quo. The madness, then, stemmed perhaps from the enormity of his vision.[77]

The novel's conclusion gives little hope that the departure of Bismarck and the end of the Anti-Socialist Law will save German society. Moments before jumping into the Spree, Carl glances at the newstands, where papers proclaim William II's social decrees of 4 February 1890. The modest reforms seem to Carl testimony to the folly of his long struggle, for they come in spite of, rather than because of, socialist action. A comment among two bystanders, that the imminent resignation of Bismarck and the lapsing of the Anti-Socialist Law will help the stock market, strengthens his determination to end his life. The society based on manipulation and betrayal still survives. Carl's friends vow to continue his work, but it is an impulsive vow, deriving from their grief. They are left with little to build on other than ideas for which the world is not ready. Far more persuasive in this novel is the implicit case for social withdrawal. And far more ominous is the vision of urban madness.

# Notes

1. Karl Gutzkow, *Die Ritter vom Geiste*, 6th ed. (Berlin, 1878), I, xv.
2. *Die neuen Serapionsbrüder*, I, 81, 132, 182.
3. Ibid., I, 125; III, 231.
4. Ibid., I, 146. On the ideas and role of Lassalle see Vernon Lidtke, *The Outlawed Party: Social Democracy in Germany, 1878–1890* (Princeton, 1966), 18–27.
5. *Die neuen Serapionsbrüder*, III, 216–219.
6. Richard Hamann and Jost Hermand, *Naturalismus* (Munich, 1972), 145. See also

Martin Halter, *Sklaven der Arbeit—Ritter vom Geiste: Arbeit und Arbeiter im deutschen Sozialroman zwischen 1840 und 1880* (Frankfurt am Main, 1983).
7. Wilhelm Raabe, *Im alten Eisen*, *Sämtliche Werke*, 3rd Series, Vol. III (Berlin, n.d.), 114–118. See also Manuel J. K. Muranga, *Großstadtelend in der deutschen Lyrik zwischen Arno Holz und Johannes R. Becher* (Frankfurt am Main, 1987), 23–52.
8. Raabe, *Im alten Eisen*, 4. See also Fritz Martini, *Deutsche Literatur im bürgerlichen Realismus, 1848–1898*, 4th ed. (Stuttgart, 1981), 715.
9. Friedrich Spielhagen, *Was will das werden?*, in *Sämtliche Romane*, Vol. XXII (Leipzig, 1895), 64, 69.
10. Adalbert von Hanstein, *Das jüngste Deutschland: Zwei Jahrzehnte miterlebter Literaturgeschichte*, 3rd ed. (Leipzig, 1905), 41. See also Carl Bleibtreu, *Revolution der Literatur* (1885; reprinted Tübingen, 1973), 36; Julius Erich Kloss, *Max Kretzer: Eine Studie zur neueren Literatur*, 2nd ed. (Leipzig, 1905), 25; Adalbert von Hanstein, *Die Sozialfrage in der Poesie* (Leipzig, 1897), 35; and Max Kretzer, "Meine Stellung zum Naturalismus," in Günther Keil, *Max Kretzer: A Study in German Naturalism* (1928; reprinted New York, 1966), 105.
11. Max Kretzer, *Die Verkommenen: Berliner Sitten-Roman*, 4th ed. (Leipzig, 1908), vii.
12. Keil, *Kretzer*, 107.
13. Annemarie Lange, *Berlin zur Zeit Bebels und Bismarcks: Zwischen Reichsgründung und Jahrhundertwende* (Berlin, 1972), 703.
14. Kretzer, *Die Verkommenen*, 247; for references to effects of economic exploitation see also 38, 100, 120, 197, 246, 406.
15. Ibid., 2. The circumstances most closely match the winter of 1876–1877. See Lange, *Berlin zur Zeit Bebels*, 293–295; 309.
16. Kretzer, *Die Verkommenen*, 102. See also Lange, *Berlin zur Zeit Bebels*, 304–305.
17. Kretzer, *Die Verkommenen*, 7.
18. Ibid., 37–38. Due to policies that led to these enormous buildings, by 1920 Berlin had a density of people per building almost 50 percent higher than any other European or American city. Werner Hegemann, *Das steinere Berlin: Geschichte der größten Mietskasernenstadt der Welt* (1930; reprinted Braunschweig, 1976), 333 and 207–220. See also Richard Dietrich, "Von der Residenzstadt zur Weltstadt: Berlin vom Anfang des 19. Jahrhunderts bis zur Reichsgründung," in *Das Hauptstadtproblem in der Geschichte, Jahrbuch für Geschichte des deutschen Ostens*, 1 (1952), 119.
19. Kretzer, *Die Verkommenen*, 38.
20. Ibid., 2; see also 65.
21. Ibid., 139–140.
22. Ibid., 238.
23. Ibid., 128, 170.
24. Ibid., 237.
25. Ibid., 275.
26. Ibid., 289–290. "Flawed victims are the most subjugated of all victims of society, because injustice damages their character as well as body," writes George Goodin in his *Poetics of Protest: Literary Form and Political Implication in the Victim-of-Society Novel* (Carbondale, Ill., 1985), 90.
27. Kretzer, *Die Verkommenen*, 440.
28. Naturalist writers in general have been plausibly described as naive in their belief that the Bismarckian state would respond to such needs as were described by Kretzer. Günther, *Literarische Gruppenbildung*, 36.
29. Kretzer, *Die Verkommenen*, 120–121.
30. Ibid., 325; see also 198.
31. Max Kretzer, *Im Sturmwind der Sozialismus: Erzählung aus großer Zeit* (Berlin, 1883), 152.

32. Ibid., 167.
33. Max Kretzer, *Meister Timpe* (Berlin, 1927), 24.
34. Ibid., 59.
35. On the *Stammtisch* discussions see, for instance, ibid., 101–109. Although critical of Kretzer's sentimentalizing the role of the artisan, Hamann and Hermand point to *Meister Timpe* as the decisive point when Kretzer's economic understanding came to maturity. Richard Hamann and Jost Hermand, *Naturalismus* (Munich, 1972), 225.
36. Kretzer, *Meister Timpe*, 149.
37. Ibid., 192; see also 124, 150, and 207.
38. Ibid., 346.
39. For an English translation of the text of the Anti-Socialist Law and an account of its passage see Lidtke, *Outlawed Party*, 339–345 and 71–78.
40. Adalbert von Hanstein, *Das jüngste Deutschland: Zwei Jahrzehnte miterlebter Literaturgeschichte* (3rd printing, Leipzig, 1905), 50–81.
41. See Vernon Lidtke, "Naturalism and Socialism in Germany," *American Historical Review*, 79, 1 (February 1974), 14–37; Helmut Scheuer, "Zwischen Sozialismus und Individualismus—Zwischen Marx und Nietzsche," in Helmut Scheuer, ed., *Naturalismus: Bürgerliche Dichtung und soziales Engagement* (Stuttgart, 1974), 150–174; Dietger Pforte, "Die deutsche Sozialdemokratie und die Naturalisten: Aufriß eines fruchtbaren Mißverständnisses," in Scheuer, *Naturalismus*, 175–205; and Josef Polácek, "Zum Thema der bürgerlich-individualistischen Revolte in der deutschen pseudosozialen Prosa: Hans Land, Felix Hollaender, John Henry Mackay," *Philologica Pragensia*, 7, 1 (1964), 1–14.
42. Hans R. Fischer, *Unter den Armen und Elenden* (Berlin, 1887); *Was Berlin verschlingt* (Berlin, 1890); *Berliner Zigeunerleben: Bilder aus der Welt der Schriftsteller, Künstler und des Proletariats* (Berlin, 1890).
43. Fischer, *Was Berlin verschlingt*, 1–2. Fischer's works received a good deal of attention among "serious circles," wrote Hanstein in *Das jüngste Deutschland*, 259.
44. Fischer, *Berliner Zigeunerleben*, 1–36. See the similar account in Eduard Bernstein, *Die Geschichte der Berliner Arbeiter-Bewegung*, Vol. II: *Die Geschichte des Sozialistengesetzes in Berlin* (Berlin, 1907), 187–188. Bernstein notes that after Bebel's attempt to speak, Robert von Puttkamer, Prussian Minister of the Interior, issued a ban on his speaking anywhere in Berlin outside the Reichstag.
45. Hofstetten is known chiefly for his lengthy conflict in the late 1860s with Lassalle's successor to leadership, Johann Baptist von Schweitzer. On his role in the movement see Bernstein, *Die Geschichte der Berliner Arbeiter-Bewegung*, Vol. I: *Vom Jahre 1848 bis zum Erlaß des Sozialistengesetzes*, 129, 170, and 192, and Franz Mehring, *Die Geschichte der Sozialdemokratie*, Vol. II (Berlin, 1960), 741.
46. Mehring, *Die Geschichte der Sozialdemokratie*, II, 631.
47. Fifteen years later Bernstein characterized this as a time of pervasive police spying and the simultaneous rise of the party. Bernstein, *Die Geschichte der Berliner Arbeiter-Bewegung*, II, 110. See also Lidtke, *Outlawed Party*, 241–248, and Dieter Fricke, *Bismarcks Prätorianer: Die Berliner politische Polizei im Kampf gegen die deutsche Arbeiterbewegung (1871–1898)* (Berlin, 1962), 179–256.
48. Hans Land, *Der neue Gott*, 2nd ed. (Berlin, 1892), 87.
49. Ibid., 191.
50. Hamann and Hermand, *Naturalismus*, 217.
51. Land, *Der neue Gott*, 73.
52. Ibid., 244.
53. Bernstein, *Die Geschichte der Berliner Arbeiter-Bewegung*, II, 213–216. See also Mehring, *Die Geschichte der Sozialdemokratie*, II, 641.
54. Land, *Der neue Gott*, 36.

55. Ibid., 93–96. The Prussian constitution categorized voters according to the taxes they paid, and weighted their votes accordingly; the numerically superior workers in Berlin were thus outweighed by the propertied classes. On the intense debate over the question of workers' participation see Lidtke, *Outlawed Party*, especially chapters 7 through 10.
56. Ironically, it was not the Lassalleans, represented by the old Berliner in Land's scene, but young radicals, the so-called *Jungen*, who would split the party in 1890 by arguing against parliamentary participation. Lidtke, *Outlawed Party*, 269. See also Bernstein, *Die Geschichte der Berliner Arbeiter-Bewegung*, II, 234–235.
57. Land, *Der neue Gott*, 242.
58. *Der neue Gott* sparked controversy among socialists when some critics argued that Land was uninformed about the realities of working-class life and activism. See, for example, Franz Mehring, "Kunst und Proletariat" (21 October 1896), in *Aufsätze zur deutschen Literatur von Hebbel bis Schweichel, Gesammelte Schriften*, Vol. XI (Berlin, 1976), 132, and Lidtke, "Naturalism and Socialism," 32–35. For a recent study of working-class society see Vernon Lidtke, *The Alternative Culture: Socialist Labor in Imperial Germany* (New York, 1985).
59. See Hanstein, *Das jüngste Deutschland*, 241; Hamann and Hermand, *Naturalismus*, 217–218; and Polácek, "Zum Thema der bürgerlich-individualistischen Revolte." Biographical information for Hollaender (1867–1931) is scant. As a student in Berlin, he gravitated to the Friedrichshagen circle of the Hart brothers, where he was exposed to socialist-anarchist ideas and literary controversies that pervaded the atmosphere. See Franz Brümmer, *Lexikon der deutschen Dichter und Prosaisten vom Beginn des 19. Jahrhunderts bis zur Gegenwart*, 6th ed. (Leipzig, 1913), III, 271; Katharina Günther, *Literarische Gruppenbildung im Berliner Naturalismus* (Bonn, 1972), 123–129; and Heinrich Hart, *Literarische Erinnerungen, Gesammelte Werke*, III (Berlin, 1907), 7.
60. Felix Hollaender, *Jesus und Judas: Ein moderner Roman* (Berlin, 1895), 205–206.
61. Ibid., 11, 48–49, 97–104. See also Theodore Ziolkowski, *Fictional Transfigurations of Jesus* (Princeton, N.J., 1972), 55–97, and Richard Hamann and Jost Hermand, *Naturalismus* (Munich, 1972), 218–219.
62. Hollaender, *Jesus und Judas*, 55, 58, 282.
63. The accuser, a villainous figure with shadowy origins in Russian anarchist movements, is part of an intricate subplot involving police spying among Russian exiles. His murderer is actually the brother of one of the Russians he had betrayed and thereby condemned to death. Ibid., 164–169, 173–176, 241–243.
64. Ibid., 287–290.
65. Ibid., 105.
66. Polácek, "Zum Thema der bürgerlich-individualistischen Revolte," 6–10.
67. Hollaender, *Jesus und Judas*, 95.
68. Ibid., 117.
69. Ibid., 318.
70. Ibid., 334.
71. Ibid., 247.
72. Ibid., 346.
73. Ibid., 347.
74. Ibid., 351.
75. Ibid., 357–358.
76. Ibid., 221.
77. On the theme of "Genie und Irrsinn" as a literary convention see Lotte Rausch, *Die Gestalt des Künstlers in der Dichtung des Naturalismus* (Dissertation, Gießen, 1931), 20, and Jochen Schmidt, *Die Geschichte des Genie-Gedankens in der deutschen Literatur, Philosophie und Politik, 1750–1945*, Vol. II (Darmstadt, 1985), 252–257.

# 7

# Dis-ease in the Metropolis

Berlin novelists of the 1890s depicted a society beset by spiritual crisis. Although greed and ruthlessness continued to form a major focus of the social criticism of some, other writers became intrigued by what they saw as an age of intense anxieties. The self-confident "children of the world" portrayed by Paul Heyse in the 1870s were thus succeeded by characters who questioned whether they could survive in a world based on purely secular or scientific values. Two words by which novelists frequently alluded to this crisis were restlessness (*Unruhe*) and sickness (*Krankheit*). The terms referred, first, to an acute sense of unease with modern society and, second, to the likelihood that the disquieting situation betokened a sickness in the human soul. The English word "disease," with its dual connotations of uneasiness and of illness, is thus an apt designation for an elusive urban condition novelists were seeking to diagnose.

Although related, however, portrayals of spiritual unease and of psychological illness in novels of the '90s evoked differing strands of German cultural heritage and resulted in differing notions of the unfinished revolution. Novelists defining the crisis in terms of unease tended to echo the call for moral renewal of the whole society, thus placing themselves in the line of writers sounding the call to social engagement. Those who depicted it in terms of illness allowed the extreme individualism of their characters to end in complete social alienation—and cultural despair. By the end of the century, novels of the second sort were proliferating. Their portrayals of madness and despair meant a dramatic diminution of the calls for national regeneration that had heretofore typified novels of Imperial Berlin.

The backdrop to this development was a city that appeared in the 1890s to have established itself as the quintessence of an exuberant nation. The onset of William II's reign and Bismarck's resignation seemed to sound the retreat of an old order. The end of the Anti-Socialist Law brought a resurgence of working-class activism, in which Berlin became the center of a burgeoning SPD. Moreover, astonishing technological advances and industrial expansion continued to transform the city into the undisputed commercial center of Germany—and even of Europe. Visible evidence of change abounded in traffic-clogged streets, an array of new hotels, and popular stand-up eating establishments, like the Aschinger chain, designed to meet the needs of harried urban dwellers.[1] Waves of new immigrants besieged the city as factories and hastily constructed Mietskasernen broke through the ring of villages that formerly comprised its outskirts. Triumphs of scientific research in the university, moreover, caused many to proclaim Berlin the leader of modern civilization's struggle to eradicate ignorance and misery. Finally, two decades of intense artistic and literary activity had confirmed Berlin as the cultural capital of Germany as well.

To many observers all this energy and activity presaged a new level of human evolution. In novels of the '90s, then, moods of despair could alternate with moods of optimism, reflecting the belief that, despite its impersonal and oppressive forces, the city would be the arena where a new humanity would find and proclaim its freedom.

To imagine how such freedom might look in an intensely irreligious age, however, posed enormous problems. Max Kretzer undertook the challenge in two Berlin novels that tried to envision a Christianity that spoke to modern ideas: *Die Bergpredigt*, (*The Sermon on the Mount*) (1890) and *Das Gesicht Christi* (*The Face of Christ*) (1896). Both asked how Christian beliefs could be renewed in a city whose prosperous inhabitants saw their condition as a sign of divine grace and whose poor were so oppressed by want that they had grown deaf to the Christian message of hope. Although both novels concern the social mission of Christianity, they have different premises. *Die Bergpredigt*, focusing on the institutional church, uses a deeply concerned Protestant pastor to advocate that organized religion must become infused with the social teachings of Jesus. The novel concludes with his suspension from his clerical post, which signifies the loss of an influence that might revivify an ineffective, complacent religious establishment. *Das Gesicht Christi* turns away from the church with a startling challenge to modern sensibilities: numerous appearances of Christ in modern Berlin. This "deus ex machina," as a recent critic called the Christ-figure, seems a sharp departure from Kretzer's usual realism, but his recourse to the device attests to the urgency driving him to fill the spiritual vacuum he saw.[2] And it attests to the difficulty of recasting traditional belief in modern terms.

Berlin society is characterized in *Die Bergpredigt* by an episode at the crowded Spittelmarkt, the heart of Berlin's commerce. People scurrying about like ants ignore an old woman trying to load a heavy sack on her back. When the protagonist, Konrad Baldus, stoops to help her, he nearly halts traffic: "Many a passerby stopped and gaped at Konrad, the woman, and her sack with that intense curiosity Berliners always show when they meet something in their path that's worth looking at." The sight of a gentleman becoming involved with the work of someone so clearly beneath his station causes one observer to comment, "Maybe it's an Englishman." Konrad, very much a German, draws a different conclusion: "The simplest human obligation, the first commandment of loving one's neighbor that Christ charged his followers to fulfill with the toilers and the oppressed, seemed to these people to be something remarkable."[3] The children of modernity, he reflects further, having outgrown belief in miracles and become deaf to promises of heavenly salvation, have also abandoned the tenets of Jesus' ministry. Konrad vows to use his new post as pastor to awaken his urban flock to the goal of Christian living: "the completely selfless deed."[4]

His task is immeasurably complicated by his own church. In insisting on the centrality of works, he seems to his critics to be subverting the Protestant doctrine of justification by faith alone. Kretzer alludes to this issue when he has the most influential cleric in Berlin, the court chaplain, dismiss Konrad's call for the selfless deed. "It's not the first time," Chaplain Bock says, "that someone has read something into the gospel that was never there. The church has endured up till now and will continue to endure without allowing her foundations to be shaken."[5] The religious establishment in Berlin clearly has no place for a theological "provocateur."

More than theological difficulties separate Konrad from churchmen who are unconcerned about genuine ministry. Konrad's older brother is a pastor whose obsession with his own security and perceptions of a church under siege typify clergymen in both Kretzer novels. Beholden to Berlin's religious leaders for his comfortable material and spiritual existence, Julius Baldus performs his duties conscientiously while devoting time and resources to his book and art collections and to an affair with his housekeeper. He advises Konrad to follow his example: "You didn't come to Berlin to turn the world upside down or to lead a battle against the church but rather to struggle on its behalf."[6] For him, the only compelling social concern is the irreligiosity of modern society. The misery of the working class, he argues, lies beyond clerical purview; it stems from moral weaknesses that church attendance would cure.

Kretzer depicts an equally reprehensible clerical type in the court chaplain. Introduced as the creator of a program to "solve the worker question," Bock is modelled after Adolf Stoecker.[7] Like his prototype, this chaplain hopes to lure the working class to a Christian socialist party by using anti-Semitism as an appeal. Kretzer, however, gives Bock none of the social compassion associated with Stoecker but describes him as one whose features bespoke something "repulsive and cruel."[8] The novel, moreover, uses him to personify an unholy alliance between church and state. The church's penchant for sanctifying the regime, as Konrad sees it, only spreads incongruities between Christ's teachings and current dogma: "The state, public life, and all society become infected."[9]

Konrad illustrates his point with a provocative idea. When Christ directed his followers to abolish the chasm between earthly and divine law, he argues, He did not intend them to forsake divine law. Equality of all people before God is fundamental, and until the state makes this law its own, it will stand in opposition to Christ's will. The modern-day church, Konrad urges, far from working to effect equality, uses its privileged position to widen social distinctions. This idea of translating spiritual into social equality amounts to a revolutionary goal, but, the mention of the state notwithstanding, equality here seems a humane ideal rather than a concrete political aim. Konrad does not mention the issue again, and a moment of potential political engagement passes.

The novel is unremitting, however, in attacking a church that caters to the privileged and ignores the teachings of Christ. The climactic episode brings these two strands together in Konrad's first sermon, which will decide whether he will be confirmed in his appointment. The description of people filing into the "Marthakirche" (whose Dance of Death frescoes identify it as the Gothic Marienkirche that still stands) emphasizes the predominance of social elites: clerics, theologians, deacons, government emissaries, delegates from the synods, merchants, and other prominent citizens. Ordinary parishioners seem of little consequence amid the panoplied officialdom. Konrad's sermon infuriates the theological dignitaries with its apparent dismissal of Christ's divinity. Christianity, he instructs the congregation, is not "a belief in the supernatural origins of the man of justice who strode as a living being across the earth and bled there."[10] Christ's ministrations to the poor, he continues, show him to be the son of God in the same sense that all who nurture these virtues and fulfill these teachings are like God. "It's scandalous to use the church for such a performance," rants the court chaplain afterward, while his sycophantic assistant gives a more telling explanation: "Well, that's modern youth for you."[11] The consistory soon notifies Konrad it has rejected his appointment. The clear message is that the real Christian has been driven from the church by the moneychangers.

Konrad tells his brother he will be a Christian outside the church. Julius mutters that that probably means he will become a socialist, but Konrad rejects that surmise, saying, "Christianity and socialism are two different things for me, even if they might lead to the same goal. Socialism seeks external happiness, and Christianity seeks it inside. Socialism makes demands on others; Christianity makes them upon itself."[12] It would be nice, he adds, if the two movements could meet each other halfway, but as with his earlier mention of the ideal of equality, he drops this musing. Instead, Kretzer reverts to a familiar theme: Konrad will carry on the struggle of transforming modern humanity by becoming a writer. While passing his former church, Konrad is struck, as always, by the beauty of its pealing bells. He is also struck, however, by an electric streetlight that illuminates the ancient brickwork: "It was as if it wanted to penetrate the innermost limits of this powerful wall to proclaim the ceaseless progress of the times."[13] As Konrad's carriage moves on, the church bells are drowned out by city noise.

*Die Bergpredigt* depicts the institutional church as a prominent source of modern crisis. The paradox of a religious institution betraying its mission is, of course, deeply embedded in Judeo-Christian tradition. The example of a rigid religious establishment parallels other fictional portrayals of oppressive academic and cultural establishments. What is unusual is the attempt to define the regeneration of German society in Christian terms. That Kretzer ran roughshod over doctrines of Christ's divinity in the process is less surprising than the fact that he focused on religion at all. Only two decades earlier Paul Heyse had his "children of the world" turn away from religion. In this novel "true Christianity" inspires a vision of the unfinished revolution.

In *Das Gesicht Christi* Kretzer, again asking how Christianity can transform modern lives, calls on people to affirm an uncompromising faith in a living Christ. Although he intended this to be a two-part novel, the first volume, which portrays the power of faith in the lives of the poor, is all that resulted. The second volume, dealing with the wealthy, was to show that among Berlin's upper classes obsession with externals had overwhelmed the teachings of Jesus.[14] The intended volume was essential to Kretzer's original purpose of developing the message that true Christianity was not a message of social complacency or acceptance of the status quo.

Standing alone, Part I subordinates any call to social engagement to its portrayal of Christ as witness to human suffering. Christ's appearances have nothing to do with the Second Coming, for, the narrator emphasizes, this is to be neither the age of last judgment nor a time of new miracles. Rather, the novel explains the sequence of appearances through Jesus' promise to be with those in spiritual and material need.[15]

Kretzer exemplifies that promise by tracing the suffering of a working-class family. Outwardly, the Andorfs resemble the Merks of *Die Verkommenen*, for the father is unemployed and the family is on the brink of starvation. The Andorfs differ, however, in the spiritual awakening that begins with the recognition of Jesus by two of the children as they walk through Berlin streets with their father. Suddenly they greet a figure with astonishment: "Master Jesus!" The vision, the narrator explains, is visible only to those "who place the hunger of the soul above that of the body in this world of dying faith."[16] A major theme links such spiritual hunger to a childlike ability to see the incomprehensible—an ability that, although usually lost in adults, can be reawakened.

Andorf, too, begins to see the Christ-figure. He first sees Him wearing a crown of thorns and peering sorrowfully through a pub window, where a chance encounter has brought him and his children a much-needed meal. Although he is awed by the sight, most of the revelers around him respond with laughter and sarcasm. When Andorf's infant dies in the wretched family quarters that night, Christ again appears silently as Andorf sits by the tiny corpse. And when he goes to the commissioner for the poor to plead for burial funds, Christ is there, too, watching as the bureaucrat evades the request. At a gathering of social democrats, He also appears as they try to induct Andorf into their cause.[17]

The most momentous appearance, however, comes as Andorf pulls a cart with his child's coffin through Berlin streets and amazed passersby see Christ following the humble procession. Some guess the figure is Brother Miericke, a tailor who stunned Berliners in the 1870s with his messianic claims. Others laugh, thinking it to be a madman. Others look for a policeman: "'Crucify him!' was out of date; fashion had now changed it into a call for the police."[18] But hundreds join the procession: "The unconscious longing for a pure, untroubled hour in life, that since the day of the crucifixion had germinated in the human breast, now burst forth powerfully."[19] At the gates of the cemetery Andorf is bewildered by the crowd that follows him, and then, when he sees Christ, he is besieged by turbulent emotions. A bystander explains the meaning of Christ's presence: "He lives for all true Christians and accompanies them along their way." Indeed, this is the hope Andorf draws from the experience: "As sure as I'm a poor man, I now believe."[20]

Through Andorf's conversion, Christ's compassion with human suffering is shown to offer a genuine hope for the transformation of the individual—and of modern society.[21] Christ's miraculous appearances in an age that discounted miracles were Kretzer's portrayals of the miracle that would occur if people perceived His presence in their daily lives.[22] The appearances of Christ give the Andorfs strength to refuse help from tainted sources. Besides rejecting a grudging offer from social democrats, Andorf also declines desperately needed money from a good-hearted prostitute. His eldest daughter, fleeing a terrible scene in which a lascivious employer dies suddenly in a frenzied act of seduction, similarly forces herself to leave his two gold pieces on the table. The newly awakened faith prevails, and the family's crisis is finally alleviated by a new job for Andorf.

This novel has been criticized as sentimental consolation literature, in which Kretzer, by preaching quiet acceptance of suffering, put his popularity in the service of those he supposedly was attacking.[23] Kretzer would have been anguished by this judgment, for he saw himself calling for a new humanity grounded in the radical demands of Christ's teachings. The knowledge of Christ's compassion and suffering was to become the foundation for bearing one's own suffering and for helping others lessen theirs. Working for social change within one's capacity was an imperative. This was less a message to Germans than to humanity and less a call to national regeneration than to spiritual awakening. Nevertheless, the Berlin setting put this call in German terms, and the ideal of a spiritual revolution placed the novel in the tradition of Berlin novels begun by Gutzkow. In the dozen years following its publication, *Das Gesicht Christi* underwent five printings—more than any other Kretzer novel in so short a time. It also aroused lengthy discussions both in the secular and the religious press.[24] In providing a challenging statement about spiritual commitment in the modern age the novel was a milestone in fictional confrontations with modernity.[25]

Predictably, however, the advocacy of Christian ideals was far from a universal answer for the spiritual quests of the 1890s. Secularization had gone too far for most writers to return to religion, but dis-ease with modern society induced some to look elsewhere. Wilhelm Bölsche's novel, *Die Mittagsgöttin* (*The Mid-day Goddess*) (1891), which examines spiritualism, is the most methodical instance of a fictional quest for a spiritual alternative to religion. Given Bölsche's long advocacy of scientific method, the novel's vindication of natural science might seem foreordained. Nonetheless, its focus on the occult, and Bölsche's own lengthy investigation of spiritualist claims, testified to a restlessness among Berlin modernists over what they saw as the primacy of scientific reality.[26]

Die Mittagsgöttin centers on the identity crisis of its narrator, a scientist-turned-writer named Wilhelm. The protagonist's name is but one of many parallels between him and the author: they were the same age, had the same educational background, shared the same intellectual interests, and lived in an uneasy relationship with Berlin.[27] The crisis of the fictional Wilhelm was surely also familiar to Bölsche, beginning as it did with his thirtieth birthday and the question, "What now?" Wilhelm remarks, while reviewing his twenties, on "how many false starts and zigzag paths; how many overthrown gods and goddesses; how many sphinx riddles that no one solves; how much carnival—and how many Ash Wednesday marks on my mind and heart."[28] His struggles, he decides, are those of his generation, whose members now sit in their various temples awaiting the call of the final bell: "ascetics in intoxication, in fantasies, in deception, in intellectual confusion; ascetics in the midst of the world's turmoil; in conventional tail-coats; in the plain gown of the academic; among the poverty-stricken."[29] Wilhelm wonders where his temple is and what bell will call him.

The call comes in the form of a birthday adventure organized by his best friend: they will attend a seance and unmask the fakery. The seance collapses as planned, but Wilhelm leaves the scene with a count, who urges him not to allow the tricks they have witnessed to obscure the existence of genuine supernatural phenomena. As they stroll along Leipzigerstraße, Wilhelm is conscious of the profusion of electric lights, a symbol, he reflects, of the "brightly shining, intellectually powerful nineteenth century."[30] Just as the count reveals he is a spiritualist, the street lights are extinguished, as they always are at midnight.

The midnight in Wilhelm's soul is reached some days later with a powerful vision of his best friend, in a distant town, mortally wounded from a duel. When his premonition is confirmed by a telegram, Wilhelm is convinced he has received knowledge through immaterial means, an experience that precipitates what he calls his "scientific bankruptcy."[31] Wilhelm finds his crisis mirrored in Berlin, whose familiar landmarks incite turbulent emotions. Like other characters in other novels, he is inspired by Brandenburger Tor and by the victory column nearby, but he now decides these monuments have been superseded by a new one: the Friedrichstraße station, a shrine to frenzied human activity. "Looming over the nearby roofs like the armored scales of an enormous lurking reptile," it might, he muses, satisfy the longings of "a forthcoming, transformed generation" better than the magnificent Greek columns of the triumphal gate.[32] His own revulsion toward the technological world provokes a deepening crisis that overcomes him when he utters Jesus' cry of despair: "My God, why hast thou forsaken me?" Like Konrad in Die Bergpredigt, he hears church bells being drowned out by city noise but knows he will find no consolation in religion.[33]

Count Otto von Land had offered an alternative on the night of the failed seance with an account of his own search for answers. He had become disgusted by his anachronistic title, the count told Wilhelm, and fallen into hedonism. Paradoxically, an encounter with disreputable women led to his first commitment by causing him to look beyond the "moral abyss" to the economic realities of their realm. This awakening provoked intensive economic studies and feverish commitment to the "sacred mission of the worker." Like early Christians, however, he began to realize that the age of fulfillment was not at hand and that it would be generations before socialism was achieved. Meanwhile, science had ripped away the veil of religion to reveal a cosmos offering no hope to those who suffered in "the terrible confusion of this earthly misery."[34] The count deduced that the durability of Christianity had to do with the belief that Jesus had conquered death. If new proof verified that life continued after death, then despite defeats in individual lives and delays of the revolution, modern humanity would have its answer. Seeking such proof, the count immersed himself in new studies of phenomena like dreaming and hypnosis. The key, however, came from a remarkable woman named Miss Lilly Jackson, whose carefully documented psychic powers had given him, he told Wilhelm, conclusive proof of life after death.

At the end of his monologue the count had begged the skeptical Wilhelm to suspend judgment long enough to visit his estate in the swamps of the Spreewald to witness the phenomena Miss Lilly revealed. This invitation established the dichotomy between science and spiritualism in geographic terms, with Berlin signifying the cold reality of modern rationalism and the tangled swamps of the Spreewald fostering the mysteries of the supernatural. After the turmoil of the intervening days, Wilhelm decides to leave Berlin to stay with the count, thereby launching his own search for a new answer to the despair he believes the modern age has engendered.

The goddess of the title resides in the Spreewald, and the count relates her legend upon Wilhelm's arrival. The palpable "mid-day enchantment," the count explains, is a sign of the presence of Psychipolniza, the goddess of the mid-day silence. A white figure who approaches a farmer taking a respite from his work, she questions him about why he works so hard and, if he cannot provide a suitable answer, strangles him. Rationalists might attribute such deaths to heatstroke, but the local Wendish peasants think differently. Although uncertain as to his own belief, the count adds, the allegory of Psychipolniza might well apply to the noon-time of civilization. Modern humanity has scant answer to give a questioning deity, but those who find one have nothing to fear from the mysterious spirit.[35]

As he settles into the quiet routine at the estate, Wilhelm believes he too has found the answer to Psychipolniza's question. The count and three other gentlemen have set up a social and scholarly regimen that includes extensive reading in the count's large library, interspersed with seances at which the resident Miss Lilly communicates with spirits of deceased persons, and followed by critical discussion and written accounts documenting the conclusions the group has reached. This enclave, Wilhelm soon learns, is but one island of a worldwide network of spiritualists who exchange written correspondence to further their belief that the human spirit will soon be understood with the same certainty by which mathematical problems are now solved.[36] But Wilhelm's newfound peace is also social. The small community affords welcome release from his isolation and from grief over his friend's death. After his first participation in one of Miss Lilly's seances Wilhelm shares a champagne toast with his new friends, who welcome him to their brotherhood with the words, "Now you are also a knight of the new spirit!"[37] Completely isolated from the turmoil of modern society, these gentlemen can hardly seem further removed from Gutzkow's spiritual knights. In their minds, however, they are preparing the way for the salvation of humankind as surely as any of their predecessors.

This idyll is short lived, but from the ordeal that ensues Wilhelm attains enlightenment. Miss Lilly's powers become suspect when her live-in companion is unmasked while mascarading as a spirit, and after a series of other crises Miss Lilly confesses to creating the seemingly supernatural phenomena. The count is so enraged that he shoots her and turns the gun upon himself. Wilhelm, having fulfilled his charge of disposing of the count's library and papers, boards a train for Berlin in the realization that for the first time he can live with the uncertainties and complexities of modernity. Far from feeling isolated, he sees himself as a member of the universal human community and commits himself to its struggles. The real ghosts belong to this world, he concludes, and can be exorcised through action. They are "the ghosts of need, of oppression, of moral darkness, of perpetual routines of conventionality, gnawing at thousands upon thousands of living hearts and minds, poisoning life in this world, and artificially cultivating the longing for a better beyond."[38] When the train pulls into the Friedrichstraße station, Wilhelm marvels at the sight that so recently disgusted him, and beholds the cavernous hall of glass and steel as "the symbol of force, the symbol of all that is possible if we only have the will."[39]

Like Kretzer's *Die Bergpredigt*, *Die Mittagsgöttin* concludes with a protagonist who, stripped of illusions, still vows to work for society's regeneration. Although both characters experience intense personal trial and intellectual questioning, their perception of a spiritually troubled society leads not to despair but to social engagement. The call for such engagement resonates through Berlin novels from Gutzkow to Spielhagen to Alberti, and, like those earlier ones, the calls in Kretzer and Bölsche are filled with hope if lacking in specifics. More striking, however, was the advent of novels that portrayed characters unable or unwilling to sustain their ties with the rest of society.

The year 1890 is best known as a political watershed, but it proved to be a cultural watershed as well. Adalbert von Hanstein characterized it as a year of fermentation with important experiments on the stage, new forms of poetry, and the popular discovery of Nietzsche: "The feverish excitement that pervaded all the literature caused us to expect a completely new experience with each new book."[40] Berlin novelists depicting the period also conveyed images of feverishness, but far from signifying energetic quests, they denoted a virulent sickness. For individual characters this sickness meant extreme alienation ending in insanity or suicide. Moreover, when they projected their symptoms onto society, they were beset by visions of apocalyptic destruction. Such images obscured attempts to envision a German revolution. Characters in novels of the '90s were discovering, wrote Hanstein, "that they lacked the knowledge and preparation for achieving genuine resolution of the social question, and that simple good intentions were no substitute for these—and many of the authors were recognizing the same thing in themselves."[41] The inability of novelists to encapsulate such a period and envision a clear direction toward regeneration is not surprising. But the despair of artist-characters in their works nevertheless blunted appeals for social engagement, and visions of urban apocalypse made a mockery of projects for reform. These reactions came at a time when engagement was sorely needed, as German society grew more rigid and self-satisfied.

A crucial element of this withdrawal was a growing notion that genuine regeneration could be achieved only through the spiritual self-assertion of the exceptional individual. The urgency given to individual inner freedom in earlier fiction intensified in the 1890s, but now novels showed individuals who yielded to irrational impulses in their rebellion against a mechanistic universe and a society governed by social convention. Nietzsche's sudden popularity, more an effect than a cause of this crisis, attested to his ability to articulate it in terms that spoke to a long German quest for individual spiritual freedom. Declaring that Western civilization had been victimized by the "slave mentality" of Judeo-Christian morality, Nietzsche specified that a new humanity, to become truly free, would have to redefine itself in radical ways. Johannes Schlaf, a writer whose work we will consider shortly, interpreted this as a call for his whole generation "to tear loose from the old cultural constraints and to come to terms with what was truly modern; to work stringently to raise oneself through this period of transition to a condition of harmonious individuality."[42]

A diverse array of Berlin novelists responded to this call and produced works that once again depicted Berlin as an arena for struggle—this time between reason and insanity. The resulting visions of urban madness contributed to the growing reputation of Berlin as the center of all that was unhealthy in German society—a reputation cultivated by an intensely anti-modernist movement.[43] A disavowal of modernity was not, however, the intent of Berlin novelists, for they distinguished themselves from their anti-modernist contemporaries by a refusal to reject the city in favor of a mythical, *völkisch* past. Their works nevertheless attest to the difficulty of sustaining a commitment to modernity in the atmosphere of the 1890s.

An ironical portrayal of the crisis unfolds in *Stilpe* (1896), a novel by Otto Julius Bierbaum. In contrast to other fictional artists and outsiders, Willibald Stilpe is pure anti-hero, beginning with the description of him as a short, hefty schoolboy with small eyes, pockmarked face, and strange, disheveled clothes. His decision to become a writer erupts impulsively while he is hiding under the schoolmaster's podium with a bewitching girl. The narrator apologizes profusely:

"Good God, I'm not trying to write a demonology, but my hero (oh, Willibald!) wants to become a poet."[44] Thus begins the caricature of the artist as fallen savior.

In this satiric *Bildungsroman* Stilpe trains for his calling with a long odyssey through German society on a ship of fools that sails a sea of absurdity. The heritage of German classicism becomes personified for the adolescent Stilpe in a Gretchen-like girl named Martha. The Gretchen-figure still lives in the German soul, he is taught at school, whereupon the narrator confirms, "we see her daily on laundry wrappers, cigar boxes, and postcards."[45] The infatuation with Martha—and with German classicism—cools, and Stilpe becomes a "raging revolutionary," then a "patriotic visionary."[46] The lure of Greece next captivates him—"What did Germany matter to him, the cosmopolitan!"—but while concocting a scheme to pursue Byron's path, he gets into trouble and ends up at another gymnasium, where he decides to become a bohemian.[47] To this end, he forms a literary circle—*cénacle*, after Henri Murger—bestowing French names on each member and designating which high priests of literature will be discussed (Ibsen, the Russians, Zola, and German naturalists) and which will be banned (Heyse heads the list). At another gathering, in which, typically, Stilpe instructs his friends to bring the food and drink while he provides the lecture, he proclaims his devotion to the religion of art. Similar ventures continue when, having somehow withstood his exams, he enters the university in Leipzig. "I am a fragmented person," he laments during one of many periods of indecision; "the curse of modern man weighs down upon me."[48] Consciously cultivating the role of outsider, he increasingly becomes one and settles into an existence of eccentric behavior, run-down clothes, and literary ravings. After three years of dissipation he is given train fare to Berlin by a friend.

Berlin works a dramatic transformation upon Willibald Stilpe. Having taken a job as a reporter, he gains enough notice to become an elegantly dressed, widely known—and widely despised—critic. Life in the cultural establishment proves irredeemably boring, however, and after donning some old clothes he resumes his bohemian life. As he puts it, "I long for disorder, for craziness, for the laughter of people with nothing to lose."[49] In a last attempt at artistic commitment, Stilpe meets with four dissolute friends to plan a new literary enterprise.[50] Drinking themselves into oblivion, they concoct increasingly absurd proposals, until they hit upon the idea of founding a cabaret. Stilpe feverishly sets about raising capital, assembling material, and hiring singers in a flurry of activity that points to a new direction for the artist: the literary cabaret as a popular art form that speaks to the "philistine" German soul.[51] The cabaret, envisioned by Stilpe as a path beneath the lofty heights of artistic messianism and above the abyss of dissipation, did in fact represent a new kind of social engagement; it would command the energies of Bierbaum and others like him. For Stilpe, however, the project is a fiasco: too much *Tingeltangel* for the critics and too much art for the audience. He is fired by the cabaret's backers and reverts to drink. Berlin has served only as a center for bohemianism on a grand scale—a natural destination for the provincial bohemian who runs out of things to do.

The odyssey ends in a café on the northern edge of Berlin, where Stilpe nightly performs a monologue of a down-and-out poet that culminates in a "suicide" from a lamp post on stage. "There's no drink strong enough to do me in," he tells the audience in Berlin dialect, "that's why I have to do myself in."[52] The description of his act is followed by a newspaper account of Stilpe's actual suicide during a performance. A rambling suicide letter acknowledges his failure to develop what talent he did possess and ponders whether he was ruined by the low-grade alcohol of his Berlin life or by the sublime punch of the *cénacle* period. This question remains unanswered.

Stilpe's letter also questions whether he was ruined by his failure to develop the virtues his education tried to instill or by the attempt to instill them. Again, no answer. By raising this question, however, Bierbaum attacks a cherished assumption about the unfinished revolution—the notion that by building on their cultural legacy, Germans would bring about the regeneration of humanity. Bierbaum's irreverence toward classical education was extreme but by no means unique.[53] As early as 1866 literary historian Julian Schmidt alluded to the dilemma of what to do with the heritage of German classicism when he wrote, "The writing of Goethe was our patent of nobility. But the proud courage of the poets and philosophers left us in the lurch when it came from establishing our real lives according to the measure of our idealism."[54] In Berlin novels this inability to apply German classicism to modern life proved a major obstacle to envisioning the cultural revolution. Stilpe's last question epitomizes the resulting ambivalence.

In other Berlin novels, images of dissolute bohemians and deranged artistic geniuses continued to proliferate, with a sharpening focus on their individual psyches. "Ho, you psychologists!" one protagonist exclaims: "Explain what is taking place in my soul. You have such a mass of psychological laws and principles. Won't you please explain?"[55] Even as characters embraced the cult of the irrational, they tried desperately to make philosophical sense of the loss of control over their own minds. Their self-destructiveness and chaotic visions of society struck heavy blows against ideals of cultural regeneration that had so recently prevailed in other Berlin novels. Psychic turmoil manifested rage and bewilderment beneath fin de siècle society.

Although rage and bewilderment are not the explicit subjects of Johannes Schlaf's *Das dritte Reich* (1900), they are ingrained in the personality of his protagonist: rage at a society that smothers the individual with its conventions and bewilderment over the means for breaking those constraints. They erupt in apocalyptic visions that form a tumultuous version of spiritual crisis. Schlaf (1862–1941), a leading Berlin naturalist, designates the novel as the first of a trilogy depicting his generation (Alberti's "generation of 1870"). Although others have already undertaken this task, Schlaf writes in the preface to the last novel, their efforts have been premature. The right time is at hand, he asserts, to show how this generation has lifted the veil to reveal a new humanity.[56]

The embodiment of that vision is Dr. Emanuel Liesegang. Although introduced as a modern-day Faust, the twenty-eight-year-old scholar sees himself not on the brink of despair but at the edge of victory. While gazing at the rows of books in his study, he recalls how he has labored to unify the diverse approaches to truth they represent: the theories of Darwin and Haeckel; the physics of Büchner and Fechner; the materialism of Strauß; and the individualist philosophies of Nietzsche and Stirner. His eyes then light on the massive family Bible, whose prominence on the shelf represents "a first and last and inalienable sign of his intellectual and spiritual formation."[57] The books of St. John with their apocalyptic prophecies and allusions to a thousand-year empire contain the key. The words of Christ hold the promise: "I have yet many things to say unto you, but you cannot bear them now."[58] The age in which humanity can bear such truth has arrived, a thought that fills Liesegang's mind with the Erda motif from Wagner's "Ring" cycle. Liesegang discovers he can manipulate the disparate tones and rhythms to form a single harmony "beyond all the contradictions of knowledge, feeling, thinking, and acting."[59] The third reich means the age that will resolve the dichotomies in the German soul.

Liesegang ponders how such dichotomies apply to him. He distinguishes one of them in types of people: "Those who find their destiny and fulfillment here and those who know it to be in the unknown realm beyond; those who possess and those who seek; the happy and the wretched; the serene and the restless; those who are at home and those who are alien."[60] Both types live in him, he realizes, but his tendency toward the latter means a life of unsettled isolation. Indeed, he links his growing alienation with another dichotomy: sickness versus health. His unremitting introspection calls forth symptoms familiar from other novels: extreme restlessness, inability to concentrate, increasing dependence on cognac and morphine, and paralyzing indecisiveness. He and his friends fear he is ill, so alienated is he from conventional middle-class society. But one conversation places the sickness elsewhere. "An age of civilization is now moribund," a friend tells Liesegang.[61] This definition makes illness merely the pain of transition to a new age and health the province of those who, like Liesegang, are striving to liberate themselves from a diseased society.

The ambiguity between sickness and health unfolds through the novel, but the view that society is diseased predominates. Two conspicuous symptoms are the acute nervousness of the modern city dweller and a lassitude that makes even pessimism exhausting.[62] Health means the opposite of these two conditions: a quietness of spirit coupled with a dynamic energy that will be released when the soul finds harmony. Liesegang believes he possesses the vision and the will to reach this condition. As he sees it, the challenges raised by philosophers like Nietzsche and Stirner correspond to biblical prophecies of a day of judgment. This day will mark the completion of humanity's inner evolution and will reveal "the sovereignty of an all-embracing individuality."[63] What such sovereignty actually means, however, proves extremely difficult for Liesegang to conceive.

Immersion in New Testament prophecies and studies of Oriental religions bring him powerful visions but few answers. At one stage, for instance, his vision of Buddha sitting under the plane tree across from his window causes him to wonder briefly whether another great religious figure is coming. Liesegang soon returns, however, to the notion that humanity must find its own salvation through the birth of an *Übermensch* who no longer damns or questions God because he has reached harmony between his own soul and the realm of nature.[64]

The dichotomy between humanity and nature, another important dimension of Liesegang's spiritual crisis, is epitomized in alternating ecstasy and terror over the city. Like Wilhelm in *Die Mittagsgöttin*, Liesegang has tumultuous encounters with Berlin, but far from causing him to seek refuge in the Spreewald, they drive him to realms within the city that speak to his inner turmoil. In his besieged mind, awe toward the city's technological wonders can be obliterated suddenly by existential terror at the realization of his extreme isolation from people around him. Had Karl Gutzkow still been alive, he would surely have diagnosed an acute stage of sidewalk disease.

On a day of especially intense mental paralysis, for instance, Liesegang decides to be led wherever instinct takes him (if he were a spiritualist, he thinks, he would be certain spirits were leading him). He traverses modern civilization: from the working-class Rosenthalerstraße, past the museums and the university, across the opulence of Unter den Linden, and into the commercial beehive of Leipzigerstraße. A bombardment of sights and impressions attests to human triumphs over nature: huge waterworks, streetcars, iron bridges, electric trams, speeding cycles. Mixed into the wonder, however, are portents of cataclysm deriving from the same marvels. He is impelled by inner furies to head toward Kreuzberg with its extraordinary panorama of Berlin, "and as if through an internal revelation he became aware of the absolute domination of the human intellect over the planet."[65] Far from exhilarated, Liesegang is terrified by the realization that no previous generation can instruct humanity in controlling the titanic power of modern civilization. "Where to now?" he asks himself, but his question is directed less to his destiny than to that of humankind. The answer comes in an onslaught of apocalyptic visions of destruction: "The thousand-year empire has arrived!" he proclaims, while stumbling down the path to the city.[66]

The Kreuzberg episode turns Liesegang from his books into the depths of his mind. He also turns away from society, convinced he must tear himself loose from the external conventions that hitherto defined his being. Those of the *Bürgertum* weigh most heavily, bringing revulsion for the center of the city with its mechanized order and trappings of material success. He is now drawn to working-class realms in north Berlin, where the sight of human castaways pursuing their dark existence causes him to feel "with some irony" that he has found his milieu. Convinced that the liberation of the masses is a mere illusion and their misery an "eternal necessity," Liesegang scoffs at the memory of his youthful faith in the future workers' state.[67] Social engagement was but a way station on the path toward absolute individuality.

Liesegang finally decides he can reach this goal only by shedding the body that chains him to a diseased world. The act of suicide, he reasons, is the next stage of his quest and "will bring him freedom and recovery from the hallucinatory delusions of his study, from this Berlin, and from the whole surrounding view of the world."[68] A last attempt at contact with his closest friend, now ensconced in a comfortable middle-class existence, only confirms his isolation and disgust for society. He returns to his apartment and shoots himself. Schlaf ends his novel as news of Liesegang's death arrives at the household of the friend he last visited. The friend reacts with middle-class practicality: "Well, it's for the best that he's dead! Nothing worse than a fellow who doesn't know what to do with himself."[69]

That Schlaf did not intend these words as his own judgment becomes apparent in his preface to the last novel of the trilogy. There he defends Liesegang against charges of succumbing to decadence or to internal emptiness, by comparing him to Moses, who after years in the wilderness finally stood on the rise that overlooked the Promised Land. Liesegang, by analogy, stood at the heights of modern human experience to gain a view of the promised land where the great problems of existence would be resolved: "And not for a moment does he lose his German reverence and piety. Despite all his weariness and martyrdom, strength and life endure to the last breath."[70] This linking of Liesegang's pursuit of truth with the German soul reveals a central dilemma. Schlaf, convinced that German intellectuals encountered the onslaught of modernity with weapons unique to their cultural tradition, sought to define that tradition. His focus on the philosophical heritage, with its profound questions about the relation of objective and subjective reality, was repeatedly diverted by the intrusion of another heritage: that of the dutiful, hard-working *Bürger*. Despite Liesegang's determination to renounce his middle-class identity, he was all too often engulfed by admiration for the *Bürger* and the energy behind his successes. Two souls clearly lived in this German breast.

Schlaf's novel shows something drastic happening to the notion of the unfinished revolution at the end of the century. The combination of the messianic expectations of earlier novels with themes of madness and social withdrawal intimated that the long-sought cultural regeneration would be a cataclysm eradicating all social forms. Apocalyptic imagery collided jarringly with the technological wonders of modernity, and the Nietzschean *Übermensch* with the down-to-earth *Bürger*. Withdrawal from social engagement, extreme individualism, the dissipation of the bohemian life, and apocalyptic images of destruction all reflected a cultural pessimism that pervaded the fin de siècle mood of European society as a whole.[71] German writers were not unique in portraying cultural institutions that censored or ignored their works, or in their depiction of lonely struggles to create artistic forms for the modern age. They were unique, however, in trying to reconcile this alienation with inherited ideals about themselves as saviors of a new nation.

While these tumultuous images of radical withdrawal were coming forth,

Berlin society continued to be reshaped by modernity. New social groups were coming to the fore, and old ones were besieged by crisis. However strong the impetus for withdrawal in novels like Schlaf's, many novelists persisted in their commitment to confronting social changes and exploring the implications for Germany's future. Three groups that became especially problematic in the context of modernization were Jews, women, and the nobility. Novelists' encounters with each group will be the subject, respectively, of the next three chapters.

## Notes

1. Annemarie Lange, *Berlin zur Zeit Bebels und Bismarcks: Zwischen Reichsgründung und Jahrhundertswende* (Berlin, 1972), 459–545.
2. Helmut Scheuer, "Zur Christus-Figur in der Literatur um 1900," in Roger Bauer et al., eds., *Fin de Siècle: Zu Literatur und Kunst der Jahrhundertwende* (Frankfurt am Main, 1977), 385.
3. Max Kretzer, *Die Bergpredigt: Roman aus der Gegenwart*, 4th ed. (Leipzig, 1901), 182–183.
4. Ibid., 57.
5. Ibid., 61.
6. Ibid., 106; see also 49–54, 85–89 and 181.
7. Ibid., 37. On Stoecker see Günter Brakelmann, *Protestantismus und Politik: Werk und Wirkung Adolf Stoeckers* (Hamburg, 1982).
8. Kretzer, *Die Bergpredigt*, 37, 74. Bock's age provides the clearest indication of the chronological setting; if calculated by Stoecker's dates (1835–1909), it places the novel in the late 1880s.
9. Ibid., 59.
10. Ibid., 364.
11. Ibid., 369–370.
12. Ibid., 410; see also 344.
13. Ibid., 416.
14. Julius Erich Kloss, *Max Kretzer: Eine Studie zur neueren Literatur*, 2nd ed. (Leipzig, 1905), 84. As late as the fifth edition, the title page of *Das Gesicht Christi* was still labeled "Part I."
15. Max Kretzer, *Das Gesicht Christi: Roman aus dem Ende des XIX. Jahrhunderts*, 5th ed. (Leipzig, 1908), 67.
16. Ibid., 1.
17. Ibid., 67, 108, 132. The counterpoint between social democracy and Christianity is a significant theme; see also ibid., 40.
18. Ibid., 179.
19. Ibid., 183.
20. Ibid., 188.
21. Ibid., 68. On literary images of Christ as "ein Opfer der Gesellschaft" see Scheuer in Bauer, *Fin de Siècle*, 382–383.
22. Kretzer's conception of Christianity bears parallels to the liberal theology preached by Berlin theologian Adolf von Harnack. See Roy Pascal, *From Naturalism to Expressionism: German Literature and Society, 1880–1918* (London, 1973), 169.
23. Scheuer in Bauer, *Fin de Siècle*, 385. On the complexities of evaluating the hopeful outcomes of such "innocent victim" novels as this see George Goodin, *The Poetics of*

Protest: Literary Form and Political Implication in the Victim-of-Society Novel (Carbondale, Ill., 1985), 43–49.
24. Kloss, Max Kretzer, 72–83. Another contemporary referred to Das Gesicht Christi as Kretzer's "most significant work." Richard Urban, Die literarische Gegenwart: 20 Jahre deutschen Schrifttums, 1888–1908 (Leipzig, 1908), 178. See the comprehensive bibliography of Kretzer's works in Günther Keil, Max Kretzer: A Study in German Naturalism (1929; reprinted New York, 1966), 108–114.
25. Das Gesicht Christi can be seen as part of a trend toward Entidealisierung of Christian tradition. Richard Hamann and Jost Hermand, Naturalismus (Munich, 1972), 92–97. On forms of religious quest in these years see Pascal, From Naturalism to Expressionism, 161–197.
26. On the widespread occultism of this period, see Pascal, From Naturalism to Expressionism, 174–179. It has been suggested that Bölsche's concern with "Realität und Spiritualität" might be considered as a "Signatur der Epoche." Klaus Günther Just, Von der Gründerzeit bis zur Gegenwart: Geschichte der deutschen Literatur seit 1871 (Bern, 1973), 176. For extensive treatment of the intellectual context of Bölsche's quests see Alfred Kelly, The Descent of Darwin: The Popularization of Darwinism in Germany, 1860–1914 (Chapel Hill, N.C., 1981).
27. Wilhelm Bölsche, Die Mittagsgöttin, 4th ed. (Jena, 1910), I, iii–v.
28. Ibid., I, 3–4.
29. Ibid., I, 10.
30. Ibid., I, 88.
31. Ibid., I, 297.
32. Ibid., I, 321–322. See also I, 266, 351; II, 140–141.
33. Ibid., I, 260–261. On the religious indifference in Wilhelm's upbringing see II, 6–10.
34. Ibid., I, 123, 115.
35. Ibid., I, 170–173.
36. Ibid., II, 111; 365.
37. Ibid., II, 63.
38. Ibid., II, 432.
39. Ibid., II, 435–436.
40. Adalbert von Hanstein, Das jüngste Deutschland: Zwei Jahrzehnte miterlebter Literaturgeschichte, 3rd ed. (Leipzig, 1905), 237.
41. Ibid., 241. On the broad question of social engagement see the fine collection of articles in Helmut Scheuer, ed., Naturalismus: Bürgerliche Dichtung und soziales Engagement (Stuttgart, 1974).
42. Johannes Schlaf, Peter Boies Freite, "Vorwort," 2nd ed. (Leipzig, 1903), 7. On the growth of Nietzsche's influence in the '90s see Fritz Martini, Deutsche Literatur im bürgerlichen Realismus, 1848–1898, 4th ed. (Stuttgart, 1981), 955–956, and Richard Frank Krummel, ed., Nietzsche und der deutsche Geist, Vol. II: Ausbreitung und Wirkung des nietzscheschen Werkes im deutschen Sprachraum vom Todesjahr bis zum Ende des Weltkrieges (Berlin, 1983).
43. On the city's reputation as a center for the "unhealthy" see Hans Herzfeld, "Berlin als Kaiserstadt und Reichshauptstadt, 1871–1945," in Hans Herzfeld, ed., Das Hauptstadt Problem in der Geschichte (Tübingen, 1952), 143–144, and Friedrich Lienhard, Die Vorherrschaft Berlins: Litterarische Anregungen (Leipzig, 1900). On anti-modernist currents see Fritz Stern, The Politics of Cultural Despair: A Study in the Rise of the Germanic Ideology (Berkeley, 1961); George Mosse, The Crisis of German Ideology: Intellectual Origins of the Third Reich (New York, 1964); and Klaus Bergmann, Agrarromantik und Großstadtfeindschaft (Meisenheim am Glan, 1970).
44. Otto Julius Bierbaum, Stilpe: Ein Roman aus der Froschperspektive, in Gesammelte Werke, II (Munich, 1921), 261. Stilpe is also a good example of the "pseudo victim,"

described in George Goodin's *Poetics of Protest*, 134–137.
45. Bierbaum, *Stilpe*, 288.
46. Ibid., 289. On autobiographical strands in *Stilpe* see the entry on Bierbaum by George Schoolfield in James Hardin, ed., *German Fiction Writers, 1885–1913* (Detroit, Mich., 1988), 20–24.
47. Bierbaum, *Stilpe*, 306.
48. Ibid., 383.
49. Ibid., 422.
50. The four characters in this scene are recognizable as well-known Berlin writers. Julius Bab, *Die Berliner Bohème*, Großstadt Dokumente, Vol. II, 3rd ed. (Berlin, 1904), 50–68.
51. Bierbaum, *Stilpe*, 448.
52. Ibid., 471.
53. The gymnasium has been described as raising "das Classicitätsdogma zur Nationalreligion." Reinhard Wittmann, "Das literarische Leben 1848 bis 1880," in Max Bucher, Werner Hahl, Georg Jäger, Reinhard Wittmann, eds., *Realismus und Gründerzeit: Manifeste und Dokumente zur deutschen Literatur, 1848–1880*, Vol. I (Stuttgart, 1976), 250.
54. From *Literaturgeschichte seit Lessings Tode*; quoted by Hanstein, *Das jüngste Deutschland*, 4. Peter Jelavich discusses the "ambiguous political implications of the German classical tradition" in his *Munich and Theatrical Modernism: Politics, Playwriting, and Performance, 1890–1914* (Cambridge, Mass., 1985), 15–19.
55. Stanislaw Przybyszewski, *Homo Sapiens: A Novel in Three Parts, Overboard*, translated from the Polish by Thomas Seltzer (New York, 1915), 43. For other such novels see also Karl Bleibtreu, *Größenwahn* (1887), Hans R. Fischer, *Berliner Zigeunerleben* (1890), Ernst von Wolzgen, *Lumpengesindel* (1892), Ulla von Eck, *Zigeuner der Großstadt* (1895), Hans von Zobeltitz, *Lichterfelderstraße Nr. 1* (1899), Hans Ostwald, *Vagabunden* (1900), Rose Austerlitz, *Café Größenwahn: Roman aus der Berliner Künstlerwelt* (1900?), Wilhelm von Polenz, *Wurzellocker* (1902).
56. Schlaf, *Peter Boies Freite*, 5–15. See also Just, *Von der Gründerzeit bis zur Gegenwart*, 179–180.
57. Johannes Schlaf, *Das dritte Reich* (Berlin, 1900), 9. In addition to Nietzsche, the other authors present on Liesegang's shelf include physicist Gustav Theodor Fechner, scientist philosopher Ludwig Büchner, anarchist writer Max Stirner, and rationalist religious scholar David Friedrich Strauss. On the importance of these figures in late-nineteenth century German culture see Pascal, *From Naturalism to Expressionism*, 16–66; and Just, *Von der Gründerzeit bis zur Gegenwart*, 57–74.
58. John 16:12; Schlaf, *Das dritte Reich*, 10.
59. Schlaf, *Das dritte Reich*, 11–12. On the spiritual and political conceptions of the third reich see Stern, *Politics of Cultural Despair*, 253–254, and Jean Neurohr, *Der Mythos vom 3. Reich* (Stuttgart, 1957). See also M. H. Abrams, *Natural Supernaturalism: Tradition and Revolution in Romantic Literature* (New York, 1971), 325–372.
60. Schlaf, *Das dritte Reich*, 246.
61. Ibid., 65–66.
62. See, for instance, Liesegang's meditation on the modern human condition, ibid., 80.
63. Ibid., 117, 31–32.
64. Ibid., 116, see also 57, 76–77, 95, 119, 243, 301. Schlaf makes an explicit connection between the end of humanity's alienation from nature and the coming of the third reich in *Peter Boies Freite*, 54. The notion that humanity can be its own messiah reaches back at least to Gutzkow. See, for instance, Karl Gutzkow, *Die Ritter vom Geiste*, 6th ed. (Berlin, 1878), III, 377.
65. Schlaf, *Das dritte Reich*, 93–94, 252.
66. Ibid., 97. On apocalyptic themes in literature see Klaus Vondung, ed., *Das wilhelmi-*

nische Bildungsbürgertum: Zur Sozialgeschichte seiner Ideen (Göttingen, 1976), 198, n2, and 199, n11. A naturalist author who earlier made frequent use of apocalyptic imagery was Conrad Alberti. See, for instance, Conrad Alberti, "Verbotene Liebe," in Riesen und Zwerge, (Leipzig, 1887), 187ff, 212, 264. On the wider manifestations of apocalyptic thinking see Lucian Hölscher, Weltgericht oder Revolution: Protestantische und sozialistische Zukunftsvorstellungen im deutschen Kaiserreich (Stuttgart, 1989).
67. Schlaf, Das dritte Reich, 170, 175–176, 146, 150. See also Helmut Scheuer, "Zwischen Sozialismus und Individualismus—Zwischen Marx und Nietzsche," in Scheuer, ed., Naturalismus, 150–174.
68. Schlaf, Das dritte Reich, 339.
69. Ibid., 341.
70. Schlaf, Peter Boies Freite, 12. The image of Liesegang as Moses also appears in the reminiscences of the protagonist. Ibid., 249. See also Susan Arnold and Elke Mohr, "Über die Dekadenz zum neuen Menschen in den frühen Romanen von Johannes Schlaf," in Dieter Kafitz, ed., Dekadenz in Deutschland: Beiträge zur Erforschung der Romanliteratur um die Jahrhundertwende (Frankfurt am Main, 1987), 125–142.
71. See, for example, Helmut Kreuzer, Die Bohème: Beiträge zu ihrer Beschreibung (Stuttgart, 1968), and Roger Bauer, et al., eds., Fin de Siècle. On the complexities of interpreting fatalism in fiction see Goodin, Poetics of Protest, 124–132.

# 8

# The Outsiders: Berlin's Jews

Jewish characters appear frequently in Berlin novels, for the most part as stereotypes, such as the manipulative speculator and the social-climbing wife. Such figures, however, are usually subsidiary to other, non-Jewish characters with similar traits. A smaller number of novels acknowledges anti-Semitism and a smaller number still deals with its victims. Novelists who concerned themselves with the situation of Jews in Berlin did so as standard-bearers of the modern age and defined the issue in terms of hopes of progress and enlightenment. Modernity, they believed, meant the dismantling of old prejudices and the rise of a new toleration they expected to extend to Jews. But even these authors found a clear vision of Jewish equality to be elusive, not least of all in themselves.

A long-standing tradition of toleration made Berlin a likely setting for the challenging of anti-Semitism. Although Jewish emancipation did not finally occur until 1869, the city became a haven for Jews in 1671, when the Great Elector invited fifty Jewish families, expelled from Vienna, to settle there. Through the eighteenth century legal restrictions still governed where Jews could live and what trades they could practice, but as Enlightenment ideals took hold, such laws seemed increasingly anomalous.[1] In particular, Lessing's tribute to the humane ideals of Berlin's most prominent Jewish thinker, Moses Mendelssohn, in "Nathan der Weise" (1779), sparked calls for Jewish emancipation. Three decades later a short-lived emancipation was achieved when the Prussian reform ministry removed most legal constraints, but the following era of reaction brought renewed restrictions that prevailed until the North German Confederation legislated equality for Berlin's—and Germany's—Jews.[2]

During the many decades leading to emancipation the Enlightenment agenda for emancipation seemed to become increasingly embedded in Berlin society. At the beginning of the nineteenth century, the acceptance of Jews seemed assured as Jewish salons became the gathering place for cultivated society.[3] As the century progressed Berlin's growing reputation as the most secular city in Germany seemed further to lessen distinctions between Jews and Christians. The influx of immigrants after unification underscored the city's tradition of welcoming outsiders, and Jews, who formed but a small segment of the population, might have been expected to end their isolation amid the capital's diversity.[4]

Berlin's rapid expansion, however, brought new prejudices. In the 1880s an outbreak of pogroms in Russia brought a throng of refugees to the city, and at the other end of the social spectrum Jewish entrepreneurs and financiers were noticeable among the brash newcomers. The prominence of Jews as patrons, critics, and producers in cultural realms further stimulated beliefs that they were causing the vulgarity that infused modern culture. Other, less definable anxieties—feelings of social alienation or political impotence, fears about German identity, economic insecurities, and tensions between generations—also contributed to the tendency to make Jews into scapegoats.[5] Novelists reacting to these developments used their works to show that anti-Semitism, far from being the province of fanatics or uneducated masses, was spreading through cultivated society. Seeing themselves as enlightened observers, they sought to educate readers by linking the rise of anti-Semitism to historical experiences, and by warning of its dangers for the moral well-being of Germany.

However well intentioned, the novelists who concern us in this chapter also yielded to anti-Jewish feelings. They too accepted the existence of the "Jewish question" (*Judenfrage*), a catchall phrase for the issue of how Jews fit into German society. By suggesting that some Jews were harmful to German well-being, they all too easily became mired in the effort to distinguish desirable Jews from the undesirable and promoted the acceptance of the "good Jews" as an answer to anti-Semites.

Paradoxically, one reason for authors' inability to champion toleration unequivocally lay in the Enlightenment heritage itself. Besides proposing ideals of toleration, its rationalist precepts defined religion as a holdover of medieval superstition. Since Judaism with its rituals and laws seemed a special threat, proponents of such rationalism argued that Jews should abandon their alien observances and assimilate into German society.[6] Berlin novelists revealed elements of this secular view, and even as they encouraged assimilation they revealed ambivalence both about the Germanness of Jews who remained within the observant fold and about the trustworthiness of those who chose conversion.[7] Some pleas for toleration thus gave unwitting support to the claim that Judaism was a scourge that should be eliminated from Germany.[8] This irony is a significant instance of the difficulties liberal Germans encountered while seeking to free themselves from the illiberal atmosphere that surrounded them.

Berlin novels conventionally linked the origins of anti-Semitism in Imperial Germany with the *Gründerjahre*. Their portrayals of the supposed role of Jews echoed notions first sounded by popular journalists like Otto Glagau, who in a widely read series of articles made the preposterous claim that ninety percent of the *Gründer* were Jews and warned that "Jewish corruption" was poisoning the atmosphere.[9] Novelists easily yielded to the temptation to portray the image of the speculator through Jewish stereotypes, and they frequently conveyed the idea of moral catastrophe through allusions to the "golden calf" around which Germans had danced.[10] The only novelist of this period to challenge the association of Jews with moral failure was Wolfgang Kirchbach, who in *Kinder des Reiches* used the instance of the Bredow family's hostility toward the son's Jewish fiancée to make a strong plea for Jewish/German harmony.[11] The elder Bredow exemplifies the Berlin tradition of toleration, and the rest of the family, by finally accepting the young woman, demonstrates that anti-Semitism can be overcome. Moreover, the fiancée's efforts at conciliation suggest the salutary role of Jews in German society. "You Jews are the cement of European humanity," one family member remarks: "You're the real unifiers of the empire and of the bickering Germans and all other peoples." By portraying Jews as positive contributors to a united Germany, Kirchbach makes it the duty of every patriot to acknowledge them as Germans.[12]

No other author of a Berlin novel made this case as explicitly, but in subsequent years others took up the charge of showing that Jews could be loyal Germans. They were, for the most part, Jewish themselves, and thus their fiction reflected dilemmas about their own identities as Jews and as Germans. A poignant degree of self-hatred is evident in frequent stereotypes of the truly alien (caftan-garbed Jews from the east) and the truly despicable (unprincipled speculators, modern legatees of the Jewish usurer). As self-consciously modern Jews, they tended to contrast an enlightened urban Jewry with an uncultivated ghetto Jewry of the east.[13] Or they distinguished between two types of modern Jews: the vulgar parvenu and the dedicated professional. When the insidiousness of anti-Semitism became apparent to them, however, self-hatred was replaced by a realization that German anti-Semitism extended to all Jews. Three authors who dealt with this crisis were Fritz Mauthner, Ludwig Jacobowski, and Conrad Alberti. Each wrote novels revealing an incipient awareness that the well-being of all Jews in Germany—both the assimilated Jew and the alien, both the "good" Jew and the "bad"—rested on the successful challenge to negative images. Their works gave voice to the anxieties of German Jews who were confronting old hatreds in a new age.

Fritz Mauthner (1849–1923) was the first novelist to concentrate on questions of Jewishness and Germanness in Imperial Berlin in his *Der neue Ahasver* (*The New Ahasverus*, 1882). The work depicts a widespread surge of anti-Jewish feeling at the end of the 1870s and uses its Jewish protagonist to explore responses to the new pressures. Mauthner underscores his social intent when he writes in the preface, "I am not thinking at all about applause from the estheticians; I want the approval of the ethicists, especially the writers of history."[14]

Ironically, one instigator of the crisis that motivated the novel came from the profession to which Mauthner appealed. In November 1879, historian Heinrich von Treitschke, a popular and widely respected professor, sparked controversy with an article entitled "Our Future Prospects." It appealed to Germans to recognize the present as a critical time for building a great culture, and to understand that the task was being impeded by what Treitschke described as an alien Jewish presence. As long as Jews maintained a separate religion and community, German nationhood would be endangered. The truth could no longer be ignored, he proclaimed: "The Jews are our national misfortune!"[15] The article provoked an onslaught of written rejoinders, meetings, and petitions, including a pamphlet by fellow historian Theodor Mommsen that attacked Treitschke on patriotic and ethical grounds.[16] Mauthner acknowledged this controversy by dedicating *Der neue Ahasver* to Mommsen and writing his preface in the form of a letter to him.

Despite divergent stances, Treitschke, Mommsen, and Mauthner all embraced assimilation as the answer for German Jews. Mommsen replied to Treitschke with the strange prescription that the "Jewish question" could be resolved if all Jews whose consciences permitted it converted to Christianity. Conversion, he argued, would lessen the distance between Jews and a society that was fundamentally "Christian." "To remain outside its boundaries and still be inside the nation is possible, but difficult and dangerous," he explained.[17] In his reply Mauthner cautiously took issue. He did agree that to be true Germans, Jews should relinquish their separate practices (including observing the sabbath), but he noted that if conversion became the goal, then as long as any Jews still adhered to their religion the "Jewish question" would remain.[18] The crux of Mauthner's case lay elsewhere, however. Just as no German emigrated to Paris during the Franco-Prussian war, he insisted that no Jew could be expected to convert in the present atmosphere in Germany: "My novel describes a case in which an individual conversion fails because of the fury of the Jewbaiters."[19] By focusing on the siege mentality induced by anti-Semitism, Mauthner implied that once the "siege" ended, obstacles to conversion would fall. This willingness to sanction any argument for conversion revealed the yearning of "modern" Jews for acceptance by their countrymen.

Mauthner was one such "modern" Jew who, educated in the German-speaking environment of Prague, developed an early enthusiasm for German culture. In 1876 he migrated to Berlin, where for three decades he contributed to cultural journals and wrote a succession of Berlin novels and novellas, of which *Der neue Ahasver* was the first.[20] The novel's title refers to the legendary Ahasverus, who was condemned to eternal wandering when Germany converted to Christianity.[21] Mauthner's "new" Ahasverus is Heinrich Wolff, who, like his creator, is a secularized Jewish immigrant to Berlin. Through him Mauthner depicts the step-by-step dissolution of a Jew's dream of participating in the building of Germany. While applauding German unification, the novel warns that national ideals are being corrupted by anti-Semitic hatreds.

Heinrich's zeal for all things modern and all things German stems from long-standing feelings of exclusion from Christian society. His early memories include the experience of going to a convent school and having to stand alone in the corridor during religious classes. The death of his father meant a move to his grandfather's house in the Jewish quarter of Prague, where the old-fashioned furnishings and cherished symbols of Jewish piety only deepen his sense of separation from the modern world. But Heinrich also becomes estranged from the traditional world of Judaism and as a medical student must bear perennial accusations from his grandfather that he has surely been baptized. Although he has not, Heinrich has tired of standing outside the mainstream of society. Assuming the old-fashioned Judaism to be the cause of his isolation, he decides upon all-out immersion in modernity. For him this means escaping not only religious bonds but Prague itself, where "the comrades of his youth were still living, out of deadening habit, as pariahs."[22]

Heinrich decides he belongs in Berlin. Arriving there about 1869 (following the emancipation law), he is convinced he will find fulfillment in joining the great struggle for German unity.[23] He enlists as a field doctor in the Franco-Prussian war, where he receives a near-fatal wound. The first Berlin scene of the novel shows him, months into a painful recuperation, in the Unter den Linden mansion of an aristocratic comrade wounded at the same time. Both heroes lie immobilized on the day the victorious army marches into Berlin, but it is noteworthy that Heinrich's wound, although incurred in the line of duty, did not come from "real" participation in the war as a German soldier. This implicit distinction between the comrades raises questions about whether even Mauthner saw his hero as truly German. Nevertheless, although the cheers outside are intended for the troops, Heinrich hears them as a tribute to his service as well and is convinced that his isolation has ended.

The first breach in this belief occurs when the kindly Jewish physician treating Heinrich warns him that equality is not yet a fait accompli. Berlin's atmosphere, he explains, is being poisoned by a few Jewish families, made wealthy by speculation, who are trying to clamber into high society. Although anti-Semitism results from unseemly activities of the few, it hurts all Jews: "Otherwise we hard-working members of the middle class would have long since been able to forget the whole thing."[24] The hollow values of the social climber, moreover, are wrongly conceived as a Jewish trait. Real Jewish ideals are realized in the bonds of family and community, the doctor reminds Heinrich, thus invoking another claim by which Jews sought to establish their credentials as genuine Germans. With such remarks the doctor distances himself from negative images of the "bad Jew."[25] Heinrich does so even more completely by dismissing the warning as no threat to him, a member of the modern generation.

The novel lends credence to the "good Jew"/"bad Jew" dichotomy with a range of characters under both categories. A negative figure is Tina Feigelbaum, who indulges in the frenzied social climbing the old doctor decried. On the other hand, Tina's Jewish husband exemplifies the positive virtues of "a cautious businessman, not a swindler."[26] Another "bad Jew," a charlatan who cadges free meals from kosher restaurants by screaming he has been served pork, is offset by a diligent artisan who believes manual labor will secure Jews their place in

Germany.[27] Such balancing of "good Jews" against "bad Jews" stresses that Jews' foibles and virtues are typical of any group. The novel also provides non-Jewish figures with proclivities for moneygrubbing and shows them also to be victims of the gold fever that swept "stormily" over Germany in the *Gründerjahre*.[28] The visibility of "bad Jews" nevertheless reinforces the notion that Jews are to blame for the rise of anti-Semitism.

Heinrich, a pillar of purposefulness and moderation, personifies the "good Jew," whom Mauthner clearly meant to promote as an exemplary German. Mauthner's main purpose, however, was to depict the forces in Germany that ruined such exemplars. With Heinrich the process begins when he falls in love with the daughter of an aristocratic household, overcomes his middle-class reluctance to court her, and then confronts his Jewishness as a second obstacle. He curses the fate that "forced him into the position of outsider—he who wanted so much to take his place in the midst of his people, the German people."[29] Soon, however, he admonishes himself that his Jewish origins should be no greater obstacle than his class.

Indeed, even the young woman's grandfather, the family patriarch, proves flexible enough to meet with Heinrich to discuss conditions for the match, but this proves to be a fateful encounter. To the grandfather's reference to religion Heinrich indicates that conversion is no obstacle for him. The issue can be best understood, he tells the old man, in the distinction between institutionalized Christianity (*Christentum*) and Christendom (*Christenheit*) as the cultural realm of Western civilization. Most German Jews embrace the latter, he asserts, clearly including himself among the supposed majority.[30] Since modern Jews and modern Christians share the same cultural heritage, there should be no obstacle to their sharing the same religion. When the grandfather asks why he has not converted sooner, Heinrich reminds him that conversion was once a weapon of intolerance. Because it is no longer forced as a social necessity, "Jews can allow themselves to be baptized without disadvantage to themselves or to Christianity."[31] Neither Heinrich nor the grandfather notices that baptism *is* being urged as a social necessity here—nor does Mauthner convey consciousness of the irony. Nevertheless, Heinrich does warn that if the old persecution revives, even "modern" Jews will rush to defend their origins.

The rest of *Der neue Ahasver* shows how the old persecution does revive with dangerous new overtones. Its onset is linked to the assassination attempts on the Kaiser in the spring of 1878. Moments before receiving news of the Kaiser's serious wounding in the second attempt, a newspaper editor remarks upon how a dramatic event, whether for good or for ill, has the effect of unifying the nation. As Mauthner portrays it, the central outcome of the furor over the shooting is to unite German Gentiles in attacks on Jews in their midst.[32] Heinrich witnesses the suddenness of this phenomenon by being absent during its beginnings. Having agreed that his young fiancée should be given time to be sure of her desire to marry him, he goes to Africa in early 1878 to study tropical diseases. Upon his return a year later he is shocked to see a nationwide obsession with the

Jews. He is most struck by the restrained language in which he hears the so-called question of the day discussed in train compartments, restaurants, bookstores, public meetings, and even drawing rooms.[33] Despite the belief of many Berliners that they are immune to intolerance, Heinrich discerns the caricatures made by radical anti-Semites beneath their euphemisms.

Heinrich's sensitivity begins to affect relations with his Gentile friends. In a melodramatic sequence the obstacles to his marriage fall, but on the evening the engagement is to be announced the modern Ahasverus emerges. Heinrich decides baptism would mean undergoing a kind of salvation he does not want: "Salvation from the age-old curse . . . Ahasverus' salvation! But the eternal Jew must not die!"[34] Seeing the spread of anti-Semitism as a sign that he will not be accepted as a German, Heinrich tells his fiancée he must become a Jew again and breaks off the engagement. A friend attempts to dissuade him by taking him to an anti-Semitic rally, which he hopes will show Heinrich that the harassment stems only from a contemptible minority. The plan seems to be succeeding as the first speakers arouse ridicule, and one speaker wins cheers even from Heinrich when he attacks the materialism sweeping Germany. The same speaker, however, brings the crowd to its feet by blaming the scourge on the Jewish race (*Volksstamm*). In an attempt to save the situation, Heinrich's friend mounts the podium and puts forth his own "modest proposal," to the effect that the answer to the Jewish question is to enslave all Jews—a move that will use their talents while putting them in their place. The audience fails to perceive his irony when he says, "We are barbarians and proud of it!"[35] Instead, they rise to cheer.

This scene destroys Heinrich's hope of being part of the German nation. At first he vows to become a wanderer, returning perhaps to his land of origin, where his father was once driven to his death for being a German. "If I am to go down because of hatred, then I want to go down as a German pursued by Slavs rather than as a Jew pursued by Germans!"[36] A new tragedy causes him to realize he has fallen victim to Germans after all. A crazed mob, incited to believe his former fiancée has been lured to a Jewish tailor to be strangled, storms toward the house. When the young woman appears at the door to reassure the crowd, she is struck by a hurled rock. Heinrich arrives to witness her dying breath: "One after the other he had lost his fatherland and his loved one. The same people had murdered both."[37] Heinrich chooses to die also by challenging one of the offenders to a duel in which he allows himself to be shot.

As the events leading up to this scene unfold, Heinrich remarks that the German in him was upset, not the Jew.[38] This outrage stems from his—and Mauthner's—view that anti-Semitism was part of a network of attitudes that contradicted the humane ideals upon which German nationhood should be based. Mauthner came closest to articulating this in the preface, when he identified 4 August 1789 as the date on which Ahasverus' death took place. By choosing the day the French National Assembly began to dismantle the regime of feudal privilege, Mauthner tied Jewish emancipation to a wider historical movement for human rights, a rare instance of a German author's invoking the French revolution as a standard for Imperial Germany. The novel itself, however, failed to develop this idea.

In making events of the late '70s the setting for the novel, Mauthner associated modern anti-Semitism with conditions of German unification. He thus put his appeal in the same context as Treitschke's but with the opposite message: anti-Semitism, not an alien Jewish presence, was the real danger for Germany.[39] The novel also warned Jews against the assumption that they were being accepted in the new Germany. However deeply Jews might want to become Germans and cease being outsiders, Mauthner cautioned that if the price was to close one's eyes to rampant anti-Semitism, it was too high.

Still, Mauthner showed himself vulnerable to the self-hatred that is so often the lot of the persecuted. As his epigraph he chose a quotation from Mommsen to the effect that his book was intended to raise the hackles not only of anti-Semites but also of "Jewlovers" (*Judenschmeichlern*).[40] The novel fulfilled this promise with its subplots of obnoxious stereotypes. A significant part of the book echoed the argument of the old doctor: some Jews' adherence to vulgar or alien ways was keeping Jews from becoming true Germans. In falling prey to the myth that Jews were in some way to blame for their victimization, Mauthner exemplified the double bind in which modern Jews could become enmeshed: to become German, they had to divest themselves of their Jewishness; but the more they sought to do so by identifying with "German" values, the more they confirmed their alienation.[41] Self-hatred was explicit in Heinrich Wolff's repeated cursing of his isolation as a Jew, but it was overcome to the extent that he affirmed his Jewishness at the end.

Jewish self-hatred reemerged in more extreme form nine years later in a widely read novel entitled *Werther der Jude* (*Werther, the Jew*) (1891). Written by a twenty-two-year-old student named Ludwig Jacobowski, it appeared during a resurgence of anti-Semitism after a decade of relative quiescence.[42] The novel depicted the effects of this resurgence on the Jewish protagonist, and announced with its title a striking conjunction of Jewishness with the sufferings of the hero of one of Germany's best known classics. Jacobowski's "Werther" is a student who, like his prototype, is driven to suicide by inner conflicts, but in his case they derive from anxieties over his Jewishness.

Leo Wolff has the trappings of a typical Berlin student. Arrived from a provincial town, he lives in a rented room in the flat of an attentive, lower-middle-class family. As a member of a fraternity he devotes much time to drinking and carousing but finds another diversion in courting his landlady's niece, a shop girl named Helene. Finally, like many other students, Leo is an incurable dreamer whose meditations about a grandiose future substitute for studying. Indeed, eight semesters into his student career Leo is only beginning to deal with his lack of discipline. Increasingly anxious queries about his progress accompany his father's monthly remittance and cause him to realize it is time to finish the work that will allow him to follow the path of his hometown mentor and become a gymnasium professor.

These qualities aside, Leo is not typical, for his Jewishness sets him apart. Even more than Mauthner's hero, Leo is thoroughly irreligious because of what he sees as the unspiritual emphases of Jewish practice. His early memories, for example, center in the tedium of Hebrew lessons from a crotchety man incapable of nurturing any religious sensibilities.[43] The resulting unbelief has made Leo into a self-perceived outsider who, when he steps into the Berlin cathedral on Reformation Day, hears the thunderous tones of "A Mighty Fortress Is Our God" as confirmation of his being "a Jew, unloved and empty."[44]

This alienation is more than spiritual, however, for Leo discerns a psychological dimension of his Jewishness as a further barrier to acceptance. The feeling is embodied in a childhood experience of a dancing lesson at which a little girl arrived whom Leo would remember as terribly ugly with Semitic features. When the newcomer tried to join the circle of chattering girls around the daughter of the school principal, she was rebuffed. Leo sprang to her defense by chiding the principal's daughter for her behavior, but as he recasts it in his memory, this brave act rebounds against him. Far from stemming from compassion, he decides, his defense of the woebegone creature is an instance of the mysterious solidarity between one Jew and another (*Gemeinsamkeitsgefühl*). Such an instinct must be overcome to make room for feelings of Germanness.[45] The image of national feeling and its incongruity with a Jewish sense of community provoke Leo's determination to purge himself of Jewishness.

Although Leo works to free himself "of all specifically Jewish traits and ways," he is repeatedly identified as a Jew.[46] When a well-meaning friend advises him to ignore it all, Leo asks how he, a Christian, can presume to know what it is like to be a Jew.[47] Rowdies on the street insult him; a fraternity brother named Max von Horst comments sotto voce that his hair and his whole manner bespeak "too much of the Jew"; his girlfriend's parents pressure their daughter to stop seeing "the Jew"; and the cool reception of aristocratic hosts of a fraternity gathering shows he has been recognized as a Jew.[48] Such episodes have terrible psychological and physical effects. In addition to being plagued by headaches, lassitude, and extreme anxiety, Leo becomes obsessed with the subject of anti-Semitism. The obverse side of this fixation is a growing bitterness aimed at two targets other than anti-Semites: first, other Jews, and second, himself.

His disdain for other Jews is manifest in his retrospective disgust for the little girl at the dancing lesson—both for her ugliness and for the knowledge that her father was one of the town's notorious cheats. Beneath the disgust, it becomes apparent, is a deep-seated fear that Jews have earned the hostility of decent people. This fear becomes acute when Leo learns that his father, an upright small-town banker, plans to transform a local chemical factory into a joint-stock company. Leo's alarm derives from three worries: that the role of "speculator" will hurt his father's carefully wrought reputation; that the eagerness of many townspeople to invest will end in a disaster for which his father will be blamed;

and that the involvement of Siegmund Königsberger, a cousin whom Leo sees as a detestable specimen of the *Ostjude*, will corrupt the venture. His worry about his father and his dislike of his cousin stem from his own acceptance of negative stereotypes. His concern for the townspeople reflects his acceptance of another myth, that respectable, hard-working Christians are the victims of Jewish swindlers. Leo's worst fears are realized when the stock collapses and wipes out the savings of the trusting townspeople, but not before the elder Wolff and his nephew have pulled out with profit. Leo interprets the episode as overwhelming evidence of Jews' responsibility for their disfavor.

This conclusion intensifies his anxieties about himself. Although Leo admits his tendency to magnify the errors of Jews and to minimize those of Christians, he rationalizes that Jews are more visible and therefore must be more careful about their behavior.[49] He thus persists in seeking out shortcomings and easily turns the compulsion against himself. "When he loosed a burst of anger against the Jews, sometimes it felt as if he were stabbing himself slowly but surely in his heart, and sometimes it felt as if he were confessing his own faults to an ideal figure inside of him who in turn sat before the figure of the ideal Jew."[50] This passage, the novel's clearest depiction of the mechanism of self-hatred, does a great deal to explain the fluctuations between Leo's self-images as the reformer of Judaism and as the embodiment of primordial Jewish sins.

Leo counters thoughts about Jewish sins with a vision of their moral regeneration that will finally bring Jews into the bosom of German society. He envisions himself as the initiator of that renewal by making good what others have destroyed.[51] He pushes himself by invoking the words "noble, helpful, and good." In Goethe's poem, "The Divine," the line defines the qualities that distinguish humans from other creatures, but Leo intends it to become the standard for the "young Jewish generation." In moments of resolve he decides he can lead the way by devoting himself to his work, by cultivating sterling friendships, by pulling back from the shallow activities of the fraternity, and by giving much-deserved attention to Helene. His assumption of responsibility for ending the causes of anti-Semitism through such a program results, of course, in frenzies of self-blame whenever he sees himself failing. He reacts to his shortcomings by wondering how others still more embittered by anti-Semitic hatreds can be expected to adhere to his principles.[52]

The collapse of the stock venture confirms to Leo the futility of looking for change among Jews who have suffered for so long and brings about his decision to have nothing more to do with them. The break takes place when he rushes back to his hometown and encounters a father bewildered by his son's rage and Siegmund, who spews justification for taking profit at the expense of Christians. Leo listens to his cousin's accented narration of growing up Jewish in Posen: being beaten for walking on the wrong street, being jeered for his Yiddish, seeing his mother kicked by so-called Christians. Leo, however, feels no vestige of solidarity with his kinsman; rather, he hears his worst fear confirmed when Siegmund screams, "Sure we betrayed [the goyim], that's great!"[53] This admission, as far as Leo is concerned, shows the chasm to be unbridgeable. Ignoring pleas about normal business practices and about Christian investors scrambling to take part, he storms out. His instinct for seeing Jews as betrayers has won out over rage at their suffering.

Leo next turns the notion of Jewish betrayal against himself. He had already applied it in unreasonable ways, as when he once decided the whole weight of working-class misery belonged on Jews' shoulders, "and he shared in the gigantic burden, whether guilty or innocent, for the guilt would be avenged into the fourth generation."[54] The collapse of his father's stock enterprise also caused him to turn the word "betrayer" into an instrument of self-flagellation.[55] Leo's genuine act of betrayal, however, has nothing to do with profiteering but comes from his treatment of Helene. First, he allowed his fraternity brothers to cajole him into mounting a sexual conquest of the innocent girl. Next, he allowed an ill-conceived passion for the wife of a mentor to cause him to drive Helene to despair. Finally, his fury over his father's collapsed enterprise caused him to remain oblivious of her pregnancy. The story has overtones of another episode in Goethe, Faust's ruin of Gretchen,[56] but as with the Werther theme, Jacobowski transforms it into a tale of the Jew's ruin in Imperial Germany. Leo's final act of self-hatred occurs when his antagonistic fraternity brother, Max von Horst, sends a clipping from a scandal sheet about Helene's ending her misery in the Spree. The vicious language about Jews' having seduced German daughters heightens Leo's sense of connection to his father and cousin as betrayers of moral well-being. His betrayal of the person he loved is proof of his inability to become "noble, helpful, and good." Like Werther, he writes farewell letters, acquires a brace of dueling pistols, and shoots himself.

*Werther der Jude* depicted the moral failures of Leo, his father, and his cousin convincingly enough to add fuel to the fires of German anti-Semitism. This, however, was no more Jacobowski's intent than it was Goethe's that his Werther should become the prescription for suicide among lovesick eighteenth-century readers. Jacobowski meant Leo to be a negative example, an admonition to young Jews to resist the rage that consumed him and prevented him from achieving his personal reformation. He also meant to show anti-Semitism as poisoning the new Germany. One passage raises the disturbing possibility that the poison might inhere in the younger generation, if they are personified in Max von Horst, "the sober German rationalist and go-getter whose hatred for Jews came both from instinct and calculation."[57] The end of the novel indicates, however, that the arrogant von Horst is not representative of the new Germany but rather the lifelong friend who discovers Leo after he shoots himself. The last sentence describes the import: "Then the young German knew he was cradling a dead person in his arms, his old friend the young Jew."[58] Thus Jacobowski promoted the belief that once the younger generation came to the fore, the hatreds would vanish. He was convinced that modernity meant a rationalism with no scope for prejudice and that the "Jewish question" would dissolve in a new age of German harmony. In his preface to the sixth printing of the novel in 1898 Jacobowski wrote that the passage of time had strengthened his belief that Jews must rigorously adhere to the path of the German spirit. He dismissed claims that the path was being closed by extreme nationalists who would deny Jews the appellation of "German." To write this, Jacobowski had to ignore evidence in his own novel.

Both Mauthner and Jacobowski, despite their attacks on anti-Semitism, showed in their works how the image of the "bad Jew" was becoming entrenched in the culture of Imperial Germany and why it was difficult to dislodge. The presence of the "bad Jew" in the form of the accented alien reflected insecurities about what was truly German and how such Germanness, whatever it was, could be protected from cultural dilution. The "bad Jew" in the person of the manipulative speculator reflected anxieties about a capitalism that seemed unresponsive to traditional values of hard work. Such clearly offensive Jewish characters in fiction nevertheless served to undermine the advocacy of toleration in much the same way Mauthner himself had worried that Mommsen's suggestion of Jewish conversion would do.

Unresolved, moreover, was the question of how "good Jews" should deal with anti-Semitism. Well-meaning friends in both novels urged the protagonists to ignore prejudice as manifestations of uneducated rabble or of a past still being eradicated. But this response ignored not only the pent-up rage that inevitably resulted but also the signs that anti-Semitism was spreading, not receding, in Imperial Germany. Although novels continued to depict such signs, they also continued to sustain the myth that anti-Semitism had its roots in the behavior of "bad Jews" and would be cured when they disappeared from German society.

The Berlin novelist who most conspicuously embraced this myth was a Jewish writer from Breslau named Konrad Sittenfeld, whom we have already encountered under the pen-name Conrad Alberti. Alberti's immersion in Darwinian ideas clearly extended to his notion of the "Jewish question," which he described in 1889 as having to do with an inferior race whose presence was contaminating the cultural and economic realms of Berlin. The "good Jews," as he described them, were those who manifested the greatest degree of biological assimilation. The recent wave of anti-Semitism, he argued, only strengthened the ties of such people to the Jewish community, thereby impeding the natural selection that eventually would cause Jews to be bred out of existence.[59] Such an argument exhibited a startling mixture of racist ideas and calls for reform. Non-Jewish Germans, Alberti continued, could weaken the bonds among Jews by ending discrimination in the officer corps and government bureaucracy and by reversing the social strictures against mixed marriages. Only Jews, however, could halt Jewish separatism, a task that modern Jews were beginning by seeing to their own "inner, spiritual self-dissolution."[60] Alberti's prescription for the destruction of Judaism by Jews, predictably, evoked outraged responses from readers,[61] but these did not deter him from incorporating his theory into his fiction.

The "Jewish question" appears three times in Alberti's fiction: in *Die Alten und die Jungen* (1889), *Schröter & Co.* (1893), and his last novel, *Ablösung vor!* (*Relief Guard, Forward!*) (1911). His treatment of the issue suggests a progression in his attitudes, beginning with an apparent acceptance of the myth of Jews' being a dissolute influence on German society, and traveling to a stage in the last novel in which an assimilated Jewish character is shown striding vigorously into the German future. Although the progression might reflect Alberti's beliefs that Jews could be bred out of existence, it also suggests his own progress against self-hatred.

*Die Alten und die Jungen* shows a growing prominence of "bad Jews," from its opening description of a ragged family of *Ostjuden* arriving in Berlin[62] to the far more visible Jarociner family enjoying the enormous wealth garnered by speculation. Each of the four Jarociners exudes the weaknesses of a particular gender and generation, but they all suggest that Jews are especially susceptible to materialism and crassness. Although vulgar anti-Semitism is attacked, the real "Jewish question" seems to concern the threat of people like the Jarociners to German society. One passage has Frau Jarociner whispering to her husband at a particularly glorious social triumph, "Today we rule Berlin! This is what I've worked for my whole life! Let them say what they will—we Jews will rule the world!"[63] This joy is premature, however, and the apparent triumph ends when the Jarociners' hollowness brings them social and financial disaster.

*Schröter & Co.* similarly portrays a complement of "bad Jews," but devotes more attention to the effects of anti-Semitism on the "good Jew." A sequel to Gustav Freytag's *Soll und Haben* (1855), the novel puts the same constellation of characters in the setting of 1878. It centers mainly on the economic pressures that incite Freytag's Anton Wohlfahrt, now a successful, middle-aged businessman, to abandon caution and plunge into a chaotic stockmarket. Anti-Semitism is thus a secondary theme, which Alberti develops at one level as a justifiable reaction against the modern legatees of the wily Jew. Freytag's beautiful but socially inferior Rosalie Ehrenthal has aged into an obese social climber, married to Isaak Blumenreich, the stock mogul who leads a naive Anton down the path to ruin. Alois Tinkely (the son of Freytag's shifty peddler, Schmeie Tinkeles), is another character who epitomizes the unrestrained opportunism of a modern type of Jew, first as a lawyer in Berlin and then, when debts force him out of his profession, as a demagogic social democrat. The wretched outcomes of all three underscore Alberti's wish to hasten the demise of the "bad Jew." Although some details suggest that their spitefulness in dealing with Christians comes from their suffering as Jews, the clear message is that their malice explains their ostracism by German society.

The "innocent" victim of anti-Semitism in *Schröter & Co.* is the Blumenreich's son Werner, who personifies the "good Jew." His troubles also signify Alberti's prescription that the way out of the vicious circle of anti-Semitism and "bad Jews" lies with Germans' complete social acceptance of young people like Werner. An upright young man who despises the behavior and values of older

Jews, he strives to be an exemplary German. When he encounters signs of anti-Semitism, he works around the obstacles it imposes. Werner's most disheartening experiences illustrate two issues Alberti alluded to in his journalism. The first involves Werner's drive to win a commission in the reserve officer corps. When his commanding officer advises him to withdraw his application (referring vaguely to "so many qualified candidates"), Werner is forced to abandon illusions about "outworn prejudice" and equality.[64] He laments his "ruined existence," but the defeat proves to be only a setback. A second episode of prejudice occurs when Werner proposes to Anton Wohlfahrt's daughter and is rejected. She lacks the will, she tells him, to live with the ongoing tension with society that mixed marriages bring. This rejection, too, proves only a temporary hindrance, for Werner soon establishes a more promising bond with her companion, an orphaned relative of a notably lower station. At the end, Werner is to be a guest in an aristocratic household whose genteel anti-Semitism has subsided in the face of his honorable bearing. This young Jew, then, seems on his way to acceptance in German society. Or, conversely, German society is progressing in the absorption of its Jews.

Almost two decades later, in his last novel, *Ablösung vor!*, Alberti once again alluded to the "Jewish question." The title, referring to the command given at the changing of a guard, represents the novel's focus on the arrival of a post-Bismarckian generation. The relative insignificance of Judaism in this novel—especially the lack of any signs of anti-Semitism—suggests that Alberti believed that the "Jewish question" had retreated with the old guard. The only Jewish character, a young archeologist named Walter Benhay, seems assimilated. Moreover, his Jewish origins play no role in the conflicts he experiences, which seems to confirm Alberti's earlier theory that Judaism was disappearing from modern society.

Nevertheless, two passages indicate that Alberti still saw a wall of separation between Walter and his non-Jewish countrymen. In one conversation about his discovery of an ancient Coptic site Walter comments laughingly to a Gentile friend on the irony of his excavating for the "goyim" their most ancient sacred writing.[65] In a more significant passage he reveals himself still further by alluding to a hidden identity within the soul of every Jew. The episode begins with a description of his apartment, a carefully contrived reflection of his personality. When a visitor asks about the meaning of the Greek citation over the entrance, Walter explains that it is a passage from the New Testament. He thereupon pulls a Bible from the shelf and reads a translation of the quotation, Romans 2:28–29: "For he is not a Jew, which is one outwardly; neither is that circumcision, which is outward in the flesh; but he is a Jew, which is one inwardly; and circumcision is that of the heart, in the spirit, and not in the letter." Walter uses this passage, which concerns Paul's efforts to clarify Judaism's relation to the new gospel, to suggest Judaism's obsolescence. Citing his father's mere outward adherence to Jewish worship, he implies that he has displayed the lines to detach himself altogether from Judaism. Suddenly, however, he compares Jewish spirituality to race: "Do you know that Judaism is to the soul what skin color is to the body? There are Jewish mulattoes, half-breeds, quadroons, and octoroons, but the color keeps reappearing in later generations."[66] This comment is ambiguous. The biblical passage suggests a positive concept of Judaism as an inner spirit. But its location in the New Testament also suggests that Jews should abandon their legalistic practices for the spiritual life of Christianity. Moreover, the racial metaphor has the negative connotation of an unwanted trait that lasts for generations. Uneasiness is evident in the notions that Jews should become Christianized and that even modern Jews may not have ceased to be Jews.[67]

The book gives one additional hint about Alberti's changing concern for his origins: its title page contains his patrimonial name, Sittenfeld, in parentheses. Was Alberti simply reaffirming the family legacy he had abandoned with the adoption of his pen name, or was he also reaffirming the legacy of Judaism? An autobiographical piece published a year later, on his fiftieth birthday, gives no hint of a religious awakening.[68] It does show, however, a man grown more tolerant and judicious than the bombastic young author who had written two decades earlier of the "superfluity, perniciousness, and decadence of Judaism."[69] It also shows a man hopeful that the humane traditions of Western culture will win out in modern Germany.

This hope was shared by all the authors discussed in this chapter. With their angry portrayals of social and institutional anti-Semitism they showed themselves to be heirs of those traditions. But their uncertainties about the meaning of that heritage for Jews obscured their message. Their own susceptibility to stereotypes showed how easily anti-Semitism grew from anxieties about the modern age. Their eagerness to encourage the dissolution of Jewish identity into Germanness showed how the legacy of toleration could be overshadowed by a fearful nationalism. Their failure to depict Jews who were committed both to their religion and to their Germanness meant a lost opportunity to counter the notion that Jews could not be Germans.[70] In short, their refusal to believe the ominous implications of their own testimony becomes a tragic irony in hindsight. Hindsight, however, must not be allowed to obscure the plausibility of their hope that Berlin would one day realize the vision of Mendelssohn and Lessing.[71]

# Notes

1. Hans Israel Bach, *The German Jew: A Synthesis of Judaism and Western Civilization, 1730–1930* (Oxford, 1984), 37, 48–49, and Annegret Ehmann et al., *Juden in Berlin, 1671–1945: Ein Lesebuch* (Berlin, 1988), 9–14.
2. On the history of Jewish emancipation in nineteenth-century Germany see Ismar Schorsch, *Jewish Reactions to German Anti-Semitism, 1870–1914* (New York, 1972), 1–13, and Reinhard Rürup, "Emanzipation und Krise—Zur Geschichte der 'Judenfrage' in Deutschland vor 1890," in Werner E. Mosse, ed., *Juden im Wilhelminischen Deutschland 1890–1914* (Tübingen, 1976), 19–20.

3. See Deborah Hertz, *Jewish High Society in Old Regime Berlin* (New Haven, Conn., 1987).
4. A statistical summary of the proportion of Jews to the total population in Berlin shows a range from 1.7 percent in 1816 to 5.1 percent in 1895, after which it declined. Peter G. J. Pulzer, *The Rise of Political Anti-Semitism in Germany and Austria* (New York, 1964), 10.
5. See Werner Jochmann, "Struktur und Funktion des deutschen Antisemitismus," in Mosse, *Juden im Wilhelminischen Deutschland*, 389–419.
6. On this "emancipation ideology" see Sanford Ragins, *Jewish Responses to Anti-Semitism in Germany, 1870–1914: A Study in the History of Ideas* (Cincinnati, 1980), 2–3; Uriel Tal, *Christians and Jews in Germany: Religion, Politics, and Ideology in the Second Reich, 1870–1914*, translated by Noah Jonathan Jacobs (Ithaca, N.Y., 1975), 16–19; Bach, *German Jew*, 74–75.
7. Bach, *German Jew*, 81. Max Kretzer is one exception; his *Die Bergpredigt* dealt more than any other novel with the religious element in anti-Semitism.
8. This has been interpreted as a collision between liberalism and *völkisch* thought in which the latter won out. George L. Mosse, *Germans and Jews: The Right, The Left, and The Search for a "Third Force" in Pre-Nazi Germany* (New York, 1970), 96.
9. Cited in Pulzer, *Political Anti-Semitism*, 89.
10. See, for example, Friedrich Spielhagen, *Sturmflut*, II, 157. Years later Spielhagen still insisted that unscrupulous Jewish profiteers were to blame for popular anti-Semitism. Hermann Bahr, *Der Antisemitismus: Ein internationales Interview* (1894; reprinted Berlin, 1979), 18.
11. Wolfgang Kirchbach, *Kinder des Reiches* (Leipzig, 1883), 49.
12. Ibid., 135. This notion of Jews as contributors to the values of Western civilization has its origins in Moses Mendelssohn. Bach, *German Jew*, 201.
13. See Steven E. Aschheim, *Brothers and Strangers: The East European Jew in German and German Jewish Consciousness, 1800–1923* (Madison, Wis., 1982), 3–16, and Sander L. Gilman, *Jewish Self-Hatred: Anti-Semitism and the Hidden Language of the Jews* (Baltimore, 1986).
14. Fritz Mauthner, *Der neue Ahasver: Roman aus Jung-Berlin* (Dresden, 1882), I, 10.
15. Heinrich von Treitschke, "Unsere Aussichten," in Walter Boehlich, ed., *Der Berliner Antisemitismusstreit* (Frankfurt am Main, 1965), 11. See also Tal, *Christians and Jews in Germany*, 50–54, and Ragins, *Jewish Responses to Anti-Semitism*, 14–17.
16. *Über unser Judenthum* is reprinted in Boehlich, *Berliner Antisemitismusstreit*, 210–225. On Treitschke's wounded reaction to Mommsen's attack see 239, 238, 247.
17. Ibid., 224–235. See also Schorsch, *Jewish Reactions to German Anti-Semitism*, 63, 99. As Bach puts it, "The defense was almost worse than Treitschke's attack." Bach, *The German Jew*, 125.
18. Mauthner's character Oswald Fränkel exemplifies the prescription that Jews should relinquish their distinctive traditions. See also Ragins, *Jewish Responses to Anti-Semitism*, 6.
19. Mauthner, *Ahasver*, I, 9.
20. On Mauthner's biography see Brümmer, IV, 396–397. On the relation of his Jewishness to his linguistic interests see Gilman, *Jewish Self-Hatred*, 227–233.
21. Another Ahasverus legend, popularized earlier by Eugene Sue, concerned a shoemaker's trek from Jerusalem to the North Pole. Karl Gutzkow modernized this version when his narrator remarked that the only frozen thing the modern Ahasverus knows are the ices at Kranzler's in Berlin. *Die neuen Serapionsbrüder* (Berlin, 1877), II, 206.
22. Mauthner, *Ahasver*, I, 60–61. See also Fritz Mauthner, *Prager Jugendjahre* (reprinted, Frankfurt am Main, 1969), 35–150, 248–254.

23. On the link between Jewish enthusiasm for modernity and the emancipation law see Hans-Joachim Bieber, "Anti-Semitism as a Reflection of Social, Economic and Political Tension in Germany: 1880–1933," in David Bronsen, ed., *Jews and Germans from 1860 to 1933: The Problematic Symbiosis* (Heidelberg, 1979), 34–35.
24. Mauthner, *Ahasver*, I, 106.
25. This distinction attests to Jews' acceptance of the *völkisch* image of the modern Jew as a soulless materialist. Mosse, *Germans and Jews*, 80–81, and Aschheim, *Brothers and Strangers*, 74–75.
26. Mauthner, *Ahasver*, I, 121.
27. Ibid., I, 247–260.
28. Ibid., I, 120. Mauthner's subsequent trilogy, *Berlin W* (1886–1890), continues to focus on the prevalence of these traits in Berlin society.
29. Mauthner, *Ahasver*, I, 209. Cursing one's Jewishness has been described as a peculiarly modern reaction. Bach, *German Jew*, 81.
30. Mauthner, *Ahasver*, II, 38. Mauthner credits Mommsen with awakening him to this conception of *Christenheit*. Ibid., I, 5. On the tradition of this distinction see Helmut Scheuer, "Zur Christus-Figur in der Literatur um 1900," in Richard Bauer et al., eds., *Fin de Siècle: Zu Literatur und Kunst der Jahrhundertwende* (Frankfurt am Main, 1977), 381–382; on social pressures on Jews to give up their "distinctiveness," see also Tal, *Christians and Jews in Germany*, 31–80.
31. Mauthner, *Ahasver*, II, 38.
32. Ibid., II, 74. Recent interpretations of the onset of modern anti-Semitism rely far more on the activities of Stoecker, the Treitschke articles, and the crisis of German liberalism as explanations. See, for example, Ragins, *Jewish Responses to Anti-Semitism*, 19–33; Schorsch, *Jewish Reactions to German Anti-Semitism*, 36–39, 54–59; and Jochmann, "Struktur und Funktion des Antisemitismus," in Mosse, *Juden in Wilhelminischen Deutschland*, 412–414.
33. Mauthner, *Ahasver*, II, 158; see also II, 202–207, 288–289.
34. Ibid., II, 258.
35. Ibid., II, 293.
36. Ibid., II, 304.
37. Ibid., II, 323.
38. Ibid., II, 205.
39. The interpretation of anti-Semitism as "a result of misguided national feeling" was not uncommon at the time. Boehlich, *Berliner Antisemitismusstreit*, 251.
40. Mauthner, *Der neue Ahasver*, I, 5. The quotation in which this term occurs comes from a footnote in Mommsen's essay. Boehlich, *Antisemitismusstreit*, 217n.
41. Gilman, *Jewish Self-Hatred*, 2–4.
42. During the next thirty years this novel was printed in seven German editions and six translations. Schorsch, *Jewish Reactions to German Anti-Semitism*, 95; see also Ragins, *Jewish Responses to Anti-Semitism*, 43–44. On the resurgence of anti-Semitism in the 1890s see Schorsch, *Jewish Reactions to German Anti-Semitism*, 36–37, 103–113, and Jochmann, "Struktur und Funktion des deutschen Antisemitismus," in Mosse, *Juden in Wilhelminischen Deutschland*, 436–460.
43. Ludwig Jacobowski, *Werther der Jude*, 6th ed. (Berlin, 1898), 48. The references in this passage to the old man's nasalized speech vividly support Gilman's thesis that language set Jews apart.
44. Ibid., 38.
45. Ibid., 33–35.
46. Ibid., 27.
47. Ibid., 46; see a similar episode on 153.
48. Ibid., 20, 9, 97, 78. See also Ehmann et al., *Juden in Berlin*, 146–148.

49. On the wider manifestations of Jewish self-criticism see Schorsch, *Jewish Reactions to German Anti-Semitism*, 47–48.
50. Jacobowski, *Werther*, 54.
51. Jacobowski, *Werther*, 59. Zionists looked surprisingly favorably on this assimilationist novel by interpreting Jacobowski's call for self-reformation as the prelude to building a new Jewish community in a new homeland. Itta Shedletzky, "Ludwig Jacobowski (1868–1900) und Jakob Loewenberg (1856–1929): Literarisches Leben und Schaffen 'aus deutscher und aus jüdischer Seele,'" in Stéphane Moses and Albrecht Schöne, eds., *Juden in der deutschen Literatur: Ein deutsch-israelisches Symposion* (Frankfurt am Main, 1986), 202–203.
52. Jacobowski, *Werther*, 197–198.
53. Ibid., 328.
54. Ibid., 57.
55. Ibid., 305.
56. One passage refers to Helene as "a blond Gretchen" who attracts him with magnetic force. Ibid., 60.
57. Ibid., 311; see also 315.
58. Ibid., 354. See also Ragins, *Jewish Responses to Anti-Semitism*, 43–44. On the controversy the novel provoked within the Jewish community see Shedletzky in Moses and Schöne, *Juden in der deutschen Literatur*, 204–207.
59. Conrad Alberti, "Judentum und Antisemitismus: Eine zeitgenössische Studie," *Die Gesellschaft*, 5, 3 (December 1889), 1718–1733.
60. Ibid., 1730.
61. See *Die Gesellschaft*, 6 (1890), 349–370, 556–566, 905–906, 1054–1058, 1355–1367, and 1822–1833.
62. Conrad Alberti, *Die Alten und die Jungen* (Leipzig, 1889), I, 6. On the immigration of eastern Jews to Berlin see Aschheim, *Brothers and Strangers*, 33–37.
63. Alberti, *Die Alten und die Jungen*, II, 132.
64. Conrad Alberti, *Schröter & Co.* (Berlin, 1893), 190–192, 237.
65. Conrad Alberti, *Ablösung vor!* (Berlin, 1911), 58.
66. Ibid., 256.
67. On the notion of inherited psychological traits see Bach, *German Jews*, 162.
68. Conrad Alberti, *Der Weg der Menschheit* (Berlin, 1912), IV, xi–xv. See also Katherine Roper, "Conrad Alberti's *Kampf ums Dasein*: The Writer in Imperial Berlin," *German Studies Review*, 7, 1 (February 1984), 75, 85–86.
69. Conrad Alberti, "Judentum und Antisemitismus," 1719.
70. One author did portray a Berlin family living quietly with both Jewishness and Germanness, in two best-selling novels set in Biedermeier Berlin. See George Hermann's *Jettchen Gebert* (1906) and *Henriette Jacoby* (1910). Recalling his own upbringing in a Jewish household in Wilhelmine Berlin, Gershom Scholem challenged the notion that most Jews wanted to assimilate. Gershom Scholem, "On the Social Psychology of the Jews in Germany: 1900–1933," in Bronsen, ed., *Jews and Germans*, 20.
71. Scholem is emphatic about the "blindness or self-delusion" of Jewish authors toward the realities of Wilhelmine Germany, but others have argued that it was plausible for Jews of Imperial Germany to believe that anti-Semitism would wane. Bronsen, ed., *Jews and Germans*, 22; Ragins, *Jewish Responses to Anti-Semitism*, 161–162; Robert Weltsch, "Nachwort," in Mosse, *Juden in Wilhelminischen Deutschland*, 700–702.

# 9

# Coming of Age: Women in Berlin Society

The production of Henrik Ibsen's *Doll's House* in Berlin was a sensational event of the winter of 1889. Six months later Conrad Alberti described its effects in terms of an epidemic he called "Noramania." The example of Ibsen's heroine striding from marital confines into an independent life was infecting countless Berlin wives, wrote Alberti, unable to hide his impatience with women who indulged in "Nora-like" fantasies.[1] Their reckless behavior, he conceded, was provoked by a society that consigned women to a state of perpetual immaturity, but despite admitting an injustice in society's treatment of women, Alberti proposed to solve the "woman question" by leaving women bound within the existing marital contract.[2] Only economic independence could justify women's demand for autonomy, he argued, but for women of the "propertied" classes marriage was clearly a more favorable state than becoming a housekeeper or seamstress (the sorts of female jobs he named).[3] In accepting the marriage contract, a woman pledged "her existence" to the man who promised to support her and thereby renounced any claim to an independent will. Modern marriage, to be sure, should be grounded in mutual love that embodied the irresistible drive of two people to merge their lives, but how such a union was to be realized by women in childlike minority or economic dependence was a question Alberti failed to raise in his article. It was a question, however, that he and a host of other novelists raised in their fiction.

Definition of the "woman question" in terms of tensions between marriage, economic independence, and personal autonomy is only part of the scope of concerns raised by and about women in Imperial Germany. During the last decades of the nineteenth century growing numbers of Germans engaged in intense and wide-ranging debate over the role of women in modern society. Pamphlets, articles, and books took on the task of exposing and challenging the multi-faceted structures of discrimination against women in educational, economic, professional, political, and cultural realms, and new reform organizations sprang forth in increasing abundance.[4] Although women's suffrage was not to be achieved during the life of Imperial Germany, the growing pressures led to significant changes, especially in legal status, education, and professional opportunities.[5]

Within this wider context debate about women's identity and its relation to marriage was carried on, and novels were a major vehicle of this discourse. Alberti's simultaneous anger against marriage as a means of oppression and against women who challenged that institution reflected an ambivalence shared by many of his literary contemporaries.[6] Novelists who were conscious of a modernizing age questioned deeply held beliefs about marriage as a religious commitment, as a moral basis for society, or as the essential means of transmitting name and property. Ideas about women's equality and marriages based on love or the pursuit of happiness caused them further confusion. But if women's possibilities of existence were not to be defined solely in terms of their relation to the home, family, and marriage, what other terms would apply? If women were to become full participants in a call to national regeneration, how would their roles be redefined?

In confronting such questions, novelists were reacting to the need to give life to their female characters. If such creations were to succeed, they could not relegate women to the periphery of human experience, as politicians, philosophers, or social scientists were wont to do.[7] Already prominent in Gutzkow's *Ritter vom Geiste*, the treatment of women's condition arose in almost every novel of Imperial Berlin. And within these fictional treatments signs of ambivalence were universal, with portrayals of legal and social entrapment being frequently offset by indications of contempt toward women's unpreparedness to deal with life and of suspicion toward the "emancipated" woman.[8] This chapter focuses on novels—all but one of them written by women—that not only depicted women's situations but articulated women's perspectives on them. It examines works that were especially explicit in portraying female characters who grappled with the social and psychological obstacles to their developing an independent identity.[9] The novels suggest that although women's idea of "coming of age" in Germany drew on the Kantian notion of maturity as a process of reaching intellectual and moral independence, it involved experiences completely foreign to that legacy.[10] Works like *Doll's House* were catalysts for defining the coming of age in particularly female terms, but novels of Imperial Berlin became a vivid instance of the power of prevailing notions to enclose this process within private spheres of domesticity rather than to open women's realm to public spheres of social engagement.[11]

Although numerous Berlin novels portrayed women's childlike state within a protective marriage and a patriarchal society, Theodor Fontane's *Effi Briest* (1895) gives the most expansive introduction to the theme. Through this novel Fontane also demonstrated the extent to which a male writer could "think" his way into portraying a woman's collision with a patriarchal society. To be sure, he elsewhere denied advocating women's emancipation and seemed to underscore it by having his heroine ultimately embrace the code of a traditional society.[12] Still, through the story of Effi Briest he questioned that code, by following a self-willed young woman's road to maturity and showing how it was impeded by the social conditions that surrounded her gender. Effi's progress toward a genuine understanding of that environment and toward defining her role in it involved a struggle with clear parallels to that of Nora. And yet, unlike Nora, her exit from a confining marriage was involuntary and her experience outside of it held none of the redefinition of women's social role that Nora's action seemed to promise.

In its outlines Effi's story is unremarkable in its conventionality.[13] An energetic seventeen-year-old daughter in the household of an unassuming member of the Prussian nobility, Effi is steered by her parents into a marriage of convenience with the much older Baron Geert von Innstetten. She languishes as a young bride on her husband's austere Pomeranian estate until she yields to the seduction of a newly arrived district commander, but she ends the affair when her husband's transfer to Berlin provides a much desired escape. Some years later, however, Innstetten discovers letters attesting to the affair, whereupon he challenges the officer, kills him in the duel, and expels Effi from his household and from contact with their daughter. In her subsequent life as a social outcast Effi declines in health and eventually dies.

The main focus of the novel concerns the conflict between a rigid social code and an ideal of individual freedom. All the characters embody this conflict, but Effi becomes its ultimate victim. Her fate, suggesting that women cannot define a social identity outside the bounds of marriage and family, unfolds in the context of three settings. The conflict begins in her childhood home on the family estate north of Berlin amid the quiet, traditional values of German family life. It grows on Innstetten's Pomeranian property, which is associated with Bismarck's estate, Varzin, and the Junker society of that era. Finally, it reaches its climax in Berlin's modern expanses. In her life the city serves two functions: first offering her liberation from the stultifying life in provincial outlands and later providing anonymity for her social exile.

The tranquil Briest estate suggests the ideal environment for a young girl to make the transition from her parental home to that of her husband. But Effi only partly reflects that environment: the placid young girl stitching an altar cloth in the garden bower moments later becomes an impetuous child who vents her energy in gymnastic stretches and bends. She is equally impetuous when the visiting Baron von Innstetten asks her parents for her hand. Effi's mother pressures her to accept the offer, and Effi quickly acquiesces because Innstetten meets her girlish expectations: "He must be an aristocrat, and he must hold an important position, and he must be good looking."[14]

The complacency with which Effi and her parents follow the well-established process contrasts with authorial warnings about the match. When she and her mother go to Berlin to shop for her trousseau, for example, Effi's exuberance over the glamor of the capital makes it clear that her restlessness will not be easily tamed in the monotony of Pomerania. For her trousseau, moreover, she wants to persuade her mother to buy her a fur coat rather than see to the practical objects of married life. More ominous still is the ease with which she glosses over her indifference to the staid Innstetten; luxury and honor, she implies, will substitute for love. She then adds another insight: Innstetten is a man who abides by clear rules of conduct. "I don't have any such principles," she confesses, "that's something that bothers and frightens me."[15] The need for distraction, the craving for position, the lack of principles—all are jarring qualities to emerge in the girl just introduced. They suggest that the conventional upbringing of young girls, however careful and well intentioned, provides an inadequate foundation for maturity.

Although Effi's apprehension is a step toward self-understanding, she must travel much further before she knows the consequences of her unpreparedness for marriage. The next stage begins with her arrival in the austere society of aristocratic Pomerania, a rural outpost whose rigid restraints become the impetus for Effi's ultimate ruin. In the drawing rooms of far-flung estates her pretentious dress gives rise to much head-shaking, as betokening a sign of the "Berlin school" with its "love of the external."[16] In turn, Effi detests the scrutiny of dull people. Her overriding feeling, however, is a fearful loneliness, intensified by Innstetten's frequent absences on official business.

Outwardly Effi progresses toward conventional womanhood in Pomerania, but her inner state remains turbulent. The birth of a daughter provides "a dear plaything" for a still childlike Effi, who works to submerge her nature in an adult role.[17] One scene shows her as a nineteen-year-old "matron" at a ball, not dancing but sitting sedately with the "old ladies."[18] Still more oppressive is a marriage that she perceives to be based on an unbalanced relation with her husband as teacher and herself as pupil. The affair with the officer becomes a much desired distraction.

Who is responsible for the adultery? The immature Effi, who yields to a craving for diversion? The worldly officer, who scoffs at society's rules? The husband, who remains oblivious to his wife's needs? The stifling atmosphere of East Pomerania? The parents, who swayed Effi into a marriage of convenience? Fontane shows all to be responsible, but he allows Effi to spare herself no illusions about her own responsibility. She is uncomfortable when Innstetten returns from an absence and exclaims how womanly she looks, and she is relieved to learn he has accepted a government position in Berlin. If the affair has brought womanly fulfillment, it has also intensified her revulsion for a life determined by conditions over which she has no say.

Effi uses the move to Berlin to take control of her life and makes each subsequent action a private declaration of independence. In a letter to the officer, she asserts her culpability and breaks off the relationship. She leaves for Berlin under the guise of making a short journey to look for living quarters, determined that the choice will be hers—not her husband's nor her mother's. Once there, she ignores her mother's advice and selects a brand-new apartment west of the Tiergarten. She then feigns an illness that will keep her in Berlin until her husband takes up his post. The day before Innstetten's arrival, she steps onto the balcony of their apartment and exclaims, "Now, God willing, a new life! Things will be different."[19]

Things are markedly better, but Effi's discovery that she feels no shame over the adultery makes her question her identity as a woman: "If all women are like that, it's terrible, and if they aren't like that—and I hope they're not—then there's something amiss in my soul."[20] Life in Berlin, however, causes such worries to wane. Innstetten proves to be more attentive, and Effi's social ambitions are satisfied when she receives complimentary words from the Kaiser himself at a court ball. The role of Berlin matron brings an end to Effi's youthful restlessness. And yet, even after more than six years of her Berlin life, a hidden part of her remains troubled. To what extent did her adulterous lapse betoken something amiss in her womanly soul?

Innstetten has no doubts about something being irredeemably amiss in his wife's integrity when he finds the letters and casts her out. When her parents reject her as well, Effi settles without demur into an isolated life in a small walk-up in old Berlin. Thus begins a period of testing that, in contrast to personal trials endured by male characters in other novels, offers no passage out of the private realm in which Effi is ensconced. Financial matters are not an issue, for despite their moral disowning the Briests provide material support. Paramount, rather, is the question of how time is to be filled by a woman cut off from her socially designated role. Hours of knitting, playing solitaire, and practicing the piano provide scant relief from the boredom. A desire to work with poor children is abandoned when she realizes she would never be accepted by the charity associations. Finally, she begins painting lessons, and, while admitting she will never be more than a dilettante, she immerses herself in the one activity that allows stimulating contact with others. Over the three years after her divorce, Effi finds the resources to make the best of her situation, but the fact that she does not overcome the obstacles between her and meaningful work testifies to the pressure of the social forces that exile her within her private sphere. Only briefly does Effi become angry: "In the end [Innstetten] was wrong. Everything that happened lay far in the past; a new life had begun; he could have let it lie; instead he cut down the poor [officer]."[21] Such anger, however, soon dissolves back into acceptance.

When Effi's health deteriorates, her parents reverse themselves and accept her back in their home. As she approaches death, she abandons any inner challenge to the traditional moral code. Let Innstetten know, she instructs her mother, that she agrees fully with what he did. Effi's coming of age, then, involved a free acceptance of a moral code, not from anyone's tutelage but through her own introspection. Coming of age meant taking responsibility for her own life—not defying the social conditions that molded it. As Fontane said, he never intended to advocate women's emancipation. Nevertheless, in showing a young woman's growing up to meet a crisis with honesty and dignity, Fontane challenged stereotypes that women were so weak as to collapse when confronted with life's realities. He left it to other authors, however, to search for means by which women might reshape realities that kept them in perpetual immaturity.

The challenge of reshaping social institutions to accord with an ideal of individual freedom for both sexes proved far more difficult than feminists of the 1890s, or even much later, envisioned.[22] Marriage remained a central part of this dilemma insofar as it consigned women to legal, intellectual, and emotional dependence. But if Nora's decision to leave her self-conceived doll's house meant her coming of age, it also meant her leaving the private domestic realm that had given social- and self-definition. If she were to succeed, she would have to acquire a new identity in a public realm that had little place for the unmarried, untrained woman, while also seeking to reinforce her belief that she was better off facing this fearsome world than enduring her marriage. Ibsen's conclusion revealed no doubt about Nora's ability to sustain her resolve, but his allowing a self-sufficient widow in the same play to end her isolation by remarrying underscored marriage as a response to deep human needs. To suggest that the independent woman should forego it was to suggest that she renounce her emotions as well as her social identity.

Few novelists of this period went so far as to advocate a woman's renunciation of marriage, but all who treated the situation of women recognized that if women were to go beyond their nonage, marriage would have to change radically. Most, however, including virtually all male authors who dealt with the issue, merely described an intractable dilemma and allowed their female characters to meet defeat and often death through natural or self-inflicted causes. The few who used their works to explore sustained struggles for women's autonomy, both inside and outside marriage, created fictional counterparts to women's movements and other writings on the condition of women. Unlike the relatively clear goals and theories of movements, novels depicted huge obstacles encountered by women; in a few cases they also depicted men who were committed to defining new relations between the sexes. Women writers proved more willing to grapple with the obstacles that hindered women from forming congruent personal and social identities, perhaps as a consequence of trying to translate personal experience into literary discourse.[23] The rest of this chapter concerns novels by three such women: Gabriele Reuter, Clara Viebig, and Jolanthe Marès; each shows women characters who travelled farther along the road to self-affirmation than Effi Briest. Each also manifests the resistances to moving self-affirmation from the private to the public realm. The entry of women into the struggle for German regeneration was to be circumscribed in the Berlin novels by a deep-seated notion that true womanhood was fundamentally alien to the strident competitiveness of the public arena.

Of the three authors Gabriele Reuter (1859–1941) was the most self-consciously feminist, but even she distanced herself from organized movements.[24] Nevertheless, her works showed a deep commitment to women's self-realization and an intense awareness of social and psychological hindrances. Reuter first attained notice in 1895, the year *Effi Briest* was published, with her novel *Aus guter Familie* (*From a Good Family*), which traces the systematic nurturing of a young girl to a role of passivity and self-denial. Of her many subsequent novels that continued to explore women's social victimization, *Ellen von der Weiden* (1900) is particularly appropriate, not only because it took up issues raised by *Effi Briest* but also because its Berlin setting specifically linked women's condition to modernization, and because its immense popularity gave its provocative questions about the nature of modern womanhood wide dissemination.[25] What emerges in the novel is both a scathing critique of women's socialized expectations of marriage and an affirmation of motherhood as their most important social responsibility.

Like Effi, Ellen von der Weiden is charming, spontaneous, and rigorously honest with herself. She also marries an older man who admires her naturalness but expects to tame it to his specifications. She also encounters untold frustrations in trying to mold her temperament to her husband's expectations, and increasingly she resents being subjected to his pedagogy. Her boredom and unhappiness also drive her to a momentary act of adultery, and although she ends the affair quickly, she searches her heart in vain for feelings of remorse. Her husband finds out about the affair, and the marriage ends in divorce, after which Ellen ultimately returns to her parental home away from Berlin.

Ellen differs from Effi, however, in being far less socially conventional and in achieving a radical resolution in unmarried motherhood. She adapts neither to married life nor to life in Berlin, and her story concludes with her facing a hopeful future outside the bounds of a traditional moral code and away from Berlin. Far from leading to an endorsement of conventional rural values, the anti-urbanism in this novel is specifically linked with the modern specter of an independent woman conscious of having arrived at a self-actualizing maturity.

Ellen is introduced as a free-spirited girl who scrambles up cliffs in her beloved Harz mountains. Her writer-father warns her against accepting the marriage offer of a staid Berlin physician, but in ignoring this advice she shows how even a girl of independent mind has been conditioned by the notion that young women will find happiness in the security of a respectable marriage. A diary entry makes her expectations plain: with her marriage her destiny has been fulfilled. But if the waiting is over, she writes, why then "does my soul listen day and night for sounds of the future?"[26] With little else to do, Ellen scrutinizes her marriage, searching for signs of love for her husband, of his love for her, and of her becoming a good wife. Convinced that marriage is a woman's most important project and that its success depends on her, she cannot fathom why peace and happiness elude her. She attempts to force serenity by resolving that "love and marriage are two different things having nothing to do with one another" and vowing to dedicate herself to becoming a cheerful, caring wife—the foundation of every good marriage.[27]

Repeatedly, however, Ellen feels unsuited to this role. Even the newness of the furniture in their Berlin apartment seems threatening, "symbols of an

existence I don't know what to do with."²⁸ More threatening still are the so-called "perfect people" around her, women like her maid and her sister-in-law who seem to carry out their respective household and wifely tasks with ease. Ellen knows she cannot achieve that ease and hopes that her husband Fritz does not place high value on her doing so, but, alas, he, too, numbers among the "perfect people." When he returns home after hours in a sweltering clinic, she is ashamed of having languished in the coolness of the apartment. Indeed, whenever she measures herself against him, she finds herself lacking. He reinforces her sense of failure with his tutelage. Marriage is a school, the young bride writes to a friend, "and Fritz reminds me daily of how much I have to learn in order to make him happy."²⁹

The thought that he might have much to learn to make Ellen happy never occurs to him. Seeing himself as a man of science in his personal as well as his professional life, Dr. Fritz Erdmannsdörfer has contact with many an "hysterical woman" and is determined that neither he nor his wife become infected by the rampant nervousness of the capital.³⁰ He does not even want a "cheerful" wife if it leads to what he sees as undignified behavior or sentimental compassion. When Ellen regales guests with her antics, Fritz admonishes her for being "unwomanly," and he refuses to tolerate her seeming to take the side of one of his "hysterical" patients.³¹

Fritz's and Ellen's views of Berlin reflect the basic conflict of their marriage. Whereas he thrives in the city as the proving ground for building a brilliant career, Ellen is terrorized by its noise, crowds, and traffic. The same young woman who fearlessly climbed mountain precipices finds herself paralyzed at the congested Leipziger Platz. But more than the chaos, the falsity of the city frightens her; after a half year in Berlin, a poet friend warns her, she will no longer know what feelings are her own.³² Ellen discovers the truth of the warning as she attempts to fulfill Fritz's desire for a household in which to recoup his energies. The renunciation of her own feelings transforms her into a moody, even "hysterical" woman (although Reuter never applies this phrase). She argues when Fritz criticizes her; she teases when he reacts jealously to other men's attentions; and she disobeys when he commands. She becomes horrified at what her vow of being a good wife entails: "the terrible possibility of dying without ever having experienced what it meant to act according to one's own nature."³³ Ellen is beset by contradictory feelings about the marriage: one moment she is comfortable with being a wife, the next she is overcome by boredom, and then she is beset by unfulfilled passion.

This "unfulfilled passion" precipitates the final crisis.³⁴ On a visit to the Harz she argues with Fritz and runs out, over his prohibition, to climb a mountain with friends to watch the moon rise. On the trek Ellen allows herself to be drawn into the woods by an artist and gives herself over to passionate embrace. Upon her return, Fritz, ignorant of what has happened, lectures her that he was thinking only of her well-being, for he has ascertained she is pregnant. The news provokes a sequence of confrontations that ends the marriage. When Ellen blurts out an account of the adulterous episode Fritz becomes obsessed, less by the act than by the mistrust it has spawned. His fear of losing his reason is the breaking point: "You go crazy; you become an animal, and, finally, you lose all self-respect."[35] The marriage, as Reuter depicts it, has been reduced to two people psychologically destroying one another. That Fritz takes the step to end the destruction, although Ellen suffered under it longer, attests to the tenacity of her illusion that it lay within her power to build a "good" marriage. In the end she understands the divorce has as much to do with Fritz's failure to acknowledge her as her own person as with her adultery. Her inability to adapt to the role of Frau Dr. Fritz Erdmannsdörfer shows that the failure of the marriage has crucial social causes.

As with Effi Briest, Ellen's coming of age takes place during the introspection and social isolation that follow her divorce. After a difficult childbirth she returns to the Harz, depressed by what she sees as her lack of love for her sickly baby. What does come forth is a compassion that sustains her during the months of nurturing upon which her child's survival depends. When her erstwhile lover visits he is shocked by the funereal atmosphere. "Something has indeed died here," she tells him: "My youth."[36] What has really died are her illusions about womanliness, love, marriage, and motherhood. Her new life begins when she enters her baby's room to find him smiling for the first time and reaching for spots of sunlight on his quilt. Filled with new hope, she no longer asks whether this is the long-awaited motherly instinct. At the height of her crisis she uttered a prayer: "Will I ever learn to have the courage to be true to myself and my own nature?"[37] The last scene shows her prayer to have been answered in the form of freely embraced motherhood. The author's resolution of Ellen's identity crisis reflected a rising concern among feminists with issues of motherhood at the beginning of the new century.[38]

Like her protagonist, Gabriele Reuter raised a child outside of marriage,[39] but she did not thereby conclude that marriage in modern society was doomed. Instead, in a pamphlet entitled "The Problem of Marriage" (1907), she defined marriage as the institution in which women would contribute most profoundly to the transformation of their own society. The essay, echoing themes of *Ellen von der Weiden*, describes inevitable clashes between men and women who seek fulfillment in an institution built on male domination and female submissiveness.[40] Reuter here implicitly takes Ellen to task, however, for having failed in a woman's most important social goal: the creation of harmony. While urging husbands to encourage their wives' individuality, she calls on women to realize their own natures through will and sacrifice within marriage. "Why," she asks, "should dusting and cooking and taking care of children hinder one's personal development? With almost all household tasks, there is time for serious thinking."[41] The domestic activities that drove Ellen to distraction are now proposed as a means of self-realization as women devote themselves to nurturing future generations. This conclusion must have been poor comfort to those who, like Ellen, were perplexed at their inability to find harmony in prescribed womanly roles. Reuter's acceptance of such prescriptions in her essay signifies a deep resistance, even by a radical feminist, to envisioning the possibility that women might enter the public arena to join in the struggle for national regeneration.

Both *Effi Briest* and *Ellen von der Weiden* portray failings in the upbringing of daughters and injustice in the perpetuated minority of wives. Although Reuter's later essay affirmed marriage as the ideal realm for women's self-realization, her understanding of needed changes in the institution went beyond Fontane's. Although she refused to define women's salvation as the achievement of prescribed rights, she was more supportive than Fontane of those who sought those rights.[42] Although she failed to explore the economic dimension of women's dependence in her novel, she at least alluded to its importance in her essay on marriage.[43] Although her notion of women's fulfillment was shown by the same essay to be closer to Fontane's than her novel suggested, she depicted a fictional situation in which an unmarried woman approached the future with hope and purpose.

Like Fontane, Reuter seemed to dismiss art as a serious womanly pursuit. To be sure, her own life clearly embodied the example of an independent woman committed to her art, but in her essay she referred disparagingly to women who allowed the pursuit of their "tiny talents" (*Talentlein*) to disrupt their marriages.[44] During her crisis Ellen von der Weiden thought about becoming an artist and pondered in her diary that art and motherhood both create new life, but she dismissed the idea by asking rhetorically how many people there were in whom art was as fruitful as motherhood.[45] The speculation raised an issue that other fictional portrayals of women took up.

Although Effi Briest found a measure of fulfillment in painting, she belittled her ability. Her self-depreciation might seem more a sign of her approach to art, however, than evidence of a lack of talent. Effi's experience, like that of most women of her times, virtually precluded her taking herself seriously and undertaking the sustained work needed to achieve artistic expression. Yet, because other realms such as higher education and the professions remained closed, artistic endeavor was the major means by which a nineteenth-century woman could attain an independent identity in the public realm.[46] Clara Viebig (1860–1952), one of the most prolific and widely read female writers of the period,[47] explored the difficulties of attaining and sustaining such an identity in two early novels: *Dilettanten des Lebens* (*Dilettantes of Life*) (1898) and *Es lebe die Kunst!* (*Long Live Art!*) (1899). Despite overtones of conventional resolution, these works offered new possibilities for reconciling women's domestic identity with their desires for self-realization in the cultural realm.

*Dilettanten* traces the development of Lena Langen from her first encounters with adult responsibilities to her affirmation of independence and a down-to-earth understanding of its limits. Lena's coming of age involves balancing her desire for a singing career against the day-to-day demands of a struggling marriage. By the time of her marriage to a young artist named Richard

Bredenhofer, she has already brought her study far enough to make a modestly successful debut before a critical Berlin audience.[48] Having ignored family opposition, the pair expects a rapturous life in which their respective talents will flourish. Although the novel's title clearly applied to a host of characters,[49] the two main "dilettantes of life" are Lena and Richard, who prove ill-prepared to deal with married life or to realize their artistic dreams within the realities of their situation.

Whatever their fantasies, their marriage exemplifies the expectation that the man's art is to be taken seriously and the woman's task is to support his endeavors. Immersed in an array of artistic projects, Richard thinks of himself as an emergent genius and expects Lena to treat him accordingly. Seeing his wife as a reflection of his own being, he decrees how "his" household will be run and becomes indifferent to Lena's musical pursuits. In his need to maintain appearances he runs up debts with tradesmen and the landlord and overrules Lena's efforts to budget their expenses. He also squelches her plan to act as accompanist to her former singing teacher because he would feel humiliation from having his wife work. Finally, when an impresario wants to arrange a concert tour for Lena, Richard announces that her music is to be performed in his house and nowhere else. Lena submits obediently, even as she recognizes their immaturity in handling their affairs and searches for practical ways to move beyond it.

Her liberation comes not from these efforts, however, but from the intervention of fate. When Richard's work fails to sell, he declines psychologically and physically until he succumbs to pneumonia. Lena's young widowhood means taking charge of her life, and, however deep her grief she clearly intends to do so. Since she is pregnant, she will depend on her own and Richard's families for support and thus quickly overcomes an inclination to reject relatives who have already caused much trouble. Rather, she begins to redefine her relationship with them in ways that will meet her own needs as well as theirs, as her reconciliation with her estranged brother shows. For the first time he offers compassion rather than advice, trusting that she has the strength to face what lies ahead.

Although Lena's commitment to music seems to have been forgotten, a brief exchange suggests otherwise. In mourning she encounters a singer with whom she once shared lessons. Now in Berlin on a concert tour, the diva asks Lena about her progress. Hearing that Lena has laid her music aside, she nevertheless offers encouragement: "Well, what hasn't happened yet may still come!"[50] Indeed, although earlier judgments about Lena's voice give scant hope that she will become a celebrated singer, evidence of genuine musicianship suggests she will make something of her talent. Whether through being an accompanist, giving singing lessons, or performing the *Leider* she sings so well, she will one day reclaim her art. Lena is no longer one of life's dilettantes.

This novel represents a halfway stage in fictional portrayals of the woman artist. It begins to reinterpret women's identity by allowing Lena to face a life not defined simply by marriage or family. It also causes her to confront her artistic limitations and to realize that less glamorous alternatives than international concert tours likely await her efforts. Still, the novel also shows Lena adapting to a role that sacrifices her artistic commitment to domestic demands. And although it leaves the door open to further artistic pursuit, the novel does not make it an explicit part of Lena's future. This omission underscores the extent to which the question of whether women could combine family and professional work had yet to be defined.

Viebig addressed this question in her next novel, *Es lebe die Kunst!* This path-breaking work sustains a focus on the relation of a woman both to her art and her family as it follows her through many confrontations with external pressures and internal doubts. Elisabeth Reinharz differs from Lena Langen in that she achieves success as a writer and thus finds herself dealing directly with Berlin's cultural establishment as an artist and as a woman. A second major difference lies in the understanding and support Elisabeth receives from close friends and, far more important, from her husband. The novel is unique in portraying a marriage that does not impede the work of a woman artist but actually fosters it.

This state is reached, however, only after a long period of crisis and adjustment. The novel introduces Elisabeth as she arrives in Berlin with the conventional expectations of a hopeful young artist. "I *had* to come to Berlin; I must accomplish something!" she exclaims to another woman author and is astonished by the reply that those are illusions they all once had.[51] Elisabeth believes she will conquer the literary world on her own terms, but she ignores subtle compromises along the way. When told she has "talent, good health, and energy" but that she needs the support of a "literary clique," she scoffs and fails to notice that her renown begins with her acceptance into an elite literary salon.[52] She resists pressures to have the arbiters of this salon determine her social life, and yet shudders when she hears a woman refer to the "literary death" that resulted from being expelled from the clique.[53] She resists publishers' advice to produce something fashionable (perhaps on the "woman question"), but does not notice that it takes the help of a detested critic to get her stories published. So self-confident is Elisabeth that she ignores the situation of women in a realm dominated by men. She fends off the advances of a famous poet but does not notice how much other interest in her also has to do with her beauty. She overlooks the irony of a male poet's dominating a gathering purportedly dedicated to the furtherance of women artists. She also fails to note that a friend expresses "approval" of women writers by warning about the dangers of shamelessly exposing themselves or trying to equal men.[54]

Elisabeth's first book is a triumph, and the only thing especially "womanly" in her exuberant reaction is her spontaneously throwing her arms several times a day around her maidservant. The next months, however, bring an antidote to the intoxicant of producing a bestseller: the first writing block. It derives in part from doubts common to both male and female authors but is worsened by obstacles particular to a woman's sustaining her artistic commitment. She needs someone, Elisabeth tells herself, to erect a wall between her and the world so she can get on with her work. The solution seems to come when she falls in love with and marries a down-to-earth bookkeeper named Wilhelm Ebel. Plenty of household help and a well-positioned writing table, however, do not result in the hoped-for creativity. Dogged effort now replaces Elisabeth's earlier naive inspiration, and this is subject to constant distractions: an overflowing drain, an argument between servants, a cry from her newborn child, an intrusive visitor. At the end of the day Elisabeth is distraught over the lack of writing to show for hours at her desk, and beset by guilt about seeming to manage things so poorly. When Wilhelm tries to comfort her she laments the fact that her work has not brought any financial contribution to the household, and frets about the toll her writing takes on him and their son.[55]

Wilhelm's quiet support becomes crucial. A less sympathetic husband, not to mention an authoritarian one, would surely have tipped the balance during this period and ended Elisabeth's writing. Instead, Wilhelm gives critical judgment when Elisabeth is tempted to accede to cultural fads and is immensely tolerant of her periods of despair. He also provides practical help, as exemplified in a unique fictional instance when he, the male, matter-of-factly states he will go make the tea. Finally, Wilhelm never wavers in his faith in his wife's talent, and when she finally perceives the depth of this faith, she recovers her creative energy. In short, Wilhelm is an unself-conscious feminist who not only does not feel threatened by his wife but is proud of her.[56]

This support is put to a severe test when Elisabeth finishes her first drama and encounters a full range of new crises in the cultural arena: having her play turned down by five producers; asking for help from a man she despises; accepting radical script changes; and finally, enduring a disastrous premiere.[57] Most of what ruins the premiere has nothing to do with her play, but her sense of failure is devastating. Even here, her womanhood does not allow her time to cope with it, for she returns home to discover the baby has suffered a severe concussion. Elisabeth spends the next days by his bed, berating herself for being negligent and determined to abandon art forever. Society's worst judgment comes from a so-called friend: "I always regretted the fact that Elisabeth had more interest in her writing than in her beautiful child. She actually should not have gotten married!"[58] The child recovers, but Elisabeth languishes, convinced she meant her vow never to write again. In this state she personifies an emerging cultural collision between ideas of the professional life of women and notions of motherhood as the expression not only of the traditional woman but of the new woman as well.

Elisabeth is one of the rare fictional characters of this period who survives the collision with both identities intact. At Wilhelm's behest the family travels to her native Rhineland, "where," as he says, "she discovered her art, and where she will also rediscover it."[59] His prediction is correct. Surrounded by warmhearted villagers and the rural landscape, she rediscovers her need to write and the depth of her husband's faith in her work. "I am thankful both to you and to art," she says to Wilhelm: "I simply cannot separate one from the other."[60] The last scene has Elisabeth and her family heading back to Berlin. The stay in the country has been restorative, but it serves to reaffirm that she belongs in the dynamic environment of the city—with her family and with her work.

Elisabeth Reinharz does not become a prototype for a fictional new woman who can reconcile creative work and marriage. Instead, novels continued to portray inherent contradictions in the goals of independence and marriage, as indicated in *Begierde* (*Desire*) (1916) by a writer named Selma Reichel, who published under the pseudonym Jolanthe Marès.[61] In dealing with four female characters, the work enunciates a paradox in the relationship between women and modernity: women's drive for self-fulfillment, having been spawned by the forces of modernization, is also being deformed by them. The city becomes the setting for this paradox, but, as in the case of Reuter's novel, the anti-urban thread does not preclude untraditional resolutions among the female characters.

The two-sided effect of the modern age on women is shown in the contrast between the utterances and the thoughts of an aunt about her adolescent niece. The aunt tells her that she envies modern young girls for the opportunities for education and career that have opened up in Berlin.[62] She is silently appalled, however, when the girl responds by equating the new woman with unrestrained freedom and the manipulation of others. She becomes frantic over what "the swamp of the metropolis" has wrought in her niece and wonders if it is possible to hold her back from a headlong rush into its evils.[63] Are modern women to be ruined by the forces supposed to liberate them? The novel answers that women *can* come to terms with themselves and modernity, but it shows the enterprise to be exceedingly difficult.

The modern *Egoismus* that in other novels has corrupted countless male characters is given specifically female attributes by Marès. She sounds this theme in the opening scene of *Begierde*, which depicts a stereotypical modern woman in the person of a cigarette-smoking American who is expounding her impressions of German women. She expresses surprise that the fabled "three K's"—*Kirche, Küche, Kinder*—do not apply at all to modern German women, many of whom are elegant, fashionable, and even flirtatious.[64] But the epitome of the woman the American so admires also epitomizes the *Egoismus* that Marès condemns. She is Thea Westphal, wife of a banker named Lukas Westphal, who presides over an elegant house, the scene of some of Berlin's most glittering parties. As a self-described "modern wife" she is freed by her affluence from household duties but has a multitude of outside commitments, including activity in the "Association for Combatting Declining Birthrates." Pointedly, her dedication to an organization committed to holding the family together supplants devotion to her own family.[65] Thea's main worry about motherhood is that people who know of her fourteen-year-old daughter can compute her age. Her husband, the source of her luxury and her escort in the social season, has become a stranger as the two frantically meet the demands of the modern metropolis. Far from bringing harmony, Thea causes unrest (*Unruhe*), which leads her daughter to remark, "We have a house, but we don't have a home."[66] When bankruptcy looms, Thea runs off to Nice with a count, and when he gambles away his fortune she heads for St. Petersburg with a wealthy Russian. "What do you expect of someone of that temperament and lack of self-discipline?" a character asks: "She's just being modern, that's all."[67]

Thea embodies the extremes to which notions of individuality and self-fulfillment can be taken, but Marès makes it clear that frantic "egoism" is a peril for all urban people who have been torn loose from "custom, morals, and a sense of duty."[68] Three other female characters find less destructive paths to self-fulfillment, but Marès does not relinquish her focus on the danger of *Egoismus* for the modern woman.

Next to Thea the character who most exemplifies this tendency is a young woman named Gerda von Wangenheim, a would-be concert singer who, at great sacrifice for her parents, is training with a master teacher in Berlin. She discovers that in addition to a strong will she needs more contact with cultural patrons and more expensive training than she anticipated. The process is an immense gamble, for even she is uncertain as to whether she has the talent to become a great singer. A major theme of Gerda's coming of age involves her finding economic support for the years of development needed before she can assess her ability. When her father dies her mother cuts off the stipend in hopes that she will forget the foolishness, return home, and marry respectably. Gerda not only ignores this parental order but also refuses to contemplate the woman's option of offering either love or favors in return for a man's financial support. When one admirer declares his love she replies she does not trust love, "because men are so dishonest about their intentions, because they seem to have lost respect for women."[69] In another instance she tests her sexual passions by asking a suitor to kiss her, and is relieved to find she feels nothing. Or again, when a lovesick man begs her to marry him she says, "Thanks for offering a golden cage, but I need my freedom."[70] A cosmic sanction for this behavior comes when a friend theorizes that Gerda has been chosen to avenge the sisterhood of women by "striding coolly over the broken lives" of her suitors.[71]

Gerda's militance against men does not save her concert career, but it preserves her independence. Through much effort she gives two recitals that are coolly received. Rather than "sell" herself to a suitor to obtain resources to find out whether more years of training will raise her above mediocrity, she decides instead to "sell" herself to the public and negotiates a contract to become a cabaret singer. The tradeoff of her concert career for her independence is preferable to the humiliation of going home to East Prussia or the imprisonment of marriage. Marès, although clearly sympathetic to Gerda's plight, shows that this bitter young woman, by renouncing love, is another victim of modern egoism.

The counterpart to Gerda is Lotte Wunsch, a sculptress who sublimates her desire for marital love into two realms: motherhood and her art. At the beginning of the novel Lotte is as cynical about love as Gerda. Her experience of being sexually assaulted in a sculptor's studio produced long-lived rage over her vulnerability as a woman: "Do you think I'm the only one that's happened to? I was horribly defiled, and I want to wash myself clean again by raising my voice in accusation."[72] Through her art she vows to rip off the mask worn by this "Moloch" of modern society and bare its countenance of "wild greed and base passions."[73] Unexpectedly, however, Lotte falls in love with an architect, and, discovering new creativity, finishes the work that has long consumed her: a bloodthirsty and grasping monster entitled "Humanity." Completion of the sculpture purges her and causes her to believe she stands on the threshold of a fulfilling life. Her fiancé, however, is awestruck in an unexpected way: "She had a vocation that she loved and that fulfilled her. To whom would she belong? To him or her art?"[74] He decides he cannot live with her dual commitment nor ask her to give up art, and he breaks the engagement. Lotte falls into the arms of another man and uses their stormy relationship to conceive the child she has always wanted. She decides to leave Berlin for a rural setting where she can devote herself to her art and her child. She has reconciled her art with her womanhood, but without the man she loves. The new woman has emerged; the new man has not. Nevertheless, at the end of the novel Lotte is planning a new sculpture to express her newfound hope for humanity.

The model for this idealistic sculpture is a fourth female character, Ebba Holm. The one character who achieves a "womanly" serenity, Ebba is problematic as a representative of the new woman, for she denies that with her ideals of woman as keeper of the home she can be called "modern." Still, she is "modern" in two respects. First, she is an unmarried woman in the metropolis. Having been deserted by a gambling husband, she moves to Berlin to be near her brother, Lukas Westphal, and sets up her life with a decisiveness that bears no trace of stereotypical female ineptitude or dependence. Second, she is modern in her ability to accept people on their own terms. Although shocked by what she sees in Berlin, she treats every person she meets with openness and respect.

Ebba nevertheless personifies a deeply rooted social value: the ideal of feminine ability to create harmony in a frantic, discordant world. She represents Marès' concerted attempt to articulate a traditional womanly ideal in a modern context. Shortly after arriving in Berlin, Ebba decides she must have her own apartment. In answer to the question of Gerda von Wangenheim as to why she would want to leave the comfort of the women's pension in which they both live, she explains she wants her own home and its daily problems. When Gerda persists, Ebba raises the issue to a universal level: "You are an artist . . . and you're allowed to think that way [about housework]. But think how sad it would be for family life if all women thought that way."[75] Conscious that she has no family to care for, Ebba defines a purpose in the creation of a home open to her family of friends. The choice of location becomes a critical element of this ideal, and Ebba rejects the "modern" west ("Berlin-W") for a flat on a quiet, tree-lined street southeast of the Tiergarten. She thrives on arranging every detail to create a serene haven to which people gravitate. Lotte Wunsch explains the achievement as Ebba's art of making others happy in an age overrun by egoism.[76]

Ebba is still beset by a sense of failure over her broken marriage and her lack of children, but she discovers her neglected niece (the daughter of Lukas and Thea Westphal) and offers the mothering that has been denied her. When Thea runs off, Ebba accepts her brother's invitation to live with him and the child. Her outpouring of love finds a permanent vessel; her life now has womanly purpose.

Each woman in *Begierde* achieves an outcome of her own making. Thea Westphal, presumably enjoying the luxury she craves in faraway Petersburg, at least no longer wreaks havoc with the lives of her husband and daughter. Gerda von Wangenheim is achieving success in her art, even if not in the realm she originally chose. Lotte Wunsch, uniting art and single-motherhood, is fulfilling a dual commitment that is radically modern, even though it culminates outside the metropolis. And Ebba Holm is contributing to the well-being of modern society by bringing her talent for cultivating harmony to a home where it is sorely needed. To the extent that each has gone outside a conventional wifely role, these characters represent the modern woman. The spectrum of their fictional destinies shows the impossibility of casting her into one mold or another.

What remained unsettled in Marès' outcomes was the question of relations between the sexes. Thea Westphal aside, the other three female characters embarked upon their new lives with vows of celibacy. Each had had bitter experiences with men, and although two of the three affirmed their need for motherhood, all three renounced marriage. Marès suggested no resolution for the contradiction between women's self-fulfillment and existing patriarchal institutions.[77]

These contradictions point to the wider difficulty of articulating the quest for individuality—a pervasive theme in Berlin novels—in terms of female experience. In novels about women the tension between individuality and dependency was defined in terms of internal familial relationships rather than in terms of the external social dependencies that beset male characters. This distinction, in turn, pointed to another: women's fictional exclusion from public realms. In Berlin novels the unfinished revolution was articulated and engaged by the two sexes in differing realms. Even in novels by radical feminists such as Reuter, women's call to social engagement is not accompanied by a call for them to participate publicly in the work of regenerating German society. Most of the female characters do not leave their domestic boundaries; the two who do, Elisabeth Reinharz with her return to literature and Lotte Wunsch through her sculpted images of humanity, are driven more by commitment to their art than by commitment to working toward a new society. While this is surely a plausible and commendable impulse, its horizons are narrower than those of male heroes in other novels. Whatever strides the new woman was making in German fiction—and they were substantial—she was still virtually excluded from the public arena in which the active struggle for nationhood was being engaged.

This exclusion perhaps represented another lost opportunity in the fictional search for the unfinished revolution. Novelists might have applied the ostensibly more humane female morality to visions of the unfinished revolution, but they did not do so precisely because it was female and thus remained firmly situated in domestic realms.

## Notes

1. Conrad Alberti, "Die Frau und der Realismus," *Die Gesellschaft*, 6, 2 (July 1890), 1023. A similarly critical essay by a female author is discussed in Marilyn Scott-Jones, "Laura Marholm and the Question of Female Nature," in Susan L. Cocalis and Kay Goodman, eds., *Beyond the Eternal Feminine: Critical Essays on Women and German Literature* (Stuttgart, 1982), 203–206.
2. Alberti, "Die Frau und der Realismus," 1023. See also Elke Frederiksen, ed., *Die Frauenfrage in Deutschland, 1865–1915: Texte und Dokumente* (Stuttgart, 1981).
3. Alberti, "Die Frau und der Realismus," 1027. See also Renate Möhrmann, "Women's Work as Portrayed in Women's Literature," in Ruth-Ellen B. Joeres and Mary Jo Maynes, eds., *German Women in the Eighteenth and Nineteenth Centuries: A Social and Literary History* (Bloomington, Ind., 1986), 61–77.
4. See Florence Hervé, ed., *Geschichte der deutschen Frauenbewegung*, 3rd ed. (Cologne, 1987), and John C. Fout, ed., *German Women in the Nineteenth Century: A Social History* (New York, 1984).
5. See, for instance, James C. Albisetti, *Schooling German Girls and Women: Secondary and Higher Education in the Nineteenth Century* (Princeton, 1988), Barbara Greven-Aschoff, *Die bürgerliche Frauenbewegung in Deutschland, 1894–1933* (Göttingen, 1981), 1–147; and Ute Frevert, *Women in German History: From Bourgeois Emancipation to Sexual Liberation*, translated by Stuart McKinnon-Evans (Oxford, 1988) 107–130.
6. Linda Schelbitzki Pickle, "Self-Contradictions in the German Naturalists' View of Women's Emancipation," *German Quarterly*, 52 (1979), 442–456.
7. Silvia Bovenschen, *Die imaginierte Weiblichkeit: Exemplarische Untersuchungen zu kulturgeschichtlichen und literarischen Präsentationsformen des Weiblichen* (Frankfurt am Main, 1979), 21–24.
8. See Roy Pascal, *From Naturalism to Expressionism: German Literature and Society, 1880–1918* (London, 1973), 208–211.
9. On the rewards and perils of "gynocriticism" see Nina Auerbach, "Engorging the Patriarchy," in Shari Benstock, ed., *Feminist Issues in Literary Scholarship* (Bloomington, Ind., 1987), 150–160. On images of resistance to marriage in fiction see Shirley Foster, "The Open Cage: Freedom, Marriage and the Heroine in Early Twentieth-Century American Women's Novels," in Moira Monteith, ed., *Women's Writing: A Challenge to Theory* (New York, 1986), 154–174, and Shirley Foster, *Victorian Women's Fiction: Marriage, Freedom and the Individual* (Totowa, N.J., 1985).
10. See Kant's "What Is Enlightenment?" and Ella Mensch's *Die Frau in der modernen Literatur* (Berlin, 1898), 13. Despite a recent warning that the phrase "coming of age" is insulting, I persist in using it because the protagonists discussed in this chapter are clearly portrayed in the processes of maturing. See Richard J. Evans, "Modernization Theory and Women's History," *Archiv für Sozialgeschichte*, 20 (1980), 499–500.
11. See Janet Wolff, "The Culture of Separate Spheres: The Role of Culture in Nineteenth-Century Public and Private Life," in John Seed and Janet Wolff, eds.,

*The Culture of Capital: Art, Power and the Nineteenth-Century Middle Class* (Manchester, 1988), 117–134.
12. Walter Müller-Seidel, *Theodor Fontane: Soziale Romankunst in Deutschland* (Stuttgart, 1975), 162.
13. On the actual scandal that inspired the novel see Horst Budjuhn, *Fontane nannte sie "Effi Briest": Das Leben der Elisabeth von Ardenne* (Berlin, 1985).
14. Theodor Fontane, *Effi Briest*, in *Sämtliche Werke*, VII (Munich, 1959), 182.
15. Ibid., 195.
16. Ibid., 223.
17. Ibid., 252.
18. Ibid., 310.
19. Ibid., 344.
20. Ibid., 359.
21. Ibid., 403.
22. I use the word "feminist" as defined by Linda Gordon: "a critique of male supremacy, formed and offered in the light of a will to change it, which in turn assumes a conviction that it is changeable." Linda Gordon, "What's New in Women's History," in Teresa de Lauretis, ed., *Feminist Studies/Critical Studies* (Bloomington, Ind., 1986), 29. "Feminism," it should be emphasized, had completely different connotations in German at the end of the nineteenth century. Richard J. Evans, "The Concept of Feminism: Notes for Practicing Historians," in Joeres and Maynes, *German Women*, 252, 247–249.
23. On the intense debate over whether a uniquely female language exists in literature see Benstock, *Feminist Issues in Literary Scholarship*, and de Lauretis, *Feminist Studies/Critical Studies*.
24. Faranak Alimadad-Mensch, *Gabriele Reuter: Porträt einer Schriftstellerin* (Bern, 1984), 115–118. On the word "feminist" see n22, above.
25. The novel was published in 65 editions. See James Hardin, ed., *German Fiction Writers, 1885–1913* (Detroit, Mich., 1988), 415.
26. Gabriele Reuter, *Ellen von der Weiden: Ein Tagebuch*, 6th ed. (Berlin, 1907), 54, 62.
27. Ibid., 139.
28. Ibid., 14. The symbol of furniture reappears in Gabriele Reuter, *Das Problem der Ehe* (Berlin, 1907), 42.
29. Reuter, *Ellen von der Weiden*, 12, 15, 28.
30. Ibid., 24.
31. Ibid., 93 and also 29–30, 52.
32. Ibid., 46 and also 14. On women's relation to the city in literature see Susan Merrill Squier, ed., *Women Writers and the City: Essays in Feminist Literary Criticism* (Knoxville, Tenn., 1984).
33. Reuter, *Ellen von der Weiden*, 142.
34. The glowing frequency of fictional allusions to women's unsatisfied sexual drives reflects a consciousness of the development of a "new" morality. See Richard J. Evans, *The Feminist Movement in Germany, 1894–1933* (London, 1976), 117, 138.
35. Reuter, *Ellen von der Weiden*, 231.
36. Ibid., 282.
37. Ibid., 244.
38. Ann Taylor Allen, "Mothers of the New Generation: Adele Schreiber, Helene Stöcker, and the Evolution of a German Idea of Motherhood, 1900–1914," *Signs*, 10, 3 (Spring 1985), 418–438.
39. Ibid., 273. Reuter described her own refusal to marry in terms of a Nietzschean rejection of bourgeois convention. Richard L. Johnson, "Gabriele Reuter: Romantic and Realist," in Cocalis and Goodman, eds., *Beyond the Eternal Feminine*, 228.

40. Reuter, *Das Problem der Ehe*, 16–24.
41. Ibid., 60.
42. See, for example, Gabriele Reuter, *Liebe und Stimmrecht* (Berlin, 1912).
43. Reuter, *Das Problem der Ehe*, 29.
44. Ibid., 59.
45. Reuter, *Ellen von der Weiden*, 150.
46. Although middle-class women's movements intensified the agitation for "Berufsfreiheit," only the medical and teaching professions became open to women in the years prior to World War I. Hervé, *Geschichte der deutschen Frauenbewegung*, 52. See also Regula Venske, "Discipline and Daydreaming in the Works of a Nineteenth-Century Author: Fanny Lewald," in Joeres and Maynes, eds., *German Women*, 175–192.
47. Hardin, *German Fiction Writers*, 471.
48. Clara Viebig, *Dilettanten des Lebens*, 5th ed. (Berlin, 1907), 34. Viebig moved to Berlin in her early twenties with her mother to study singing. Franz Brümmer, *Lexikon der deutschen Dichter und Prosaisten vom Beginn des 19. Jahrhunderts bis zur Gegenwart*, 6th ed. (Leipzig, 1913), I, 430.
49. For example, Lena's older brother remarks, "Wir sind alle Dilettanten des Lebens!" Viebig, *Dilettanten des Lebens*, 328.
50. Ibid., 321.
51. Clara Viebig, *Es lebe die Kunst!*, 4th ed. (Berlin, 1905), 25.
52. Ibid., 83.
53. Ibid., 146.
54. Ibid., 68–69, 99, 101–103. See also Patricia Herminghouse, "Women and the Literary Enterprise in Nineteenth-Century Germany," in Joeres and Maynes, *German Women*, 78–93.
55. Viebig, *Es lebe die Kunst!* 293–294, 301. Elisabeth's experiences might be analyzed in terms of the female anxieties of authorship identified in Sandra M. Gilbert and Susan Gubar, *The Madwoman in the Attic: The Woman Writer and the Nineteenth-Century Imagination* (New Haven, Conn., 1979). See also Adele Gerhard and Helene Simon, *Mutterschaft und geistige Arbeit*, 2nd ed. (Berlin, 1905).
56. Viebig, *Es lebe die Kunst!*, 271, 413.
57. Ibid., 375–400.
58. Ibid., 413.
59. Ibid., 432.
60. Ibid., 465.
61. A full title, *Begierde: Ein Berliner Roman aus der Zeit vor dem großen Kriege*, is given in Hans Zopf and Gerd Heinrich, eds., *Berlin Bibliographie (Bis 1960)* (Berlin, 1965), 471. The edition I used is subtitled simply *Ein Berliner Roman*. Despite the intriguing reference of the other subtitle, the work gives no hint of the approaching war.
62. Jolanthe Marès, *Begierde: Ein Berliner Roman*, edition containing numbers 21. bis 30. Tausend (Berlin, n.d.), 75–76.
63. Ibid., 83.
64. Ibid., 5–6.
65. Ibid., 35. On the theme of "busy leisure" see Sibylle Meyer, "Die mühsame Arbeit des demonstrativen Müßigangs: Über die häuslichen Pflichten der Beamtenfrauen im Kaiserreich," in Karin Hausen, ed., *Frauen suchen ihre Geschichte: Historische Studien zum 19. und 20. Jahrhundert* (Munich, 1983), 172–194. On feminist reactions to the so-called "Geburtenrückgang" see Ann Taylor Allen, "German Radical Feminism and Eugenics, 1900–1918," *German Studies Review*, 11, 1 (February 1988), 31–56.
66. Marès, *Begierde*, 85; see also 178.
67. Ibid., 197.

68. Ibid., 24–25.
69. Ibid., 43.
70. Ibid., 176.
71. Ibid., 251. On the wider reaction against the example of women using men see Pascal, *From Naturalism to Expressionism*, 207.
72. Marès, *Begierde*, 55, 20.
73. Ibid., 54, 26, 108, 113.
74. Ibid., 149–150.
75. Ibid., 49.
76. Ibid., 69.
77. A successful resolution does take place within the marriage of a supporting character (Suse Wolf) in Marès' novel *Lillis Ehe* (Berlin, 1914), but the title character ends in suicide.

# 10

# The Aristocracy: A Crisis of Honor and Means

Although Karl Marx pronounced the death of feudalism in the 1840s, the landed nobility was still very much alive in Germany at the turn of the century. To be sure, the last vestiges of legal serfdom had been abolished, and income from estates had often been reduced by indifferent management, falling agricultural prices, or increasing indebtedness. The idea of a hereditary aristocracy, moreover, was being attacked as anathema to modern ideals of opportunity and merit. But strong forces worked in the opposite direction. Bismarck's constitution, by creating a ministerial government responsible only to the monarch and by creating as one of its two deliberative bodies a Federal Council (*Bundesrat*) dominated by Prussian aristocrats, ensured the political power of the nobility throughout the life of Imperial Germany. The military establishment continued to be controlled by an officer corps that was an aristocratic domain. In the late '70s the land-owning nobility launched a successful campaign for agrarian tariffs that, along with the application of modern farming technology, stemmed much of the economic threat, at least for large estate owners. A series of new policies and administrative changes by Bismarck, begun in 1879, further consolidated aristocratic political rule.[1] Finally, what popular energies did exist were channeled by Bismarck against the supposed threat of socialist anarchism. In short, developments after unification served to strengthen aristocratic preeminence.

Historians have described the results as a "feudalization" of German society in which the middle class not only entered a period of political collaboration with the aristocracy but fortified aristocratic rule by emulating aristocratic values and pastimes.[2] Literary evidence for such feudalization can be seen in the unabated fascination of novelists and their readers with the world of the nobility. Such fascination, however, did not resolve the aristocracy's role in the modern age, for the center of modernity, the city, refused to be "feudalized," even under the pressure of literary imagination. Collisions of aristocratic with middle-class values and a crisis of means for a dispossessed urban nobility appeared repeatedly in Berlin novels, showing how apparent the anachronism of a hereditary nobility was to contemporaries. But even as novels suggested the long-term impossibility of aristocratic rule, their resolutions tended to sanction its continued existence. The fictional treatment of the nobility provides another instance of novelists' resistance to pursuing the implications of situations they portrayed.

The final scene of *Eysen* (the second novel in Georg Freiherr von Ompteda's trilogy *Deutscher Adel um 1900* [*German Nobility in 1900*]) depicts one such situation—a group of young barons walking eastward through the Tiergarten after having left their uncle's apartment in the middle-class Hansa district. Their ears ring with his sobering lecture on the challenges that face their 800-year-old family:

> They went through Brandenburger Tor, through which their fathers' generation had passed into Berlin after the war. Unter den Linden now pulsated with the frantic traffic of the metropolis: wealth, poverty, diligence, troubles, seriousness, joy, the striding businessman and the dawdler, prince and beggar—all thronging together. The young Eysens were walking against the current of life flowing toward them, a current that would wash them away if they failed to understand their era, but, if they went along with it, would carry them on its surface as it had done for almost a millennium.[3]

Three crucial attitudes can be discerned in this passage. First, to the young men, Brandenburger Tor symbolized *their* fathers' triumph. The blood and iron of Bismarck's speech meant the blood of the Prussian nobility and the "iron heart" of their heritage. In the words of their uncle, these traits had "shaken off the old weaknesses and disunity to establish the empire."[4] Second, as they strode along the route of their fathers' triumphal march they entered the chaotic reality of the metropolis. Experiencing a form of Gutzkow's "sidewalk disease," they became aware that they, the nobility, could not remain aloof from this reality, however alien to their traditions. And third, with the image of the swirling current they manifested confidence in their ability to stay on top of a tumultuous modernity.

Few novels so clearly articulated the intention of sustaining aristocratic rule—perhaps because relatively few had aristocratic authors—but the problematic existence of the hereditary aristocracy was not thereby resolved. As this and the other novels treated in this chapter document, the intrusion of modernity wrought too many breaches for the closed world of the nobility to remain intact.

A good example of this intrusion comes in *Spitzen* (*Summits*), published in 1888 by Paul Lindau (1839–1919), a critic, novelist, and dramatist whose popularity during the period of this study was enormous. *Spitzen* came two years after Lindau's best-selling *Der Zug nach dem Westen* (*The Westward Procession*), which will concern us in the next chapter, and the success of the earlier work ensured numerous printings and a wide readership for this one.[5] The novel, which focuses on aristocratic life and its code of honor, demonstrates the extent to which novelists could envision a nobility that still determined its own existence, oblivious to the transformations of modernity. But although Lindau appears to glorify values others saw as outmoded, the novel implicitly acknowledges their incongruity with modernity.

The year is 1879 and the setting is the most prestigious location in Berlin: a Wilhelmstraße mansion whose garden overlooks the Tiergarten. The magnificent palace has recently been acquired from a ruined speculator by Graf Albrecht von Iseneck, a cabinet minister of distinguished lineage. Living amid the mansion's elegant furnishings and attended by its liveried servants is Iseneck's beautiful young wife, Juliane, whose graciousness corresponds to the surroundings. This splendor does not preclude conflict, however, and from his title Lindau derives three meanings to develop a crisis of values that ruins the enviable pair. First, the word refers to the summit of society, as when the narrator remarks that "the highest levels [Spitzen] of Berlin society are gathered in the ballroom."[6] Equally significant is the second connotation of Spitzen as fine lacework. The collection of antique lace, Juliane's passion, epitomizes the ideal diversion of a lady of the leisure class. A third use of Spitzen, denoting the figurative spikes that drive into Juliane's head as she goes mad, becomes a violent image of the psychological conflict to which her aristocratic ennui leads.

The crisis of aristocratic honor develops from the conjunction of Juliane's dalliance with a young count and a burglary of the mansion under the direction of an underworld figure of Berlin. The action progresses to a perjury trial in which Ulrich von Engernheim, the count in question, is accused of lying about his whereabouts on the night of the burglary in order to preserve the honor of Juliane. Thanks in part to the perjured testimony of a criminal and in part to the defense attorney's aspersions on the social status of Ulrich's accusers, Ulrich is acquitted and celebrates his victory with honor and duty intact.[7] The celebration is cut short, however, by a letter from Count von Iseneck that asks Ulrich to swear on his honor that he was not at the mansion on the night of the burglary. Although his presence was due to extenuating circumstances, Ulrich cannot lie as he did before the court, and the ritual of satisfaction is thereby set in motion. Lindau provides his readers with a detailed narrative of meetings among seconds to arrange for the duel. Although Ulrich ponders the unfairness of a code that imposes such a drastic penalty for a foolhardy lapse, he permits himself no thought of violating it as he had the civil code. In a last letter to his wife he entreats her to respect the code's tragic effects and reminds her, "you are the daughter and the wife of a nobleman."[8] With that he rides to a meadow west of Berlin, where he dies instantly from Iseneck's shot.

In this novel the nobility still lives in an encapsulated world. Noblemen can compromise, even lie, in the surrounding world, if such serves their separate code of honor. But even though Lindau's sympathy with the absolute demands of this code is apparent, his novel still fails to resolve the contradiction between it and modern urban society. At the end of the novel Juliane is hopelessly insane, Ulrich is dead, and Iseneck is left alone with his honor. The mansion on Wilhelmstraße, had Lindau pursued the implications of his conclusion, would be sold to the highest bidder. Insofar as it implied the permanent ascendancy of the nobility, the feudalization of Berlin society failed even in this sympathetic portrayal.

The affair of honor, nevertheless, remained a frequent convention among portrayals of the nobility, many times following its prescribed course to a fatal outcome in which no court or judge intervened. There were, of course, numerous variations. In Max Kretzer's *Drei Weiber* (*Three Women*) (1886), for instance, secrecy is maintained by the method of a duel by lot, but the terms are as fatal to the loser as a dawn encounter.[9] In Fritz Mauthner's *Der neue Ahasver* (*The New Ahasverus*) (1882) the duel in which Heinrich Wolff is mortally wounded is unusual because of its non-aristocratic participant, but the code of honor nevertheless supersedes civil law.[10] And Hans Hopfen, in his *Der Väter zweie* (*The Fathers of Two*) (1899), provides his readers with a climactic double duel that results from intricate dealings between "impoverished aristocrats and industrial knights."[11] The outcome is one death, two injuries, and no apparent civil repercussions. In such treatments the matter-of-factness with which the duel is accepted by characters—and ostensibly, their authors—might have allowed readers to forget the fundamental conflict between such practice and the modern legal system. The secrecy surrounding the ritual, however, attests to the fact that modern society cannot tolerate aristocratic modes of justice.

A few novels articulate this contradiction by allowing modernity to intrude in the affair of honor. One has the press get word of the duel just as the prospective combatants have reconciled. Their demand for satisfaction having been exposed, they are compelled to carry on a farcical encounter for fear of seeming cowardly to the Berlin public.[12] In another novel a duel results in one participant being wounded and his opponent being brought to trial and dutifully serving a three-month jail term.[13] The most jarring collision between the affair of honor and modernity, however, is ridicule. In one such instance a businessman confronts an officer with evidence of the officer's affair with his wife. When the officer responds by asking the businessman if he would like to seek satisfaction, the other is incredulous: "That's a good one! You gentlemen just don't have any other answer! Slashing, stabbing, shooting—that's your justification for everything you aren't capable of defending with reason . . . . Whoever attacks me in my realm has to give me satisfaction in terms of my code, the one that applies to people like me: not in Grunewald or Jungfernhaide, but in the office of your solicitor, and that's where we'll next see each other!"[14] Such moments baldly exposed the anachronism of the affair of honor.

Other literary conventions for portraying the nobility implied similar anachronisms. A major issue of all fictional treatments of the nobility was its claim of superiority in a democratizing age. A clear boundary between nobility and commoners was essential to maintaining such superiority, and yet novels showed this boundary beginning to blur. Gutzkow had long since characterized Berlin as a city in which the egalitarianism of the sidewalks brought people from across the social spectrum together, to force a kind of democratic consciousness, whatever the contrary inclinations of particular classes.

Most fictional aristocrats, however, still shunned the sidewalks in favor of their exclusive salons, officer clubs, and ballrooms. The secrecy of such sanctuaries could help maintain superiority, and novels simultaneously breeched and validated such secrecy.[15] By depicting events lavish with displays of refined taste and opulence, novels perpetuated the notion that these attributes exemplified the nobility's superiority. Through portrayals of aristocratic leisure they also underscored the notion of a class set apart from commoners. Outward signs of this leisure in fiction included varied forms of conspicuous and wasteful consumption: meticulous attention to dress, jewelry, and furnishings; servants devoted to visibly non-productive tasks; pursuits exemplifying leisured accomplishments; and pastimes conventionally reserved for the aristocracy, such as horse racing.[16] Portrayals of such leisured refinements contributed to notions about the distinctiveness of urban aristocrats, who were uprooted from the traditional signs of authority enjoyed by the landed nobility. Novels also conveyed images of aristocratic existence as a consciously created work of art in which surroundings, dress, and manners combined to create an esthetic whole by which true aristocracy could be recognized. Although some novels expressed middle-class disgust over aristocratic displays, many seemed to serve as the vehicle for "a secret wish fulfillment" into which readers could momentarily escape.[17] Any interest and envy of other classes that such depictions aroused implicitly substantiated aristocratic claims of inherent superiority.

Simultaneously, however, novels also challenged notions of aristocratic superiority by allowing commoners to enter, if only vicariously, an exclusive world. The visibility of aristocratic lives in novels lessened their distance from the rest of society. The fictional catalogues of aristocratic practices encouraged commoners to emulate them. And, finally, fictional portrayals of an urban aristocracy became an especially strong incitement to democratization by showing the jarring incursions by other classes into previously closed aristocratic preserves.

In *Der Klatsch* (*Gossip*) (1888) Theophil Zolling depicted such an incursion in one Berlin matron's salon. While her husband, a court chamberlain, was still alive, Irma von Aldringen restricted her salon to "essentially the same society one would see at the royal balls, especially, of course, the peers of her husband, other high representatives of the aristocratic and diplomatic world, and the best of the young cavaliers."[18] After his death, however, in a desire to bring new brilliance to her soirées Irma opens the door to carefully selected guests from outside aristocratic ranks—not to members of the "aristocracy of money," of course, but to notables from realms not normally included in court circles, such as the university, the Reichstag, or the art academy. Even these cautious undertakings ultimately prove fatal to the standing of the salon: increasing numbers of the court aristocracy stay away and more and more "undesirable" elements appear.

The alternative of maintaining exclusivity, however, is shown to have its own perils. The hostess who restricts her drawing room to members of the aristocracy inevitably runs the risk of having conversation languish at the hands of ill-informed guests, such as a general's daughter who "could not be moved to talk about anything beyond her flowers, the wonders of the royal theater, and her last trip to Ems to take the waters."[19] A disgruntled lieutenant leaves the gathering, thinking, "tonight he had been in irreproachable company, which once seemed so respectable, exemplary, and refined (*vornehm*), and now, for the first time, had thoroughly bored him." Notably, however, the boredom of the aristocratic drawing room drives this character disastrously to the lair of a bourgeois socialite. More threatening to the nobility as a class, however, is the likelihood of its so isolating itself from intellectual and artistic currents that its pretense to superiority will be as laughable as that of the general's daughter.

Whereas many novelists stressed the enviable qualities of aristocratic existence, others spewed venom at its ostentation and hypocrisy. Max Kretzer's *Drei Weiber*, for example, in a sixty-page passage describes a lavish dinner in which a multitude of gossipy conversations are interspersed with descriptions of each elaborate course.[20] In giving such prominence to the event, Kretzer underscored its importance to the stature of the aristocratic hostess, which in turn served to demonstrate his certitude of the nobility's vacuousness. This use of the convention of the *dîner*, perhaps unintentionally, also revealed the extent to which aristocratic superiority had devolved into an easily imitated opulence.

The ball, another convention for portrayals of the aristocracy, further underscored the vulnerability of aristocratic activities to middle-class intrusions. In novels the ball was often portrayed as the major endeavor of an aristocratic house in a social season; it became the most visible display of a family's taste, its social command (who was invited, who actually came), and its wealth.[21] Although aristocratic balls were modeled after the premier event of the social season, the royal ball for court nobility, the extraordinary financial cost of such undertakings made them among the first aristocratic activities to be successfully imitated by the wealthy bourgeoisie. In fact, two novels at either end of the period of this study, Spielhagen's *Sturmflut* (1876) and Ompteda's *Droesigl* (1909), depict spectacular bourgeois balls to which Berlin's highest society flocks. In other words, the ball, once testimony to aristocratic supremacy, increasingly became another literary indication of its loss of monopoly over such forms.

First appearances to the contrary, fictional portrayals of Berlin's nobility can be seen as democratizing influences that revealed to the masses at the lending library lives guarded by liveried servants at the entrances of Berlin's palaces and mansions. The actual nineteenth-century heirs of the feudal nobility might have been more successful in keeping outsiders from their ranks and their mansions, but fiction became an important sign of their inability to keep them uninitiated to the symbols of aristocratic preeminence or to prevent commoners from realizing they could also acquire those symbols (or at least passable imitations thereof). Aside from actual patents of nobility, which were difficult to obtain, everything requisite to aristocratic life, including an array of honorific titles, could be invented, imitated, or bought.[22] Novels were excellent catalogues and textbooks.

• • •

Wealth was an attribute the nobility had no possibility of monopolizing in the modern age, but another aristocratic realm that seemed far less vulnerable to middle-class encroachment was the officer corps. Visitors to Berlin were invariably struck by the high visibility of officers, who thronged Berlin streets, crowded the opera, and predominated in many restaurants. The feudal tradition of the warrior caste had evolved in the eighteenth century into a powerful component of Prussia's rise as a great power, and the officer corps of Imperial Germany continued to claim this tradition as an aristocratic preserve.[23] Some officers likely interpreted their prominence in the most elegant locations in the capital as society's reward for the loyal service of the caste, but their insistent presence could also be seen as a sign of the nobility's awareness of "the threat to its ruling position."[24] Both explanations, that the officer corps was reaping its reward for past service and that it was there to shore up its crumbling position, point to the problematic aspect of its place in the metropolis. As Walter Kiaulehn later diagnosed it, "the separateness of the aristocratic officer was not only painful for all other social groups but it brought a grotesque, caricature-like feature into public life."[25] It was a problem no fictional portrayal of the officer corps could overlook.

The most common message conveyed by the fictional treatment of officers was that the glamorous side of their existence consumed a vast amount of time and enormous quantities of money. One Berlin historian's remark that honor was the only reward given for an officer's service was certainly confirmed by novels, in which officers' stipends were so small as to be usually unmentioned.[26] The unending round of social activity—theater visits, late-night suppers of champagne and oysters, gaming at officers' clubs, standing invitations to Berlin's most elegant drawing rooms, maintaining a stable of horses or even an equipage—all entailed seemingly limitless expenditures that even in the world of fiction few could afford. The officer in Berlin confronted demands that the psychologically immature or financially strapped young man could rarely meet, leading to countless tales of ruin caused by the sins of do-nothingness and profligacy.

The "do-nothingness" (*Nichtstuerei*) associated with so many officer-characters in novels could be interpreted as a "conspicuous abstention from labor," by which they confirmed their superiority over the laboring classes,[27] but it also became a target of ridicule. Far removed from their caste's original warring role, such characters seem to vie for the dubious honor that a bourgeois character in one novel levies on a particularly arrogant nobleman: "He does nothing, but he does it in a masterly way."[28] Another author makes the same point by putting *Arbeitszimmer* (study or work room) in quotation marks every time he refers to the place to which his lieutenant retreats.[29] And a remark in another novel, although it refers to a civilian character, documents the resentment that conspicuous abstention from work could raise in a work-oriented society: "The deep hatred against the compulsive do-nothingness of wealth that had filled his whole life now was aimed at his friend."[30]

More dangerous than the possibility of provoking resentment from middle-class onlookers are the financial pitfalls associated with flourishing do-nothingness. Bankruptcy from monumental gambling debts is but the last station along the treacherous road taken by countless fictional lieutenants (those who make captain seem rather more immune!). Their examples show the enormous financial outlays the officer—or, more accurately, his family—will have to make to further a career either in the infantry or the cavalry (the latter being more prestigious but incomparably more costly). Part of the problem concerns changing times, as one young lieutenant asserts when reminded that his father made do with a fraction of the stipend he receives from his family.[31] But much of it reflects the expensive attractions of Berlin, attractions deemed essential to living in a style appropriate to the aristocratic estate (*standesgemäß*). Novels show that the necessities include eating regularly at the officers' casino, maintaining appropriate quarters and engaging a manservant, acquiring expensive dress uniforms, and subscribing to charity balls and comparable events. Such expenses represent mere subsistence living, some novels suggest; a young man who wants to give the appearance of wealth incurs mountains of additional obligations.[32]

A particularly explicit interpretation of the vicious circle in which Berlin officers meet their ruin is the case of Reinhard von Steffani, a character in Fedor von Zobeltitz's *Der Hetzjagd* (*The Frantic Hunt*) (1913). After his father's financial folly dissipated the family fortune, Reinhard must struggle perennially to maintain his career. He convinces himself that he wants only to achieve a serene existence and that "the fear of a sudden financial collapse [is] paralyzing his feelings and will, never letting him get beyond his insecurity."[33] The only way he can conceive of obtaining enough wealth to overcome such insecurity is through a timely marriage. In launching his hunt for a wealthy bride, he constructs a chain of lies that begins with his pretending to be rich. Predictably, these pursuits collide with the officer's code of honor. Although a frequent instance of the crisis of honor originates with the Jewish usurer to whom insurmountable gambling debts have been referred, in this novel it occurs over the scandal of Reinhard visiting a marriage broker. His commanding officer confronts him, saying, "Our honor is not of this world, in which people count with false quantities and weights. It is rock solid and whoever tries to shake it must go."[34] Reinhard, of course, goes. The inner conflict that led to his disgrace is due, however, not only to moral weakness on his part but also to an external conflict between the honorific status of the officer and his financial inability to uphold it. It culminates in his suicide.

All such fictional situations show that a nobleman could not live by honor alone, but particularly not an immature and impecunious young officer who tasted the expensive fruits offered by Berlin society. Many also indicate how difficult it was for a warrior caste to sustain itself in an age in which the rewarding of land, the feudal means of sustenance, was disappearing and in which the seeking of most alternative means of wealth was deemed dishonorable.[35] That the first years of the twentieth century brought only a heightening of the tension is suggested in one novel by the thoughts of the lone civilian at a military funeral. He is disgusted by the pervasive arrogance: "All they know is just playing, barracks, parades, maneuvers—more or less official leisure." And he extends his criticism to the city as well: "The present-day officer corps, of which only a small fraction has ever faced the enemy, is like present-day Berlin: it has no tradition, no respect for the older generation to whom it owes everything."[36] The abandonment of tradition, compounded by more than three decades without military action, this thinking implies, has taken its toll on a once-proud institution. Aside from the dangerous notion that what the officers need is a good war, this critical view of a corrupted tradition points to the unanswered question of the place of a feudal warrior caste in urban society. The possibilities for honor and glory in twentieth-century Berlin seemed to fictional officers to be restricted to the dueling field or the gaming table.

From the 1890s onward novelists increasingly looked at the problems of the nobility not in terms of a moral crisis of individuals but in terms of a capitalist economic system that had dire implications for the whole class. Although Berlin novels allude to the economic concerns of the land-owning nobility, their main focus is on those who through mismanagement or bad luck have become dispossessed of their land or have otherwise dissipated family fortunes. They are now in the city seeking to regain lost means of sustenance or at least to live out their lives in the "brilliant misery" that circumstances have brought them. From such portrayals three basic reactions to the crisis unfold: dedication to maintaining aristocratic appearances despite genteel poverty, improvement of fortune through misalliance, and capitulation to the burgher's road to economic security (*Verbürgerlichung*).[37] As the mere enumeration of these alternatives indicates, none represented a happy solution to the nobility's dilemma.

The title of Hans Hopfen's three-volume novel *Glänzendes Elend* (*Brilliant Misery*) (1893) was a popular term for characterizing the straits of Berlin's most privileged poor. Hopfen applies it to an aristocratic family living far from the elegance of the Wilhelmstraße in a modest apartment in the Hansa district northwest of the Tiergarten. The father, having been expelled from the officer corps because of unpaid debts, attempts unsuccessfully to maintain his family on a small military pension. Despite the desperate efforts of the one responsible family member, his daughter Runhilt, to manage the household frugally and to provide for the family through her paltry earnings as a writer, the situation only worsens. They are forced to sell most of their belongings and finally to undergo weeks of near-starvation as one financial disaster follows another. Through it all the father maintains a dress uniform to wear each month when he races through much of his pension by reliving the old days of champagne suppers with his military cronies. The mother, meanwhile, escapes into morphine addiction. Sustained by a deeply engrained sense of duty (*Pflichtgefühl*), Runhilt avoids the temptation to jump out the third-floor window and doggedly carries on.

The crisis is resolved by the intervention of a middle-class character. When

Runhilt's editor learns of the family's plight (she has been too proud to tell anyone who might have helped), he, the self-made man, rescues the family by paying off their debts and offering her a position as his private secretary. That this resolution implies a humiliating defeat for the once distinguished family is evident in that the secretarial job was earlier refused by another down-and-out aristocrat offended by the idea: "That a Rabenegger would enter into the personal service of such a parvenu seemed to him from the first a degrading prospect, even in his present straits."[38] And yet Hopfen induces readers to look at the *Verbürgerlichung* of the nobility not as a humiliation but a salvation in the concluding lines: "Now the brilliance became real and the old misery had come to an end."

In his portrayal of a similar situation in *Die Poggenpuhls* (1896), Theodor Fontane also provides a "happy ending," but one that implicitly leaves the problem of aristocratic impoverishment intact. Like the family depicted by Hopfen, the Poggenpuhls have been put into dire straits by the father's inability to manage a failing situation. After his death the bourgeois mother maintains a household of genteel poverty through an array of frugal measures. The only visible remnant of former times is the small "ancestors' gallery," whose centerpiece is a painting that depicts a Poggenpuhl defending a castle in the wars of liberation. The hero is caught in a surprise attack in his nighttime underwear, which evokes an image of the emperor without clothes.[39] The treasured painting makes a telling comment on the state of the nobility.

In this novel, remarkable for its lack of plot and action in the conventional sense, Fontane portrays the irreversible decline of the nobility and expresses his simultaneous challenge to them to reform their ways.[40] His development of the reactions of four of the five Poggenpuhl children to their family's situation ranges from the snobbish insistence of the oldest daughter on maintaining aristocratic appearances to the conventional foibles of the younger son who piles up debts in the officer corps. The end of the novel brings a small bequest from the fortune of a middle-class aunt that will allow each family member a modest degree of security. Each in his own way continues the struggle for aristocratic survival. Fontane's resolution vests the survival of the family in dependence on a non-aristocratic outsider—a resolution that offers scant hope for the prospects of the next generation of Poggenpuhls.

Marriage was the most viable means of escaping such poverty, and novelists had frequent recourse to misalliance to underscore their perception of the aristocracy's declining situation. They also showed the extreme dangers of such marriages, since the existence of a hereditary aristocracy rested on family line. Fontane's extraordinarily popular *Irrungen, Wirrungen* (*Differences, Confusions*) (1888) depicts the triumph of duty over love in the acquiescence of a young nobleman to his parents' wishes that he conclude a marriage of convenience with a cousin rather than follow the dictates of his heart and marry a commoner. The latter also acknowledges the impossibility of their love, but the confusion referred to by the title applies in part to a society in which the rationale for such sacrifice has become questionable.

A far more common situation, however, involves a marriage of convenience outside the aristocracy. Hopfen's *Glänzendes Elend* shows the difficulty of one impecunious aristocratic family concluding an alliance with another when Runhilt's father explains his refusal of an aristocrat's offer: "I have nothing. He has nothing. And to unite nothing with nothing means propagating misery and putting new proletarians into the world."[41] The most realistic hope is that family name can be merged with bourgeois fortune to mutual benefit.

Since the exchange is far more desirable if a title is involved, the more common convention is between aristocratic sons and bourgeois daughters. Max Kretzer portrays an extreme example of this in *Millionenbauer* (*Millionaire Farmer*) (1890), in which the son of one of the oldest aristocratic families in Berlin marries the daughter of a coarse peasant who has made millions by selling his suddenly valuable Schöneberg farm at the height of the *Gründer* speculation. Despite the repeated bailouts of his son-in-law, however, at the end of the novel the ex-farmer is still being snubbed by the young man's father, an impecunious baron and retired officer. With such distaste the nobility accepts their salvation.

The reverse situation—in which a bourgeois son and an aristocratic daughter are allied—can be no less distasteful, as shown in Georg von Ompteda's *Eysen*, when Gisela von Eysen marries Heinrich Gideon, the bourgeois buyer of her family's estate. An exemplary representative of the *Bürgertum*, Heinrich has none of the parvenu about him: he is the son of a wealthy industrial family, a former corps student, a doctor of laws and philosophy (two degrees!), a reserve lieutenant in the prestigious Dragoner-regiment, the holder of a new patent of nobility, and most important of all, a man of "humility and will."[42] The uncomfortable meeting of the two families at the wedding dinner in a hotel on Unter den Linden, however, is but the beginning of the social tensions, which extend to the refusal of the aristocratic society surrounding the estate to acknowledge the presence of its new neighbor. Heinrich does assimilate gradually into this society, however, and the novel promotes him as a founder of a new aristocratic line (*Stammesgründer*) that will infuse much-needed new blood into the German nobility.

This "feudalization" of the bourgeoisie also implies the embourgeoisement (*Verbürgerlichung*) of the aristocracy, for Ompteda lectures his aristocratic readers that if they are to survive they must welcome the Gideons into their midst. In a later novel he underscores this message when a high-ranking minister assures the aristocratic wife of millionaire Ludwig Droesigl of her husband's forthcoming patent of nobility: "We need fresh blood, families who still have the necessary funds. You, my dear lady, are of an old family just as I am, almost too old because the powder has been shot. Now new families are coming forth. The Droesigls are a good, Christian family, the type we need to draw into our midst. Whether they're old or new will soon be forgotten."[43] The implication that the nobility had better quickly forget the arrival of newcomers to their midst ignored the obvious question of how such a dilution would affect the premise of a hereditary ruling class.

Ompteda experienced further difficulties when he tried to envision how aristocratic sons might ensure their future while still maintaining their class identities. In the first novel of his trilogy on the German nobility, *Sylvester von Geyer* (1908), he establishes an ongoing debate between two middle-aged brothers, Gottfried and Hanns von Geyer, over the proper career for Sylvester, the young heir to the family name. Gottfried's disgust over the unproductive activity of the nobility is invariably countered by Hanns' insistence on the need for it to maintain its dignity through remaining in such conventional realms as the officer corps.[44] Although Hanns' own career has been marked by a humiliating early retirement, poor management of the waning family fortune, and "brilliant misery" for the whole family, he refuses to consider an alternative to the officer corps for his son. While Ompteda seems to condemn Hanns' rigidity as well as his willingness to see his family suffer dreadful privations for the sake of "dignity," by the end of the novel Sylvester is well into his officer's career, destined for the war academy in Berlin. He dies unexpectedly of a ruptured appendix, but the author implies that had tragedy not intervened, years of struggle and hard work would have brought the young man success in the endeavor forced upon him.

In *Eysen*, the next novel of the trilogy, Ompteda pursues the issue through numerous characters of the Eysen family, young and old, urban and rural. At the end, distraught over the suicide of one young Eysen and the scandal of another family member, an uncle, the family patriarch, convenes all the younger males in the scene described at the beginning of this chapter. Pointedly, the gathering is held in the uncle's apartment in the Hansa district away from the symbolic temptations of Unter den Linden and without the symbols of leisure-class affairs: "This time it was not a lively celebration in the 'Römischen Hof,' not a dinner with champagne and toasts but a quiet, intimate gathering in which there would be serious talk." In his lengthy address the uncle urges upon his young charges the need to prepare themselves to meet the challenges of the new century: "Whoever works will rise up; whoever doesn't work will sink down, unsalvageable—so, work, I tell you!"[45] Although the traditional occupations—estate ownership, civil service, or the officer corps—remain honorable endeavors for sons of the nobility, the young men must not to limit their vision to tradition, he warns: "We are watching the memory of the middle ages sinking, and with the new century, a new age is dawning. Do we want to stay with the status quo? Do we want to remove ourselves from other people, do we want to stand aside, idle, too refined [*vornehm*] to take part? Do we want to watch the times passing us by? You Eysens, do you want to be thrown away as scrap iron [*alten Eisen*]?"[46] The patriarch's answer to these rhetorical questions is to entreat the young Eysens to involve themselves in the forefront of the new age: in technology, industry, art, commerce. Thereupon the young men stride toward Brandenburger Tor, inspired by their mission.

What they (and Ompteda) fail to see is the unlikelihood of their uncle's vision being realized. The various members of the Eysen family are shown to consist of vastly uneven quantities of the needed virtues of talent, intelligence, willingness to work, and commitment to aristocratic ideals. The diversity makes them no more likely to stand in the forefront of the new age than the members of any particular bourgeois family.

The feudalization of German society had not occurred. In repeatedly demonstrating the connection of money and social prestige, and in repeatedly showing the impossibility of the aristocracy's obtaining money through its leisured pastimes, novels demonstrated that the aristocracy as a class could not hope to prevail. While novels allowed the wealthy nobility to retreat into exclusivity, they forced a growing number to confront fictionally the conflict between their aversion to bourgeois endeavor and their need for bourgeois prosperity. On the other hand, in largely ignoring the institutional powers of the nobility (particularly its essential ties to the monarchy), novels neglected a crucial element of its dominance in the society of Imperial Germany.[47] The effect of 1870 had been to give the aristocracy another moment of glory by cementing its superiority into the constitution. Yet its preeminence was being threatened by the explosion of new economic and social forces that followed Germany's triumph, as the novels of Berlin imply through their many portrayals of how the urban nobility was oscillating between the alternatives of frivolous leisure and bourgeois work.

While the frivolous activities could be discounted as signs of individual corruption, the bourgeois alternative to such a life contained its own perils even for middle-class authors. A plausible explanation for the failure of novelists to challenge the aristocracy more consistently lies not so much in a feudalization of their attitudes as in the crystallization of their fear of the parvenu. The transformation of the middle class by modernity represented a threat to deeply held values, as the fictional treatments of this class show. The contrast between a wastrel nobility and the diligent burgher could be easily overshadowed by the apparently more frightening contrast between the refinement of the aristocracy and the vulgarity of the newly rich. Although fear of the parvenu was not the sole reason for middle-class tolerance of aristocratic ascendancy, it was especially strong in German society. A militant aversion to the parvenu colored the perceptions of many novelists, who used Berlin, with its spreading reputation as a parvenu city, as a setting for the unfolding of their fears.

# Notes

1. See Gordon A. Craig, *Germany, 1866–1945* (New York, 1978), 98–100, and also Francis L. Carsten, *A History of the Prussian Junkers* (Aldershot, Hants, England, 1989), 115–151.
2. Karl Erich Born, "Structural Changes in German Social and Economic Development at the End of the Nineteenth Century," in James J. Sheehan, ed., *Imperial Germany* (New York, 1976), 25–26. For a critique of the concept of feudalization see David Blackbourn and Geoff Eley, *The Peculiarities of German History: Bourgeois Society and Politics in Nineteenth-Century Germany* (Oxford, 1984), 228–237.

3. Georg Freiherr von Ompteda, *Eysen* (Berlin, 1908; 14th ed., 1909), II, 294. See also Arno J. Mayer, *The Persistence of the Old Regime: Europe to the Great War* (New York, 1981).
4. Ompteda, *Eysen*, II, 287.
5. Ernst Wechsler, *Berliner Autoren* (Leipzig, 1891), 300–301. See also Roland Berbig, "Paul Lindau—eine Literatenkarriere," in Peter Wruck, ed., *Literarisches Leben in Berlin, 1871–1933* (Berlin, 1987), I, 88–125.
6. Paul Lindau, *Spitzen* (Berlin, 1926), 106.
7. Ibid., 491. The attorneys' addresses to the jury enunciate the conflict between social attitudes and the legal system in the case. Ibid., 470–493.
8. Ibid., 527. See also V. G. Kiernan, *The Duel in European History: Honour and the Reign of Aristocracy* (Oxford, 1988).
9. Max Kretzer, *Drei Weiber* (Jena, 1886). A duel by lot substitutes for unacceptable combat between nobleman and commoner in Karl Frenzel's *Geld* (Berlin, 1885). A similar arrangement is referred to as an "American duel" in Theophil Zolling's *Bismarcks Nachfolger* (Berlin, 1891), 451–455.
10. Fritz Mauthner, *Der neue Ahasver* (Dresden, 1882), II. 331. This and the duel cited in note 13 are two rare instances of a Jew participating in an affair of honor.
11. Hans Hopfen, *Der Väter Zweie* (Stuttgart, 1899), II, 134.
12. Artur Landsberger, *Lu, die Kokotte* (Munich, 1912).
13. Conrad Alberti, *Schröter & Co.* (Leipzig, 1893), 262–270.
14. Conrad Alberti, *Wer ist der Stärkere?* (Leipzig, 1888), II, 263, 293. A recent study reminds us, however, of the extent to which *bürgerlich* ideals of duelling developed in nineteenth-century Germany through socialization in the military and the universities. Ute Frevert, "Bürgerlichkeit und Ehre: Zur Geschichte des Duells in England und Deutschland," in Jürgen Kocka, ed., *Bürgertum im 19. Jahrhundert: Deutschland im europäischen Vergleich* (Munich, 1988), 101–140.
15. *The Sociology of Georg Simmel*, translated and edited by Kurt Wolff (Glencoe, Ill., 1950), 321–324, 361–376. For an application of Simmel's theory of secret societies to an aristocracy see Domna Stanton, *The Aristocrat as Art: A Study of the Honnête Homme and the Dandy in Seventeenth- and Nineteenth-Century French Literature* (New York, 1980), 77–78.
16. On these categories see Thorstein Veblen, *The Theory of the Leisure Class* (1899; reprinted Boston, 1973).
17. Patricia Herminghouse, "Schloß oder Fabrik?" in Peter Uwe Hohendahl and Paul Michael Lützeler, eds., *Legitimationskrisen des deutschen Adels, 1200–1900* (Stuttgart, 1979), 248–255.
18. Theophil Zolling, *Der Klatsch* (Leipzig, 1889), 208–210. On the reaction of a long-time British observer to the exclusiveness of Berlin salons see Henry Vizetelly, *Berlin under the New Empire* (London, 1879), I, 86.
19. Alberti, *Wer ist der Stärkere?*, I, 229–230.
20. Kretzer, *Drei Weiber*, I, 41–100. On the importance of such details in fiction see Walter Müller-Seidel, *Theodor Fontane: Soziale Romankunst in Deutschland* (Stuttgart, 1975), 183.
21. See Veblen, *Leisure Class*, 65.
22. Blackbourn and Eley, *Peculiarites of German History*, 229, 237.
23. Vizetelly, *Berlin*, I, 21. On counter-evidence of the embourgeoisement of the officer corp see Blackbourn and Eley, *Peculiarites of German History*, 245.
24. See, respectively, Eda Sagarra, *A Social History of Germany, 1648–1914* (New York, 1977), 202, and Golo Mann, *Deutsche Geschichte des 19. und 20. Jahrhunderts* (1958; Hamburg, 1969), 412.
25. Walter Kiaulehn, *Berlin: Schicksal einer Weltstadt* (Munich, 1958), 130.

26. Hans Otto Modrow, *Berlin 1900: Querschnitt durch die Entwicklung einer Stadt um die Jahrhundertwende* (Berlin, 1936), 252.
27. Veblen, *Leisure Class*, 28–29, 43–47.
28. Karl Bleibtreu, *Die Auskunftei* (Munich, 1910), 175.
29. Max Kretzer, *Millionenbauer* (Leipzig, 1906), 257 and passim.
30. Adalbert von Hanstein, *Zwei Welten*, (Berlin, 1898), I, 65.
31. Friedrich Spielhagen, *Sturmflut*, in *Sämtliche Werke*, XIII, (Leipzig, 1883), 244.
32. The most detailed fictional portrayal of financial demands on aspirants to the officer corps occurs in Georg von Ompteda, *Sylvester von Geyer* (Berlin, 1908). The novel is set in Dresden and Meissen, but occasional references suggest that the already difficult demands for the officer of a provincial regiment are much greater in the impossibly more expensive environment of Berlin.
33. Fedor von Zobeltitz, *Die Hetzjagd* (Berlin, 1913), 86. See also Wechsler, *Berliner Autoren*, 319.
34. Zobeltitz, *Die Hetzjagd*, 372.
35. On aristocratic disdain for middle-class notions of work see John Kautsky, "Funktionen und Werten des Adels," in Hohendahl and Lützeler, *Legitimationskrisen des deutschen Adels*, 9–10.
36. Karl Bleibtreu, *Geist* (Berlin, 1906), 14, 35. On Bleibtreu as a portrayer of "Prussianism" in literature, see M. G. Conrad, *Von Emile Zola bis Gerhart Hauptmann: Erinnerungen zur Geschichte der Moderne* (Leipzig, 1902), 76.
37. On the notion of the *Verbürgerlichung* of the nobility see Hohendahl and Lützeler, *Legitimationskrisen des deutschen Adels*, xiv–xvii, and Werner Mosse, "Adel und Bürgertum im Europa des 19. Jahrhunderts: Eine vergleichende Betrachtung," in Kocka, ed., *Bürgertum im 19. Jahrhundert*, II, 276–314.
38. Hans Hopfen, *Glänzendes Elend* (Berlin, 1893), III, 55.
39. The image is suggested by Alan Bance in his *Theodor Fontane: The Major Novels* (Cambridge University, 1982), 166–167.
40. See Peter Uwe Hohendahl, "Fontane und der Standesroman," in Hohendahl and Lützeler, *Legitimationskrisen des deutschen Adels*, 271, and Müller-Seidel, *Fontane*, Chapter 8.
41. Hopfen, *Glänzendes Elend*, II, 105.
42. Ompteda, *Eysen*, II, 125, 72–77.
43. Georg von Ompteda, *Droesigl* (Berlin, 1909), 369–370. See Hohendahl in Hohendahl and Lützeler, *Legitimationskrisen des deutschen Adels*, 272.
44. For examples of their respective attitudes see Ompteda, *Sylvester von Geyer*, I, 142, 191, 203, 340. For further analysis of this tension within the nobility see Carl Brinkmann, "Die Aristokratie im kapitalistischen Zeitalter," in *Grundriß der Sozialökonomik*, 9, 1 (Tübingen, 1926), 23–30.
45. Ompteda, *Eysen*, II, 287.
46. Ibid., II, 289–290.
47. See Born, "Structural Changes in German Social and Economic Development," in Sheehan, ed., *Imperial Germany*, 24. Gutzkow's *Die Ritter vom Geiste* and Hesekiel's *Von Brandenburg zu Bismarck* are two exceptions to the tendency of novels to neglect the monarchy's importance to the nobility.

# 11

# The Westward Procession: Into the Idler's Paradise

As the nineteenth century drew to a close a host of newcomers sprang forth from the pages of Berlin novels. Heedlessly discarding the cultivated simplicity of Athens-on-the-Spree, they were shown amassing new riches whose corruptive influence dwarfed previous experience. Moreover, by increasingly equating such parvenu figures with Berlin itself, novelists articulated new criticisms about the city's role and about cultural failure in German society. A character in one novel denotes the connection by referring to "Spree-Parvenupolis,"[1] and a character in another, designating Berlin as "the parvenu among world cities," states the implications:

> "All around us we see and hear the powerful drive of this huge city; here world peace is negotiated, and politics and history are made; here is the center for the intellectual and artistic flowering of our nation . . . But our civilization has not yet become a noble culture, and our society remains petty, lowly, and mean . . . . Despite all our great men, we will remain barbarians as long as we allow the get-rich spirit, the social fawning, and the back-biting to reign among us."[2]

This passage demonstrates the ease with which novelists could progress from condemning the parvenu to blaming Berlin and then to disparaging Germany. Newness at all three levels became equated not only with a lack of culture but also with a lack of moral integrity.

Novels symbolized this crisis of newness through the westward direction of the expanding city.[3] As early as 1850 Karl Gutzkow identified the west, or Berlin W as it became known, with new money. Into the 1880s novels showed the Tiergarten district beyond Potsdamerplatz being invaded by the newly rich, but even so, an atmosphere of gentility prevailed. All this changed in 1886, when Paul Lindau published *Der Zug nach dem Westen* (*The Westward Procession*), whose title came to denote Berlin's headlong rush toward the twentieth century, with Berlin W epitomizing the parvenu mentality. Novelists' abhorrence of this mentality translated into two basic reactions: sentimental portrayals of "real" Berliners, whose humble values kept them uncontaminated by the new frenzy, and fatalistic images of parvenuism sweeping the society. Both reactions muffled calls to social engagement.

This is not immediately apparent in novels that combatted parvenuism with the "real" Berliner (*echt Berliner*), a down-to-earth type whose humble virtues were credited with bringing the city through many a hardship.[4] Such figures can be seen as offering a mooring point for readers adrift in modern seas—and thus as another dimension of fictional calls for national regeneration. But they also can be interpreted as justifications for a nostalgic withdrawal from the public arena. Leberecht Hühnchen, one of the most beloved of all Berlin characters, exemplifies both these implications. Heinrich Seidel (1842–1906) introduced him in February 1880 in a series of novellas; the manifold printings made Hühnchen into a German rival of Sherlock Holmes as the fictional character whose fame most surpassed that of his creator.[5] Although the improbable name, with its conjunction of the Puritanical sounding "right-living" and the diminutive of "hen," suggests Seidel was belittling his character, the author clearly meant him to be a model for all Germans who wished to "live right." The satire is directed against pretension, a quality that anyone with such a silly name could scarcely foster. Indeed, it is difficult to imagine a less pretentious person than Leberecht Hühnchen. A cultural counterweight to the greedy and ambitious characters populating other Berlin novels, he copes with the economic and social uncertainties of his age through his "talent for sucking honey out of all flowers, even out of the poisonous ones."[6]

The antidote for too much honey is self-irony—a quality that, despite his Mecklenburg origins, gives Hühnchen entry into the ranks of "real" Berliners. One day, for example, he greets the narrator by asking, "Can't you see from a block away that I'm a landowner and a homeowner?"[7] Indeed, he has succeeded in buying a small, ugly house in Steglitz (a suburb whose southwestern location connoted newness but lacked the prestige of the more elegant districts of Berlin W). He proudly calls his house "Villa Hühnchen," although by his own admission the critical elements of a villa, "columns and caryatids and sculptured vegetation" are lacking.[8] The "wine harvest celebration" that marks the villa's first social event gives further scope to self-irony, as well as permitting a thinly veiled attack on the ostentation in Berlin's real villas. Only two guests beyond the Hühnchen family take part, but Hühnchen has prepared written programs and menus. The welcoming ceremony is followed by a showing of the menagerie (consisting of a rabbit, a starling, and a tree frog) and then the harvest, which involves plucking the fifteen grapes produced by the new vine.[9] Similarly modest events ensue, each affectionately recounted under their grandiose titles.

Beneath the fantasy and self-irony lies a still more important quality: an overweening compassion for others' needs. For example, upon hearing of a draftsman whose fear of his fiancée's father has caused his engagement to stretch on for twenty-five years, Hühnchen decides to hold a "silver anniversary engagement party" for the middle-aged couple. The suitor, presenting his fiancée for the first time, is suddenly infused, the narrator reports, with that rare feeling expressed by Goethe's lines: "Here I am truly human; here I am allowed to be so."[10] Hühnchen repeatedly provides such haven for lonely souls in episodes that enshrine the humane instincts of the Berlin *Kleinbürger*.

Another of Hühnchen's Berlin qualities is a realism that tells him when to let go of fantasy. One such moment comes when he acknowledges that Berlin's inexorable expansion will overwhelm his modest property. Typically, he resists such knowledge by commenting that the huge new building on the adjoining property has brought an unexpected benefit: the sun's reflection on the expanse of windows gives his house more light. But he finally realizes he must sell his property, for he cannot bear to watch his fruit trees' dying struggles against the encroachment. Clearly, Seidel meant Hühnchen's acceptance of this urban tragedy to guide his readers in making their own way, perturbed but not destroyed by the disruptions of modernity.

While Hühnchen seems to yield to the reality of modern Berlin, he actually finds a means of escaping it. The last episode has him buying new property beyond the southern edge of the city. This house will also be engulfed by Berlin, he admits, but the property is large enough to protect its garden from urban depredations. Seidel's failure to acknowledge the contradiction implied in giving his humble Berliner the wherewithal to buy his way out of the city thus mixes wish-fulfillment with his message. His admonition to readers to cultivate modest pleasures rather than pursue profit[11] is offset by an enticing vision of the idyllic surroundings such profit could buy.

Whatever the implications of Hühnchen's move, his humane qualities prevail. His virtues presumably would prevail in any environment, but it is no accident that Hühnchen shuns the prestigious districts of Berlin W. Paul Lindau's *Zug nach dem Westen* gives a graphic portrayal of the perils that await "real" Berliners who transplant themselves into its realms. A peripheral character articulates the assumption behind the title:

> "The metropolitan society is following the same direction established in migrations of long ago, and it seems to have been learned from the sun: the great westward procession. The present-day Berlin that our generation has brought to above the million mark, was formed almost completely by immigration from the east . . ., and the great tide maintains its direction within the city as well. There, too, the same westward procession is characteristic: from the part of Berlin that is hard-working and frugal to the part that is pleasure-seeking and extravagant."[12]

Ignoring the wider aspects of this theory, Lindau focuses on intra-city movement to Berlin W, whose society he shows to consist of newcomers to wealth and position. "Our Berlin, the Berlin in which we are living," a resident comments, "still doesn't have a well-defined character, and I can imagine that there are a lot of people who don't like it at all."[13] The novel explains that remark by depicting the effects of Berlin W on the lives of five major characters and numerous lesser ones.

Maximilian and Stephanie Wilprecht are prototypes of the inhabitants of Berlin W. The son of a hard-working lumber dealer who built a prosperous trade on the right bank of the Spree, Maximilian sold the business after his father's death at the height of the *Gründerjahre*. The fortune allows him to build a spectacular mansion on the Tiergartenstraße, and his social ascent seems beyond doubt when he attains the title of commercial councillor (*Kommerzienrat*). Stephanie Wilprecht is introduced as an unstinting social climber who is presiding as a worried hostess over the first ball at the new mansion. Her intuitive worry is shown to have good cause, for the episode gives readers a glimpse of the Wilprechts' precarious balance in Berlin society. Most guests are awed by the splendor of the scene, but those who really matter are less impressed: "Nowadays it was no great achievement to acquire good taste; you only had to put your hands in your lap and not interfere with the architect and decorator: they'd take care of everything!"[14] Unaware of such slurs, the Wilprechts have worked to acquire the trappings of culture by attending theatrical premieres, filling their salon with luminaries, ostentatiously patronizing the arts, and lining library shelves with lavishly bound—but unread—German classics. None of these activities covers the lack of insight beneath the "worn-out generalities" of the Wilprechts' cultural discourse,[15] but the couple finally gains entrée into an aristocratic drawing room. In this society *Bildung* can be bought.

The Wilprechts' pretension to good taste is but one symbol of the social deception that pervades Berlin W. Another manifestation of this deception, "the art of the social lie," includes Stephanie's ability to hide her hurt when a much-sought ambassador fails to appear at the ball, or her loathing for a guest whom she welcomes effusively. At the other extreme, deception comes at the expense of deep feelings. For instance, Stephanie learns of her father's death just before a long-awaited *dîner* at an ambassadorial mansion. Unable to relinquish this social moment, she decides to conceal the news until the next day, when she can begin mourning in earnest. The deception works; the fact that several close observers become aware of Stephanie's moral callousness does not impede her social ascent. Nevertheless, she cries heartfelt tears upon realizing the enormity of her covering up her father's death. Her husband, on the other hand, reveals no redemptive qualities. Although vengeful toward anyone who impedes his own amorous pursuits, Maximilian is ruthless in turning others' social deception into scandal. Lindau exacts no poetic justice from the Wilprechts; their shallow, self-serving lives seem to be their own punishment, but the couple is too blind to realize it.

The counterpoint to Maximilian Wilprecht is Gustav Ehrike, whose arrival in Berlin W was preceded by a lifetime of hard work in the Wilprecht lumber firm and an early marriage to the boss's daughter, Maximilian's stern older sister, Adelheid. Unquestioningly, he endured the regime she imposed: "He lived comfortably, worked comfortably, ate a lot and well, competed with his wife in steadily gaining weight, and missed his freedom as little as the canary crawling from its egg into a cage. He lived contentedly on Koppenstraße . . . in a Berlin that ended for him beyond the palace on the other side of the Spree."[16] This matrimonial morality tale ended ironically, however, when, on the couple's silver anniversary celebration, Adelheid died of an acute bilious attack from the unaccustomed lobster salad. Gustav's staid life changed radically when Maximilian persuaded him to move into a townhouse by the Tiergarten, sell his share of the lumber business, and live off the long-accrued profits. The new townhouse attracted genuine admiration for its elegance, taste, and lack of pretension. But Gustav's new surroundings alienated him from his old cronies, and they were supplanted by a host of young artists eager to partake of his hospitality. Still lonely, Gustav embarked upon the courtship of the 19-year-old daughter of the bookkeeper from the Wilprecht firm. Lolo, as the beautiful girl was known, hesitated but briefly before marrying Gustav and entering the glamorous world of Berlin W.

In contrast to Stephanie Wilprecht, Lolo Ehrike manifests genuine *Bildung*. Her father's efforts to provide her with the best education available to young girls, coupled with her innate tastefulness, enable her to establish "one of the best and most enjoyable [salons] in the cultivated society of the city."[17] Far from being a calculated pose, Lolo's involvement with the arts is a natural expression of her interests. In contrast to the clichés uttered by other Berlin W residents, she thrives on discussions in which she expounds ideas resting "on an independent artistic taste and feeling, [and on] a well-educated understanding."[18] That Gustav is openly bored by such exchanges is taken amiss by no one, since he does not interfere.

Both Ehrikes fall victim to the affliction of self-deception. Gustav has deceived himself in assuming that the vivacious Lolo will remain content with his kind attentions. Lolo has deceived herself by marrying a stodgy old man she does not love. This self-deception reaches a crisis when a young composer, Georg Nortstetten, meets Lolo in a Berlin drawing room and they fall in love. Lolo heedlessly carries on their relationship beneath her husband's nose. After a long build-up of gossip Gustav discovers the couple in a sexually innocent rendezvous in Georg's apartment and commands Lolo never again to darken his door. His command echoes through other houses as well, for, as a self-righteous Maximilian Wilprecht puts it, "Every man of honor has the duty of making it his humble endeavor to keep the hearth of his loved ones clean."[19]

Lolo and Georg show their own deference to this rigid code by embarking on a program to minimize the social damage of their having violated it. Their breach is underscored when Lolo's brother-in-law refuses to allow her to spend even one night under his roof and when Georg's father likewise refuses to receive her. Lolo gratefully accepts an offer of refuge from Georg's uncle, a stern Protestant pastor in a provincial town. Upon her arrival at the parsonage, he informs her that he expects her to engage in rigorous moral cleansing to detach herself from the environment of universal lying that got her into trouble. Lolo willingly assents and begins a routine of household tasks, attending church, reading spiritual tracts, and self-examination. Her break with her past becomes clear one evening as she plays hymns on the harmonium for the pastor and his wife. She thinks of how Berlin acquaintances would laugh at the homely scene and yet notes that she is genuinely glad to be part of it.

Were this scene a manifestation of conventional anti-urbanism, *Der Zug nach dem Westen* might have ended here, with Lolo rehabilitated and Georg joining her. But a move to the provinces—or even to old Berlin in the east—is not the answer, for working in Berlin is vital to Georg's artistic development, "and only the western part of the city was considered by them to be the essence of Berlin."[20] They thus decide to settle in the Hansa district, which although west seems far removed from the superficial people of the Tiergarten district. Here, too, the novel might have ended, for Georg and Lolo, now married, begin a life of "pure, true, untroubled happiness." The contrast with their former lives is profound: "They did not go out and also held no parties," the narrator reports, describing how they received only close friends for comfortable evening conversations.[21] Removed both from the philistine atmosphere of eastern Berlin and the social frenzy of Berlin W, their household symbolizes Lindau's prescription: a joining of the quiet cultivation of the old Berlin with the sophistication of the modern metropolis.

Lindau's conclusion, however, produces an image of the westward procession that diffuses his social message. Five days after giving birth to a daughter, Lolo dies in an agony of "childbed fever" and is taken to her grave in a "mournful procession to the west." Lindau did not intend Lolo's death to be a cosmic judgment, for he allowed even the country pastor to be won over by her virtuous spirit. Moreover, the funeral procession hardly betokened the death of Berlin W, since its real representatives, the Wilprechts, still lived in undisturbed social glory. Lindau's use of the funeral as a symbol of westward movement seems an afterthought, for it is the one migration whose precise destination is unspecified. Lindau's abandonment of his focus on the cultural dichotomy between east and west allowed social criticism to dissipate into sentimentality.

Some of Lindau's contemporaries criticized the novel on this score, as in Fritz Mauthner's comment that the novel sailed under a false flag because the issue of east versus west Berlin had no real bearing on the story of Lolo and Georg.[22] In turn, however, Mauthner encountered similar difficulties in sustaining contrasts between specifically west- or east-Berlin traits in his trilogy, *Berlin W*. Despite such problems and despite sharp controversies over the literary worth of *Zug nach dem Westen*, Lindau's novel came to stand at the head of a long line of other novels that attacked Berlin W as a center of materialism, parvenuism, and social deception. But as with Lindau's novel, such attacks did not end in fictional reversals of the westward movement. Instead, novelists were far more likely to confront the realization that the conventions of eastern Berlin provided scant solution to the vulgarity and materialism of Berlin W, so inadequate were they to modern realities. What resulted were portrayals of a full-blown crisis in the middle class.

• • •

One of the best examples of this crisis occurs in Theodor Fontane's *Frau Jenny Treibel* (1892), which portrays what Fontane calls the bourgeois mentality as an insidious force that threatens the values of the *Bildungsbürgertum* both from within and without.[23] Its depiction of this triad—bourgeoisie, *Bildungsbürgertum*, and the city—offers a complex rendition of German cultural tradition's being molded by modernity. Although Fontane uses the term "bourgeoisie" to denote the alien nature of the new middle class, he chooses two native Berliners as its paragons: Jenny Treibel and her factory-owner husband, whose entrepreneurial success has garnered him the coveted title of *Kommerzienrat* (Commercial Councillor). Although the Treibels engage in manifold struggles for social position, both also manifest elements of Berlin tradition, with Jenny striving to exhibit the ideals of Athens-on-the-Spree and her husband revealing at key moments the Berliner's inclination to shun pretension. In contrast to other novels about the bourgeoisie, moreover, Fontane has the Treibels living not in Berlin W but on Köpenickerstraße in the southeast.

The Treibel villa reflects the character of its mistress. Its rooms of "beautiful simplicity" and park-like gardens are meant to radiate refinement, but it also betrays the taint of the 1870s, when "the attitudes of the *Gründer* began to rule even the most sober heads."[24] That Jenny's head was so ruled is suggested by the information that she originally wanted to decorate the dining room with reliefs by Reinhold Begas, Berlin's most sought-after sculptor. Her husband had vetoed the idea with the droll observation that Begas pieces were inappropriate in the house of a *Kommerzienrat* and should be postponed until he received the title of *Generalkonsul*, a day that at the time of the novel, sixteen years later, had yet to arrive. Still, more than a few traces of bourgeois pretension appear in the giant vases of lilacs gracing the dining room; in the garden fountain bouncing a small sphere in its stream; and in the cockatoo carried out to a garden perch every morning to serve as decoration. A jarring incongruity is the adjoining Treibel dye factory, whose smokestacks blow a foul odor over the house in northerly winds. Those winds, however, are "notoriously rare," and besides, Treibel alleviates the nuisance by building the factory chimneys taller each year.

Jenny's image of herself, like that of her surroundings, the novel makes clear, is nothing less than "sweet self-delusion."[25] She constantly finds opportunities to claim that her position as *Kommerzienrätin* has not affected her and repeatedly affirms that "money is only a burden and that happiness lies in a completely different realm."[26] This affirmation is belied by her calculated struggle to rise above her origins as a grocer's daughter. She also constantly refers to the "little blossom," first cultivated by her childhood sweetheart Willibald Schmidt, that grew into her "God-given" sense of the good, the true, and the beautiful.[27] In truth Jenny actually fosters only a profuse sentimentality that is ritualized in every social gathering in the villa. At a prescribed point in the evening she imposes upon an aging tenor to sing, and he responds with a rendition of the same three *Lieder*. Other guests perform similarly standard offerings to polite applause. Then Jenny is beseeched to sing "her" song, which she invariably does, singing in a thin voice words written for her many years earlier by Schmidt:

> Happiness, of your thousand poses
> I choose but one for me,
> What matters gold? I wish roses
> my humble adornment to be.[28]

The song always elicits wistful comments about a bygone era, and Jenny revels in the image of herself as a woman stifled by a prosaic marriage, who instills poetry into the lives of those around her.

Although *Kommerzienrat* Treibel seems unpretentious, he too proves susceptible to the activity of promoting the Treibels—or *Treibelei*, as one observer calls it. His involvement is clear, for instance, as he mentally surveys the guests of an approaching *dîner*. The guest of honor, an Englishman bearing the venerable name of Mr. Nelson, will bring an international dimension. A retired Lieutenant Vogelsang may be enlisted to help Treibel win a Reichstag seat in a nearby district, which Treibel sees as the prelude to being named a *Generalkonsul*. Finally, two former ladies-in-waiting will confer an unprecedented aristocratic presence in the Köpenickerstraße, well worth the expense of sending a coach west to fetch the pair. Clearly, Treibel envisions the evening as a significant moment in the family's social fortune.

Although Fontane intended his novel as an attack on the bourgeoisie, he also gently criticized the *Bildungsbürgertum*. "I hate what is bourgeois with a passion that would belong to a sworn social democrat," he wrote, but elsewhere he compared that feeling to his dislike of "professorial wisdom, professorial ignorance, and professorial liberalism."[29] In *Frau Jenny Treibel* gymnasium professor Willibald Schmidt seems the counterpoint to the bourgeois Treibels, but he harbors traits that make him less far-removed than he suspects. He is as meticulous in planning his social evenings as any *bourgeoise*, preparing for a gathering with fellow professors by scrupulously arranging crystal wine glasses, porcelain vases filled with flowers, and brass lamps on the table. Although he detests the ostentation of a bourgeois *dîner*, he is obviously proud of his fresh crawfish and carefully selected Mosel. When one guest chides the host for conversing about the food "as if [he] belonged to the bankers and money princes," Schmidt finds grounds for defending himself, but the point has been made.[30] In another exchange Schmidt reproaches a fellow professor for denigrating the archeology of "an untutored millionaire" like Heinrich Schliemann, but he acknowledges his own aversion to the idea that someone who "once filled shopping bags and sold raisins is now digging up venerable old Priam."[31] Snobbery clearly is not a monopoly of the bourgeoisie.

Fontane's portrayal of the small-town character of Berlin further satirizes cultural affectation. The novel is concentrated in the east, where both the Treibel and Schmidt houses are located, but it makes no mention of such famed sites as Brandenburger Tor or Unter den Linden.[32] A *Landpartie* to the westerly

Halensee provides the only foray out of old Berlin, and the scene there confirms the impression of a city of almost poignant pretensions. Surrounded by "a sandy panorama criss-crossed by railway dikes and asparagus beds," the small lake cannot even be seen from most parts of the restaurant in which the party assembles.[33] A shooting gallery and a bowling alley on the opposite shore form the view from the table they choose, and when members of the party climb onto chairs to try to see the water, they spot two swan houses—but no swans. Willibald Schimdt's comment on the folly of trying to dress up a place with "swan houses and bowling alleys" seems to pertain all too well to Berlin as a whole.[34]

Berliners' defensiveness about their city extends to allusions to its sorry comparison with cities of a more venerable reputation. When a young woman from Hamburg visits the Treibel household, she heeds Berlin sensitivities by avoiding overt comparisons with Hamburg and by complimenting such cultural achievements as the Treibels' coffee service. Even so, her Hamburger pride shows itself when an engagement announcement arrives in the mail and she finds herself compelled to question a detail of its presentation. To show her that it actually conforms to current standards of propriety, Treibel hands it to her, saying wryly that she must keep it, "as a souvenir of your Berlin stay and as proof of the gradual progress of its native culture. Of course, we're still a good bit behind, but we're getting there."[35] In Treibel's case, then, humor substitutes for anger, perhaps because, unlike his wife, he ultimately prefers the "simpler" ways of Berlin.

The themes of the Treibels, the Schmidts, and Berlin converge in a crisis of *Treibelei* over whom the younger son Leopold will marry. Eight years earlier the elder son had married a prim, self-assured young woman from Hamburg whose visible pride in her patrician origins became for Jenny an ongoing reproach against the Treibels and Berlin. Jenny declares that one daughter-in-law from Hamburg is enough and refuses to consider matching Leopold with the younger sister.[36] Suddenly, however, Leopold becomes engaged to Willibald Schmidt's daughter Corinna, and Jenny is outraged at the notion of a Treibel marrying a socially obscure Schmidt. "Treibels simply do not grow on trees, to be shaken to the ground by anyone who happens to walk by," she shouts at Leopold.[37] At first Jenny's husband reacts with his unassuming nature, declaring, "We aren't Bismarcks or Arnims or some other Markish nobility; we're the Treibels with our factory chemicals; and you're a Bürstenbinder from Adlerstraße. Now being a Bürstenbinder is quite all right, but a Bürstenbinder can't possibly be higher than a Schmidt."[38] Later, however, he has second thoughts: "What if she were right after all!" This denial of his instincts, the narrator explains, is inevitable: "For after all, the good Treibel was still the product of three generations that had grown increasingly wealthy in manufacturing, and despite all his good-hearted qualities, the bourgeois mentality was as deeply rooted in him as in his sentimental wife."[39] Ultimately, the match disintegrates when Corinna sees that Leopold cannot stand up to his mother, and soon a second connection between the Treibels and the Hamburg family is in the offing. Jenny would sooner have her son marry the daughter of a socially prominent family she despises than the daughter of an unknown gymnasium professor for whom she professes lifelong affection and admiration.

Academicians are shown also to have their own prejudices about a suitable match, as is clear from Schmidt's relief when Corinna abandons thoughts of marrying Leopold in favor of a liaison with her cousin, Marcell Wedderkopp. The young man in question is depicted as an unexciting suitor whose modest situation as a teacher at a girls' school holds no attraction for Corinna. Just as her stalemate with the Treibels is becoming tedious, however, Marcell receives a stipend to join the Schliemann excavations in Greece—an honor that will assure him a gymnasium post. Corinna switches her attentions to him. "That's what I call a good match," Schmidt tells his housekeeper.[40] Like any good bourgeois, Schmidt cannot resist welcoming his daughter's marriage to a man of stature—even if the stature is academic, not social. Delighted by Corinna's "return to reason," he welcomes her back with fatherly guidance that his absent-minded upbringing has neglected. "Become the person you are," Schmidt tells her, adding that Pindar's prescription will bring far more happiness than *Treibelei*.[41]

*Frau Jenny Treibel* also contains a subtle antidote to the strident nationalism of the 1890s in a conclusion that alludes to a "real" Germany as unprepossessing as the "real" Berlin. The wedding of Corinna and Marcell has taken place, and most participants, including the bridal pair, have left. Only Schmidt and a few old friends remain, swapping stories "from the treasure chest of the German nation."[42] Their camaraderie reflects an ideal of Germans without pretension, enjoying their common heritage. Schmidt suddenly asks the old tenor to sing Jenny's song, and as the words pour forth he allows himself some sentimental tears. It's not a bad song, he muses, for everything beyond one's own nature *is* meaningless—money, learning, even professorships. The last word, then, is given to the professor, but it is noteworthy that *Kommerzienrat* Treibel is also among the old friends. The bourgeois and the *Bürger* can be brothers if they abandon pretensions and self-pride. Although "real" Berliners may become infected by modern ways, this novel urges, they can avoid losing themselves in pursuit of externals by coming back to their simple ideals. By subtly raising this message to a national level, Fontane warned not only Berliners but Germans. But this novel also suggested that the *Gemütlichkeit* of German tradition had little chance of surviving onslaughts like those of the Berlin bourgeoisie with their social climbing, of Hamburger patricians with their English ways, or even of gymnasium professors with their elite ideas of *Bildung*. To that extent it became an expression of quiet resignation.

Most novels nevertheless continued to portray parvenus as the greatest threat. Max Kretzer exemplified the growing obsession when in the late 1880s he turned away from working-class Berlin to examine the spreading influence of the parvenu. His novel *Drei Weiber* (1886) focused most explicitly on Berlin W, with its details of the social comings and goings in a splendid house on Potsdamerstraße. Depicting a world of ostentation, insincerity, and corruption, Kretzer placed at its center a young widow named Frieda von Setzen, whose husband made her executor of his fortune on behalf of his daughter from a previous marriage. Frieda's reckless maneuvers to secure her own ambitions before the child comes of age cause one observer to comment that "there are salon whores who have their procurors just like every other whore."[43] A prominent dimension of Frieda's hypocrisy is her self-serving involvement in charitable associations that supposedly work for the protection of wayward girls, prison reform, or the rehabilitation of ex-convicts. Even after ruining her step-daughter's life, Frieda still faces bankruptcy. She avoids it by yielding to the advances of a disgusting speculator whose prison record does not deter her from concluding a match that allows her to set up fashionable new quarters near the zoological garden. This westward move signifies both social success and utter degradation. A parade of other characters shows that Frieda is only a part of a widespread depravity beneath the cultivated surface of Berlin W.

A more innocent—but more uncouth—version of the parvenu emerges in Kretzer's *Millionenbauer* (1890). Published seventeen years after the crash, this novel gave new force to the notion that the sins of the *Gründerjahre* had irretrievably damned Berlin society.[44] The title character, Hans Köppke, had been a simple farmer, tilling land garnered by generations of Köppkes in Schöneberg, the village bordering southwestern Berlin. Suddenly the value of his land began to multiply because of its proximity to the Potsdam and Anhalter railroads. After unification, Köppke, like many other Schönebergers, found himself awash in riches as he sold his farmland to speculators. "Berlin's gobblin' everything up," Köppke comments wryly about the phenomenon that has changed his life.[45]

Hardly the embodiment of the traditional *Bürger*, Köppke is a newcomer both to urban and to well-to-do society. His routine of introducing himself as "Köppke of Schöneberg" evokes the ironic narrational comment that "'Goethe of Weimar' could not have sounded more splendid or more convincing."[46] His expensive dress and newly acquired taste for cognac cannot hide his boorish manners, nor does the expansive villa he builds reveal anything but unrefined extravagance. The Köppkes, it seems, are not even able to buy good taste.

They can, however, buy social connections, and the novel centers on Köppke's efforts to do so by arranging an aristocratic match for his elder daughter. An appropriately desperate young nobleman with gambling debts responds, and, despite the repugnance of the young man's proud but impoverished father, the marriage takes place. To his consternation, Köppke finds himself the object of repeated humiliations by his new in-laws, and also realizes that his son-in-law is running up more debts at his expense. He responds by precipitating a melodramatic sequence of exchanged insults, blackmail, marital crises, family ruptures, and suicide threats—all of which finally reach happy resolution. The last scene has the millionaire farmer being snubbed anew, but this time he takes the insult philosophically: "After all, he was the one who was rich and that couldn't be changed . . . . He would continue to amuse himself on his own terms—he, Hans Köppke of Schöneberg!"[47] Kretzer thus gives the new Berlin the last word; the age of the parvenu has arrived. He is, these lines suggest, the inevitable product of modernity.

The most virulent fictional portrayal of a triumph of parvenuism in Berlin came ten years later, when Heinrich Mann (1871–1950) published his first novel, *Im Schlaraffenland* (1900). Freely translated as *In the Idler's Paradise*, its title clearly states Mann's judgment on a society completely transformed by ill-distributed capitalist wealth.[48] Berlin W, the center of this society, is populated by self-absorbed upstarts devoted to elaborate rituals of pleasure and devoid of moral principles. This domain is shown within the wider context of a German nation that wildly applauds such exploits—a nation eager, in what the narrator calls its mood of "hurrah-patriotism," to overlook the cultural demolition taking place.

Mann examines Schlaraffenland by tracing the odyssey of his protagonist Andreas Zumsee through its realms. The novel becomes a satirical morality tale on the hubris of someone who mistakenly equates the trappings of social ascendancy with genuine power. A poor student from a small Rhineland town, Andreas is something of a Candide traveling to a German version of El Dorado. But he resembles Stendhal's Julien Sorel even more, for beneath his naiveté he possesses a calculating instinct for upward mobility and a readiness to adopt whatever hypocritical pose will best serve that instinct. In contrast to Julien, Andreas decides that success in Schlaraffenland is not to be attained through the church, the crown, or the aristocracy but rather by associating with the manipulators of two new institutions: a stockmarket representing the financial treasury of the German nation and a mass press, its cultural counterpart. Although ceaselessly amused by "the pleasure of seeing through people," Andreas fails at crucial junctures to employ this ability with regard to himself and thus experiences a dizzying social ascent and crashing fall that only Berlin W can offer. The milestones are designated in geographic terms: four changes of residence, each reflecting a different social status.

The novel opens in 1894, with Andreas living in a cramped room in a northern working-class neighborhood. A year at the university has made him desperate over the prospect of a supposed future in his native town of Gumplach as a humble schoolmaster. Daydreaming about how to escape this fate, Andreas decides that as a drama critic he could gain "power, influence, a good income and a respected place in Berlin society."[49] With new resolve he makes contact with literary café society, presents himself at the offices of the *Berliner Nachtkourier* (touted by its editor-in-chief as "the voice of German civilization"), and gains introduction to the house of *Generalkonsul* James Türkheimer, a stock mogul whose immense wealth has made him one of the most powerful men in

Berlin. Türkheimer's nod of approval or that of his wife Adelheid, Andreas is told, will provide instant social stature for the most obscure young man. At his first Türkheimer soirée Andreas decides to cultivate Adelheid, since she seems vulnerable to his naive good looks. He also meets an array of other important people and manages to win two thousand marks at the gaming table. This, then, is Schlaraffenland—a world in which money and position are there for the taking. Power, essential to sustaining one in this world, is far less accessible, as Andreas will learn.

Andreas marks his entry into this world by moving to a room in the much more respectable Dorotheenstraße, near Unter den Linden, and by accepting Adelheid's veiled invitation to outfit himself at her tailor's. Arrayed in his frock coat, he glances at his old clothes, thinking, "That was actually his old self, lying there all sunken together."[50] The Dorotheenstraße period is marked by Andreas' campaign to cultivate Adelheid's attention and thereby to penetrate to the center of Berlin society. Deciding he must have a *Marotte*, or a personal hallmark, to set him apart, he concocts a trait that is indeed eccentric: he declares himself to be a devout Catholic. This improbable role, he reasons, will highlight his one source of superiority over the inhabitants of Schlaraffenland: his origins in the much older culture of the Rhineland. This gambit proves a stroke of genius. Adelheid is at first disbelieving when he declines to attend a Sunday performance because of his religious obligations; then she is intrigued to find him in his room dressed as a monk with a "bleeding crucifix" hanging above his desk; finally, she concludes that the piety is "actually chic."[51] Andreas, of course, does not allow his *Marotte* to interfere with the passionate lovemaking that ensues. In the next weeks Adelheid's secretive visits to Dorotheenstraße are punctuated by Andreas' appearances at the Türkheimer mansion, which signify what seems to be his full-fledged entry into the society of Schlaraffenland.

Not content simply to be the lap dog of a society matron, Andreas seeks to attain independent power by transforming himself into a famous *Literat*. The process, he discovers, has nothing to do with artistic talent or with producing serious work, but involves gaining the notice of the right people in a society characterized by cultural shallowness.[52] From all sides he is told that the theater is the quickest route to fame, and he sees this precept confirmed when he witnesses the adulation a dramatist receives at a premiere.[53] The successful rendition of his initial poetic efforts in the Türkheimer salon causes Adelheid to pressure him to write a play in time for a dramatic evening eight weeks hence. She exclaims, "Then we will have been in love for three months. What a long time! Then you'll become rich and famous."[54] Although Andreas' new life gives him little time or inclination for such work, he finally sits at his desk long enough to complete a dramatic poem about the current fashionable subject: the misunderstood woman. All of Berlin society seems to be present when the work is performed on a makeshift stage at the Türkheimers'. Andreas' reputation seems secured when Türkheimer spends five minutes congratulating him, after which he is besieged by well-wishers, drama critics, and journalists. Such is the birth of the cultural hero in Schlaraffenland. Andreas becomes Berlin's—and Germany's—favorite dramatist overnight.

Andreas marks his arrival at the summit of Schlaraffenland society with a move to an elegant apartment in Berlin W, which Adelheid furnishes in a masterpiece of interior design. Andreas, however, is so absorbed in fantasies about "the mechanism of a whole cultural realm" working for his enjoyment that he has little time for his mistress.[55] Occasionally he puts on a show of working, but the main work in Schlaraffenland is maintaining appearances—a task at which he excels. When Adelheid beseeches him to tell her what will make him happy, he requests notebooks for every room so he can write down ideas that occur during moments of feverish creativity. She fulfills the request, little suspecting that the notebooks will serve only to make laundry lists. "You only have to look happy in Schlaraffenland in order really to become happy," an acquaintance tells Andreas, and each new episode of enjoyment seems to confirm that statement.[56]

A ceaseless observer as well as partaker, Andreas continues to ponder the relation of power to money in Schlaraffenland. Advised to partake in "the Türkheimer national endowment,"[57] he has begun to benefit from a strange kind of communism in Schlaraffenland. Adelheid funnels large amounts of money to him, claiming that she took the last hundred-mark note from his one-time gambling winnings, gave it to her husband to invest in the "Texas-Bloody-Bank-Corporation," and now, a week later, is returning the fivefold profits it has reaped. Andreas easily accepts the story and rationalizes that, "Here, where gold pieces rolled under furniture in unfathomable ways, no one took any personal responsibility; one lived under the hand of a higher destiny."[58] Although he sees the corrupt means by which fortunes are secured, the closer he gets to the source, the easier it becomes to praise the methods. He is enraged, for example, to learn that Türkheimer has manipulated the price of a popular stock by planting false information in the press. But when he learns Türkheimer has taken him along on the profitable ride, he gushes: "It's incalculable what an acquaintance with a genius of action like you is worth to a poet! You allow us debilitated moderns the privilege of looking upon a conqueror, a renaissance man!"[59] Andreas thus continues to feed at the Türkheimer trough.

Andreas' growing belief that he has achieved wealth and fame through his own efforts is the beginning of his downfall. All along he has resented Türkheimer because of his "eastern" [Jewish] origins.[60] Now he becomes convinced that he is helping the Türkheimers with his literary renown, rather than vice-versa, and decides to demonstrate his power over Türkheimer's realm. The opportunity arises when Türkheimer acquires a 17-year-old, working-class girl as a mistress. Achnes Matzke, or "Little Matzke," as she is called, is the extreme example of the rise and fall of human fortune in Schlaraffenland. One day she is living a poverty-stricken existence, and the next she presides over a villa in Westend on Berlin's westernmost border. When Andreas seeks her out she delightedly gives him a tour of her elegant and tasteful surroundings. With her magnificent wardrobe she also looks like a true lady. As another character proposes, women are classless by nature and therefore easily assume the identity of any class.[61] As soon as Little Matzke opens her mouth, however, all illusion vanishes, for she spews forth unrelieved triviality in heavy Berlin dialect. Andreas nevertheless decides that his "man-of-the-world upbringing" will be complete only when he possesses this empty-headed creature, and he dutifully begins his "high corruption."[62]

Andreas' life in Schlaraffenland ends when the two Türkheimers learn of his flagrant affair with Little Matzke and overcome their mutual betrayals by uniting against him. The sweetest revenge for his multi-faceted assault on the family honor, they decide, will be to demonstrate their power by driving him into the life of a *Kleinbürger*. They will put him into a humble editorial post at the *Berliner Nachtkourier* and force him to marry Little Matzke. So much will he fear losing these tokens of social respectability that he will never reveal what he has seen of the Türkheimer family. Thus ejected from Schlaraffenland, Andreas moves to a nondescript apartment, where he endures the inept cooking of his new wife and the shrewishness of the housekeeper she has managed to bring with her. In addition to the similarity with Candide's ending up with the now-ugly Cunegonde, another Candide-like irony emerges. While performing his editorial duties at the *Nachtkourier*, Andreas suddenly realizes that all has happened for the best: this tumultuous journey has spared him the fate of becoming a Gumplacher schoolmaster.

Lest such rationalizations obscure the real victor, however, Mann interrupts them with a loud fanfare on the street. All in the office rush to the window and see a large open carriage with four liveried trumpeters heralding its progress through the city. In it sits Türkheimer next to a visiting dignitary whom someone identifies as the Prince of Wallachia, coming to Berlin to solicit support for the modernization of his realm. Not only is Türkheimer presiding over this pageant, but the streets are lined with people shouting wild approval in a demonstration of the "hurrah patriotism" sweeping Germany. Türkheimer has become a "mythical symbol," and his carriage vanishes in a rosy cloud of dust, "just like the apotheosis at the end of a fairytale."[63] More than that, he has fulfilled his long-sought dream of receiving a royal order. Schlaraffenland has prevailed in a Germany whose ideals of an unfinished revolution have been forgotten.

The worst fears enunciated by novelists of the *Gründerjahre* have thus been realized in the eyes of a turn-of-the-century observer. In contrast to earlier authors, Mann provides no sign of a redemptive *Bürgertum* to counteract the specter of a vulgar and corrupt bourgeoisie mesmerizing the rest of German society. Other novels of the early 1900s reinforced the image with scathing treatments of two new districts that symbolized the triumph of Berlin W. Replacing the Tiergarten as the habitation of the arriviste was Grunewald, a cluster of ostentatious villas located on the extreme western edge of Berlin's administrative boundary. More vulgar still was Kurfürstendamm, the boulevard designed to link Grunewald with the Tiergarten district. Intended by its creators to rival Paris' Champs Elysées, "Kudamm" received only derision in novels for its mishmash of architectural styles and the ornate, cheaply built facades of its buildings.[64] The westward procession thus completed the vulgarization of Germany's capital.

Im Schlaraffenland added another ominous dimension by emphasizing the procession of immigrants from the east and equating their arrival with the ruination of Berlin. Others added fuel to this fire, most notably the cultural critic Karl Scheffler, who, in 1910, devoted an entire book to attacking Berlin as a "colonized city" (Kolonialstadt). He blamed the situation on a stampede of newcomers who were overrunning the city with "bestial roughness": "This Berlin middle class belongs to the most evil phenomena wrought by modern times."[65] The human invasion reawakened the "barely dozing parvenu instincts" throughout Berlin and its society. Not only was Berlin not civilized, Scheffler argued, it was not even truly German because of the procession of non-German immigrants from the east.[66] And finally, "While Berlin's modern development can be seen on the one hand as proof of the powerful workforce and entrepreneurial spirit of the modern age, on the other hand, it serves as proof of a lack of culture that seems to have risen in places to a level of barbaric monumentality."[67]

Such statements show how the sentiments portrayed in novels like Mann's could merge with strident attacks on modernity and on groups associated with it. Although Mann was criticizing the "hurrah-patriotism" he described, such criticism could easily be ignored by anti-modernist critics who saw their own denunciations of the city sustained. Novels like Schlaraffenland, whatever their authors' critical intentions, implied a resignation that reinforced trends toward new visions of German society, based on a virulent nationalism aimed against perceived alien influences. In the shadow of such visions ideals of the unfinished revolution could seem ridiculously irrelevant.

## Notes

1. Karl Bleibtreu, Geist: Geschichte einer Mannheit (Munich, 1906), 45.
2. Theophil Zolling, Der Klatsch: Ein Roman aus der Gesellschaft (Leipzig, 1889), 112, 467.
3. On the history of Berlin's westward expansion see Walter Kiaulehn, Berlin: Schicksal einer Weltstadt (Munich, 1958), 42–57.
4. An outspoken critic of the new Berlin pointed to William I as the embodiment of the unpretentiousness, the austerity, and the prosaic bearing that characterized vormärzliche Berliners. Karl Scheffler, Berlin: Ein Stadtschicksal (Berlin, 1910), 164. See also Theodor Fontane, "Die Märker und das Berlinertum," Aus dem Nachlaß von Theodor Fontane (Berlin, 1908), 295–312.
5. Klaus Günther Just, Von der Gründerzeit bis zur Gegenwart: Geschichte der deutschen Literatur seit 1871 (Bern, 1973), 49. "The best known of the unknown" Berlin

novels, *Leberecht Hühnchen* exceeded a million copies by 1958. Kiaulehn, *Berlin*, 337.
6. Heinrich Seidel, *Leberecht Hühnchen*, Jubilee edition (Jubiläumsausgabe) (Stuttgart, 1942), 9.
7. Ibid., 60. On Berlin humor see Fontane, "Die Märker und das Berlinertum," 301–305.
8. Seidel, *Hühnchen*, 80, 61.
9. On love of gardening as a Berliner trait see Hans Otto Modrow, *Berlin 1900: Querschnitt durch die Entwicklung einer Stadt um die Jahrhundertwende* (Berlin, 1936), 104–111.
10. Seidel, *Hühnchen*, 55.
11. An echo of this ideal is sounded in a remark by Julius Rodenberg: "The picture of a modest middle-class contentment is the most precious to me of all the pictures of Berlin life." Julius Rodenberg, *Bilder aus dem Berliner Leben in einer Auswahl* (Berlin, 1892), 69.
12. Paul Lindau, *Der Zug nach dem Westen* (Berlin, 1886), 74. On further dimensions of the east-west myth see Russell A. Berman, *The Rise of the Modern German Novel: Crisis and Charisma* (Cambridge, Mass., 1986), 12–24.
13. Lindau, *Der Zug nach dem Westen*, 30.
14. Ibid., 4. On the transformation of *Bildung* into *Besitz* in German culture see Walter Müller-Seidel, *Theodor Fontane: Soziale Romankunst in Deutschland* (Stuttgart, 1975), 285–300.
15. Lindau, *Der Zug nach dem Westen*, 126.
16. Ibid., 56.
17. Ibid., 69, 73.
18. Ibid., 126.
19. Ibid., 260.
20. Ibid., 369.
21. Ibid., 377.
22. Fritz Mauthner, *Von Keller zu Zola: Kritische Aufsätze* (Berlin, 1887), 106.
23. A good treatment of this theme is given in W. H. Bruford, *The German Tradition of Self-Cultivation: 'Bildung' from Humboldt to Thomas Mann* (Cambridge, 1975), 190–205.
24. Theodor Fontane, *Frau Jenny Treibel*, *Sämtliche Werke*, VII (Munich, 1959), 15.
25. Ibid., 124.
26. Ibid., 12.
27. Ibid., 11. Jenny's botanical metaphor for *Bildung* first appeared in Johann Friedrich Blumenbach's *Über den Bildungstrieb*, a work frequently cited by Goethe. Müller-Seidel, *Theodor Fontane*, 286. See also, Gunhild Kübler, *Die soziale Aufsteigerin: Wandlungen einer geschlechtsspezifischen Rollenzuschreibung im deutschen Roman, 1870–1900* (Bonn, 1982), 40–45.
28. Fontane, *Frau Jenny Treibel*, 43.
29. Letters of 25 August 1881, and 18 April 1884; quoted in Müller-Seidel, *Theodor Fontane*, 303, and Bruford, *German Tradition of Self-Cultivation*, 192. Willibald Schmidt echoes the first statement in the novel. Fontane, *Frau Jenny Treibel*, 142.
30. Fontane, *Frau Jenny Treibel*, 64–65.
31. Ibid., 57.
32. For further analysis of the roles of the houses' locations see Marilyn Sibley Fries, *The Changing Consciousness of Reality: The Image of Berlin in Selected German Novels from Raabe to Döblin* (Bonn, 1980), 51–53.
33. Fontane, *Frau Jenny Treibel*, 99.
34. Ibid., 138.

35. Ibid., 162. For other instances of the Berlin-Hamburg tension see 73–78, 80, 95, 104, 144.
36. Ibid., 108; see also 73–78.
37. Ibid., 126.
38. Ibid., 131.
39. Ibid., 132.
40. Ibid., 153.
41. Ibid., 159.
42. Ibid., 165.
43. Max Kretzer, *Drei Weiber*, 3rd ed. (Leipzig, 1912), 105.
44. On the importance of the *Gründer* image in literature of this period see Richard Hamann and Jost Hermand, *Naturalismus* (Munich, 1972), 37–47.
45. Max Kretzer, *Der Millionenbauer* (Leipzig, 1890), 25.
46. Ibid., 16; see also 58, in which an aristocratic mother emphasizes to her son that *their* house is located in Berlin, not Schöneberg.
47. Ibid., 354.
48. The title of the English translation published in 1929 is *In the Land of Cockaigne*. See also Roger Hillman, *Zeitroman: The Novel and Society in Germany, 1830–1900* (Bern, 1983), 119–141.
49. Heinrich Mann, *Im Schlaraffenland: Ein Roman unter feinen Leuten* (Berlin, 1968), 7.
50. Ibid., 89.
51. Ibid., 132.
52. Ibid., 14; see also 128, 161, 297.
53. This episode satirizes the Freie Bühne and the popular enthusiasm for naturalist dramas. Roy Pascal, *From Naturalism to Expressionism: German Literature and Society, 1880–1918* (London, 1973), 34, 129, 271.
54. Mann, *Schlaraffenland*, 178.
55. Ibid., 317–318.
56. Ibid., 263.
57. Ibid., 183.
58. Ibid., 190.
59. Ibid., 254.
60. Ibid., 85–86, 190, 293. See also Pascal, *Naturalism to Expressionism*, 82.
61. Mann, *Schlaraffenland*, 267, 270.
62. Ibid., 285, 311.
63. Ibid., 373. An early passage explains the nickname of a "Café Hurra" as a reflection of changes after 1890, when revolutionary ideas went out of fashion, to be replaced by "hurrah-patriotism." Ibid., 11–12.
64. See, for example, Rudolf Lothar, *Kurfürstendamm* (Berlin, 1910).
65. Scheffler, *Berlin*, 154–155. See also Friedrich Leyden, "Berlin als Beispiel einer wurzellosen Großstadt," *Zeitschrift für Geopolitik*, 10, 3 (1933), 175–188.
66. Scheffler, *Berlin*, 18.
67. Ibid., 143–145.

# 12

# The Changing of the Guard

Berlin novelists depicted the crash of 1873 as a moral crisis that impeded true German unity for years. Some, like Friedrich Spielhagen, looked in vain through the 1880s for an end to the crisis. Others, like Julius Stinde, embraced the Bismarckian regime as the fulfillment of German greatness. And others, like Conrad Alberti, identified William II's accession as the time when Germany's moral trial was coming to an end. The salvation was not only a new emperor but also a new generation that would lead Germany toward a cultural glory commensurate with its military victories. Alberti concluded *Die Alten und die Jungen* (1889), as we have seen, by enshrining the changing of the generational guard in Berlin symbolism. The sight of William II riding through Brandenburger Tor becomes a conversion experience for the protagonist, who dedicates himself to working for a spiritual German victory.[1] Without a trace of irony the novel's conclusion implies that Germany's troubled times are over with the ascendancy of the so-called generation of 1870.

Even as such hopes were appearing in novels, new political crises such as Bismarck's resignation and the end of the Anti-Socialist Law were bringing new tensions.[2] Count Leo von Caprivi and Prince Hohenlohe, Bismarck's two successors as chancellor, were colorless, dogmatic figures whose ineffective leadership caused some to see a chance for the Reichstag to assert itself. A true parliamentary government, to be sure, was impeded by constitutional limitations and by the inability of opposition parties to form a coherent majority, but, despite its lack of authority over the imperial cabinet, the Reichstag remained a strong force. Social democrats were especially visible, and their surging electoral gains seemed to confirm fears of revolution, or, worse still, of anarchy. When unemployed workers took to the streets of Berlin in February 1892, their attempt to call attention to their plight was widely seen as a portent of the violent future that awaited Germany if she did not contain social democratic pressures.

Novels portrayed the immediate post-Bismarckian years as a time as decisive for Germany as the *Gründerzeit*. Although a dramatic moment comparable to the crash of 1873 did not occur, the disappearance of the generation that brought unification was depicted as equally critical. This perspective is particularly evident in Alberti's last novel, *Ablösung Vor!* (*Relief Guard, Forward!*) (1911), whose title signifies his continued fascination with generational transition. Although written more than two decades after *Die Alten und die Jungen*, the novel has a chronological setting only two or three years later, and in contrast to the optimism at the end of the earlier novel it portrays a loss of direction. *Ablösung Vor!* sets the stage for what appears to be a normal transition: an aging Berlin manufacturer, personifying an exhausted older generation, is preparing to turn the family business over to his energetic son, just returned from America filled with ideas about new technology and management techniques. "Maybe youth will be successful!" Karl Ambühl tells his long-time manager: "We elders have to abdicate sometime. 'Relief guard, forward!' is not only a command in the military but also in civilian life."[3] As father and son approach the transition, however, both contribute to growing conflict: the elder by rigid adherence to outmoded ways and the younger by an inability to adapt new approaches to existing realities. The threat of bankruptcy forces them to yield the business to the control of a banker, and the son ends by marrying the banker's daughter, a match he once strenuously opposed. This generational transition, among several others, points to an unsettling changing of the guard. By the end, which generation is "on watch" remains unclear.

Such uneasiness is not unique to Alberti's novel. The rapid succession of William I's death and the departure of Bismarck raised questions about what political approaches the post-Bismarckian generation would bring to a modern, prospering nation. Three novels dealing with these questions provide the focus for this last chapter. Published over a twenty-year period, Theodor Fontane's *Der Stechlin* (1899), Theophil Zolling's *Bismarcks Nachfolger* (*Bismarck's Successor*) (1895), and Heinrich Mann's *Der Untertan* (*The Loyal Subject*) (1914) all portrayed the early 1890s as a critical turning point. In contrast to the images of Berlin as a center of parvenuism or of cultural malaise, they portrayed Berlin as the progenitor of a dynamic national identity, which extended its influence through the rest of Germany. Their emphasis on this influence returns our focus to the national implications of novels of Imperial Berlin.

All three novels use the same chronological setting, the post-Bismarckian era, to announce that the age of the masses has irrevocably arrived and to portray widespread fears over the specter of *Umsturz* (the word by which all three denote violent revolution). But they offer differing prognoses for the changing of the guard. Fontane, a member of the Bismarckian generation, depicts a Germany in which popular parties are in the ascendancy, and yet he reveals cautious optimism about what he sees as a democratizing era. Zolling, a member of the generation reaching middle age in the 1890s, articulates hopes for genuine popular participation but abandons any notion that this will be achieved by the ineffectual politicians who have succeeded Bismarck. Instead, he offers the vision of a German youth that will be inspired to serve the nation through a Bismarckian populism somehow detached from the sham politics Zolling has portrayed in the Reichstag. Mann, a generation younger than Zolling, sees bankruptcy in all this and depicts instead a polity manipulated by ruling groups that are transforming Germans into a multitude of little kaisers. He portrays the ascendancy of a generation that offers Germany not selfless service but mindless subservience. The path from Fontane's cautious hope to Zolling's apolitical fantasies to Mann's portrayal of pandemic national delusion represents a final defeat for fictional hopes for the unfinished revolution in Imperial Germany.

Near the end of Fontane's *Der Stechlin*, a bridal couple has left for the obligatory wedding trip to Italy. The bride's sister proposes that although the train has not yet reached Wittenberg, her sister probably already misses Berlin. She follows this remark with one of the asides that often give keys to Fontane novels: "Before you say a final goodbye to an old life, you indulge yourself in a last deep longing for it."[4] *Der Stechlin*, Fontane's last, longing look at an era he knows has passed, forms not only the testament of a writer feeling his own mortality (he died before the book was in print) but the summing up of an era for a Germany heading into a new century.

Although most of *Der Stechlin* is set outside of Berlin, several elements justify characterizing it as a Berlin novel. The political contact between the capital and the countryside is of greatest interest here, but other connections include the service of the protagonist's son in a Berlin regiment, his courtship there of two daughters in an aristocratic household, a host of Berlin characters including a prototypical landlady, and the theme of Berliners' spreading into the Markish countryside, especially evident in a stereotypical Berlin parvenu who shocks rural society with her "Berlin style." The constant intrusion of Berlin influences into the novel's provincial setting suggests a nation being formed in the image of its capital.

The novel's title refers to an unprepossessing lake in the countryside some distance north of Berlin. The Stechlin See has a peculiar quality: whenever a catastrophe occurs somewhere in the world, it responds by shooting a waterspout from its depths. Although usually couched in terms of seismic upheavals such as volcanic activity or the surge of a faraway geyser, links are suggested with political upheaval when the pond is referred to as a "true revolutionary who rumbles along anytime something breaks loose somewhere."[5] The lake does not perform during the novel, but visitors to the lake and readers alike are put in a state of expectation that it could burst forth at any time. The lack of activity clearly corresponds to the outwardly quiescent situation in Germany in the 1890s.

More reactive than the pond, however, is Dubslav von Stechlin, the estate owner who presides over the wonder. Like "his" lake, Dubslav responds to distant events, and through his person the novel develops multi-layered themes of connections: the countryside to the outside world (especially Berlin), the older generation to the younger, tradition to modernity.[6] The last theme is particularly problematic, for Dubslav exemplifies a tradition that is passing and yet one, the novel suggests, that Germany can abandon only at grave peril.

The elements of this legacy are manifest in Dubslav's personality. A measure of *Berlinertum* remains from his years in the venerable Nicholas Regiment in

Berlin, which surely strengthened his capacity for self-irony and tolerance for diversity of opinion.[7] Dubslav is also Markish to the core, for, since resigning his commission shortly after the Schleswig-Holstein war, he has lived on his estate, where he always delights in showing visitors the local wonders: the view from a tower on the estate, the nearby elementary school, the church and its graveyard, the glassworks (the landmark of industrialization in the district), and, of course, the Stechlin See. Dubslav also harbors Prussian loyalties, refusing, for example, to change the black and white Prussian flag on his estate into a German one by adding a red stripe. The flag would be too heavy, he explains, and would probably rip. A particular focus of his Prussianism is Frederick II, whose reign, despite gentle criticisms of its authoritarian methods, he sees as an era of heroism.[8] The flag issue aside, Dubslav also shows a streak of German patriotism, as when he recalls the winter of 1870 as "a wonderful time" that put him in touch with the rest of the world.[9] Another time he allows a concern about possible German excesses to be overruled by national pride, commenting that "we Germans are on top again, a little too much in fact. But better too much than too little."[10]

The novel focuses on Dubslav's final months, with his death signifying the passing of an old Prussian generation and the succession of a new in the person of his son, Woldemar. Another change of guard takes place earlier, however, when Dubslav runs as the conservative candidate for the district's supposedly safe Reichstag seat. At first he protests he knows nothing about politics, but supporters respond with a story in which Bismarck was said to have assured a similarly reluctant figure, "That is exactly why I am choosing you, my dear man."[11] Dubslav thereupon agrees to run, the old military man in him seeming to accept the idea that "in the modern civic state elections were as good as battles."[12] The analogy between military glories and electoral campaigning holds true when Dubslav's supporters show up at a meeting bedecked in medals, but it does not extend to the creation of finely honed strategies or heroic dedication to the campaign. Dubslav and his supporters expect him to win and see no need for "traveling around" and "speechmaking."[13] On the evening of the election they are shocked by the news that Feilenhauer Torgelow, an unknown social democrat from Berlin, has won. The assurances about not needing to understand politics suddenly ring hollow. A new age of electioneering has dawned.[14]

Two things defeat Dubslav. First, the conservatives prove to be divided and ineffective, with some even working against him because they fear a man of his moderate inclinations will betray their principles. Second, the victory of the unknown Torgelow over a locally respected Stechlin shows that voters are thinking ideologically, not personally.[15] Dubslav, although philosophical about his defeat, remains convinced he has more concern than Torgelow for the well-being of the local citizenry, and regrets he failed to communicate this to voters. His failure to do so suggests the contradiction between the mythology of 1813, of all classes united under the leadership of a reform-minded nobility, and the reality of modern parties' appealing to class interests.

Dubslav realizes he is too old to change, but at least he avoids yielding to the anti-democratic instincts of other aristocratic characters. To this extent his gentle resignation reflects that of the author. Despite democratic impulses, Fontane, too, was unexcited over the prospects of an inexperienced electorate's being swayed by promises and appeals. Yet he was also critical of a nobility that proposed to respond to the masses only by continuing their patriarchal rule. The nobility, whether humane or indifferent, *Der Stechlin* showed, could not sustain its rule in an age of universal suffrage.

This recognition comes most directly from a middle-aged pastor named Lorenzen, who, despite the designation of "almost a social democrat," also shows a reluctance to embrace democracy.[16] The best example of this comes when Melusine, a visitor to the Stechlin estate, calls at the parsonage just after seeing the ice-covered Stechlin See. Her experience provokes a chain of meditations on the old and the new that begins with her recounting how she expressed disappointment at the lake's placidity. Someone offered to chop a hole in the ice in hope of encouraging the waterspout, but she protested that nature should not be disturbed. Lorenzen takes up the theme but suggests that frozen beliefs from the past must now give way. Specifically, he lists the achievements of Prussian history: Frederick William I laying the foundations of the state, Frederick II achieving military greatness, and the Prussian Enlightenment bringing rational ideals. These once progressive developments, however, are now past. The "battalions," Lorenzen declares, must yield to "discoverers and inventors," adding that "our regime is trying to give what is in decline an artificial ascendancy. . . . It's possible," he tells Melusine, "that aristocratic rule will come back, but for now, wherever we look we find signs of a democratic ideal. A new era is beginning. I think it's a better and happier one. But even if not happier, it's at least an era with more oxygen in the air, a time in which we can breathe more freely. And the more freely we breathe, the more alive we are."[17] The difficulties of a conversation that moves from a frozen lake to a tentative espousal of democracy reflect Fontane's own difficulties in reconciling his conservative inclinations with his conviction that popular sovereignty was inevitable. Lorenzen's conclusion, however, suggests an underlying faith on Fontane's part that democratizing change was for the better.

Dubslav's son Woldemar is a young man who seems able to combine the old and the new. Having been tutored by Lorenzen, he is more open to modern ideas than his father. He joins an exclusive Berlin regiment known for its members' proclivity for radical political notions. He ignores his aunt's injunction "to marry Lutheran, marry Markish, or better still, marry *Mittelmarkisch*,"[18] and courts the daughter of a cosmopolitan diplomat. And he spends several months in England as a regimental envoy, to see firsthand the world's most advanced civilization. One character's remark about England—"Everything is modern and at the same time everything is old, rooted, stabilized"—seems to epitomize Fontane's ideal for Germany.[19] The succession of Woldemar to the estate reflects the ideal of new outlooks prevailing in old surroundings, but the novel's last lines suggest that even new outlooks will not maintain the reign of the nobility. They consist of a note from Melusine to Lorenzen: "It is not necessary for the Stechlin family to continue to exist, but long live the Stechlin See."[20] What is certain is that there will continue to be upheavals throughout the world, and they will continue to be felt in this corner of Germany.

This political novel remains in the private realm. It neither focuses on politicians nor, with the exception of the election, portrays day-to-day political events. August Bebel and the retired Bismarck receive fairly frequent mention, but only one reference to Prince Hohenlohe identifies the chancellorship under which it takes place.[21] William II, moreover, is absent from conversations, a sign of Fontane's disapproval of the emperor's militaristic bluster and another instance of his inclination to view politics from a distance.[22]

Novels that deal with the public political realm further underscore the difficulties German authors had in envisioning the transition from an authoritarian past into a democratic future. Theophil Zolling's *Bismarcks Nachfolger*, whose title announces the focus, gives an unusually detailed portrayal of politicians and political institutions.[23] This work is notable for the political confusion beneath its startling combination of attitudes: wholehearted admiration for Bismarck, belief that Bismarck simply neglected to train Germans for the time of democracy that has arrived, and contempt for the institutions that might foster such democracy. Zolling's apparent lack of awareness of incongruities among these assumptions points to internal obstacles that confronted democratically minded critics of Wilhelmine Germany who tried to formulate new visions.

Reverence for Bismarck is evident in the saintly and heroic images with which Zolling depicts him. First described as a titan striding into a polling place in the elections of February 1890, Bismarck injects a Christlike prophecy by telling poll workers this is the last time they will see him there.[24] In another parallel to Christ's passion it is implied that the surly people who line the streets to witness Bismarck's departure have betrayed their leader. In contrast, Bismarck alights at the station, "an imposing figure, strong and upright," his face illuminated by rays from the setting sun.[25] The new age, the novel proposes, should resurrect Bismarckian leadership in democratic form. As Fritz Hornung, a newly elected Reichstag representative, proclaims, "[Bismarck] put us into the saddle; now he will teach us to ride, something he neglected to do in the press of state affairs."[26] Clearly unaware that Bismarck was considering the overthrow of the Reichstag at the end of his career, Zolling's protagonist believes that if he remains to "advise, lead, and inspire" the German people, they will learn to govern themselves. So towering was Bismarck's image that Zolling could transform it into that of a democratic teacher even while acknowledging that he as chancellor had failed in such education.

Zolling's desire for a responsible political system competes with his veneration of Bismarck, however, and he uses the novel to search the political landscape for a leader or institution with the stature to qualify as Bismarck's successor. All but the final pages are set in Berlin, and when the protagonist finally leaves the capital Zolling's survey seems to have arrived at a dead end, having shown all nominees to the successorship of Bismarck to be wanting in the qualities of service and self-sacrifice the author sees as essential to the future well-being of Germany. The search for Bismarck's successor offers a detailed account of a process of political disillusionment.

Three conspicuous successors are the new chancellor, General Leo Count von Caprivi, a responsive cabinet government, or the Kaiser himself, but the novel rejects all of them. Caprivi is portrayed as a political dilettante whose military bearing provides no leadership for a peacetime government. Hornung's observation of him using "the large yellow pencil of his predecessor" to sketch trees during a debate suggests an ineffectiveness that will prevent solid political achievements.[27] Through a newly appointed minister of culture Zolling gives slightly more consideration to a cabinet government as Bismarck's successor, but also abandons that alternative. His portrait of the old-guard figure, with "his military moustache and his student dueling scars," suggests a man unsuited to his post,[28] but when the minister shows unexpected integrity he falls victim to palace intrigues. As he tells his wife,

> "I have opponents among my colleagues, the other ministers, and invisible enemies as well. They are the unanswerable advisers who have the ear of the Kaiser and whose secret power extends much further than the influence of the appointed civil servants. They are everywhere: on back stairways of the palace, on the train between Berlin and Potsdam, in the imperial entourage. They offer their wisdom in congenial chitchats and refer to the ministers as if they were only there to carry out orders."[29]

When the minister decides that independence and dedication to new programs are not wanted by the regime, he resigns.[30] The Kaiser makes an even briefer appearance amid protesting masses. Fritz Hornung witnesses the situation:

> He saw the Kaiser, surrounded by the poor and the wretched, as the leader and savior of his people—serious, willful, an ideal in his heart of love for his people. The Iron Chancellor had created internal political unity and external power; the Kaiser should save his people economically. . . . Bismarck's successor was not the new chancellor, not the ministers, and least of all the Reichstag. But that figure over there could be it, could be his own chancellor, if only he wanted to. . . .[31]

The trailing phrase, "if only he wanted to," suggests Zolling's elimination of the most obvious claimant to succession: the imperial system.

Mass action is also rejected. The scene of Bismarck's departure ends with the arrival of a trainful of workers: "The day of one-man rule had passed. The mighty leader is going into exile, and the masses are coming forth into the capital of the Reich."[32] But other scenes suggest a rowdy, angry populace whose presence on the political stage is destructive. Zolling's sympathy for the misery of Berlin's unemployed is countered by a now familiar repugnance toward the "animal instincts" that drive the masses when they take to the streets. The novel's depiction of the demonstrations of February 1892 shows how a march on the palace leads to destruction, looting, and death.[33] By giving force to the notion that social democratic politics, anarchism, and mobs are all of a piece, the scene reinforces middle-class horror at the prospect of revolution as Bismarck's successor.

The major political hope seems to lie with the Reichstag, but Fritz Hornung's inexorable disillusionment defeats it. Instead of a body working together to secure Germany's best interest, Hornung finds squabbling factions, trivial debates, and thriving particularism. Apathetic members, with their inattentiveness and absences, compound the inability of the Reichstag to transact business. At times the novel overestimates the role of the Reichstag by implying that with a few procedural changes it will equal the English parliament.[34] Elsewhere it ridicules members foolish enough to believe they have real political power. As Hornung sees it, such arrogance only confirms the Reichstag's failure to pursue "constitutional logic and come forth as the successor of Bismarck."[35] Hornung personifies an alternative political type who vows at the outset to struggle for the "well-being of his people and the greatness of his fatherland" by advocating a "great national constitutional party" that would form a majority of moderates.[36] He ignores pressure to join existing factions, which makes it difficult for him to get the floor as an unallied member, but he nevertheless makes a maiden speech with a patriotic lesson in a debate over the new Reichstag building. Arguing for stone as the material of choice, Fritz compares it to genuine German unity as opposed to plaster's superficiality. The tepid response strengthens his conviction that his peers are a mindless herd, and drives him further into impotent isolation.

Berlin is central to Hornung's despair, as he contemplates his situation on long walks past the city's landmarks. In his forlorn state he sees the capital as a giant spider whose web extends through Germany, "bloodthirsty, seductive, ruinous to everything."[37] On a moonlit night he sees the city as a cemetery, its darkened buildings representing gravestones for German law, drama, art, and liberty.[38] Another symbol of his disillusionment is the new Reichstag building, which to Hornung exemplifies the external bluster and internal impotence of the German parliament. Surrounded by its own web of scaffolding, the building is useless for parliamentary work, "with its front steps only good for parade viewing and its real entrance hidden confusedly in a narrow back street."[39] This architectural travesty causes him to ask if parliamentarianism has any future in Germany at all. He enumerates alternatives—Referendum? Absolute monarchy? Socialism? Anarchism?—and walks away.

In the end Hornung leaves Berlin, convinced that Bismarck's successor must be sought elsewhere. He commits himself to educating the German people "for public life, for pure, selfless politics."[40] On the train ride home his hope takes form when he sees Bismarck at the Weimar station, making a triumphal tour of Germany. In contrast to the angry crowds in Berlin, a cheering throng now greets the "great outlaw and exile." German youth, Hornung decides, "will keep the legacy sacred and in difficult times will repay the loyalty of [Bismarck's] long service with equal loyalty."[41] The conclusion that Bismarck's successor is a new generation of German youth comes at the expense of the immediate post-Bismarckian generation, whose members stand condemned.[42] Instead of pursuing the road to responsible institutions upon which it set out, *Bismarcks Nachfolger* turns away from them as inefficient and divisive. The novel's concluding vision describes a German youth that will dedicate itself to a national ideal under the inspiration of a single leader. The safeguards of a responsible political system are not in evidence as the creator of an admittedly authoritarian system is mythologized.

Heinrich Mann, a member of the generation Zolling idealized, gave a far more ominous portrayal of the 1890s in *Der Untertan* (*The Loyal Subject*) by placing a theatrical William II at the head of a new guard of slavish imitators. Its bitter satire depicts the step-by-step descent of the young generation into a mindless view of themselves as loyal subjects of a ruler filled with Germany's mission. Having destroyed any ideal of revolution, the new generation, Mann argued, has transformed Germany into a belligerent sham of a body politic.

As in *Der Stechlin*, Berlin is the setting for only part of *Der Untertan*, but the novel develops an even clearer reciprocal relationship between Berlin and the countryside. The provinces are shown as a breeding ground for a personality that Berlin forms into the loyal German subject. Once so formed, this subject returns to his hometown and works to transform provincials into replicas of himself. By depicting Berlin's imperialistic influence as a continuum of traditional values emanating from all German society, Mann created intricate connections between the crisis of individualism, inherited tradition, Berlin's modern identity, and German nationhood.

At the center of this network is Diederich Heßling, the personification of the novel's original subtitle, "History of the Public Soul under William II." As this subtitle suggests, Mann's examination of Diederich merges into a pathology of the German nation, "leaving us in no doubt," as a critic has written, "that the aggression which is directed outward in the name of nationalism, militarism, imperialism and German idealism . . . must end in self-destruction. The history of the 'Untertan' reveals itself as the history of the Kaiserreich."[43]

Diederich, who is characterized by a complex bundle of fears, guilt, and hatreds, constitutes the first portrait in German literature of the authoritarian personality. The first two chapters of *Der Untertan*, a densely packed account of his early life, show his character, far from being an aberration, to be a direct product of hallowed German institutions—the patriarchal family, the education system, the student fraternity, and the army. In each of these realms he confronts an unyielding system of authority to which he reacts with rage, but also with a curiously enthusiastic allegiance, that springs from a realization that his impotence as subject can be mitigated by a vicarious sharing in the exercise of power. This development culminates in Diederich's awakening to the existence of a national pyramid of power, at the peak of which stands William II. Diederich internalizes the specter of the Kaiser exhorting his subjects to loyalty and obedience and carries his pose back to Netzig, his hometown. There a guilt-ridden weakling becomes transformed into a strutting champion of imperial authority.

The formation of this "German public soul," Mann shows, begins in childhood, which is an ongoing lesson in the simultaneous terrors and enticements of power. The lesson begins with Diederich's authoritarian father, a factory owner in whose office the boy voluntarily appears whenever he knows he has committed an offense. His presence alerts his father to the fact of wrongdoing, causing him to reach routinely for the whipping stick. The boy's resentment against this paternal authority is offset by the perceived rewards of being subject to such power. When he emerges from his father's office to find workers laughing at his punishment, he gloats, "You'd be happy if you could get a whipping from him, but you're too unimportant for that."[44]

This lesson is expanded when Diederich enters school, a terrible realm that "devours the whole person."[45] Being caned is a usual occurrence here also, but so is the chance for vicarious participation in power. Diederich learns to imitate the powerholders by wielding authority over those inferior to him. One day, when he forces the sole Jewish pupil to kneel before a cross, the cheers of his classmates intoxicate him: "How marvelous to be part of a shared responsibility and a collective consciousness!"[46] The masters also approve, which leads him to build on the new-found favor by becoming an informer of other pupils' activities. Countering feelings of guilt, Diederich justifies himself as a "dutiful performer of a difficult necessity."[47] Active submission to the cruelties of the schoolmasters becomes an avenue of success that extends to academics. The calculated fulfillment of assigned tasks (but nothing beyond) allows Diederich to pass his examinations.

Berlin now becomes the major influence on Diederich's further development, when the elder Heßling sends him there to study. Although an academic title will be important, the more significant education occurs in further encounters with systems of power outside the lecture hall and laboratory. Three such encounters lead to the revelation that his highest destiny lies in unquestioning devotion to the Kaiser: the experience in a student fraternity, a brief episode in the army, and, finally, a day of awakening in the workers' demonstrations of February 1892.

Association with the "New Teutons" solidifies Diederich's realization that power resides in the group. The emotional intoxications of his schoolboy years now are recast by a group whose sense of community is grounded in endless rounds of drinking. Diederich discovers that alcohol raises him above life's demands, where exams are as good as passed, careers are achieved, great thoughts spring forth, and even where God is to be found. Despite his fear of dueling, he is drawn into full membership and undergoes a "training" that involves submission to the dictates of the group and to delusions about its supposed ideals. When Diederich is "allowed" to become the lackey of an older member, far from being humiliated by the menial tasks, he feels privileged to serve the man whose fearlessness epitomizes the honor of the New Teutons. The limitless demands of the group, far from bringing a sense of loss, infuse him with self-worth. The highest moment comes when an obese New Teuton suffers a fatal seizure from too much drinking. Diederich is solemnly assured that their comrade, in giving the highest sacrifice to the manly ideals of the New Teutons, has died on the field of honor.[48] Thus ends the first stage of Diederich's training in German honor.

The next stage involves an encounter with the military. Diederich is ambivalent about his obligatory year of service, his outward enthusiasm masking a fear of the physical demands. Attempts to get a medical exemption fail, however, and he soon finds himself living in a Berlin barrack, undergoing basic training. Well schooled by now, Diederich sees that military training rests on the same principle as fraternity training, only carried out more cruelly. The systematic denigration of recruits' sense of self-worth, far from enraging Diederich, impresses him. His fervor does not sustain him through the physical rigors, however, and a foot injury convinces him that his patriotic duty lies in being discharged. The army is not so easily convinced, but eventually Diederich has the father of a fraternity brother write the letter that brings his discharge. What should have been a disgraceful entry in the annals of German courage becomes a new instance of what Mann sees as the German proclivity for self-delusion. Diederich resumes his drinking bouts and quickly converts his sorry military record into tales of sacrifice, devotion to duty, and heroism.

The mythologizing of weakness reaches its highest level when Diederich comes face to face with William II. The episode begins with the demonstrations of February 1892, in which, obsessed with ideas about subversive dangers and how they must be crushed, Diederich takes to the streets. When he finds himself surrounded by demonstrators he is driven into a crazed ecstasy at the thought that the day of reckoning has arrived. The sight of the Kaiser making his way on horseback toward Brandenburger Tor sends him into paroxysms. He shoves a worker who sneers at the Kaiser's arrival; he commiserates with a grizzled veteran of Sedan over the outrage; he waves his hat and cheers. The frenzy climaxes with a wave of revelations about the German soul:

> There on the horse rode Power, through the gateway of triumphal entries, with dazzling features but graven as in stone. The Power which transcends us and whose hoofs we kiss, the Power which is beyond the reach of hunger, spite and mockery! Against it we are impotent, for we all love it! We have it in our blood, for in our blood is submission. We are an atom of that Power, a diminutive molecule of something it has given out. Each one of us is as nothing, but massed in ranks . . . we taper up like a pyramid to the point at

the top where Power itself stands. . . . In it we live and have our being, merciless towards those who are remote beneath us, and triumphing even when we ourselves are crushed, for thus does power justify our love for it![49]

So wildly does Diederich wave that he lands in a mud puddle, causing the Kaiser to laugh. As in the affair with the army, Diederich covers the indignity with delusions of himself, the loyal subject, heroically joining forces with the Kaiser to defeat the internal enemy. This encounter could hardly contrast more sharply with the scene of the Kaiser at Brandenburger Tor in Alberti's *Die Alten und die Jungen*. That Mann was parodying a novel whose literary sensation lay a quarter of a century in the past is unlikely, but he uses the same situation to encapsulate a graphic instance of the German mythologizing of authority.

The rest of *Der Untertan* develops the effects of Diederich's conversion to the imperial ideal. He remains in Berlin long enough to seduce a vulnerable girl named Agnes and to finish his doctorate, but, his father having died in the meantime, it is clear he must return to Netzig to take charge of the factory. As with the episode at Brandenburger Tor, Diederich acknowledges this turning point with an internal monologue. This one delineates the import of his Berlin "education":

A girl like Agnes . . . would have rendered him unfit for these difficult times. These difficult times—the phrase always reminded Diederich of Unter den Linden with its mob of unemployed, women and children, of want and fear and disorder—and all that quelled, tamed into cheering by the power, the all-embracing superhuman power, massive and flashing, which seemed to place its hoofs upon those heads . . . . Diederich was proud and glad of his excellent training. The students' corps, his military service and the atmosphere of imperialism, had educated him and made him fit. He resolved to give effect to his well-earned principles at home in Netzig, and to become a pioneer of the spirit of the times.[50]

Such a "pioneer," Diederich decides, believes "unconditionally" in what the Emperor believes, and that includes imitating his appearance, gestures, and words as closely as possible. He thus ends his Berlin years by having his moustache refashioned to turn upward in the manner of the Kaiser's. The result gives him a "tigerish and threatening" look that both frightens and pleases him.[51] It also symbolizes his approach to dealing with the people of Netzig.

Mann's old and new guards in Netzig resemble Alberti's generations of '48 and '70, but Mann is more sympathetic than Alberti toward the older generation, which he shows to be motivated by democratic and humane impulses that the heirs completely lack. The defeat of such impulses, the novel suggests, heralds the ruination of Germany. It takes the form of the social and political annihilation of Herr Buck, the novel's representative of the older generation. Not only did Buck evade a death sentence in 1848, he transmuted his revolutionary renown into wealth, social stature, and political influence. Diederich returns to Netzig still harboring childhood memories of him, attired in silk hat and accepting respectful nods from every passing townsperson. Now Buck receives

Diederich warmly and tries to win him over to views that bespeak the heritage of '48: commitment to popular rule; opposition to notions of blood and iron; resistance toward the Junker establishment. The German people, lacking political education, Buck tells Diederich, have reacted to nationhood by falling victim to reactionary forces.[52] Buck mistakenly believes he has a new ally, but once out of Buck's presence Diederich seeks out other town leaders Buck has just warned against.

Diederich coordinates his attack on the Buck family with a self-proclaimed drive to infuse Netzig with the new German spirit.[53] By this time readers have been trained to recognize Diederich's high-flown interpretations of tawdry realities. Far more than being permeated by a new spirit of sacrifice, Netzig's fate is guided in the next months by corrupt property deals and other acts of self-interest. The elections of 1893 offer particular scope for such activities, for Diederich secretly offers the support of his imperial party to the social democratic candidate in common cause against the liberals, whose control of key parcels of property is at stake. The social democrat is elected, but since he, too, is a cynical participant in the power plays, Diederich and his nationalist allies are unperturbed. The ill-concealed financial maneuvers, plus increasing favor from the government in Berlin, bring huge profits, and the resulting rush of economic activity makes Netzig a microcosm of the burgeoning German prosperity. Culturally, too, the town is transformed, and a local production of *Lohengrin* brings Diederich to ecstasy. A thousand such productions would win over every last soul in Germany to the Kaiser's cause, he gushes.[54]

Diederich's own situation parallels Netzig's transformation. His political and financial maneuvers, including a crucial measure of concern for the interests of the local deputy of the imperial government, pay off. Diederich controls the rival paper factory, holds membership on the town council, has married the town's most eligible heiress, and has received a coveted royal order. The town's growing subjugation to the imperial government is reflected in Diederich's unabated identification of himself with the person of the Kaiser. One theme concerns Diederich's use of the Kaiser's words as his own, made shockingly suggestive by Mann's use of actual speeches of William II.[55] So adept does Diederich become at mouthing these words that at times he no longer knows whether they are his own or the monarch's.

The novel culminates in episodes surrounding the building of a monument to commemorate the centenary of William I. The project results from sordid maneuvers that begin with a complicated exchange of land parcels to determine the property upon which the monument will be located. The construction is a plum recklessly promised to all the contractors in town in exchange for political support. While the monument is being built, a barrage of accusations reveals the scandals, but the main beneficiaries survive unscathed. Still, by 22 March 1897, the day of the centenary, the monument is far from finished, with pieces of statuary scattered about: lions, eagles, a defeated Napoleon III, a triumphal chariot. Two figures approach: a weary and defeated Herr Buck and his son

Wolfgang, a lawyer-turned-actor. Surveying the chaos, they comment on its symbolism. The father chides his son for leaving the political stage to the likes of Diederich, but Wolfgang replies that acting—either in public life or in the theater—is the lot of his generation. Gesturing at the beasts of prey, the elder Buck says Wolfgang must not leave the field to them, but he answers they have already secured the field by indulging the masses with social legislation. Again, the father pleads for him to work for the cause of humanity: "When the catastrophe is over which they think they can avoid, you may be sure that humanity will not consider the causes leading to [1848] more shameless and stupid than the conditions that [are now] ours."[56] This last plea of the generation of 1848 receives no answer.

The belated dedication ceremony of the monument some months later provides a vivid symbolic preview of the catastrophe foretold by Buck. Descriptions of the procession and seating arrangements leave no doubt that the officer corps and the nobility are the real rulers of Germany. Diederich is abashed at being seated in the civilian section, but the sight of high-ranking officers causes his instinctive enthusiasm for authority to take over: "There are the pillars of our power!"[57]

The epitome of the loyal subject, Diederich plays a central role in the ceremony. Not only is he to give the dedication speech, but afterward he will be decorated with a second imperial order. His speech is a display of rhetorical frenzy that exalts every sign of German achievement: new prosperity, the upsurge of nationalism, the naval expansion, the end of the humanitarian weaknesses of the older generation, the heights of Germanic master-culture, and, of course, the grandson of the emperor they are memorializing. Driven by a crescendo of applause (signaled each time by the local *Oberpräsident*), Diederich invokes historical times of testing for the Germanic race and draws the moral that the long-standing endeavor to defeat a decadent French democracy is supported by the Almighty Himself.[58] Germany's trials have not ended, Diederich continues; only unwavering dedication to "German manliness and German idealism" will eradicate the French scourge, allowing each German "to stand with good conscience at that last divine rollcall before his God and his old emperor."[59]

So intoxicated has Diederich become by ideas of Germany's divine mission that he fails to notice the heavens' answer. The sky has clouded and his words are interspersed with thunderclaps and bolts of lightning. When at last he signals the unveiling of the monument, the heavens let loose. The ceremony dissolves into chaos as driving rain causes awnings to collapse and stands to buckle. Dignitaries flee in panic, with officers using their swords to push aside ladies in their way. The narrator, describing the scene in terms of mounting ruin (*Umsturz*), repeatedly uses the word that has designated "revolution" throughout the novel. The band keeps playing the anthem, dutifully ignoring the collapse of "the military cordon and the world order."[60] An astonished Diederich is convinced the apocalypse has come when he peers from beneath the lectern to see people stampeding the bunting-decorated fences, "lashed by whips from above, these streams of fire, this breaking up like the end of a drunken masquerade: nobles, commoners, the most distinguished uniform and the citizen aroused from his slumbers, pillars of the state and heaven-sent statesmen, ideal riches, hussars, lancers, dragoons and army service corps!"[61]

This time, the narrator reports, the four horsemen ride on.[62] To Diederich's amazement the emperor's statue still stands, surrounded by all the trappings of power. The last scene seals the warning for the future, however. On his way home Diederich passes the Buck house, whose door is ajar. He steals inside and looks into the room of Buck's deathbed. Buck, in his dying moment, sees Diederich at the door with his red, black, and white sash and drops back in horror. "He's seen the devil!" cries Buck's daughter when she observes her father's final agony. With these words the changing of the guard is complete.

In January 1914 a Munich periodical began serializing *Der Untertan*, but with the outbreak of war the editors informed Mann they could not continue to publish such a provocative satire in a time of national emergency. Mann agreed to the suspension of publication with the proviso that no editorial explanation be appended to the last instalment. Readers were thus left with the impression that the novel ended with a libel trial that ruined Herr Buck, an episode some fifty pages before the actual conclusion. The complete novel appeared only after the war, when its publisher advertised it as "*the* German novel of the post-*Gründer* era." It became an immediate bestseller, and Mann was proclaimed the prophet of Germany's downfall.[63] Ironically, Mann said after the war, even he failed to believe his own prophecy.[64]

This failure underscores the fact that even the clarity of insights such as Mann's were insufficient to turn Imperial Germany from its disastrous course in 1914, nor would the less drastic or less conscious warnings of the two other novelists examined in this chapter do so. Nevertheless, all three gave urgently needed attention to questions of what constituted German greatness and how it could be cemented in the post-Bismarckian era. Despite evident democratic leanings in all three authors, each found cause to dismiss the possibilities of parliamentary democracy.

Fontane came the closest of the three to embracing the notion that an age of electoral politics had arrived, but his uneasiness over this phenomenon was clear. Even he seemed to suggest—when Dubslav shrugged off his defeat—that real power lay elsewhere, but where remained unclear. The hope at the end resided in the ability of Woldemar von Stechlin to combine his father's legacy of humane conservatism with his own liberalism to meet the needs of the modern age. The last line, however, suggesting the possible end of the Stechlin family but not of its remarkable pond, forewarned of upheavals to come.

Zolling's concern with the Reichstag seemed to announce an age of parliamentary politics, but the expansive account of its failures made his rejection explicit. In contrast to Fontane, Zolling acknowledged the ascendancy of William II—indeed, whether from conviction or fear of censorship, he dutifully devoted a paragraph to promoting him as Bismarck's successor—but he simultaneously boldly attacked the spying and favoritism surrounding the imperial throne. Seemingly in desperation, Zolling found wish-fulfillment in Bismarck by designating him as the man who would somehow teach the Germans what he had rigorously denied them the means to do while in power: to govern themselves.

In Der Untertan, Mann echoed the belief articulated in Zolling's novel, that electoral politics offered only maneuvering room to the selfish interests of the few. Elections were portrayed as a sham that hardly concealed the contempt of German elites for democratic notions. The novel showed how easily Germans were translating anti-French feelings into anti-democratic ideas. It showed how the Kaiser's bluster encouraged Germans to believe that by rejecting democratic ideals they were marching toward strength and greatness. The changing of the generational guard in Mann's view meant the final surrender to this delusion. Umsturz, the novel proposed, would not come from violent revolution but rather from the subservience of German society to the idea of national power. The elements Fontane and Zolling portrayed as venerable German tradition became transformed by Mann into the roots of German downfall. The time so many celebrated as Germany's arrival as a great power was depicted by Mann as the prelude to calamity. It is little wonder that even Mann agreed to suspend the publication of Der Untertan when the guns of August sounded.

The reason for the inability of novelists to portray a humane outcome to the German revolution is suggested by the novels treated not only in this chapter but in the whole study: the weight of inherited values combined with the awesome power of a modern, united Germany was too great to be easily cast aside. Even ardent critics failed to envision a positive alternative to the rule of traditional elites over a restless populace. Confronted by the specter of party and class conflict, critics chose either resignation or a mythical ideal of national solidarity that rested on internal oppression and external belligerence. If Der Untertan gives the most complex rendition of the network of threads in this tapestry, the other Berlin novels reveal much of the same fabric.

# Notes

1. Conrad Alberti, Die Alten und die Jungen (Leipzig, 1889), II, 284. For the events leading up to this scene see above, 87.
2. On the political tensions of the 1890s see Gordon A. Craig, Germany: 1866–1945 (New York, 1978), 171–179, 224–230, 251–265.
3. Conrad Alberti, Ablösung vor! (Berlin, 1911), 220. On the wider consciousness of a changing of the guard in German society see Martin Doerry, Übergangsmenschen: Die Mentalität der Wilhelminer und die Krise des Kaiserreichs (Weinheim, 1986), 30–43.
4. Theodor Fontane, Der Stechlin, Sämtliche Werke, VIII (Munich, 1959), 286.
5. Fontane, Der Stechlin, 49, 124. For a discussion of the lake as a social/political allegory see Walter Müller-Seidel, Theodor Fontane: Soziale Romankunst in Deutschland

(Stuttgart, 1975), 450–452, and Karla Müller, *Schloßgeschichten: Eine Studie zum Romanwerk Theodor Fontanes* (Munich, 1986), 108–113.
6. On the development of the Old-New theme see Roger Hillman, *Zeitroman: The Novel and Society in Germany, 1830–1900* (Bern, 1983), 93–97.
7. These traits correspond to central characteristics Fontane delineated in his essay "Die Märker und das Berlinertum," *Aus dem Nachlaß von Theodor Fontane* (Berlin, 1908), 295–312.
8. Fontane, *Der Stechlin*, 283. Other references to "old Fritz" include passages on pages 39, 55, 121, 173, 252, 316. See also Kenneth Attwood, *Fontane und das Preußentum* (Berlin, 1970), and Gordon A. Craig, "Irony and Rage in the German Social Novel: Theodor Fontane and Heinrich Mann," in Gary D. Stark and Bede Karl Lackner, eds., *Essays on Culture and Society in Modern Germany* (Arlington, Tex., 1982), 103–107.
9. Fontane, *Der Stechlin*, 283.
10. Ibid., 55.
11. Ibid., 150. On scholarship about Fontane's politics see Gudrun Loster-Schneider, *Der Erzähler Fontane: Seine politischen Positionen in den Jahren 1864–1898 und ihre ästhetische Vermittlung* (Tübingen, 1986), 9–19.
12. Fontane, *Der Stechlin*, 170. See also an encounter with a schoolboy, in which, after questioning the boy on dates of important battles, Dubslav remarks that another time is coming, implying that knowing the dates of battles may not be enough. Ibid., 54–55.
13. Ibid., 152–156, 176.
14. A by-election in Ruppin-Templin in May 1896 influenced Fontane's decision to make the social democrat of his fictional election the winner, instead of the originally planned progressive candidate. See Eda Sagarra, *Theodor Fontane: 'Der Stechlin'* (Munich, 1986), 115–120.
15. See, for instance, Fontane, *Der Stechlin*, 34, 64, 161–162, 170–171, 179–180, 186. For further discussion of this episode see Henry Garland, *The Berlin Novels of Theodor Fontane* (Oxford, 1980), 258, and Loster-Schneider, *Der Erzähler Fontane*, 193–196.
16. Fontane, *Der Stechlin*, 124.
17. Ibid., 253–254. See also Loster-Schneider, *Der Erzähler Fontane*, 85–92.
18. Fontane, *Der Stechlin*, 149.
19. Ibid., 236.
20. Ibid., 361. See also Francis L. Carsten, *A History of the Prussian Junkers* (Aldershot, Hants, England, 1989), 125–126.
21. Fontane, *Der Stechlin* 95. For a discussion of what makes this a political novel, see Müller-Seidel, *Fontane*, 429–433, and Loster-Schneider, *Der Erzähler Fontane*, 163–164.
22. An implicit reference to William II denigrates him in comparison to his grandfather, whom Dubslav refers to as the last "real person" in contrast to the "so-called supermen." Fontane, *Stechlin*, 272. See also Loster-Schneider, *Der Erzähler Fontane*, 178–182; Gordon A. Craig, *The End of Prussia* (Madison, Wisc., 1984), 59–69; and Willy Schumann, "Wo ist der Kaiser? Theodor Fontane über Kaiser Wilhelm II," *Monatshefte*, 71 (1979), 161–171.
23. Theophil Zolling (1849–1901) became well known to the literary public when he succeeded Paul Lindau in 1881 as the editor of the literary periodical *Gegenwart*. Two other novels treating electoral politics are Botho von Pressentin, *Apokalypse* (Berlin, 1889), and Rudolph Stratz, *Die letzte Wahl* (Stuttgart, 1898).
24. Theophil Zolling, *Bismarcks Nachfolger* (Berlin, 1895), 75. See also a glorifying scene of Bismarck in the Reichstag in Theophil Zolling, *Der Klatsch* (Leipzig, 1889), 11.
25. Zolling, *Bismarcks Nachfolger*, 87.

26. Ibid., 90.
27. Ibid., 100, 107. On Caprivi's chancellorship see Craig, *Germany*, 230–261.
28. Zolling, *Bismarcks Nachfolger*, 156.
29. Ibid., 498–499. For a critical evaluation of the influence of court circles on William II's political regime see John C. G. Röhl, *Kaiser, Hof und Staat: Wilhelm II und die deutsche Politik* (Munich, 1987), 125–140.
30. The episode clearly refers to a political uproar of early 1892, following the introduction of a controversial school bill by the Prussian Minister of Education, Count Robert von Zedlitz-Trützschler. Craig, *Germany*, 254.
31. Zolling, *Bismarcks Nachfolger*, 510–511. This idealized portrayal may also reflect a realistic fear of being charged with *Majestätsbeleidigung*.
32. Ibid., 97.
33. Ibid., 544. For a description of the demonstrations of 1892 that lends much credence to Zolling's portrayal see Annemarie Lange, *Berlin zur Zeit Bebels und Bismarcks: Zwischen Reichsgründung und Jahrhundertwende* (Berlin, 1972), 727–730.
34. Zolling, *Bismarcks Nachfolger*, 375, 408.
35. Ibid., 560. Whether parliamentarianism was the "constitutional logic" German political reformers might have been expected to pursue has been the subject of intense recent debate; see, for example, David Blackbourn and Geoff Eley, *The Peculiarities of German History: Bourgeois Society and Politics in Nineteenth-Century Germany* (Oxford, 1984), 278–285.
36. Zolling, *Bismarcks Nachfolger*, 23, 125.
37. Ibid., 524.
38. Ibid., 526.
39. Ibid., 517–518.
40. Ibid., 561.
41. Ibid., 563.
42. This attitude toward the older generation resurfaces in novels of the Weimar republic. See Katherine Roper, "Images of German Youth in Weimar Novels," *Journal of Contemporary History* 13, 3 (July 1978), 512, especially notes 32 and 33.
43. David Roberts, *Artistic Consciousness and Political Conscience: The Novels of Heinrich Mann, 1900–1938* (Bern, 1971), 100, and Ulrich Weisstein, "Satire und Parodie in Heinrich Manns Roman 'Der Untertan'," in Klaus Matthias, ed., *Heinrich Mann, 1871/1971* (Munich, 1973), 125. For an analysis of the *Untertanmentalität* in Wilhelmine Germany see Doerry, *Übergangsmenschen*, 44–65.
44. Heinrich Mann, *Der Untertan* (Berlin and Weimar, 1965), 5. See also Roberts, *Artistic Consciousness*, 93–95.
45. Mann, *Der Untertan*, 8.
46. Ibid., 11.
47. Ibid., 12.
48. Ibid., 32–33.
49. Ibid., 56. The translation of this passage comes from Heinrich Mann, *Little Superman*, translated by Ernest Boyd (New York, 1945), 45. This translation of the novel omits some interesting (but obscure to English readers) political and social details about subsidiary characters and subplots.
50. Mann, *Der Untertan*, 90–91; *Little Superman*, 74.
51. On the new moustache see Mann, *Der Untertan*, 91, 130, 158.
52. Ibid., 107.
53. Ibid., 210. On the resulting economic nationalism see Harold James, *A German Identity: 1770–1990* (New York, 1989), 83–84.
54. Mann, *Der Untertan*, 323–324. On the political implications of the *Lohengrin* episode see Weisstein, "Satire und Parodie," 134–136.

55. See, for instance, a speech he made twice to workers in the paper factory. Mann, *Der Untertan*, 78, 396. See also Weisstein, "Satire und Parodie," 143.
56. Mann, *Der Untertan*, 417. The translation, slightly modified, is from *Little Superman*, 301–302.
57. Mann, *Der Untertan*, 425. On the plethora of such monuments and ceremonies in this period see George L. Mosse, *The Nationalization of the Masses: Political Symbolism and Mass Movements in Germany from the Napoleonic Wars through the Third Reich* (New York, 1975), especially 47–99.
58. The reference to "the great Ally" echoes an actual speech by William II to the navy. Roberts, *Artistic Consciousness*, 115. For further analysis of Diederich's reference to the decadence of French society, see Lorenz Winter, *Heinrich Mann and His Public: A Socioliterary Study of the Relationship between an Author and His Public*, translated by John Gorman (Coral Gables, Fla., 1970), 71.
59. Mann, *Der Untertan*, 430–431.
60. Ibid., 433. The comment that the band "played like the orchestra on a sinking ship" surely was meant to evoke images of the recent "Titanic" disaster.
61. Ibid., 434.
62. On the pervasiveness of apocalyptic imagery during this period see Klaus Vondung, "Deutsche Apokalypse 1914," in Klaus Vondung, ed., *Das wilhelminische Bildungsbürgertum: Zur Sozialgeschichte seiner Ideen* (Göttingen, 1976), 153–171, and Lucian Hölscher, *Weltgericht oder Revolution: Protestantische und sozialistische Zukunftsvorstellungen im deutschen Kaiserreich* (Stuttgart, 1989).
63. Weisstein, "Satire und Parodie," 128–130.
64. "I ought to have foreseen [the war], because it was announced in *Der Untertan*." Quoted in Winter, *Heinrich Mann*, 72.

# Conclusion

The novels of Imperial Berlin allow historians access into a stormy cultural arena in which alternative German identities were being contested. Authors confronted with signs of countless social wrongs, outmoded relationships, and immense new economic forces reacted by depicting the conditions they saw and exploring prospects for the future of German society. By creating fictional representations of their society, they not only reflected values of their times but were molding them as well by contributing to the social discourse in which they evolved. The myriad strands of social criticism running through their novels show that German encounters with modernity could provoke ideals of individual liberty, social justice, and popular political participation. At the same time, the many instances in which authors abandoned the implications of social situations and left ideals unrealized show the strength of cultural counterforces to these trends. As we have seen, traumatic historical events, cultural legacies, powerful mythologies, social anxieties, and traditions of political passivity intruded into fictional visions of a humanistic and democratic Germany.

To create these visions, Berlin novelists crossed back and forth over three levels of human experience: that of self-conscious individuals striving to assert their autonomy against an array of social and cultural constraints; that of Berliners being assaulted by the stresses and enticements of the modernizing metropolis; and that of Germans confronting a new nation-state whose identity was still unformed. The tangled connections authors drew between individuality, urban modernity, and nationhood manifested their need to discern the interaction of each of these realms upon the other and to induce readers to think about the nature of these links in their own lives. Wolfgang Kirchbach's old postmaster in *Kinder des Reiches*, for example, escaped personal crises by making an odyssey through a burgeoning capital; that, in turn, awakened his consciousness of a Germany poised on the edge of greatness. Or, to take a negative version of these interactions, Diederich Heßling, with his self-deceptions, was depicted by Heinrich Mann as a direct product of national values transmitted through his experiences in Berlin. But beyond these two figures, virtually all the other characters we have looked at can similarly be analyzed in terms that link their individual difficulties to wider urban crises and national dilemmas. The crisis of German nationhood, then, became intricately linked with moral crises of individuality and with social and economic crises of modernity.

The aggregate of these fictional connections suggests that in most authors' minds no doubt arose over whether Germany was following a unique path. The novels are replete with allusions to assumptions of particular cultural legacies from the Enlightenment onward that should mold the emergent nation. The only question was whether Germans would use these legacies to consummate their unfinished revolution, or whether they would betray them in favor of the soulless materialism of the metropolis and the hyper-nationalism of a Germany grasping for power. The novels we have dealt with attest to an evolution on the part of authors from the optimistic hope for a humane German revolution to the pessimistic abandonment of that hope, with 1890 representing the approximate turning point. The stages by which Berlin novelists faltered in their attempts to fuse humanistic values with modern realities are of vital interest to historians because they reveal perceptions of diminishing alternatives and growing disillusionment at a time when vigorous social engagement was sorely needed. The resulting crisis of confidence among these modernist critics signified a crucial setback in an ongoing struggle over German identity that continues to be waged in the late twentieth century.[1]

Novels from the Bismarckian period have given us extensive testimony to a widely held notion that German unification was incomplete and that true German unity would be achieved only with a complete regeneration of social and moral values. The belief that the German revolution was still unrealized, articulated with such intensity in Karl Gutzkow's *Die Ritter vom Geiste*, resonated in subsequent Berlin novels. Despite much uncertainty over the future, novelists in the crucial period following unification conveyed the optimism of a society with choices to make and alternatives to be explored. Protagonists like Julius Rodenberg's George Grandidier, making his rounds of Prussian monuments in the celebration of 1871, and Conrad Alberti's Franz Treumann, vowing to work for a new Germany at the Brandenburger Tor in 1888, exemplified the confidence that an age of moral greatness would result from the dedication and work of individual German citizens. In such characters individual identity became vested in working to create a worthy national identity.

Such manifestations of hopefulness, however, were countered by detailed portrayals of crises that obstructed the unfinished revolution. The social, political, and cultural dimensions of these fictional crises have offered abundant evidence of what authors saw as the problematic aspects of modernity and nationhood. By focusing on pertinent sections from a spectrum of novels, we have seen how the ambivalences of the authors were conveyed through such means as their depictions of Berlin, their treatment of distinct historical episodes in Berlin's development as German capital, and the diverse themes that signified authors' consciousness of modernity and nationhood. No single work, of course, exemplifies the change from Rodenberg's vision of new German harmony at the moment of unification to Mann's apocalyptic scenario of the turn of the century, but myriad images of Berlin, of historical experiences, and of social themes show the elements of that change.

The profuse Berlin imagery in the novels we have dealt with serves as a fundamental indicator of authorial perspectives on modernity as it was incorporated in the city. Every Berlin novel depicts houses, neighborhoods, and landmarks. Such depictions yield diverse impressions of the city, whether it be Berlin as a small town in the guise of a metropolis (Stinde), as the progenitor of German industrialization (Gutzkow), as Athens-on-the-Spree (Heyse), as a locus of aristocratic refinement (Lindau), as a concentration of urban misery (Kretzer), or as a prototype of parvenu vulgarity (Mann). Each setting sounds a tone that resonates beneath the motifs of the plot. Despite the differing tones, however, all the novels reverberate with a common theme: Berlin as center of German modernity. In the array of portrayals of the modernizing capital the evolution from hope to disillusionment is clearest.

Few passages exceed the opening chapters of Alberti's *Alten und die Jungen* for sheer exuberance, as a wide-eyed Franz Treumann arrives in the bustling, elegant metropolis for the first time. But many other novelists used similar images of the city to exemplify the hope that the extraordinary technological progress of their times heralded a new age of human well-being. To be sure, the physical disruptions of the modernizing city—demolished buildings, torn-up streets, and new construction—profoundly disrupted the lives of its fictional inhabitants. But even when a life was destroyed by these disruptions, as in the case of Kretzer's Meister Timpe, novels of the 1870s and '80s were likely to conclude with an affirmation of the modernity that had wrought such havoc. The scene of Timpe's suicide, for example, was eclipsed by a final scene of nearby crowds who were cheering the maiden journey of the new streetcar.

As the 1890s approached, depictions of Berlin increasingly became a barometer for the stormy psychological and moral state of individual characters. Scenes of modernity became the impetus for despair, as when the glass-and-steel expanses of the Friedrichstraße station came to embody the revulsion Wilhelm Bölsche's troubled protagonist felt for his age. His revulsion ultimately yielded to affirmation, when in the last scene the technological wonder of the railway station came to symbolize the limitless potential of humans to improve their world. In other novels of these years, however, such revulsion for the city escalated into the existential terror of a completely isolated individual. At the turn of the century, for instance, the Berlin odyssey of Johannes Schlaf's protagonist, Liesegang, traversed modern civilization. The ubiquitous signs of cultural opulence and commercial vigor that he passed might have suggested the exhilarating culmination of the Berlin-in-progress seen by Kirchbach's protagonist a quarter of a century earlier. But for Liesegang they symbolized only a colossal power with cataclysmic consequences for humanity if it lost control of this power. This individual's confrontation with Berlin thus became an apotheosis of *fin de siècle* despair. Although prophetic of the twentieth century, this sort of intensely psychological confrontation with modernity represented a sharp divergence from the social criticism that more usually typified Berlin novels.

A far more frequent outcome in turn-of-the-century works—and one that stayed more closely with the modernist tradition of social criticism—was disgust with Berlin as a city of parvenus. Parvenu imagery, already evident in Gutzkow, pervaded novels of the Wilhelmine period and contributed to the growing disillusionment with the city they manifested. Few statements regarding the parvenu were as explicit as the question of the Alberti character who, contemplating a particularly offensive specimen of new wealth, asked himself, "This man, . . . [w]hy wasn't he named 'Berlin'?"[2] Countless other novels portrayed the city with images of tawdry buildings with lavish façades, extravagant mishmashes of architectural styles, and tasteless displays of newly acquired wealth—all representing a new breed of inhabitant now seen to be in control. Such fictional portrayals helped strengthen cultural notions that parvenuism was in the ascendancy and that Berlin, its center, was becoming its ruinous conduit to the rest of Germany. The final scene of *Schlaraffenland* epitomizes the cynical notion that people like Türkheimer, having bought control of Berlin society, were now able to preside as potentates in a parvenu nation. Although not identical, the arriviste, the city, and the nation thus became linked by their newness. Such imagery completely transformed the notion of a new Germany, from the hopeful expectations of earlier novels to scornful contempt for the very condition of newness.

A significant reason for this transformation lies in the fact that the conceptions of newness changed over the decades. Germany in 1871 was literally a new national creation, whose identity was shown to be still undefined in novels that treated that period. The Germany of 1900 had matured into a well-established presence in European affairs, defined by astonishing economic, diplomatic, and military power. These attributes of political capital were increasingly identified in later novels with images of a parvenu nation. This transformation has proven particularly evident in fictional treatments of a succession of distinct historical episodes in the life of Imperial Germany.

Surely the most decisive historical experience for novelists of Imperial Berlin was the short-lived *Gründer* era with its precipitous ending in the crash of 1873. Although relatively few novels portrayed the actual crash, the motif of unbridled speculation that preceded it surfaced in a multitude of subsequent works. Countless fictional references to this period advanced notions of Berlin—and Germany—as entities tainted by a *Gründermentalität* that spelled moral catastrophe for all of German society.

Fictional depictions of other historical experiences revealed perceptions of subsequent fateful moments at which Germany continued to lose her innocence as a newborn nation. We have seen how some novelists used the assassination attempts on the Kaiser in 1878 to document an extension of the police state or an intensified anti-Semitism. Others turned to the political realignments of 1879 to suggest that the politics of self-interest were eclipsing any possibility of a responsible German government. Still others interpreted the repressions of the Anti-Socialist Law or the working-class demonstrations of 1892 as signs that the social harmony envisioned by proponents of the unfinished revolution was receding with each new symptom of class conflict. Even the politically sensitive topic of the ascendancy of Hohenzollern rulers to the imperial throne evolved through the pens of Berlin novelists, from enthusiastic tribute (Alberti) to notable silence (Fontane) to audacious parody (Mann). Such specific events,

## Conclusion

then, deeply affected how some novelists portrayed a changing Germany.

For all Berlin novelists, however, confrontation with the times extended far beyond the depiction of specific historical episodes. I have used the term "modernity" to characterize the focus of their concerns, and, as we have seen, their notions of what constituted the modern age ranged widely. Sometimes they were epitomized in a fleeting image or exchange, such as Kretzer's electric light that illuminated the walls of an ancient church, or Alberti's businessman who scoffed at an aristocrat's offer of a duel. But more often they were embedded in an overall crisis whose development involved the interaction of characters with a network of social phenomena by which each author chose to represent his or her notion of modernity. The novels are far too diffuse to offer an orderly, coherent concept of modernity. But, like the kaleidoscope, which shifts the same pieces through differing arrangements, they treat the same issues in differing fictional contexts. The many "encounters" with modernity were thus comprised of shifting combinations of economic, social, political, and cultural elements, each of which cast their particular shadows on authorial hopes for Germany.

Central to the growing pessimism toward modernity was the novelists' dissatisfied acceptance of a rampant capitalism as the wave of the German future. Images of a mushrooming industrial capitalist economy appeared in virtually every novel of Imperial Berlin in the form of enormous factories belching smoke, of an expansive new stock exchange, of crowded new department stores, or of luxurious villas erected by commercial magnates. Fictional evidence of such wealth reflected an important dimension of Germany's emerging identity: that her position as a great power was being secured through her astonishing rate of industrialization. Berlin novelists, however, saw this achievement as problematic. Not only had the new concentrations of wealth produced an epidemic of parvenuism, but even more threatening to any vision of national harmony, the scramble for such wealth had unleashed Darwinian struggles for survival that extended through all levels of society. Unbridled competition, unparalleled greed, and brutal human exploitation repeatedly were identified as hallmarks of a system that represented a scourge upon the nation. Extensive anti-capitalist imagery, contained in countless tales of desperation and ruin, competed, often within the same novel, with depictions of tangible marvels wrought by economic developments. Few Berlin authors allowed their ambivalences over capitalism to result in a socialist critique, and fewer still reacted by renouncing the fruits of industrialization for some sort of mythological agrarianism. But the virulent portrayals of what they discerned clouded any visions of the unfinished German revolution.

Equally destructive to such visions were perceptions of crisis among and within the social classes of modern urban society. Characters from the whole social spectrum populated the novels of Imperial Berlin, and their typical representations show an overweening perception of middle-class ascendancy in modern society. Simultaneously, there emerged fear that such ascendancy meant a dire threat to German well-being. Some novelists, to be sure, depicted alternatives to middle-class dominance, either in a working class that was beginning to assert itself politically or in an aristocracy that steadfastly maintained the means of its social control, but such portrayals involved dilemmas that by implication left the field to the middle classes.

Although all novelists who depicted living conditions of the working class did so with obvious sympathy, they also revealed middle-class fears that workers would be unruly, susceptible to demagogic manipulation, or inherently inferior in the economic *Kampf ums Dasein*. Hans Land's depiction of a genuine worker conducting an effective and successful campaign for the Reichstag was far outnumbered by portrayals by other authors of working-class violence, ineptitude, or degradation. Despite a widespread acknowledgment that the age of the masses meant a new stage in the evolution of human freedom, authors generally remained unable to create positive images of the masses asserting themselves.

At the other end of the social spectrum, the fascination of novelists with the lifestyles of the nobility was countered by many signs that the indefinite continuance of aristocratic rule was unthinkable. An array of arrogant aristocratic characters who asserted their social superiority met with economic—and therefore social—ruin. Or they were forced to compromise their elite status with distasteful marriages of convenience. Affairs of honor, although still a popular literary convention, were universally depicted as secretive encounters, made anachronistic by the constraints of a modern legal system. At its most ridiculous, the nobility was shown to be isolated in drawing rooms, its inane conversation hopelessly far removed from modern realities. Even the most sympathetic portrayals showed that aristocrats would have to adopt middle-class ways to survive economically and would have to infuse their caste with new blood from the middle class as well.

All this lends support to recent arguments that the society of Imperial Germany *did* undergo a successful middle-class revolution. Indeed, the Berlin novels are filled with middle-class characters whose material success, professional prominence, cultural visibility, and/or social ascendancy leave no doubt about authors' perceptions of a modernity dominated by middle-class values and activity. It is equally clear, however, that authors perceived not one middle class but many and that they vested their hopes for a positive German identity in the triumph of what they depicted as *bürgerlich* values over those of the so-called bourgeoisie. The distinction sometimes took the form of cultural contrasts between cultivated middle-class characters and social climbers who exuded shallow pretensions. But it also cut in other directions, as when hard-working manufacturers or artisans were contrasted with unscrupulous speculators or financiers. The negative imagery suggested less a perception of middle-class failure than a perception that the "wrong" middle classes were prevailing. Different characters exemplified differing middle-class vices—social ambition, cultural philistinism, moral rigidity, economic ruthlessness, vulgar materialism—but when such vices were depicted increasingly as ascendant in

Berlin society, any notion of middle-class revolution became transformed from one of a regenerative to a degenerative force in Germany. Traditional *bürgerlich* virtues, if they triumphed in fiction, increasingly did so in private spheres far removed from the German public soul.

Perceived distance between private and public spheres was also evident in the apparent disinterest among many novelists in confronting political themes as a dimension of the unfinished revolution. Nevertheless, a substantial number did address political issues. The various treatments suggest a common belief that for better or worse modernity meant that a democratic age was emerging; responsible Germans, they implied, should help steer it toward genuine human freedom. Political novels of the Bismarckian era displayed a spectrum of ideological alternatives that still seemed open to Germany despite the existence of the new constitution, and they recounted political debates about which of these might best serve Germans of all classes. Post-1890 novels demonstrated less concern with ideology, as we have seen, but they nevertheless showed increasing acceptance of electoral politics as a hallmark of the age of the masses. Such acceptance was fraught with ambivalence, however, that derived from authors' doubts about the political maturity of the lower classes or of all of German society, from disgust with what they saw as selfish or ineffectual elected representatives, and from cautious criticism of the regime of William II and its perceived failure to deal effectively with urgent social issues. To the extent that these ambivalences implied support for political withdrawal, they weakened any advocacy within the novels of institutional change. Moreover, although all political themes involved criticism, democratic impulses in many Berlin novels all too often became submerged in the hazy political ideas of their authors.

Not surprisingly, fictional challenges to the cultural status quo far outweighed those to the political status quo. Although the ideal of a spiritual knighthood enunciated by Gutzkow was explicitly invoked in only a few subsequent novels, the moral dimension of that ideal permeated virtually all of them and attested to their authors' commitment to the notion of spiritual struggle as essential for Germany's unfinished revolution. That this spiritual struggle would take place in the cultural realm became clear not only in the several portrayals of unfit leadership in the religious realm but in the many depictions of cultural combatants who challenged a shallow, over-commercialized cultural establishment. That many novelists envisioned themselves as possible saviors of the German nation was evident from successive instances of messianic imagery applied to young artists and intellectuals. But what began as a confident belief that such cultural figures could transform Germany evolved by the turn of the century into the satire of Otto Julius Bierbaum or the nihilism of Johannes Schlaf. Nevertheless, belief in the regenerative role of culture continued to be manifest, even in a late scene of Mann's *Der Untertan*, when the old fighter of 1848 was still trying to persuade his son to work for the cause of humanity. The disparity between expectations about what a cultural revolution could accomplish and the realization that even the most profound artistic creations could not effect a social transformation thus became another implicit inducement to resignation.

Each fictional encounter with modernity in the novels of Wilhelmine Berlin articulated problems in such a way as to close off possibilities still open in novels of the unification era. The search to bring order to chaotic experiences and to bring understanding to social questions created successive novelistic versions of an unfolding social reality. As blank spaces were filled in on what in 1871 had been the canvas of the future, less and less room was left for visionary hopes of national regeneration. In the environment of the turn of the century, idealistic hopes about German unity seemed a distant memory and expectations for moral regeneration were forgotten.

Social engagement, but one dimension of imaginative literature, offers a means of assessing changing attitudes toward German nationhood and modernity in a significant body of cultural discourse. The fact that novelists used the interaction of encounters with modernity and with nationhood to enunciate calls for national regeneration becomes important evidence of the extent to which an emergent German identity could be driven by modernist ideas.[3] In addition, however, the growing doubt about the value of social engagement in later novels vividly confirms the difficulty—and ultimate failure during the years of the Second Reich—of creating a German identity that fused cultural legacies of the Enlightenment with modern experience. We have seen innumerable instances in which social criticism in novels yielded to abandonment of the implications, as authors ignored the evidence in their own works. Challenges to the political system yielded to acquiescence to imperial authority. Challenges to social injustice yielded to fears of mass movements in general and social democracy in particular. Challenges to the impersonal forces of the city yielded to extreme individualism and social withdrawal. Challenges to the cultural establishment yielded to spiritual crisis and despair. Challenges to anti-Semitism and the oppression of women yielded to resignation and bewilderment. Appeals to traditions of simplicity and humility yielded to images of ostentation and arrogance.

Literature is not compelled to offer programs of social reform or prescriptive visions, but the ultimate failure of Berlin novelists to do so meant their forsaking an attempt to carry out the call for national regeneration that Gutzkow and so many of his successors had raised. Although they proved unable to create a genuinely humanistic identity for Imperial Germany, however, their novels provided a cultural legacy for future attempts to do so. The collapse of the imperial system interrupted such fictional encounters with nationhood and modernity, but these would be resumed by literary successors of the Weimar years in even more tumultuous circumstances. Günter Grass's call for similar visions in the midst of the German upheavals of the 1990s shows that the legacy lives on.[4]

## Notes

1. For a provocative hypothesis about cycles in the struggle for German identity see Harold James, *A German Identity: 1770–1990* (New York, 1989).
2. Conrad Alberti, *Die Alten und die Jungen* (Leipzig, 1889), II, 8.
3. In his study of perceptions of the modern city Andrew Lees clearly distinguishes between anti-urbanism as a conservative reaction against modernity and criticisms of the city by "urban partisans" who sought to reform perceived evils. In treating German culture, however, he tends to understate the number of novelists among the latter group. Andrew Lees, *Cities Perceived: Urban Society in European and American Thought, 1820–1940* (New York, 1985), 84–85, 123, 272–278.
4. "Viel Gefühl, wenig Buwußtsein," *Der Spiegel*, 47/1989 (20 November 1989), 75, cited in Gordon A. Craig, "A New, New Reich?" *New York Review of Books* 36, 21–22 (18 January 1990), 32.

# Bibliography

### NOVELS USED IN THIS STUDY

First editions cited here; the editions actually used are cited in the notes.

Alberti, Conrad. *Ablösung vor!* (Berlin, 1911).
———. *Die Alten und die Jungen*, 2 vols. (Leipzig, 1889).
———. *Maschinen* (Leipzig, 1894).
———. *Mode* (Berlin, 1892).
———. *Plebs* (Leipzig, 1887).
———. *Das Recht auf Liebe* (Berlin, 1890).
———. *Riesen und Zwerge* (Berlin, 1889).
———. *Schröter & Co.* (Leipzig, 1893).
———. *Wer ist der Stärkere? Ein sozialer Roman aus dem modernen Berlin*, 2 vols. (Leipzig, 1888).
Baluschek, Hans. *Spreeluft* (Berlin, 1913).
Bierbaum, Otto Julius. *Stilpe: Ein Roman aus der Froschperspektive* (Berlin, 1897).
Bleibtreu, Karl. *Die Auskunftei* (Munich, 1910).
———. *Bismarck: Ein Weltroman in 4 Bänden* (only 3 published) (Berlin, 1915).
———. *Geist* (Munich, 1906).
———. *Größenwahn*, 3 vols. (Leipzig, 1887).
Böhme, Margarete. *Millionenrausch* (Berlin, 1919).
Bölsche, Wilhelm. *Die Mittagsgottin: Ein Roman aus dem Geisteskampf der Gegenwart*, 2 vols. (Stuttgart, 1891).
Eck, Ulla von (pseudonym for Binzer, Ina Sofie Amalie von). *Zigeuner der Großstadt* (Berlin, 1895).
Fischer, Hans R. *Berliner Zigeunerleben* (Berlin, 1890).
———. *Unter den Armen und Elenden* (Berlin, 1887).
———. *Was Berlin verschlingt* (Berlin, 1890).
Fontane, Theodor. *L'Adultera* (Berlin, 1891).
———. *Effi Briest* (Berlin, 1895).
———. *Frau Jenny Treibel* (Berlin, 1892).
———. *Irrungen, Wirrungen* (Berlin, 1888).
———. *Die Poggenpuhls* (Berlin, 1896).
———. *Der Stechlin* (Berlin, 1899).
Frenzel, Karl. *Geld* (Berlin, 1885).
Gutzkow, Karl. *Die neuen Serapionsbrüder*, 3 vols. (Breslau, 1877).
———. *Die Ritter vom Geiste*, 4 vols. (Leipzig, 1850).
Hanstein, Adalbert von. *Zwei Welten*, 2 vols. (Berlin W, 1898).
Hart, Julius. "Kein Ideal," *Deutsche Monatsblätter*, I, 2 (May 1878), 115–143.
Heiberg, Hermann. *Esthers Ehe* (Leipzig, 1886).
Hermann, Georg (pseudonym for Georg Hermann Borchardt). *Einen Sommer lang* (Berlin, 1917).
———. *Henriette Jacoby* (Berlin, 1910).
———. *Jettchen Gebert* (Berlin, 1906).
———. *Kubinke* (Berlin, 1910).
Hesekiel, Ludovika. *Von Brandenburg zu Bismarck*, 2 vols. (Berlin, 1873).

Heyse, Paul. *Kinder der Welt*, 2 vols. (Berlin, 1873).
Hille, Peter. *Die Sozialisten* (Leipzig, 1886).
Höcker, Paul Oskar. *Dem Glücke nach* (Berlin W, 1893).
———. *Musikstudenten* (Stuttgart, 1910).
Hoffmann, Hans. *Das Gymnasium zu Stolpenburg* (Berlin, 1891).
Hollaender, Felix. *Frau Ellin Röte: Ein Ehe Roman* (Berlin, 1893).
———. *Jesus und Judas* (Berlin, 1891).
———. *Der Weg des Thomas Truck*, 2 vols. (Berlin, 1902).
Hopfen, Hans. *Glänzendes Elend*, 3 vols. (Berlin, 1893).
———. *Der Väter zweie: Eine Geschichte aus dem modernen Berlin*, 2 vols. (Stuttgart, 1898).
Hyan, Hans. *Arme Sünder* (Berlin, 1906).
———. *Gold! Berliner Roman* (Lichterfelde, 1905).
Jacobowski, Ludwig. *Werther der Jude* (Berlin, 1893).
Kirchbach, Wolfgang. *Kinder des Reiches*, 2 vols. (Leipzig, 1883).
Kretzer, Max. *Die beiden Genossen* (Berlin, 1881).
———. *Die Bergpredigt* (Dresden, 1890).
———. *Die Betrogenen* (Berlin, 1882).
———. *Die Buchhalterin* (Dresden, 1894).
———. *Drei Weiber* (Jena, 1886).
———. *Das Gesicht Christi* (Leipzig, 1897).
———. *Im Sturmwind des Sozialismus* (Berlin, 1883).
———. *Die Madonna von Grunewald* (Leipzig, 1901).
———. *Der Mann ohne Gewissen* (Berlin, 1905).
———. *Meister Timpe* (Leipzig, 1888).
———. *Der Millionenbauer* (Leipzig, 1891).
———. *Die Verkommenen* (Berlin, 1883).
Land, Hans. *Der neue Gott* (Dresden, 1890).
Landsberger, Artur. *Lu, die Kokotte: Berliner Roman* (Munich, 1912).
———. *Millionäre* (Munich, 1913).
Lindau, Paul, *Arme Mädchen* (Stuttgart, 1887).
———. *Die blaue Laterne*, 2 vols. (Berlin, 1907).
———. *Spitzen* (Stuttgart, 1888).
———. *Der Zug nach dem Westen* (Stuttgart, 1886).
Lothar, Rudolf. *Kurfürstendamm: Ein Berlin W-Roman* (Berlin, 1910).
Mann, Heinrich. *Im Schlaraffenland* (Munich, 1900).
———. *Der Untertan* (Munich, 1914).
Marès, Jolanthe. *Begierde: Berliner Roman aus der Zeit vor dem großen Kriege* (Berlin, 1916).
———. *Lilli. Ein Sittenbild aus Berlin W* (Berlin, 1914).
———. *Lillis Ehe* (Berlin, 1914).
Mauthner, Fritz. *Die Fanfare* (Dresden, 1889).
———. *Der neue Ahasver: Roman aus Jung-Berlin*, 2 vols. (Dresden, 1882).
———. *Das Quartett* (Dresden, 1893).
———. *Der Villenhoff* (Dresden, 189?).
Ompteda, Georg von. *Droesigl* (Berlin, 1909).
———. *Eysen* (Berlin, 1900).
———. *Sylvester von Geyer* (Berlin, 190?).
Polenz, Wilhelm von. *Wurzellocker* (Berlin, 1902).
Pressentin, Botho von. *Apokalypse* (Berlin, 1889).
Przybyszewski, Stanislaw. *Im Malstrom* (Berlin, 1896).
———. *Über Bord* (Berlin, 1896).
———. *Unterwegs* (Berlin, 1895).

Raabe, Wilhelm. *Deutscher Adel* (Berlin, 1876).
———. *Im alten Eisen* (Berlin, 1887).
———. *Der Lar* (Braunschweig, 1889).
———. *Villa Schönow* (Braunschweig, 1884).
Reuter, Gabriele. *Ellen von der Weiden: Ein Tagebuch* (Berlin, 1901).
———. *Frauenseelen: Novellen* (Berlin, 1910).
Rodenberg, Julius. *Die Grandidiers* (Stuttgart, 1879).
———. *Klostermanns Grundstück* (Berlin, 1891).
———. *Unter den Linden* (Berlin, 1888).
Roßneck, Friedrich. *Mimi Schlichting* (Berlin, 1887).
Saudek, Robert. *Dämon Berlin* (Berlin, 1906).
Schlaf, Johannes. *Das dritte Reich: Ein Berliner Roman* (Berlin, 1900).
———. *Peter Boies Freite* (Leipzig, 1903).
———. *Die Suchenden* (Berlin, 1903).
Schneideck, Gustav Heinrich. *Im Osten Berlins* (Leipzig, 1892).
Seidel, Heinrich. *Leberecht Hühnchen* (Berlin, 1882).
Spielhagen, Friedrich. *Ein neuer Pharao* (Leipzig, 1889).
———. *Sturmflut*, 2 vols. (Leipzig, 1876).
———. *Was will das werden?* 2 vols. (Leipzig, 1886).
Springer, Robert. *Bankier und Schriftsteller* (Berlin, 1877).
Stinde, Julius. *Die Familie Buchholz: Aus dem Leben der Hauptstadt*, 2 vols. (Berlin, 1883).
———. *Der Liedermacher* (Berlin, 1893).
Stratz, Rudolf. *Für Dich!* (Berlin, 1908).
———. *Die letzte Wahl* (Stuttgart, 1898).
———. *Unter den Linden!* (Berlin, 1893).
Tovote, Heinz. *Im Liebesrausch* (Berlin, 1890).
———. *Mutter!* (9th ed., Berlin, 1906).
Viebig, Clara. *Die vor der Toren* (Berlin, 1910).
———. *Dilettanten des Lebens* (Berlin, 1899).
———. *Elisabeth Reinharz' Ehe: Es lebe die Kunst!* (Berlin, 1899).
———. *Das tägliche Brot* (Berlin, 1900).
Wildenbruch, Ernst von. *Schwester-Seele* (Stuttgart, 1904).
Wolzogen, Ernst von. *Die kühle Blonde* (Stuttgart, 1891).
———. *Lumpengesindel* (Berlin, 1892).
Zobeltitz, Fedor von. *Die Hetzjagd* (Berlin, 1913).
Zobeltitz, Hanns von. *Lichterfeldstraße Nr. 1* (Stuttgart, 1899).
Zolling, Theophil. *Bismarcks Nachfolger* (Berlin, 1891).
———. *Der Klatsch* (Leipzig, 1889).

## Bibliography of Cited Non-Fiction Works

Abrams, M. H. *Natural Supernaturalism: Tradition and Revolution in Romantic Literature* (New York, 1971).
Alberti, Conrad. *Der moderne Realismus in der deutschen Litteratur und die Grenzen seiner Berechtigung* (Hamburg, 1889).
———. *Natur und Kunst: Beiträge zur Untersuchung ihres gegenseitigen Verhältnisses* (Leipzig, 1890).
———. "Zwölf Artikel des Realismus," *Die Gesellschaft*, 5, 1 (January 1889), 2–11.
Albisetti, James C. *Schooling German Girls and Women: Secondary and Higher Education in the Nineteenth Century* (Princeton, 1988).
Alimadad-Mensch, Faranak. *Gabriele Reuter: Porträt einer Schriftstellerin* (Bern, 1984).

Allen, Ann Taylor. "German Radical Feminism and Eugenics, 1900–1918," *German Studies Review*, 11, 1 (February 1988), 31–56.

———. "Mothers of the New Generation: Adele Schreiber, Helene Stöcker, and the Evolution of a German Idea of Motherhood, 1900–1914," *Signs*, 10, 3 (Spring 1985), 418–438.

Appleby, Joyce. "One Good Turn Deserves Another: Moving beyond the Linguistic," *American Historical Review*, 94, 5 (December 1989), 1326–1332.

Arnim, Bernd von, and Knilli, Friedrich. *Gewerbliche Leihbüchereien: Berichte, Analysen und Interviews* (Gütersloh, 1966).

Aschheim, Steven E. *Brothers and Strangers: The East European Jew in German and German Jewish Consciousness, 1800–1923* (Madison, Wisc., 1982).

Attwood, Kenneth. *Fontane und das Preußentum* (Berlin, 1970).

Bab, Julius. *Die Berliner Bohème, Großstadt Dokumente*, Vol. II, 3rd ed. (Berlin, 1904).

Bach, Hans Israel. *The German Jew: A Synthesis of Judaism and Western Civilization, 1730–1930* (Oxford, 1984).

Bahr, Hermann. *Der Antisemitismus. Ein internationales Interview* (Berlin, 1894).

Bauer, Roger, et al. *Fin de Siècle: Zu Literatur und Kunst der Jahrhundertwende* (Frankfurt am Main, 1977).

Becker, Eva D., and Dehn, Manfred. *Literarisches Leben: Eine Bibliographie* (Hamburg, 1968).

Becker, Eva D. "'Zeitungen sind doch das Beste': Bürgerliche Realisten und der Vorabdruck ihrer Werke in der periodischen Presse," in Helmut Kreuzer, ed., *Gestaltungsgeschichte und Gesellschaftsgeschichte: Literatur-, Kunst- und Musikwissenschaftliche Studien* (Stuttgart, 1969), 382–408.

Behrend, Friedrich. *Die Geschichte des Tunnels über der Spree* (Berlin, 1919).

Bendix, Reinhard. "Tradition and Modernity Reconsidered," *Comparative Studies in Society and History*, 10, 3 (April 1967), 292–346.

Benstock, Shari, ed. *Feminist Issues in Literary Scholarship* (Bloomington, Ind., 1987).

Berger, Peter; Berger, Brigitte; and Kellner, Hansfried. *The Homeless Mind: Modernization and Consciousness* (1973; reprinted New York, 1974).

Bergmann, Klaus. *Agrarromantik und Großstadtfeindschaft* (Meisenheim am Glan, 1970).

*Berlin-Bibliographie bis 1960*, ed. Hans Zopf and Gerd Heinrich. Veröffentlichungen der Historischen Kommission zu Berlin, 15 (Berlin, 1965).

*Berlin-Bibliographie: 1961 bis 1966*, ed. Ursula Scholz and Reinald Stromeyer. Veröffentlichungen der Historischen Kommission zu Berlin, 43 (Berlin, 1973).

*Berlin-Bibliographie: 1967 bis 1977*, ed. Ursula Scholz and Reinald Stromeyer. Veröffentlichungen der Historischen Kommission zu Berlin, 58 (Berlin, 1984).

*Berlin-Bibliographie: 1978 bis 1984*, ed. Ute Schäfer and Reinald Stromeyer. Veröffentlichungen der Historischen Kommission zu Berlin, 69 (Berlin, 1987).

Berman, Marshall. *All That Is Solid Melts into Air: The Experience of Modernity* (New York, 1982).

Berman, Russell A. *Between Fontane and Tucholsky: Literary Criticism and the Public Sphere in Imperial Germany* (New York, 1983).

———. *The Rise of the Modern German Novel: Crisis and Charisma* (Cambridge, Mass., 1986).

Bernstein, Eduard. *Die Geschichte der Berliner Arbeiter-Bewegung*, 3 vols. (Berlin, 1907–1910).

Blackbourn, David, and Eley, Geoff. *The Peculiarities of German History: Bourgeois Society and Politics in Nineteenth-Century Germany* (Oxford, 1984).

Bleibtreu, Karl. *Revolution der Literatur* (Leipzig, 1885; reprinted, Tübingen, 1973).

Boehlich, Walter, ed. *Der Berliner Antisemitismusstreit* (Frankfurt am Main, 1965).

Bölsche, Wilhelm, ed. *Darwin, seine Bedeutung im Ringen um Weltanshauung und Lebenswert:*

6 *Aufsätze* (Berlin, 1909).
———. *Haeckel, His Life and Work*, translated by Joseph McCabe (Philadelphia, 1906).
———. *Hinter der Weltstadt: Friedrichshagener Gedanken zur ästhetischen Kultur* (Leipzig, 1901).
———. *Die naturwissenschaftlichen Grundlagen der Poesie: Prologemena einer realistischen Aesthetik* (Leipzig, 1887).
Bogdal, Klaus-Michael. *"Schaurige Bilder": Der Arbeiter im Blick des Bürgers am Beispiel des Naturalismus* (Frankfurt am Main, 1978).
Bovenschen, Silvia. *Die imaginierte Weiblichkeit: Exemplarische Untersuchungen zu kulturgeschichtlichen und literarischen Präsentationsformen des Weiblichen* (Frankfurt am Main, 1979).
Bowler, Peter J. *The Non-Darwinian Revolution: Reinterpreting a Historical Myth* (Baltimore, 1988).
Brakelmann, Günter. *Protestantismus und Politik: Werk und Wirkung Adolf Stoeckers* (Hamburg, 1982).
Bramsted, Ernest K. *Aristocracy and the Middle-Classes in Germany: Social Types in German Literature, 1830–1900* (1937; reprinted, Chicago, 1964).
Brauneck, Manfred, and Müller, Christine, eds. *Naturalismus: Manifeste und Dokumente zur deutschen Literatur, 1880–1900* (Stuttgart, 1987).
Brinkmann, Carl. "Die Aristokratie im kapitalistischen Zeitalter," in *Grundriß der Sozialökonomik*, 9, 1 (Tübingen, 1926), 22–34.
Bronsen, David, ed. *Jews and Germans from 1860 to 1933: The Problematic Symbiosis* (Heidelberg, 1979).
Brude-Firnau, Gisela, and MacHardy, Karin J., eds. *Fact and Fiction: German History and Literature, 1848–1924* (Tübingen, 1990).
Brümmer, Franz. *Lexikon der deutschen Dichter und Prosaisten vom Beginn des 19. Jahrhunderts bis zur Gegenwart*, 8 vols., 6th ed. (Leipzig, 1913).
Bruford, W. H. *The German Tradition of Self-cultivation: "Bildung" from Humboldt to Thomas Mann* (Cambridge, 1975).
Bucher, Max; Hahl, Werner; Jäger, Georg; and Wittmann, Reinhard, eds. *Realismus und Gründerzeit: Manifeste und Dokumente zur deutschen Literatur, 1848–1880*, 2 vols. (Stuttgart, 1976).
Budjuhn, Horst. *Fontane nannte sie "Effi Briest": Das Leben der Elisabeth von Ardenne* (Berlin, 1985).
Büsch, Otto, and Sheehan, James J., eds. *Die Rolle der Nation in der deutschen Geschichte und Gegenwart* (Berlin, 1985).
Bull, J. A. *The Framework of Fiction: Socio-Cultural Approaches to the Novel* (London, 1988).
Bußmann, Walter. "Das deutsche Nationalbewußtsein im 19. Jahrhundert," in Werner Weidenfeld, ed., *Die Identität der Deutschen* (Munich, 1983), 64–82.
Carsten, Francis L. *A History of the Prussian Junkers* (Aldershot, Hants, England, 1989).
Cocalis, Susan L., and Goodman, Kay, eds. *Beyond the Eternal Feminine: Critical Essays on Women and German Literature* (Stuttgart, 1982).
Conrad, Michael Georg. *Von Emile Zola bis Gerhart Hauptmann: Erinnerungen zur Geschichte der Moderne* (Leipzig, 1902).
Conze, Werner, and Kocka, Jürgen, eds. *Bildungsbürgertum im 19. Jahrhundert*, Part I: *Bildungssystem und Professionalisierung in internationalen Vergleichen* (Stuttgart, 1985).
Craig, Gordon A. *The End of Prussia* (Madison, Wisc., 1984).
———. *The Germans* (New York, 1982).
———. *Germany, 1866–1945* (New York, 1978).
———. "Irony and Rage in the German Social Novel: Theodor Fontane and Heinrich Mann," in Gary Stark and Bede Karl Lackner, eds., *Essays on Culture and Society in Modern Germany* (Arlington, Tex., 1982), 98–121.

## Bibliography

———. "A New, New Reich?" *New York Review of Books*, 36, 21–22 (18 January 1990), 28–33.
DeLauretis, Teresa, ed. *Feminist Studies/Critical Studies* (Bloomington, Ind., 1986).
Denkler, Horst, ed. *Romane und Erzählungen des Bürgerlichen Realismus: Neue Interpretationen* (Stuttgart, 1980).
Dietrich, Richard, ed. *Berlin: Zehn Kapitel seiner Geschichte* (Berlin, 1981).
Doerry, Martin. *Übergangsmenschen. Die Mentalität der Wilhelminer und die Krise des Kaiserreichs* (Weinheim, 1986).
Drewitz, Ingeborg, ed. *Die deutsche Frauenbewegung: Die soziale Rolle der Frau im 19. Jahrhundert und die Emanzipationsbewegung in Deutschland* (Bonn, 1983).
Dukes, Jack R., and Remak, Joachim, eds. *Another Germany: A Reconsideration of the Imperial Era* (Boulder, Colo., 1988).
Eagleton, Terry. *Literary Theory: An Introduction* (Minneapolis, 1983).
Ehmann, Annegret, et al. *Juden in Berlin, 1671–1945: Ein Lesebuch* (Berlin, 1988).
Eley, Geoff. *From Unification to Nazism: Reinterpreting the German Past* (Boston, 1986).
Engelberg, Ernst. *Bismarck: Urpreuße und Reichsgründer* (Berlin, 1985).
Engelhardt, Ulrich. *"Bildungsbürgertum": Begriffs- und Dogmengeschichte eines Etiketts* (Stuttgart, 1986).
Escarpit, Robert. *The Book Revolution* (London, 1966).
———. *Sociology of Literature*, translated by Ernest Pick (Painesville, Ohio, 1965).
Evans, Richard J. *The Feminist Movement in Germany, 1894–1933* (London, 1976).
———. "Modernization Theory and Women's History," *Archiv für Sozialgeschichte*, 20 (1980), 492–514.
Faden, Eberhard. "Berlin: Hauptstadt—seit wann und wodurch?" *Jahrbuch für brandenburgische Landesgeschichte*, I (1950), 17–34.
Fontane, Theodor. "Die Märker und das Berlinertum," *Aus dem Nachlaß von Theodor Fontane* (Berlin, 1908), 295–312.
Foster, Shirley. *Victorian Women's Fiction: Marriage, Freedom, and the Individual* (Totowa, N.J., 1985).
Fout, John C., ed. *German Women in the Nineteenth Century: A Social History* (New York, 1984).
Frederiksen, Elke, ed. *Die Frauenfrage in Deutschland, 1865–1915: Texte und Dokumente* (Stuttgart, 1981).
Frevert, Ute. "Bürgerlichkeit und Ehre: Zur Geschichte des Duells in England und Deutschland," in Jürgen Kocka, ed., *Bürgertum im 19. Jahrhundert: Deutschland im europäischen Vergleich* (Munich, 1988), 101–140.
———. *Women in German History: From Bourgeois Emancipation to Sexual Liberation*, translated by Stuart McKinnon-Evans (Oxford, 1988).
Fricke, Dieter. *Bismarcks Prätorianer: Die Berliner politische Polizei im Kampf gegen die deutsche Arbeiterbewegung (1871–1898)* (Berlin, 1962).
Fries, Marilyn Sibley. *The Changing Consciousness of Reality: The Image of Berlin in Selected German Novels from Raabe to Döblin* (Bonn, 1980).
Friesen, Gerhard K. *The German Panoramic Novel of the 19th Century* (Bern, 1972).
Fügen, Hans Norbert, ed. *Wege der Literatursoziologie* (Neuwied, 1968).
*Fünfzig Jahre Deutsche Romanzeitung: Festschrift zum 50-jährigen Jubiläum* (Berlin, 1913).
Funke, Rainer. *Beharrung und Umbruch, 1830–1860: Karl Gutzkow auf dem Weg in die literarische Moderne* (Frankfurt am Main, 1984).
Gall, Lothar. *Bismarck: Der weiße Revolutionär* (Frankfurt am Main, 1980).
Garland, Henry. *The Berlin Novels of Theodor Fontane* (Oxford, 1980).
Gasman, Daniel. *The Scientific Origins of National Socialism: Social Darwinism in Ernst Haeckel and the German Monist League* (London, 1971).
Geiger, Ludwig. *Berlin 1688–1840: Geschichte des geistigen Lebens der preußischen Hauptstadt*, 2 vols. (Berlin, 1892–1895).

Gerhard, Adele, and Simon, Helene. *Mutterschaft und geistige Arbeit*, 2nd ed. (Berlin, 1905).
Gilbert, Sandra M., and Gubar, Susan. *The Madwoman in the Attic: The Woman Writer and the Nineteenth-Century Imagination* (New Haven, Conn., 1979).
Gilman, Sander L. *Jewish Self-Hatred: Anti-Semitism and the Hidden Language of the Jews* (Baltimore, 1986).
Girardi, Maria-Rita, et al., eds. *Buch und Leser in Deutschland: Schriften zur Buchmarkt-Forschung*, 4 (Gütersloh, 1965).
Glagau, Otto. *Der Börsen und Gründungsschwindel in Berlin* (Leipzig, 1876).
Goldfriedrich, Johann. *Geschichte des Deutschen Buchhandels vom Beginn der Fremdherrschaft bis zur Reform des Börsenvereins im neuen Deutschen Reiche (1805–1889)* (Leipzig, 1913; reprinted, 1970).
Goodin, George. *The Poetics of Protest: Literary Form and Political Implication in the Victim-of-Society Novel* (Carbondale, Ill., 1985).
Gottschall, Rudolf von. "Die Lektüre des heutigen Lesepublikums," *Deutsche Revue*, 33, 1 (1908), 156–169.
Greven-Aschoff, Barbara. *Die bürgerliche Frauenbewegung in Deutschland, 1894–1933* (Göttingen, 1981).
Grimm, Reinhold, and Hermand, Jost, eds. *Popularität und Trivialität* (Frankfurt am Main, 1972).
Gross, David. *The Writer and Society: Heinrich Mann and Literary Politics in Germany, 1890–1940* (Atlantic Highlands, N.J., 1980).
Günther, Katharina. *Literarische Gruppenbildung im Berliner Naturalismus* (Bonn, 1972).
Gutzkow, Karl. *Deutschland am Vorabend seines Falles oder seiner Größe* (Frankfurt am Main, 1848), 156–162.
———. Rückblicke auf mein Leben, 1829–1849, in Peter Müller, ed., *Gutzkows Werke*, IV (1875; Leipzig, n.d.).
———. *Vor- und Nach-Märzliches* (Leipzig, 1850).
Hackmann, Rudolf. *Die Anfänge des Romans in der Zeitung* (Dissertation, Berlin, 1938).
Halter, Martin. *Sklaven der Arbeit—Ritter vom Geiste. Arbeit und Arbeiter im deutschen Sozialroman zwischen 1840 und 1880* (Frankfurt am Main, 1983).
Hamann, Richard, and Hermand, Jost. *Die Gründerzeit* (Berlin, 1965).
———. *Naturalismus* (Munich, 1972).
Hamburger, Michael. *From Prophecy to Exorcism: The Premisses of Modern German Literature* (London, 1965).
Handlin, Oscar, and Burchard, John, eds. *The Historian and the City* (Cambridge, Mass., 1963).
Hanstein, Adalbert von. *Das jüngste Deutschland: Zwei Jahrzehnte miterlebter Literaturgeschichte*, 3rd ed. (Leipzig, 1905).
———. *Die Sozialfrage in der Poesie* (Leipzig, 1897).
Hardin, James, ed. *German Fiction Writers, 1885–1913* (Detroit, 1988).
Harlan, David. "Intellectual History and the Return of Literature," *American Historical Review*, 94, 3 (June 1989), 581–609.
Hart, Heinrich, and Hart, Julius, eds. *Kritische Waffengänge*, Heft 6 (1884): "Friedrich Spielhagen und der deutsche Roman der Gegenwart," 3–74.
Hasubek, Peter. *Karl Gutzkows Romane "Die Ritter vom Geiste" und "Der Zauberer von Rom": Studien zur Typologie des deutschen Zeitromans im 19. Jahrhundert* (Dissertation, Hamburg, 1964).
*Das Hauptstadtproblem in der Geschichte.* Festschrift für Friedrich Meinecke, *Jahrbuch für Geschichte des deutschen Ostens*, 1 (1952).
Hausen, Karin, ed. *Frauen suchen ihre Geschichte: Historische Studien zum 19. und 20. Jahrhundert* (Munich, 1983).

Heer, Friedrich. *Die Rolle des Buches in der Geistes- und Meinungsbildung* (Vienna, 1962).
Hegemann, Werner. *Das steinere Berlin* (Berlin, 1930; reprinted, Braunschweig, 1976).
Hermand, Jost. "Grandeur, High Life und innere Adel, 'Gründerzeit' im europäischen Kontext," *Monatshefte*, 69 (1977), 189–206.
Hervé, Florence, ed. *Geschichte der deutschen Frauenbewegung*, 3rd ed. (Cologne, 1987).
Herzfeld, Hans. "Berlin als Kaiserstadt und Reichshauptstadt," in *Das Hauptstadtproblem in der Geschichte, Jahrbuch für Geschichte des Deutschen Ostens*, I (Tübingen, 1952), 142–165.
Herzfeld, Hans, and Heinrich, Gerd, eds. *Berlin und die Provinz Brandenburg im 19. und 20. Jahrhundert* (Berlin, 1968).
Heyse, Paul. *Jugenderinnerungen und Bekenntnisse* (Berlin, 1900).
Hillman, Roger. *Zeitroman: The Novel and Society in Germany, 1830–1900* (Bern, 1983).
Hobsbawm, Eric, and Ranger, Terence, eds. *The Invention of Tradition* (Cambridge, 1983).
Hodeige, Fritz. "Die Stellung von Dichter und Buch in der Gesellschaft: Eine literarsoziologische Untersuchung," *Archiv für Geschichte des Buchwesens*, 1 (1956–1958), 141–170.
Hölscher, Lucian. *Weltgericht oder Revolution: Protestantische und sozialistische Zukunftsvorstellungen im deutschen Kaiserreich* (Stuttgart, 1989).
Hofmann, Walter. *Die Lektüre der Frau: Ein Beitrag zur Leserkunde und zur Leserführung* (Leipzig, 1931).
Hohendahl, Peter Uwe. *Building a National Literature: The Case of Germany, 1830–1870*, translated by Renate Baron Franciscono (Ithaca, N.Y., 1989).
———. "Bürgerliche Literaturgeschichte und nationale Identität: Bilder vom deutschen Sonderweg," in Jürgen Kocka, ed., *Bürgertum im 19. Jahrhundert: Deutschland im europäischen Vergleich* (Munich, 1988), III, 200–231.
———, ed. *Sozialgeschichte und Wirkungsästhetik* (Frankfurt am Main, 1974).
Hohendahl, Peter Uwe, and Lützeler, Paul Michael, eds., *Legitimationskrisen des deutschen Adels, 1200–1900* (Stuttgart, 1979).
Holborn, Hajo. *A History of Modern Germany: 1840–1945* (New York, 1969).
Hollinger, David A. "The Return of the Prodigal: The Persistence of Historical Knowing," *American Historical Review*, 94, 3 (June 1989), 610–621.
Hübener, Erhard. *Die deutsche Wirtschaftskrise von 1873, Rechts- und Staatswissenschaftliche Studien*, 30 (Berlin, 1905).
Institut für Zeitgeschichte. *Deutscher Sonderweg—Mythos oder Realität?* (Munich, 1982).
Jäger, Georg, and Schönert, Jörg, eds. *Die Leihbibliothek als Institution des literarischen lebens im 18. und 19. Jahrhundert: Organisationsformen, Bestände und Publikum* (Hamburg, 1980).
James, Harold. *A German Identity: 1770–1990* (New York, 1989).
Jaye, Michael, and Watts, Ann Chalmers, eds. *Literature and the Urban Experience: Essays on the City and Literature* (New Brunswick, N.J., 1981).
Jelavich, Peter. *Munich and Theatrical Modernism: Politics, Playwriting, and Performance, 1890–1914* (Cambridge, Mass., 1985).
Joeres, Ruth-Ellen B., and Maynes, Mary Jo, eds. *German Women in the Eighteenth and Nineteenth Centuries: A Social and Literary History* (Bloomington, Ind., 1986).
Just, Klaus Günther. *Von der Gründerzeit bis zur Gegenwart: Geschichte der deutschen Literatur seit 1871* (Bern, 1973).
Kafitz, Dieter, ed. *Dekadenz in Deutschland: Beiträge zur Erforschung der Romanliteratur um die Jahrhundertwende* (Frankfurt am Main, 1987).
Kaiser, Nancy A. *Social Integration and Narrative Structure: Patterns of Realism in Auerbach, Freytag, Fontane, and Raabe* (New York, 1986).
Kastan, Isidor. *Berlin wie es war* (Berlin, 1919).

Kavanagh, R. J. "Portrait of the Artist as a Young German: Karl Gutzkow's Political Attitudes and 1848," in Francis Barker, et al., *1848: The Sociology of Literature* (Essex, 1978).
Keil, Günther. *Max Kretzer: A Study in German Naturalism* (New York, 1966).
Kelly, Alfred. *The Descent of Darwin: The Popularization of Darwinism in Germany, 1860–1914* (Chapel Hill, 1981).
Kiaulehn, Walter. *Berlin: Schicksal einer Weltstadt* (Munich, 1958).
Kiernan, V. G. *The Duel in European History: Honour and the Reign of Aristocracy* (Oxford, 1988).
Klemperer, Victor. *Die Zeitromane Friedrich Spielhagens und ihre Wurzeln* (Weimar, 1913).
Kloss, Julius Erich. *Max Kretzer: Eine Studie zur neueren Literatur* (Leipzig, 1905).
Klotz, Volker. *Die erzählte Stadt: Ein Sujet als Herausforderung des Romans von Lesage bis Döblin* (Munich, 1969).
Knilli, Friedrich, and Nerlich, Michael, eds. *Medium Metropole: Berlin, Paris, New York* (Heidelberg, 1986).
Kocka, Jürgen, ed. *Bürger und Bürgerlichkeit im 19. Jahrhundert* (Göttingen, 1987).
———, ed. *Bürgertum im 19. Jahrhundert: Deutschland im europäischen Vergleich*, 3 vols. (Munich, 1988).
Kohn, Hans. *The Mind of Germany: The Education of a Nation* (New York, 1960).
Krausnick, Michail. *Paul Heyse und der Münchener Dichterkreis* (Bonn, 1974).
Kreuzer, Helmut. *Die Bohème: Beiträge zu ihrer Beschreibung* (Stuttgart, 1968).
———, ed. *Gestaltungsgeschichte und Gesellschaftsgeschichte*, Festschrift for Fritz Martini (Stuttgart, 1969).
Krieger, Leonard. *The German Idea of Freedom: History of a Political Tradition* (Boston, 1957).
Krummel, Richard Frank, ed. *Nietzsche und der deutsche Geist*, Vol. II: *Ausbreitung und Wirkung des nietzscheschen Werkes im deutschen Sprachraum vom Todesjahr bis zum Ende des Weltkrieges* (Berlin, 1983).
Kübler, Gunhild. *Die soziale Aufsteigerin: Wandlungen einer geschlechtsspezifischen Rollenzuschreibung im deutschen Roman, 1870–1900* (Bonn, 1982).
Kummer, Friedrich. *Deutsche Literaturgeschichte des 19. und 20. Jahrhundert nach Generationen dargestellt*, 2 vols. (Dresden, 1922).
LaCapra, Dominick. *History and Criticism* (Ithaca, N.Y., 1985).
Lange, Annemarie. *Berlin zur Zeit Bebels und Bismarcks: Zwischen Reichsgründung und Jahrhundertwende* (Berlin, 1972).
———. *Das wilhelminische Berlin: Zwischen Jahrhundertwende und Revolution* (Berlin, 1967).
Langewiesche, Dieter, ed. *Liberalismus im 19. Jahrhundert: Deutschland im europäischen Vergleich* (Göttingen, 1988).
Langland, Elizabeth. *Society in the Novel* (Chapel Hill, N.C., 1984).
Larkin, Maurice. *Man and Society in Nineteenth-Century Realism: Determinism and Literature* (London, 1977).
LaVopa, Anthony J. "The Politics of Enlightenment: Friedrich Gedike and German Professional Ideology," *Journal of Modern History*, 62 (March 1990), 34–56.
Lees, Andrew. *Cities Perceived: Urban Society in European and American Thought, 1820–1940* (New York, 1985).
———. "The Civic Pride of the German Middle Classes, 1890–1918," in Jack R. Dukes and Joachim Remak, eds., *Another Germany: A Reconsideration of the Imperial Era* (Boulder, Colo., 1988), 41–59.
———. "Debates about the Big City in Germany, 1890–1914," *Societas* (Winter 1975), 31–47.
Levesque, Paul. "*Jahrhundertwende, Fin de Siècle*, Wilhelminian Era: Re-examining

German Literary Culture 1871–1918," *German Studies Review*, 13, 1 (February 1990), 9–25.
Levine, George. *Darwin and the Novelists: Patterns of Science in Victorian Fiction* (Cambridge, Mass., 1988).
Leyden, Friedrich. "Berlin als Beispiel einer wurzellosen Großstadt," *Zeitschrift für Geopolitik*, 10, 3 (1933), 175–188.
Lidtke, Vernon. *The Alternative Culture: Socialist Labor in Imperial Germany* (New York, 1985).
———. "Naturalism and Socialism in Germany," *American Historical Review*, 79, 1 (February 1974), 14–37.
———. *The Outlawed Party: Social Democracy in Germany, 1878–1890* (Princeton, 1966).
Lienhard, Fritz. *Die Vorherrschaft Berlins: Litterarische Anregungen* (Leipzig, 1900).
Little, David Bruce. *The Parvenu in the Berlin Novel, 1871–1918* (Dissertation, Madison, Wisc., 1977).
Loewenstein, Bedrich. *Der Entwurf der Moderne: Vom Geist der bürgerlichen Gesellschaft* (Essen, 1987).
Löwenthal, Leo. *Erzählkunst und Gesellschaft: Die Gesellschaftsproblematik in der deutsche Literatur des 19. Jahrhunderts* (Neuwied in Berlin, 1971).
Loster-Schneider, Gudrun. *Der Erzähler Fontane: Seine politischen Positionen in den Jahren 1864–1898 und ihre ästhetische Vermittlung* (Tübingen, 1986).
McFarlane, James. "Berlin and the Rise of Modernism," in Malcolm Bradbury et al., eds., *Modernism, 1890–1930* (London, 1978).
Maenner, Ludwig. *Karl Gutzkow und der demokratische Gedanke* (Munich, 1921).
Mann, Golo. *Deutsche Geschichte des 19. und 20. Jahrhunderts* (1958, Hamburg, 1969).
Marris, Peter. *Loss and Change* (New York, 1974).
Martini, Fritz. *Deutsche Literatur im bürgerlichen Realismus, 1848–1898*, 4th ed. (Stuttgart, 1981).
Masur, Gerhard. *Imperial Berlin* (New York, 1970).
Mauthner, Fritz. *Prager Jugendjahre* (Frankfurt am Main, 1969).
———. *Von Keller zu Zola: Kritische Aufsätze* (Berlin, 1887).
Mayer, Arno J. *The Persistence of the Old Regime: Europe to the Great War* (New York, 1981).
Meckseper, Cord, and Schraut, Elisabeth. *Die Stadt in der Literatur* (Göttingen, 1983).
Mehring, Franz. *Die Geschichte der Sozialdemokratie*, Vol. II (Berlin, 1960).
Mensch, Ella. *Die Frau in der modernen Literatur* (Berlin, 1898).
Merbach, Paul Alfred. "Der Berliner Roman: Eine Skizze seiner Entwicklung," *Groß Berliner Kalender* (Berlin, 1913), 190–198.
Miles, David H. "Literary Sociology: Some Introductory Notes," *German Quarterly*, 48, 1 (1975), 1–35.
Modrow, Hans O. *Berlin 1900: Querschnitt durch die Entwicklung einer Stadt um die Jahrhundertwende* (Berlin, 1936).
Moe, Vera Ingunn. *Deutscher Naturalismus und ausländische Literatur: Zur Rezeption der Werke von Zola, Ibsen und Dostojewski durch die deutsche naturalistische Bewegung (1880–1895)* (Frankfurt am Main, 1983).
Monteith, Moira, ed. *Women's Writing: A Challenge to Theory* (New York, 1986).
Mork, Gordon R. "The Prussian Railway Scandal of 1873: Economics and Politics in the German Empire," *European Studies Review*, I, 1 (1971), 35–48.
Moses, Stéphane, and Schöne, Albrecht, eds. *Juden in der deutschen Literatur: Ein deutsch-israelisches Symposion* (Frankfurt am Main, 1986).
Mosse, George L. *German Jews beyond Judaism* (Bloomington, Ind., 1985).
———. *Germans and Jews* (New York, 1970).

———. *The Nationalization of the Masses: Political Symbolism and Mass Movements in Germany from the Napoleonic Wars through the Third Reich* (New York, 1975).
Mosse, Werner E. "Adel und Bürgertum im Europa des 19. Jahrhunderts: Eine vergleichende Betrachtung," in Jürgen Kocka, ed., *Bürgertum im 19. Jahrhundert* (Munich, 1988), II, 276–314.
———, ed. *Juden im wilhelminischen Deutschland, 1890–1914* (Tübingen, 1976).
Müller, Karla. *Schloßgeschichten: Eine Studie zum Romanwerk Theodor Fontanes* (Munich, 1986).
Müller-Jabusch, Maximilian. *So waren die Gründerjahre* (Düsseldorf, 1957).
Müller-Seidel, Walter. *Theodor Fontane: Soziale Romankunst in Deutschland* (Stuttgart, 1975).
Münch, Richard. *Die Kultur der Moderne*, Vol. II: *Ihre Entwicklung in Frankreich und Deutschland* (Frankfurt am Main, 1986).
Muranga, Manuel J. K. *Großstadtelend in der deutschen Lyrik zwischen Arno Holz und Johannes R. Becher* (Frankfurt am Main, 1987).
Neumann, Bernd. "Friedrich Spielhagen: *Sturmflut* (1877): Die 'Gründerjahre' als die 'Signatur des Jahrhunderts'," in Horst Denkler, ed., *Romane und Erzählungen des Bürgerlichen Realismus: Neue Interpretationen* (Stuttgart, 1980), 260–273.
Neurohr, Jean. *Der Mythos vom 3. Reich* (Stuttgart, 1957).
Nichols, J. Alden. *The Year of the Three Kaisers: Bismarck and the German Succession, 1887–1888* (Urbana, Ill., 1987).
Niemann, Hans-Werner. *Das Bild des industriellen Unternehmers in deutschen Romanen der Jahre 1890 bis 1945* (Berlin, 1982).
Ostwald, Hans, ed. *Großstadt Dokumente* (Berlin/Leipzig, 1904ff).
Otto, Hans. *Gründerzeit: Aufbruch einer Nation* (Bonn, 1984).
Paret, Peter. *Art as History: Episodes in the Culture and Politics of Nineteenth-Century Germany* (Princeton, 1988).
———. *The Berlin Secession: Modernism and Its Enemies in Imperial Germany* (Cambridge, Mass., 1980).
Pascal, Roy. *From Naturalism to Expressionism. German Literature and Society, 1880–1918* (London, 1973).
Pfannschmidt, Martin. "Probleme der Weltstadt Berlin," in Joachim Schultze, ed., *Zum Problem der Weltstadt* (Berlin, 1959), 1–16.
Pickle, Linda Schelbitzki. "Self-Contradictions in the German Naturalists' View of Women's Emancipation," *German Quarterly*, 52 (1979), 442–456.
Pike, Burton. *The Image of the City in Modern Literature* (Princeton, 1981).
Plessner, Helmuth. *Die verspätete Nation: Über die politische Verfürhrbarkeit bürgerlichen Geistes* (Stuttgart,.1959).
Polácek, Josef. "Zum Thema der bürgerlich-individualistischen Revolte in der deutschen pseudosozialen Prosa: Hans Land, Felix Hollaender, John Henry Mackay," *Philologica Pragensia*, 7, 1 (1964), 1–14.
———. "Zur Problematik des deutschen Abkehrromans," *Philologica Pragensia*, 14, 1 (1971), 16–29.
Pulzer, Peter G. J. *The Rise of Political Anti-Semitism in Germany and Austria* (New York, 1964).
Ragins, Sanford. *Jewish Responses to Anti-Semitism in Germany, 1870–1914: A Study in the History of Ideas* (Cincinnati, 1980).
Rausch, Lotte. *Die Gestalt des Künstlers in der Dichtung des Naturalismus* (Dissertation, Gießen, 1931).
Reissner, Alexander. *Berlin, 1675–1945: The Rise and Fall of a Metropolis—A Panoramic View* (London, 1984).
Ribbe, Wolfgang, ed. *Geschichte Berlins*, 2 vols. (Munich, 1987).

Richter, Claus. *Leiden an der Gesellschaft: Von literarischem Liberalismus zum poetischen Realismus* (Kronberg, 1978).
Rodenberg, Julius. *Bilder aus dem Berliner Leben in einer Auswahl* (Berlin, 1892).
———. *Unter den Linden: Bilder aus dem Berliner Leben* (Berlin, 1888).
Röhl, John C. G. *Kaiser, Hof und Staat: Wilhelm II und die deutsche Politik* (Munich, 1987).
Roper, Katherine Larson. "Conrad Alberti's *Kampf ums Dasein*: The Writer in Imperial Berlin," *German Studies Review*, 7, 1 (February 1984), 65–88.
Rosenhaupt, Hans Wilhelm. *Der deutsche Dichter um die Jahrhundertwende und seine Abgelöstheit von der Gesellschaft* (Dissertation, Bern, 1939).
Rothfels, Hans, ed. *Berlin in Vergangenheit und Gegenwart* (Tübingen, 1961).
Rucktäschel, Annamaria, and Zimmermann, Hans Dieter, eds. *Trivialliteratur* (Munich, 1976).
Ruprecht, Erich, ed. *Literarische Manifeste der Jahrhundertwende: 1890–1910* (Stuttgart, 1970).
Sagarra, Eda. *A Social History of Germany, 1648–1914* (New York, 1977).
———. *Theodor Fontane: "Der Stechlin"* (Munich, 1986).
———. *Tradition and Revolution: German Literature and Society, 1830–1890* (New York, 1971).
Scheffler, Karl. *Berlin: Ein Stadtschicksal* (Berlin, 1910).
Schenda, Rudolf. *Die Lesestoffe der kleinen Leute: Studien zur populären Literatur im 19. und 20. Jahrhundert* (Munich, 1976).
———. *Volk ohne Buch: Studien zur Sozialgeschichte der populären Lesestoffe, 1770–1910* (Frankfurt am Main, 1970).
Scherpe, Klaus R., ed. *Die Unwirklichkeit der Städte: Großstadtdarstellungen zwischen Moderne und Postmoderne* (Reinbek bei Hamburg, 1988).
Scheuer, Helmut, ed. *Naturalismus: Bürgerliche Dichtung und soziales Engagement* (Stuttgart, 1974).
———. "Zur Christus-Figur in der Literatur um 1900," in Roger Bauer et al., eds., *Fin de Siècle: Zur Literatur und Kunst der Jahrhundertwende* (Frankfurt am Main, 1977).
Schmidt, Günther. *Die literarische Rezeption des Darwinismus: Das Problem der Vererbung bei Emile Zola und im Drama des deutschen Naturalismus* (Berlin, 1974).
Schmidt, Jochen. *Die Geschichte des Genie-Gedankens in der deutschen Literatur, Philosophie und Politik: 1750–1945*, Vol. II: *Von der Romantik bis zum Ende des Dritten Reichs* (Darmstadt, 1985).
Schoeps, Hans Joachim, ed. *Zeitgeist im Wandel: Das Wilhelminische Zeitalter* (Stuttgart, 1967).
Schorsch, Ismar. *Jewish Reactions to German Anti-Semitism 1870–1914* (New York, 1972).
Schumann, Willy. "Wo ist der Kaiser? Theodor Fontane über Kaiser Wilhelm II," *Monatshefte*, 71 (1979), 161–171.
Schutte, Jürgen, und Sprengel, Peter, eds., *Die Berliner Moderne, 1885–1914* (Stuttgart, 1987).
Seed, John, and Wolff, Janet, eds. *The Culture of Capital: Art, Power and the Nineteenth-Century Middle Class* (Manchester, 1988).
Sennett, Richard, ed. *Classic Essays on the Culture of Cities* (New York, 1969).
Sharpe, William, and Wallock, Leonard, eds. *Visions of the Modern City: Essays in History, Art, and Literature* (New York, 1983).
Sheehan, James J. *German Liberalism in the Nineteenth Century* (Chicago, 1978).
———, ed. *Imperial Germany* (New York, 1976).
Showalter, Dennis E. "Army, State and Society in Germany, 1871–1914," in Jack R. Dukes and Joachim Remak, eds., *Another Germany: A Reconstruction of the Imperial Era* (Boulder, Colo., 1988).

Sichelschmidt, Gustav. *So schrieb Berlin: Eine Geschichte der Berliner Literatur* (Berlin, 1971).
Simmel, Georg. "Die Großstadt und das Geistesleben," in *Vorträge und Aufsätze zur Städteausstellung* (Dresden, 1903), 188–206.
———. "The Metropolis and Mental Life," in Richard Sennett, ed., *Classic Essays on the Culture of Cities* (New York, 1969), 47–60.
———. *The Sociology of Georg Simmel*, translated and edited by Kurt Wolff (Glencoe, Ill., 1950).
Spielhagen, Friedrich. *Beiträge zur Theorie und Technik des Romans* (Leipzig, 1883; reprinted, Göttingen, 1967).
———. *Finder und Erfinder: Erinnerungen aus meinem Leben*, I (Leipzig, 1890).
———. "Wie ich zu dem Helden von 'Sturmflut' kam," *Neue Beiträge zur Theorie und Technik der Epik und Dramatik* (Leipzig, 1898), 208–224.
Spiero, Heinrich. *Julius Rodenberg. Sein Leben und seine Werke* (Berlin, 1921).
———. *Das poetische Berlin: Alt-Berlin* (Munich, 1911).
———. *Das poetische Berlin: Neu-Berlin* (Munich, 1912).
———. "Vom Berliner Roman: Rückblicke und Ausblicke," *Germanisch-romanische Monatsschrift*, 6 (1914), 212–219.
Spranger, Eduard. *Berliner Geist* (Tübingen, 1966).
Springer, Robert. *Berlin: Die deutsche Kaiserstadt* (Darmstadt, 1878).
———. *Berlin wird Weltstadt* (Berlin, 1868).
Squier, Susan Merrill. "Literature and the City: A Checklist of Relevant Secondary Works," in Susan Merrill Squier, ed., *Women Writers and the City: Essays in Feminist Literary Criticism* (Knoxville, Tenn., 1984).
Stanton, Domna. *The Aristocrat as Art: A Study of the Honnête Homme and the Dandy in Seventeenth- and Nineteenth-Century French Literature* (New York, 1980).
Stark, Gary D. "The Censorship of Literary Naturalism, 1885–1895: Prussia and Saxony," *Central European History*, 18, 3/4 (September/December 1985), 326–343.
———. ed. *Essays on Culture and Society in Modern Germany* (Arlington, Tex., 1982).
Stern, Fritz. *Dreams and Delusions: The Drama of German History* (New York, 1987).
———. *The Politics of Cultural Despair: A Study in the Rise of the Germanic Ideology* (Berkeley, 1961).
Stern, Joseph Peter. *On Realism* (London, 1973).
Strieder, Agnes. *"Die Gesellschaft": Eine kritische Auseinandersetzung mit der Zeitschrift der frühen Naturalisten* (Frankfurt am Main, 1985).
Striedeck, Werner F. "Wolfgang Kirchbach and the 'Jüngstdeutschen,'" *Germanic Review*, 22 (February 1947), 42–54.
Stürmer, Michael. *Das ruhelose Reich: Deutschland, 1866–1918* (Berlin, 1983).
Stühler, Friedbert. *Totale Welten: Der moderne deutsche Großstadtroman* (Regensburg, 1989).
Tal, Uriel. *Christians and Jews in Germany: Religion, Politics, and Ideology in the Second Reich, 1870–1914*, translated by Noah Jonathan Jacobs (Ithaca, N.Y., 1975).
Thienel, Ingrid. *Städtewachstum im Industrialisierungsprozeß des 19. Jahrhunderts: Das Berliner Beispiel* (Berlin, 1973).
Timms, Edward, ed. *Unreal City: Urban Experience in Modern European Literature and Art* (New York, 1985).
Unseld, Siegfried. *The Author and His Publisher*, translated by Hunter Hannum and Hildegarde Hannum (Chicago, 1980).
Urban, Richard. *Die literarische Gegenwart: 20 Jahre deutschen Schrifttums, 1888–1908* (Leipzig, 1908).
Veblen, Thorstein. *The Theory of the Leisure Class* (1899; reprinted, Boston, 1973).
Vizetelly, Henry. *Berlin under the New Empire*, 2 vols. (London, 1879).

Vodosek, Peter, ed. *Auf dem Weg zur öffentlichen Literaturversorgung: Quellen und Texte zur Geschichte der Volksbibliotheken in der zweiten Hälfte des 19. Jahrhunderts* (Wiesbaden, 1985).
Vondung, Klaus, ed. *Das wilhelminische Bildungsbürgertum: Zur Sozialgeschichte seiner Ideen* (Göttingen, 1976).
Wechsler, Ernst. *Berliner Autoren* (Leipzig, 1891).
Wehler, Hans-Ulrich. *Das Deutsche Kaiserreich, 1871–1918* (Göttingen, 1973).
———. *Modernisierungstheorie und Geschichte* (Göttingen, 1975).
———. "Sozialdarwinismus im expandierende Industriestaat," Imanuel Geiss and Bernd Jürgen Wendt, eds., *Deutschland in der Weltpolitik des 19. und 20. Jahrhunderts* (Düsseldorf, 1973), 133–142.
Weidenfeld, Werner, ed. *Die Identität der Deutschen* (Munich, 1983).
Weisstein, Ulrich. "Satire und Parodie in Heinrich Manns Roman *Der Untertan*," in Klaus Matthias, ed. *Heinrich Mann, 1871–1971: Bestandsaufnahme und Untersuchung. Ergebnisse der Heinrich-Mann-Tagung in Lübeck* (Munich, 1973), 125–146.
White, Hayden. *The Content of the Form: Narrative Discourse and Historical Representation* (Baltimore, 1987).
Winkler, H. A. "Bürgerliche Emanzipation und Nationalerziehung," in H. Böhme, ed. *Probleme der Reichsgründungszeit, 1868–1879* (Cologne, 1968).
Winter, Lorenz. *Heinrich Mann and His Public: A Socioliterary Study of the Relationship between an Author and His Public*, translated by John Gorman (Coral Gables, Fla., 1970).
Wittmann, Reinhard, and Hack, Bertold, eds. *Buchhandel und Literatur. Festschrift für Herbert G. Göpfert zum 75. Geburtstag* (Wiesbaden, 1982).
Wittmann, Reinhard. *Buchmarkt und Lektüre im 18. und 19. Jahrhundert: Beiträge zum literarischen Leben, 1750–1880* (Tübingen, 1982).
Wolf, Eva. *Der Schriftsteller im Querschnitt: Außenseiter der Gesellschaft um 1900?: Ein systematischer Vergleich von Prosatexten* (Munich, 1978).
Wruck, Peter, ed. *Literarisches Leben in Berlin, 1871–1933*, 2 vols. (Berlin, 1987).
Ziegler, Klaus. "Die Berliner Gesellschaft und die Literatur," in Hans Rothfels, *Berlin in Vergangenheit und Gegenwart* (Tübingen, 1961).
Ziolkowski, Theodore. *Fictional Transfigurations of Jesus* (Princeton, 1972).

# Index

Ablösung vor! See under Alberti, Conrad
Action: versus electoral politics, 121; novelists' ambivalence toward, 26, 33–34, 59, 115; literature as a form of, 121; working-class, 33–34, 218, 224–25
Acts (New Testament), 76, 79, 80
Adultery, 167, 168, 171–72
Ahasverus, 149
Alberti, Conrad (pseud. of Konrad Sittenfeld), 2, 51, 85, 104, 135, 148, 164–65; Ablösung vor!, 159–60, 218–19; Die Alten und die Jungen, 86–87, 100–104, 158, 218, 229, 238, 239, 240; appeals for moral transformation, 87; Kampf ums Dasein cycle, 98–99; "Majestätsbeleidigung," 42, 51–52, 86, 87; Plebs, 51; Schröter & Co., 158–59, 188; Wer ist der Stärkere?, 99–100, 188, 189–90, 241
Alcohol: and the artist, 114, 137–38; as power, 227–28; and the working class, 113
Alexanderplatz, 51
Alexis, Willibald, 24
Alienation, 135, 139, 141; Jewish, 152, 154
Alsace, 45, 46
Alten und die Jungen, Die. See under Alberti, Conrad
Ambition, social, 211–14; of bourgeoisie, 31–32, 100, 203, 206–9; as hallmark of Gründerjahre, 67
Anti-modernism, and criticism of Berlin, 136, 215
Anti-Semitism: and Christian Socialism, 129; experience of, 154–57, 159; in Imperial Germany, 49, 147, 151–53; and liberalism, 81
Anti-Socialist Law, 76, 84, 117–23; end of, 123, 127, 218
Apocalypse, imagery of, 64, 83, 116, 136, 139, 140, 231–32
Apprenticeship, artistic, 102
Aristocracy, 26, 185–97, 220–23; criticism of, 29–30, 80, 190, 191–92, 242; economic straits of, 185, 191–95, 242; power of, 29–30, 185, 222, 231, 239; reformers in, 30–31, 80, 120, 221; spiritual, 29, 43; Verbürgerlichung of, 194, 195, 242
Artisan class, 116. See also Kleinbürger
Artist: as cultural combatant, 91–105; economic struggles of, 93–94; as messiah, 77, 104; woman as, 173–79. See also Novelists
Assimilation, Jewish, 147, 149, 150–51, 158–59
Athens on the Spree, 23, 56, 57, 200, 206, 239
Authority, systems of, 226–28

Ball, as literary convention, 63, 190, 203
Bebel, August, 118, 223
Begas, Reinhold, 206
Begierde. See under Marès, Jolanthe
Bereavement, as social model, 41. See also Loss and change
Bergpredigt, Die. See under Kretzer, Max
Berlin: under Anti-Socialist Law, 119–20; as capital of Germany, 24, 40, 47–49, 127–28; as capital of Prussia, 21, 24; as center of German struggle, 80; as center of modernity, 1, 3, 23, 237, 239; as city of immigrants, 44–46, 103, 158, 215; compared to other cities, 27, 47–48, 208; conflicting identities of, 23, 41, 48, 50; districts of, 21, 23, 40–41; history, 21–23, 146–47; and Hohenzollerns, 21; imagery, 4, 43, 57, 238–39; influence on German identity, 34–35, 219, 220, 225, 229, 240; landmarks, 4, 21, 40–41, 133, 225; as liberation, 102, 128, 166, 168, 239; old, disappearance of, 50, 51, 116, 193; old, mythology of, 48, 58–59; as parvenu city, 103, 200, 215, 239–40; as reflector of mood, 103–4, 133, 140, 171, 225, 239; secularism of, 130,

260

133, 146; as small town, 23, 75, 207–8, 239; as symbol of sickness, 103, 114, 136, 171; tradition of toleration, 49, 146; transformation of, 40, 41, 47, 49, 239; as *Weltstadt*, 40–52, 127; westward expansion of, 21, 200, 202. *See also* Athens on the Spree; Berlin W; individual districts and landmarks
Berlin novel: criteria for, 5, 24, 57, 220, 226; as historical source, 1, 4, 6, 16, 237–44; *Die Ritter vom Geiste* as prototype of, 7, 24–25
Berlin novelist: legacy of, 244; as proponent of modernity, 3. *See also* Novelists; Writer
Berlin W, 21, 179, 205, 210, 211, 213; society of, 202–4, 210, 211–15
Berliner, traits of, 22, 23, 49, 75, 206; the "real," 48–49; 58–59, 201
*Besitzbürgertum* (propertied middle class), 9, 55, 69, 203. *See also* Bourgeoisie
Betrayal: as literary theme, 93, 121–23; notions of Jewish, 156
*Betrogenen, Die. See under* Kretzer, Max
Biblical passages, in novels, 76, 82, 85, 121, 133, 139, 159
Bierbaum, Otto Julius, 137; *Stilpe*, 136–38, 243
*Bildung* (self-cultivation, education), 13, 55, 56, 203, 204, 210
*Bildungsbürgertum* (cultivated middle class), 9, 55, 69, 206
Bismarck: and aristocracy, 185; criticism of, 62, 80, 82, 103; fictional parallel to, 35; idealization of, 46, 75, 218, 223–24; as populist leader, 226; resignation of, 127, 218; in retirement, 223, 226; as revolutionary, 45–46, 74; successor to, 224–26; as unifier of Germany, 44, 46, 50, 73, 75, 78, 83
*Bismarcks Nachfolger. See under* Zolling, Theophil
Bleibtreu, Karl: *Die Auskunftei*, 16, 191; *Geist*, 192, 200
Bloch, Marc, 6
Bohemian life, 93; 137–38, 141
Böhlau, Helene, 88
Bölsche, Wilhelm, 97, 132–33, 135; *Die Mittagsgöttin*, 132–35, 239; *Die naturwissenschaftlichen Grundlagen der Poesie*, 97–98, 104
Book trade, controversies within, 10–11
Books: purchase of as patriotic duty, 12; retail cost of, 10, 13
Borsig machine works, 32, 41
Bourgeoisie, 31–32, 206, 207, 242
Brandenburg, Count Friedrich Wilhelm von, 44
Brandenburger Tor (Brandenburg Gate), 4, 21, 40, 104, 133, 186, 196; William II at, 87, 218, 228–29
Büchner, Ludwig, 139
Buddha, 140
*Bürger*, idealization of, 31, 60, 64, 67, 116, 195, 242
*Bürgerstolz* (middle-class pride), 61
*Bürgertum*: alienation from, 140; ambivalence toward, 141; versus bourgeoisie, 31–32; political passivity of, 59, 75–76

Cabaret, 137
Campaign, electoral, 221–22
Capitalism: and the aristocracy, 193; criticism of, 28, 65, 83, 112–13, 116–17, 241; and nationhood, 55–56, 69
Caprivi, General Leo Count von, 218, 224
Careerism, 67, 74, 212–13
Censorship, 10–11, 25, 122
Charlottenburg, 21, 57–58, 60
Christian Socialism, 129
Christianity: criticism of, 28, 128–30; early, as revolutionary, 79, 80, 122; early, and socialism, 115, 121, 130, 131, 134
City novel: in German culture, 24; history of, 23
Classicism, German, 78, 138; satirized, 137; and science, 98
Colportage novel, 5, 14, 113, 114
Commercialism: artist's dislike of, 66, 93; and novel-writing, 9
Confusion: of ideas, 28, 78, 79, 133; political, 223
Connections, made in novels, 3–4, 49–50, 56, 57, 91, 226, 237, 240
Conrad, Michael Georg, 97
Conradi, Hermann, 91
Conservatism, 50, 83–84, 232
Constitution, 74, 185

Contentment, middle-class, 201–2
Conversion, as goal for Jews, 149, 151
Copyright Law of 1867, 10
Crash of 1873, 52, 56, 63–67, 218, 240
Cultural revolution: as hallmark of nationhood, 1, 82, 98, 104; failure of expectations for, 243

Darwin, Charles, 94–95, 139
Darwinism, 91, 94–95, 157, 241. *See also* Struggle for survival
Deception, social, as hallmark of Berlin, 203
Delusion: in colportage novels, 113; as German trait, 101, 228, 233. *See also* Self-deception
Democracy: ambivalence toward, 29, 75; as ideal, 82
Democratization, 222, 243; and the aristocracy, 188, 189; through novels, 190; political education, 223; of reading, 13
*Deutsche Rundschau* (cultural periodical), 47
Dialect, Berlin, 49, 50, 214
*Dichter* (writer or poet), versus *Schriftsteller*, 8, 11
*Dilettanten des Lebens. See under* Viebig, Clara
Discourse, social, in novels, 2, 5, 8, 237
Disease, mental. *See* Madness
Disunity, as German trait, 103, 105, 225
Divorce, 168, 172
Do-nothingness: by aristocracy, 191; by parvenu, 212
Dorotheenstadt (district), 21
Dorotheenstraße, 212
Dostoyevsky, Feodor, 24
*Drei Weiber. See under* Kretzer, Max
*Dritte Reich, Das. See under* Schlaf, Johannes
Duel, 152, 187–88, 228, 242

Education: German, 138, 226–27; of girls, 167; and the working class, 113–15
*Effi Briest. See under* Fontane, Theodor
*Egoismus*, dangers of, 65, 96, 100, 177–78
Electoral politics, 74, 230, 221–22, 232–33, 243; antipathy toward, 31; and the working class, 120–21

Electric streetlight, as symbol of modernity, 130, 133
*Ellen von der Weiden. See under* Reuter, Gabriele
Emancipation, Jewish, 146, 152–53
Embourgeoisement. *See Verbürgerlichung*
Engagement, social: abandonment of, 136, 140, 201; ambivalence toward, 68–69, 244; as literary ideal, 82, 91, 102, 130, 135; and women, 180
England, as epitome of modernity, 222
Enlightenment: Berlin, 22; Prussian, 222; German, 78, 146, 147
Equality, as social ideal, 129
*Es lebe die Kunst! See under* Viebig, Clara
Escarpit, Robert, 15
Establishment: academic, 99, 207; cultural, 100, 175, 212–13, 243
Evolution, notions of, 91
Exodus (Old Testament), 82, 85
Exploitation, of workers, 112
*Eysen. See under* Ompteda, Georg Freiherr von

Faith, religious, 130–32
*Familie Buchholz, Die. See under* Stinde, Julius
Father, authoritarian, 227
Fechner, Gustav Theodor, 139
Feminism, in Imperial Germany, 169
Feudalization, 185–86, 195, 197
Fichte, Johann Gottlieb, 22
Fischer, Hans R., 118
Fontane, Theodor, 5, 219–20; on the Berliner, 22; *Effi Briest*, 165–69; *Frau Jenny Treibel*, 206–9; *Irrungen, Wirrungen*, 11, 194; *Die Poggenpuhls*, 194; *Der Stechlin*, 219, 220–23, 240
Forms, literary, 7
48er. *See* Revolution of 1848, participants in
Founders' era. *See Gründerjahre*
France: conflicts with, 45, 231, 233; cultural rivalry with, 99; indemnity from, 56, 63, 65
Franco-Prussian war, 46–47, 78, 150
Frankfurt, Berlin compared to, 48
Frankfurt Assembly, 62, 77, 83
Frankfurter Tor, 41
Fraternity, student, 153, 227–28
*Frau Jenny Treibel. See under* Fontane, Theodor

Frederick II, 22, 49, 73, 221, 222
Frederick III, 86, 102
Frederick William I, 222
Frederick William III, 58
Frederick William IV, 23, 26, 30
Freedom, spiritual: as German ideal, 3, 55, 77; for women, 166. *See also* Innerlichkeit
French Revolution, 4 August 1789, 152
Freytag, Gustav, *Soll und Haben*, 2, 158
Friedrichstadt (district), 21
Friedrichstraße, 41, 114; station, 133, 135

Gedike, Friedrich, 22
Generation: of 1813, 86; of 1848, 86–87, 100–101, 229, 231, 232; of 1870, 86, 101–4, 116, 138–39, 229
Generations: changing of, 219, 222–23, 226; conflict of, 94, 100–104, 219; literary, 7, 85, 92, 104, 219–20
Genius: ambivalence toward, 102; artistic, 100, 101; and madness, 101, 123; and struggle for survival, 97, 104
Gerichtstraße, 112
German culture, subverted by French influence, 103
German identity. *See* Identity, German
German revolution: Bismarck as fulfillment of, 35, 46, 74; cultural, 102, 104, 243; fictional search for, 3, 26, 79, 80, 85, 136, 233; as spiritual, 29, 243. *See also* Unfinished revolution
Germans: as lacking political education, 223, 225–26, 230; parallels to Jews, 50
Germany: as aimless, 79; anti-Semitism as danger for, 148, 153, 156, 157; aristocratic dominance in, 197; Berlin as summation of, 24, 83, 103, 200, 209, 214, 219, 235, 240; compared to England and France, 81; as imperious, 82–83, 87, 99, 226–33, 238, 240; industrialization of, 32, 241; as a pariah nation, 50; as parvenu, 240; as peaceful, 75; and Prussia, 44, 45; spiritual victory of, hopes for, 104, 218, 238, 243; triumphant path of, 44, 48, 66, 79, 85–86; unique path of, 23, 237–38
*Gesellschaft, Die* (naturalist periodical), 14; influence of, 97

*Gesicht Christi, Das. See under* Kretzer, Max
*Gewerbefreiheit* (free enterprise), in publishing industry, 10
Glagau, Otto, 147–48
*Glänzendes Elend. See under* Hopfen, Hans
Goethe, Johann Wolfgang von, 22, 78, 98, 138, 155, 202; *Die Leiden des jungen Werthers*, 153, 156
*Grandidiers, Die. See under* Rodenberg, Julius
Grass, Günter, 244
Great Elector, 44, 45, 96, 146
*Gründerjahre*, 56, 60–69, 109; and anti-Semitism, 148; imagery of, 151; as moral judgment, 211. *See also* Crash of 1873; Mentality, *Gründer*-
Grunewald (district), 214
Gutzkow, Karl, 25–26, 104, 135; *Die neuen Serapionsbrüder*, 65–67, 74–75, 92, 95, 109; *Die Ritter vom Geiste*, 7, 25–35, 109, 165, 200, 238, 239
Gymnasium, the German, 137

Haeckel, Ernst, 95, 139
Hallesches Tor, 41
Hamburg, Berlin compared to, 208
Hansa district, 186, 193, 196, 205
Hanstein, Adalbert von, 135; *Zwei Welten*, 191
Harmony: as creation of women, 172, 178, 179–80; as ideal of individuality, 59–60, 101; social, as German value, 65, 66, 156, 240
Hart, Heinrich, 85
Hart, Julius, 85; "Kein Ideal," 95–96
Hegelianism, as world-view, 121, 122
Herder, Johann Gottfried, 34
Hesekiel, Georg, 42
Hesekiel, Ludovika, *Von Brandenburg zu Bismarck*, 42–44
*Hetzjagd, Der. See under* Zobeltitz, Fedor von
Heyse, Paul, 104, 137; *Kinder der Welt*, 56–60, 67, 92, 127, 239; serialization of *Kinder der Welt*, 11, 57
Hoffmann, E. T. A., 66
Hofstetten, Johann Baptist von, 118
Hohenlohe-Schillingsfürst, Prince Chlodwig zu, 218, 223
Hohenzollern dynasty: imagery of, 86;

popular loyalty to, 51, 86; portrayed by novelists, 240; as Prussian salvation, 43
Hollaender, Felix, *Jesus und Judas*, 121–23
Holz, Arno, 98
Homer, imagery of, 65, 84
Honor, affair of. *See* Duel
Honor: aristocratic, 187–88, 192; as German value, 228
Hopfen, Hans: *Glänzendes Elend*, 193–94, 195; *Der Väter zweie*, 188
Huguenots, in Berlin, 44
Human nature, optimistic versus pessimistic notions of, 27–28
Humiliation, as German experience, 48, 50
Hurrah patriotism, 211, 214, 215, 230–31
Husband: as feminist, 176; as teacher of wife, 167, 171

Ibsen, Henrik, 96, 137
Idealism, German, 78; versus science, 96, 97–98
Ideas, clutter of, as characteristic of 19th century, 28
Identity, German: Berlin's influence on, 219; crisis of, 69; formation of, 3, 4, 6, 16, 46, 237; longing for, 68; and middle-class crisis, 69; and modernity, 4, 244
Identity, Jewish, 159–60
Ideology, distrust of, 85, 88, 225
*Im alten Eisen. See under* Raabe, Wilhelm
*Im Schlaraffenland. See under* Mann, Heinrich
*Im Sturmwind des Sozialismus. See under* Kretzer, Max
Immigrants to Berlin: Germans, 45; Huguenots, 44; Jews, 49, 103, 158, 215
Implications, social, abandoned in novels, 59, 157, 160, 205, 237, 244
Independence, as goal of women, 178
Individuality: as middle-class ideal, 55, 237; Nietzschean, as an ideal, 127, 139–41; quest for by women, 180
Industrialization, 32, 93–94, 241
*Innerlichkeit* (inwardness), 3, 57, 136
Institutions, failure of novels to challenge, 68, 74, 115, 169, 186, 197, 243

Intrigues, court, 224

Jacobowski, Ludwig, 148, 156–57; *Werther der Jude*, 153–57
Jesuitism, 28
Jesus Christ: imagery of, 92, 131–32, 223; as prophet, 102, 123; social teachings of, 128–30, 131; as a true socialist, 115. *See also* Messiah, imagery of
*Jesus und Judas. See under* Hollaender, Felix
"Jewish question," 147, 156, 157–60
Jews, 146–60; conversion to Christianity, 149, 151; as "dissolute" influence in Germany, 149, 158; as German, 149–50, 152, 153, 154, 156, 158, 160; "good versus bad," 81, 147, 148, 150–51, 157, 158–59; as immigrants to Berlin, 49, 103, 158, 215; the "modern," 149–51, 153; parallels to Germans, 50; self-hatred of, 148
John (New Testament), 139
Joint stock companies, as negative image, 62, 67, 154, 213
Judas, image of, 122, 123
*Judenfrage. See* "Jewish question"

*Kampf ums Dasein. See* Struggle for survival
Kant, Immanuel, 34, 165
Kiaulehn, Walter, 21, 191
*Kinder der Welt. See under* Heyse, Paul
*Kinder des Reiches. See under* Kirchbach, Wolfgang
Kirchbach, Wolfgang, 42, 50–51; "Reichshauptstadt," in *Kinder des Reiches*, 48–50, 148, 237, 239
*Klatsch, Der. See under* Zolling, Theophil
*Kleinbürger*: idealized, 202; ruination of, 116–17
Klotz, Volker, 23
Knights, spiritual, 29, 134
Knights of St. John, 29
*Kolonialstadt*, Berlin as, 215
Köpenick (district), 23
Köpenickerstraße, 206
Koppenstraße, 203
Kretzer, Max, 5, 92–93, 104, 135; *Die beiden Genossen*, 115; *Die Bergpredigt*, 128–30, 135, 241; *Die Betrogenen*, 92, 104; compared to Zola, 111; *Drei Weiber*, 188, 190, 209–10; *Das Gesicht*

Christi, 130–32; Im Sturmwind des Sozialismus, 115–16; Meister Timpe, 116–17, 239; Der Millionenbauer, 191, 195, 210–11; Die Verkommenen, 111–15, 131, 239
Kreuzberg, 41, 43, 49, 140
Kreuzzeitung (conservative newspaper), 83
Kurfürstendamm, 214–15

Land, Hans, Der neue Gott, 118–21, 242
Landpartie (Berlin outing), 57–58, 207–8
Landsberger, Artur, Lu, die Kokotte, 188
Lasker, Eduard, 63
Lassalle, Ferdinand, 109, 121
Leberecht Hühnchen. See under Seidel, Heinrich
Leibniz, Gottfried von, 22
Leihbibliotheken. See Library, lending
Leipzigerstraße, 40, 113, 133, 140
Leisure, aristocratic, 189. See also Do-nothingness
Lese majesty (Majestätsbeleidigung), 11, 51–52
Lessing, Gotthold Ephraim, 22, 78, 146, 160; Nathan der Weise, 22
Liberalism, 77, 81, 88, 232
Library, lending (Leihbibliotheken), 11–12
Lindau, Paul: Spitzen, 186–87, 239; Der Zug nach dem Westen, 5, 186, 200, 202–5
Literacy, 13
Literature, national: as cultural ideal, 10; healthiness in, 97–98
Loss and change, 48, 50
Loyalties: dynastic, 51, 86; particularist, 45; Prussian, 78, 221

Madness, images of, 122–23, 127, 187
"Majestätsbeleidigung." See under Alberti, Conrad
Manchesterism, 83. See also Capitalism
Mann, Heinrich, 219–20; Im Schlaraffenland, 211–15, 240; Der Untertan, 8, 219, 226–32, 237, 240, 243
Marès, Jolanthe (pseud. for Selma Reichel), 169; Begierde, 177–80
Marriage: failure of, 171–72; imagined as stifling, 207; modern, 164–65; women's expectations of, 170–71, 173–74
Marriage of convenience: by aristocracy, 194–95, 242; by the bourgeoisie, 208–9, 210; for women, 166–67
Marris, Peter, 41–42, 52
Marx, Karl, 109, 185
Masses, the age of, 32, 219. See also Working class
Maturity, and women, 165
Mauthner, Fritz, 148–49, 205; Der neue Ahasver, 148–53, 188
Megalomania, German, 103
Mehring, Franz, 119
Meister Timpe. See under Kretzer, Max
Mendelssohn, Moses, 22, 146, 160
Mentality, Gründer-, 65, 67, 206, 240
Merbach, Paul Alfred, 24
Messiah: artist as, 77, 91, 101, 102, 104, 137; imagery of, 29, 77, 92, 120, 122–23. See also Jesus Christ, imagery of
Metropolis. See Weltstadt
Middle class: ascendancy of, 241–42; crisis of values, 26, 31, 52, 55–69, 205–11; linked to crisis of nationhood, 56; and social reform, 120. See also Besitzbürgertum; Bildungsbürgertum; Bürgertum; Bourgeoisie
Mietskasernen, 33, 112
Milieu, theory (of Taine), 96
Militarism, 80, 226
Millionenbauer, Der. See under Kretzer, Max
Misalliance, by aristocracy, 194–95
Misery, working-class, 33, 111–13
Mittagsgöttin, Die. See under Bölsche, Wilhelm
Moabit (district), 23, 80, 99, 120
Modern society, as monster, 179
Modernity: ambivalence toward, 8, 24, 27; and aristocracy, 186; Berlin as center of, 1, 3, 23, 237, 239; collision of with tradition, 8; conceptions of, 2, 4, 5–6, 241; encounters with in novels, 2–4, 7, 241–44; and German identity, 4, 244; and toleration, 156
Modernization, German, 1
Mohammed, 102, 123
Mommsen, Theodor, 149
Monarchism, 43, 78
Monuments: in Imperial Germany, 76; victory, 65–66, 87; to William I, 230–31
Moses, imagery of, 50, 141
Mosse, George, 68

Motherhood, 170, 172, 176, 177–78
Mozart, Wolfgang Amadeus, 101
Munich, Berlin compared to, 48
Murger, Henri, 93, 137
Mythology: of authority, 226, 229; in colportage novels, 113; of historical experience, 73, 22–23, 221; of individual weakness, 228; of old Berlin, 58–59

Napoleon III, 45
Nationalism, strident, 48, 83, 209, 226, 231, 238
Nationhood, German: and generational struggle, 91; ideals of, 152, 209; linked to middle-class crisis, 56; search for, 1, 3, 7, 35, 77, 244. See also Identity, German
Natural selection, 95, 157
Naturalism, 92–105; as anti-ideological, 85; ideals of in music, 101; literary controversies of, 50–51, 85; and socialism, 117–18
*Nebeneinander*, 26
*Neue Ahasver, Der*. See under Mauthner, Fritz
*Neue Gott, Der*. See under Land, Hans
*Neuen Serapionsbrüder, Die*. See under Gutzkow, Karl
*Neuer Pharao, Ein*. See under Spielhagen, Friedrich
New Testament, in novels, 121. See also Biblical passages
New World, exile or emigration to, 82, 84, 99
Newness, as crisis, 200, 240
Nicolai, Friedrich, 22
Nietzsche, Friedrich, 135, 136, 141
Nihilism, 123
Nobel Prize, awarded to Paul Heyse, 56
Nobility. See Aristocracy
Novel: components of as a social product, 8; as democratizing influence, 190; as a historical source, 1–2, 237; and national identity formation, 16; production and publication of, 11–12; readership of, 13–16; selection of for this study, 5–7; serialization of, 11; as social discourse, 2–3, 5, 15, 24; social implications of outcomes, 52, 60, 64, 68–69, 94, 180, 194, 196–97. See also Berlin novel; City novel

Novelists: attitudes of toward modernity, 9, 24, 51, 136; professional identity of, 9; relation to publishers, 10; social origins, 9; social responsibility of, 2–3, 82, 91, 97–98, 104, 148, 232; and socialism, 109; women as, 169. See also Berlin novelist; Writer

Occult, the, 132
Officer corps, 78, 79; as aristocratic realm, 185, 191–93, 196; decline of tradition, 193; power of, 231
Olmütz, 44, 48
Ompteda, Georg Freiherr von: *Droesigl*, 190; *Eysen*, 186, 195–97; *Sylvester von Geyer*, 196
Oranienburger Tor, 40–41
*Ostjude*, 103, 155–56, 158, 213
Outcomes, in novels, social implications of, 52, 60, 64, 68–69, 94, 180, 194, 196–97

Painting, styles of, 93–94
Paris, Berlin compared to, 27
Parliamentarianism, 74, 77, 218, 225, 232–33
Particularism, obstacle to unity, 45
Parvenu: Berlin as, 103, 200, 215, 239–40; fear of, 197; Germany as, 240
Parvenuism, 100, 200, 210–15, 239–40
Patriotism, as social value, 61, 75
Persecution, political, in Berlin, 59, 117–20
Pessimism, cultural, 8, 141, 241–42
*Poggenpuhls, Die*. See under Fontane, Theodor
Police: persecution by, 117–20; spying, 34, 119
Political themes, in novels, 73–88, 218–33
Political tradition, German, formation of, 73
Potsdamer Tor (Potsdam Gate), 21, 40
Potsdamerstraße, 210
Poverty: aristocratic, 192, 193–94, 196; for the artist, 93; working-class, 33, 111–12
Power: in Berlin society, 212–13; systems of, 227–29
Pride, wounded German, 50, 66, 78
Private versus public sphere, 243
Prizes, literary, 10–11

"Problem der Ehe, Das." See under
  Reuter, Gabriele
Proletariat. See Working class
Protectionism, 84
Prussia: centrality to unification, 44, 45; and German tradition, 44, 73, 86; loyalties to, 43–44, 221; three-class voting system, 120
Psychology, as new science, 138
Public versus private sphere, 243
Publishers, 10
Puttkamer, Robert von, 119

Raabe, Wilhelm, 11; *Im alten Eisen*, 41, 110
Railway, elevated (*Stadtbahn*), 51
Railway project, Pomeranian, 63
Readership, of novels, 10, 12–16; class and gender, 13–14
Realism, artistic, 93–94; literary, German, 2; musical, 101
Reception, literary, 12–16
Reform, social: advocated in novels, 34, 80, 110, 115; by William II, 123
Reform era (1806), Prussian, 30, 73, 75, 146
Regeneration, German, 8, 34, 66, 75, 91, 104; from Berlin, 34; through Christianity, 130; through culture, 97, 100; disillusionment with, 244; through traditional virtues, 201; and women, 169. See also German revolution; Unfinished revolution
Reichel, Selma. See Marès, Jolanthe (pseud.)
*Reichsgründung, die zweite* (the second founding of the reich, 1879), 84, 240
"Reichshauptstadt." See under Kirchbach, Wolfgang
Reichstag, 74, 225, 232; building, 225
Religion: attacks on, 28, 129–30; rejection of, 59, 128, 133
Republicanism, 62, 77, 83; as alien to Germany, 78; of the spirit, 34
Resignation, in novels, 75, 209, 215, 222
*Reubund* (League of Remorse). See *Treubund*
Reuter, Gabriele, 169, 172–73; *Ellen von der Weiden*, 170–73; "Das Problem der Ehe," 172–73
Revolution: failed expectations, 81; from above, 11, 30, 73, 81; middle-class, 242; middle-class notions of, 55, 225; reading, 13–14; spiritual, 74, 132, 243. See also Christianity, early, as revolutionary; German revolution; *Umsturz*; Unfinished revolution
Revolution of 1848: as historical experience, 3, 23, 27, 73, 75; legacy of, 76, 82, 83; participants in, 45, 46, 61, 77, 82–84, 229–30, 243; as tragedy for Prussia, 42
Rhineland, culture of compared to Berlin's, 212
*Ritter vom Geiste, Die*. See under Gutzkow, Karl
Roberts, David, 226
Rodenberg, Julius, 47; *Die Grandidiers*, 42, 44–47, 238
*Roman expérimental* (of Zola), 96–97
Romans (New Testament), 159
Rosenthalerstraße, 140

Salon, aristocratic, 189–90; the Berlin, 94; Jewish, in Berlin, 22
Scheffler, Karl, 215
Schiller, Friedrich von, 22, 78, 98, 101
Schlaf, Johannes, *Das dritte Reich*, 138–41, 239, 243
Schliemann, Heinrich, 207
Schmidt, Julian, 138
Schöneberg, 195, 210, 211
School, as system of authority, 227
*Schriftsteller* (writer), versus *Dichter*, 8, 11
*Schröter & Co*. See under Alberti, Conrad
Schücking, Levin, 15
Science: and German classicism, 98; versus idealism, 96
Secrecy, as an aristocratic prerogative, 188–90
Secularization: in Berlin, 93, 132, 133; as dimension of modernity, 59, 77, 92; of Jewish character, 154
Sedan, 79
Seidel, Heinrich, *Leberecht Hühnchen*, 201–2
*Selbstbestimmung* (self-determination), as middle-class ideal, 62, 65, 68, 237
Self-actualization, women's, 168, 172–73, 174, 176–77, 180
Self-cultivation. See *Bildung*
Self-deception, as hallmark of Berlin, 204, 206–7

Self-delusion. *See* Delusion
Self-hatred, Jewish, 148, 153, 154–56
Self-made man, 60, 61, 194
Serialization of novels, 11, 13, 25, 57
Sexuality, of women, 171
Sickness: of an era, 135; versus health, in literature, 97–98; versus health, in society, 139. *See also* Madness
Sidewalk disease, 67, 140, 186
Sittenfeld, Konrad, 157–58, 160. *See also* Alberti, Conrad (pseud.)
Smithing, imagery of, 81, 82
Social Democratic Party. *See* SPD
"Social question," 110
Socialism: and Christianity, 130, 131; as moral force, 115; and naturalism, 117–18. *See also* SPD; Anti-Socialist Law; Action, working-class
Society, modern: as diseased, 139; as monster, 179
*Sozialfrage, die*, 110
SPD (Sozialdemokratische Partei Deutschlands), 109, 117, 121–22, 218, 221; Berlin as center of, 118, 127; electoral victory, 121, 221
Speculation: as immoral, 62, 80, 213; and Jews, 154
*Spenersche Zeitung*, 11, 57
Spielhagen, Friedrich, 5, 13, 104, 135; criticism of by naturalists, 85; *Ein neuer Pharao*, 76, 82–85, 92; and legacy of 1848, 87; *Sturmflut*, 60–66, 67, 69, 84, 95, 190; *Was will das werden?*, 76–82, 92, 111
Spiritual crisis, and modernity, 127–42
Spiritualism, 132–35
Spittelmarkt, 128
*Spitzen*. *See under* Lindau, Paul
Spreewald, as spiritualist symbol, 134–35
Springer, Robert, 40
Status quo, fictional support for, 76, 85
*Stechlin, Der*. *See under* Fontane, Theodor
Steglitz, 201
*Stilpe*. *See under* Bierbaum, Otto Julius
Stinde, Julius, *Die Familie Buchholz*, 75–76, 218, 239
Stirner, Max, 139
Stoecker, Adolf, 111, 129
Storm, imagery of, 63, 78, 117, 151
Strasbourg, German conquest of, 47
Strauß, David Friedrich, 139
*Strebertum*, 74

Strike, 99, 115–16
Struggle for survival (*Kampf ums Dasein*), 7, 8, 96, 241, 242; aristocratic, 194; by artists, 91–105; as model for conservative versus liberal, 88; optimistic versus pessimistic notions of, 27, 95–96, 98–99; and working class, 110, 112–14, 121
Suicide, 117, 138, 156, 192; as liberation, 141; in Spree, 123, 156
*Sylvester von Geyer*. *See under* Ompteda, Georg Freiherr von

Taine, Hippolyte, 96
Tempelhof, 26, 41
Tenement. *See Mietskasernen*
Testing, time of: for the artist, 93, 102; for women, 168
Third reich, imagery of, 139, 140
Tiergarten (district), 23, 60, 167, 179, 200, 204, 205; as symbol of bourgeoisie, 32
Tiergartenstraße, 203
Toleration, as Berlin tradition, 49, 146
Tradition: collision of with modernity, 8, 220; German cultural, 141; Prussian, 23, 77, 79
Traffic, as symbol of modernity, 40, 127, 171
Treitschke, Heinrich von, 41, 148–49
*Treubund* (League of Loyalty), 30, 43
*Trottoirkrankheit*. *See* Sidewalk disease
Tunnel über der Spree, 42
Turgenev, Ivan, 96

Übermensch, 140, 141
*Umsturz*, 219, 231
Unemployment, 112–13, 123
Unfinished revolution, 7, 27, 76, 87, 111, 238, 240; abandoned, 215; through Christianity, 130; and generational struggle, 91; and nationhood, 3, 35; obstacles to, 7–8, 35, 136, 223, 238, 241; and women, 180. *See also* German revolution
Unification (1870–1871): from above, 73, 77; effect on Berlin, 1, 56; as historical experience, 3, 85–86, 221; as loss and change, 43, 44, 45–46; linked with 1848, 62; and middle-class crisis, 68. *See also* Nationhood, German

# Index

Unity, German: as an ideal, 225, 233, 238; political versus moral, 74
Unruhe (unrest), as image, 127, 171, 178
Unter den Linden, 21, 140, 150, 186, 195, 196
Untertan, Der. See under Mann, Heinrich
Uprising of 1813. See Wars of liberation (1813)

Verbürgerlichung, of aristocracy, 194, 195, 242
Verkommenen, Die. See under Kretzer, Max
Victim, of society, 113–14, 132
Victory column, the, 133
Viebig, Clara, 169; Dilettanten des Lebens, 173–75; Es lebe die Kunst!, 173, 175–77
Vienna, Berlin compared to, 27, 47
Vision, novelists' failure to pursue, 116. See also Implications, social
Volk: conception of, 43; and unification, 78
Von Brandenburg zu Bismarck. See under Hesekiel, Ludovika
Vornehmheit, 43, 58–60, 190

Wagner, Richard, 102, 139; and the German spirit, 230
Wars of liberation (1813), as historical experience, 4, 23, 73, 74–75, 221; and character of the Berliner, 22–23
Was will das werden?. See under Spielhagen, Friedrich
Wedding (district), 112
Weimar, Berlin compared to, 48
Weltstadt (world-city), Berlin as, 27, 40, 51, 128–29
Wer ist der Stärkere?. See under Alberti, Conrad
Werner, Anton von, 73
Werther der Jude. See under Jacobowski, Ludwig
Westend (district), 213
Westward expansion: Berlin, 21, 200; move by characters, 203–4, 210, 213
Wife, role in marriage, 167, 170–71, 174, 176
Wilhelmstraße, 40, 43–44, 50, 62, 187
William I: assassination attempts on (1878) as historical experience, 4, 51, 82, 84, 151; representative of generation of 1813, 86; role in German unification, 44, 73, 75, 86
William II: accession as turning point, 4, 87, 127, 218; at Brandenburger Tor, 87, 228–29; criticism of, 223, 243; power of, 224, 227; representative of generation of 1870, 86; his social decrees of 1890, 123; speeches of, 230
Wish-fulfillment, through novels, 15, 76, 189, 202, 233
Withdrawal, political, 31, 59, 122; social, 123, 136, 140–41, 243
Wittmann, Reinhard, 13–14
"Woman question," 164
Women, 164–81; as artists, 173–79; as creators of harmony, 172, 178, 179–80; and economic dependence, 164, 173, 178; identity of reinterpreted, 174–75; and public versus private spheres, 165, 169, 176–77, 180–81; as readers of novels, 14; socially imposed limitations of, 42, 168; and work, 169, 176–77, 193–94; working-class, 94, 114
Women's movements, 164
Work ethic, problems of, 9, 102; and the aristocracy, 196, 197
Working class, 26, 32–34, 105, 109–23; age of, 224–25; ambivalence toward, 34, 110, 111, 242; conditions endured by, 112; demonstrations of 1892, 218, 224–25, 228–29, 240
World-city. See Weltstadt
Writer: social responsibility of, 130; women as, 173–77

Young Germans, 25

Zerrissenheit (inner strife): cultural, 101, 141; national, 47
Zobeltitz, Fedor von, Der Hetzjagd, 192
Zola, Émile, 96–97, 137; Max Kretzer compared to, 111
Zolling, Theophil, 219–20; Bismarcks Nachfolger, 219, 223–26; Der Klatsch, 189, 200
Zug nach dem Westen, Der. See under Lindau, Paul